GLOBAL

NATIONAL SECURITY AND INTELLIGENCE AGENCIES HANDBOOK

VOLUME 1

STRATEGIC INFORMATION AND CONTACTS

International Business Publications, USA
Washington, DC USA

GLOBAL

NATIONAL SECURITY AND INTELLIGENCE AGENCIES HANDBOOK

VOLUME 1 STRATEGIC INFORMATION AND CONTACTS

UPDATED ANNUALLY

We express our sincere appreciation to all government agencies and international organizations which provided information and other materials for this handbook

Cover Design: **International Business Publications, USA**

2019 Updated Reprint International Business Publications, USA
ISBN 0-7397-6707-0

For additional analytical, business and investment opportunities information,
please contact Global Investment & Business Center, USA
at (703) 370-8082. Fax: (703) 370-8083. E-mail: ibpusa3@gmail.com
Global Business and Investment Info Databank - www.ibpus.com

Printed in the USA

GLOBAL

NATIONAL SECURITY AND INTELLIGENCE AGENCIES HANDBOOK

VOLUME 1

STRATEGIC INFORMATION AND CONTACTS

TABLE OF CONTENTS

NATIONAL SECURITY: STRATEGIC INFORMATION INFORMATION

NATIONAL SECURITY FUNDAMENTALS

National security refers to the security of a nation state, including its citizens, economy, and institutions, and is regarded as a duty of government. National security of any suvereign state is the essential requirement to maintain the survival of the nation-state through the use of economic, military and political power, intelligence and military capabilities and diplomacy. The concept developed mostly in the United States of America after World War II. Initially focusing on military might, it now encompasses a broad range of facets, all of which impinge on the military or economic security of the nation and the values espoused by the national society. Accordingly, in order to possess national security, a nation needs to possess economic security, energy security, environmental security, etc. Security threats involve not only conventional foes such as nation-states but also non-state actors such as terrorist organizations, narcotic cartels and multi-national organizations; some authorities including natural disasters and events causing severe environmental damage in this category.

Measures taken to ensure national security include:

- using diplomacy to rally allies and isolate threats
- marshalling economic power to facilitate or compel cooperation
- maintaining effective armed forces
- implementing civil defense and emergency preparedness measures (including anti-terrorism legislation)
- ensuring the resilience and redundancy of critical infrastructure
- using intelligence services to detect and defeat or avoid threats and espionage, and to protect classified information
- using counterintelligence services or secret police to protect the nation from internal threats

DEFINITIONS

There is no single universally accepted definition of "National Security". A typical dictionary definition, in this case from Farlex dictionary, defines national security as the following:

> "the requirement to maintain the survival of the nation-state through the use of economic, military and political power and the exercise of diplomacy."

However, a variety of definitions provide an overview of the many usages of this concept. The concept still remains ambiguous, having originated from simpler definitions which initially emphasised the freedom from military threat and political coercion to later increase in sophistication and include other forms of non-military security as suited the circumstances of the time.[:1-6:52-54]

Walter Lippmann gave one of the early definitions in 1943 in terms of a nation and war:[:5]

> "A nation has security when it does not have to sacrifice its legitimate interests to avoid war, and is able, if challenged, to maintain them by war."

A later definition by Harold Lasswell, a political scientist, in 1950, looks at national security from almost the same aspect, that of external coercion:[:79]

> "The distinctive meaning of national security means freedom from foreign dictation."

Arnold Wolfers (1960), while recognising the need to segregate the subjectivity of the conceptual idea from the objectivity, talks of threats to *acquired values*:

> "An ambiguous symbol meaning different things to different people. National security objectively means the absence of threats to acquired values and subjectively, the absence of fear that such values will be attacked."

The 1996 definition propagated by the National Defence College of India resembles the accretion of the elements of national power:

> "National security is an appropriate and aggressive blend of political resilience and maturity, human resources, economic structure and capacity, technological competence, industrial base and availability of natural resources and finally the military might."

Harold Brown, U.S. Secretary of Defense from 1977 to 1981 in the Carter administration, defined national security in his 1983 book *Thinking about national security: defense and foreign policy in a dangerous world*. The definition includes elements such as economic security and environmental security

> "National security then is the ability to preserve the nation's physical integrity and territory; to maintain its economic relations with the rest of the world on reasonable terms; to preserve its nature, institution, and governance from disruption from outside; and to control its borders."

In Harvard history professor Charles Maier's definition of 1990, national security is defined through the lens of national power

> "National security... is best described as a capacity to control those domestic and foreign conditions that the public opinion of a given community believes necessary to enjoy its own self-determination or autonomy, prosperity and wellbeing."

The United States Armed Forces defines national security (of the United States) in the following manner :

> **national security** — A collective term encompassing both national defense and foreign relations of the United States. Specifically, the condition provided by: a. a military or defense advantage over any foreign nation or group of nations; b. a favorable foreign relations position; or c. a defense posture capable of successfully resisting hostile or destructive action from within or without, overt or covert.

In 2010, Barack Obama included an all-encompassing world-view in his definition of America's national security interests as:

- The security of the United States, its citizens, and U.S. allies and partners;
- A strong, innovative, and growing U.S. economy in an open international economic system that promotes opportunity and prosperity;
- Respect for universal values at home and around the world; and
- An international order advanced by U.S. leadership that promotes peace, security, and opportunity through stronger cooperation to meet global challenges.

HISTORY OF THE NATIONAL SECURITY CONCEPT

The origin of the modern concept of "national security" as a philosophy of maintaining a stable nation state can be traced to the Peace of Westphalia, wherein the concept of a sovereign state, ruled by a sovereign, became the basis of a new international order of nation states.[:19]

As an academic concept, national security can be seen as a recent phenomenon which was first introduced in the United States after World War II,[:2-4] and has to some degree replaced other concepts that describe the struggle of states to overcome various external and internal threats. The earliest mention of the term national security, however, was made in Yale University in 1790 wherein reference was made to its relation with domestic industries.[:52]

The concept of national security became an official guiding principle of foreign policy in the United States when the **National Security Act of 1947** was signed on July 26, 1947 by U.S. President Harry S. Truman.[:3] Together with its 1949 amendment, this act created important facets for American national security such as the precursor to the Department of Defense), subordinated the military branches to the new cabinet level position of the Secretary of Defense, established the National Security Council and the Central Intelligence Agency. The Act did not define national security which was conceivably advantageous as it's ambiguity made it a powerful phrase to invoke whenever issues threatened by other interests of the state, such as domestic concerns, came up for discussion and decision.

The realisation that national security encompasses more than than just military security was present, though understated, from the beginning itself. The US National Security Act of 1947 was set up "to advise the President on the integration of domestic, military and foreign policies relating to national security".

In India, the Institute for Defence Studies and Analyses realised in 1965 that "national security is a wider concept than defence."

Gen Maxwell Taylor's essay of 1974 titled "The Legitimate Claims of National Security" has this to say:

> The national valuables in this broad sense include current assets and national interests, as well as the sources of strength upon which our future as a nation depends. Some valuables are tangible and earthy; others are spiritual or intellectual. They range widely from political assets such as the Bill of Rights, our political institutions and international friendships, to many economic assets which radiate worldwide from a highly productive domestic economy supported by rich natural resources. It is the urgent need to protect valuables such as these which legitimizes and makes essential the role of national security.

NATIONAL SECURITY AND RIGHTS & FREEDOMS

The measures adopted to maintain national security in the face of threats to society has led to ongoing dialectic, particularly in liberal democracies, on the appropriate scale and role of authority in matters of civil and human rights.

Tension exists between the preservation of the state (by maintaining self-determination and sovereignty) and the rights and freedoms of individuals.

Although national security measures are imposed to protect society as a whole, many such measures will restrict the rights and freedoms of all individuals in society. The concern is that where the exercise of national security laws and powers is not subject to good governance, the rule of law, and strict checks and balances, there is a risk that "national security" may simply serve as a pretext for suppressing unfavorable political and social views. Taken to its logical conclusion, this view contends that measures which may ostensibly serve a national security purpose (such as mass surveillance, and censorship of mass media), could ultimately lead to an Orwellian dystopia.

In the United States, the politically controversial USA Patriot Act and other government action has brought some of these issues to the citizen's attention, raising two main questions - to what extent, for the sake of national security, should individual rights and freedoms be restricted *and* can the restriction of civil rights for the sake of national security be justified?

TECHNICAL ASPECTS OF NATIONAL SECURITY

Because of the highly competitive nature of nation states, national security for countries with significant resources and value is based largely on technical measures and operational processes. This ranges from information protection related to state secrets to weaponry for militaries to negotiations strategies with other nation states. The national security aparatus depends largely on combinations of management practices, technical capabilities, the projection of images both internally and externally, and the capacity to gain enough of the will of the people to gather taxes and spend them on useful efforts. While some nation states use power to gain more power for their leadership, others provide quality of life improvements to their people, thus creating larger geopolitical conflicts between types of governments. These all have foundations in internal education and communications systems that serve to build the nation states on strategic and tactical bases and create the conditions for success and failure of the nation state. Increasingly the world is replacing transportation with communication and thus the ability to communicate effectively and convey messages in the information environment is critical to national security for the Western nations. Issues like global warming and research priorities increasingly dominate the reality of competition between nation states. All of these lead to the need to have a clear understanding of the technical issues underlying national security in order to create and sustain the institutions that ultimately feed the future of the nation state.

BASIC ELEMENTS OF NATIONAL SECURITY

As in the case of national power, the military aspect of security is an important, but not the sole, component of national security. To be truly secure, a nation needs other forms of security. Authorities differ in their choice of nation security elements. Besides the military aspect of security, the aspects of diplomacy or politics; society; environment; energy and natural resources; and economics are commonly listed. The elements of national security corelate closely to the concept of the elements of national power. Romm (1993) lists security from narcotic cartels, economic security, environmental security and energy security as the non-military elements of national security.[:v, 1-8]

MILITARY SECURITY

Military security implies the capability of a nation-state to defend itself, and/or deter military aggression. Alternatively, military security implies the capability of a nation-state to enforce its policy choices by use of military force. The term "military security" is considered synonymous with "security" in much of its usage. One of the definitions of security given in the *Dictionary of Military and Associated Terms*, may be considered a definition of "military security":

> A condition that results from the establishment and maintenance of protective measures that ensure a state of inviolability from hostile acts or influences.
>
> —Dictionary of Military and Associated Terms

This is traditionally, the earliest recognised form of national security.[:67] Military security implies the capability of a nation to defend itself, and/or deter military aggression. Alternatively, military security implies the capability of a nation to enforce its policy choices by use of military force. The term "military security" is considered synonymous with "security" in much of its usage. One of the definitions of security given in the *Dictionary of Military and Associated Terms*, may be considered a definition of "military security":

> A condition that results from the establishment and maintenance of protective measures that ensure a state of inviolability from hostile acts or influences.
>
> —Dictionary of Military and Associated Terms

POLITICAL SECURITY

The political aspect of security has been offered by Barry Buzan, Ole Wæver, Jaap de Wilde as an important component of national security, Political security is about the stability of the social order. Closely allied to military security and societal security, other components proposed in a framework for national security in their book "Security: a new framework for analysis", it specifically addresses threats to sovereignty. System referent objects are defined, such as nation-states, nations, transnational groups of political importance including tribes, minorities, some religious organisations, systems of states such as the European Union and the United Nations, besides others. Diplomacy, negotiation and other interactions form the means of interacion between the objects,

ECONOMIC SECURITY

Economic security or **financial security** is the condition of having stable income or other resources to support a standard of living now and in the foreseeable future. It includes

- probable continued solvency
- predictability of the future cash flow of a person or other economic entity, such as a country
- employment security or job security

Financial security more often refers to individual and family money management and savings. Economic security tends to include the broader effect of a society's production levels and monetary support for non-working citizens.

Historically, conquest of nations have made conquerors rich through plunder, access to new resources and enlarged trade through controlling of the conquered nations' economy. In today's complex system of international trade, characterised by multi-national agreements, mutual inter-dependence and availability of natural resources etc., the freedom to follow choice of policies to develop a nation's economy in the manner desired, forms the essence of economic security. Economic security today forms, arguably, as important a part of national security as military security.

COMPONENTS OF INDIVIDUAL ECONOMIC SECURITY

In the United States, children's economic security is indicated by the income level and employment security of their families or organizations. Economic security of people over 50 years old is based on Social Security benefits, pensions and savings, earnings and employment, and health insurance coverage.

In 1972, the state legislature of Arizona formed a Department of Economic Security with a mission to promote "the safety, well-being, and self sufficiency of children, adults, and families". This department combines state government activities previously managed by the Employment Security Commission, the State Department of Public Welfare, the Division of Vocational Rehabilitation, the State Office of Economic Opportunity, the Apprenticeship Council, the State Office of Manpower Planning, and the State Department of Mental Retardation.

The Minnesota Department of Economic Security was formed in 1977 from the departments of Employment Services and Vocational Rehabilitation, the Governor's Manpower Office, and the Economic Opportunity Office, which administered anti-poverty programs. In 1985, State Services for the Blind was included in this department. In 2003, the Minnesota Department of Economic Security and Minnesota Department of Trade and Economic Development were merged to form The Minnesota Department of Employment and Economic Development.

ECONOMIC SECURITY OF COUNTRIES

Economic security, in the context of **politics** and international relations, is the ability of a nation-state to follow its choice of policies to develop the national economy in the manner desired. Historically, conquest of nations have made conquerors rich through plunder, access to new resources and enlarged trade through controlling of the conquered nations'economy. In today's complex system of international trade, characterised by multi-national agreements, mutual inter-dependence and availability of natural resources etc, Economic security today forms, arguably, as important a part of national security as military policy.

Economic security has been proposed as a key determinant of international relations, particularly in the geopolitics of petroleum in American foreign policy after September 11, 2001.

In Canada, threats to the country's overall economic security are considered **economic espionage**, which is "illegal, clandestine or coercive activity by a foreign government in order to gain unauthorized access to economic intelligence, such as proprietary information or technology, for economic advantage

ENVIRONMENTAL SECURITY

Environmental security deals with environmental issues which threaten the national security of a nation in any manner. The scope and nature of environmental threats to national security and strategies to engage them are a subject of debate.[:29-33] While all environmental events are not considered significant of being categorised as threats, many transnational issues, both global and regional would affect national security. Romm (1993) classifies these as :[:15]

- *Transnational environmental problems that threaten a nation's security, in its broad defined sense.* These include global environmental problems such as climate change due to global warming, deforestation and loss of biodiversity, etc.[:15]
- *Environmental or resource problems that threaten a nation's security, traditionally defined.* These would be problems whose outcomes would result in conventional threats to national security as first or higher order outcomes. Such disputes could range from heightened tension or outright conflict due to disputes over water scarcity in the Middle East, to illegal immigration into the United States caused by the failure of agriculture in Mexico[:15]. The genocide in Rwanda,indirectly or partly caused by rise in population and dwindling availability of farmland, is an example of the extremity of outcome arising from problems of environmental security.
- *Environmentally threatening outcomes of warfare*, e.g. Romans destroyed the fields of Carthage by pouring salt over them; Saddam Hussein's burning of oil wells in the Gulf War;[:15-16] the use of Agent Orange by the USA in the Vietnam War for defoilating forests for military purposes.

SECURITY OF ENERGY AND NATURAL RESOURCES

A resource has been defined as:

> "...a support inventory... biotic or abiotic, renewable or expendable,... for sustaining life at a heightened level of well-being."
>
> —Prabhakaran Paleri (2008)

Resources include water, sources of energy, land and minerals. Availability of adequate natural resources is an important for a nation to develop its industry and economic power. Lack of resources is a serious challenge for Japan to overcome to increase its national power. In the Gulf War of 1990, fought over economic issues, Iraq captured Kuwait in order to capture its oil wells, among other reasons. Water resources are subject to disputes between many nations, including the two nuclear powers, India and Pakistan. Nations attempt to attain energy and natural resource security by acquiring the needed resources by force, negotiation and commerce.

- Resource security
- Demographic security
- Disaster security

ENERGY SECURITY

Access to cheap energy has become essential to the functioning of modern economies. However, the uneven distribution of energy supplies among countries has led to significant vulnerabilities. Threats to **energy security** include the political instability of several energy producing countries, the manipulation of energy supplies, the competition over energy sources, attacks on supply infrastructure, as well as accidents,natural disasters, the funding to foreign dictators, rising terrorism, and dominant countries reliance to the foreign oil supply. The limited supplies, uneven distribution, and rising costs of fossil fuels, such as oil and gas, create a need to change to more sustainable energy sources in the foreseeable future. With as much dependence that the U.S. currently has for oil and with the peaking limits of oil production; economies and societies will begin to feel the decline in the resource that we have become dependent upon. Energy security has become one of the leading issues in the world today as oil and other resources have become as vital to the world's people. However with oil production rates decreasing and oil production peak nearing the world has come to protect what resources we have left in the world. With new advancements in renewable resources less pressure has been put on companies that produce the worlds oil, these resources are, geothermal, solar power, wind power and hydro-electric. Although these are not all the current and possible future options for the world to turn to as the oil depletes the most important issue is protecting these vital resources from future threats. These new resources will become more useful as the price of exporting and importing oil will increase due to increase of demand.

SECURITY THREATS

One of the leading threats to energy security is the significant increase in energy prices, either on the world markets – as has occurred in a number of energy crises over the years – or by the imposition of price increases by an oligopoly or monopoly supplier, cartel or country. In some cases the threat might come from a single energy superpower – those states able to significantly influence world markets by their action alone. Rather than just manipulating prices, such suppliers might go beyond this by suspending or terminating supplies. This has been done to apply pressure during economic negotiations - such as during the Russia-Belarus energy dispute - or to apply political pressure, for example by OPEC in response to Western support for Israel in the Yom Kippur War. Suspension of supplies may also come about as a result of worldwide international sanctions against a country.

Energy plays an important role in the national security of any given country as a fuel to power the economic engine. Hence, threats to energy security can also result from physical damage to the energy infrastructure either of the supplier, or of the importer as a result of natural events, misfortune, terrorism, or warfare. The political and economic instability caused by war or other factors such as strike action can also prevent the proper functioning of the energy industry in a supplier country. One example of this would be the United states, the U.S. has over 60% of its imported oil from OPEC countries and have been increasingly more dependent over the last 20 years.

New threats to energy security have emerged in the form of the increased world competition for energy resources due to the increased pace of industrialization in countries such as India and China. Although still a minority concern, the possibility of price rises resulting from the peaking of world oil production is also starting to attract the attention of at least the French government.

Increased competition over energy resources may also lead to the formation of security compacts to enable an equitable distribution of oil and gas between major powers. However, this may happen at the expense of less developed economies. The Group of Five, precursors to the G8, first met in 1975 to coordinate economic and energy policies in the wake of the 1973 Arab oil embargo, a rise in inflation and a global economic slowdown.

NATO leaders meeting in Bucharest in April 2008 may discuss the possibility of using the military alliance "as an instrument of energy security." One of the possibilities include placing troops in the Caucasus region to police oil and gas pipelines.

ENERGY SECTOR

The energy sector for not only the U.S. but for many other countries fuel the economies in the 21st century. Without these resources and the money coming in from them health and overall welfare will be risked world-wide. Oil has become what oxygen is to humans but for the economy. As the resources near peak production levels the U.S. economy will be threatened and will force other resources and big oil producing companies to start researching new sources of fuel to help revitalize the economy. The energy infrastructure is divided into three interrelated segments: electricity, petroleum and natural gas. Natural gas although very efficient is in decline and becomes very hard to harvest and very dangerous to store. Electricity when produced is very harmful to the environment due to all the greenhouse gases leaked into the atmosphere. With these concerns the U.S. and other countries including Russia and China have been researching new methods of creating electricity in a more clean way.

LONG TERM SECURITY

Long term measures to increase energy security center on reducing dependence on any one source of imported energy, increasing the number of suppliers, exploiting native fossil fuel or renewable energy resources, and reducing overall demand through energy conservation measures. It can also involve entering into international agreements to underpin international energy trading relationships, such as the Energy Charter Treaty in Europe. All the concern coming from security threats on oil sources long term security measures will help reduce the future cost of importing and exporting fuel into and out of countries without having to worry about harm coming to the goods being transported.

The impact of the 1973 oil crisis and the emergence of the OPEC cartel was a particular milestone that prompted some countries to increase their energy security. Japan, almost totally dependent on imported oil, steadily introduced the use of natural gas, nuclear power, high-speed mass transit systems, and implemented energy conservation measures, It has become one of the world leaders in the use of renewable energy. The United Kingdom began exploiting North Sea oil and gas reserves, and became a net exporter of energy into the 2000s.

In other countries energy security has historically been a lower priority. The United States, for example, has continued to increase its dependency on imported oil although, following the oil price increases since 2003, the development of biofuels has been suggested as a means of addressing this.

Increasing energy security is also one of the reasons behind a block on the development of natural gas imports in Sweden. Greater investment in native renewable energy technologies and energy conservation is envisaged instead. India is carrying out a major hunt for domestic oil to decrease its dependency on OPEC, while Iceland is well advanced in its plans to become energy-independent by 2050 through deploying 100% renewable energy.

SHORT TERM SECURITY: PETROLEUM

Petroleum or otherwise known as "crude oil" has become the resource most used by countries all around the world including Russia, China and the United States of America. With all the oil wells located around the world energy security has become a main issue to ensure the safety of the petroleum that is being harvested. In the middle east oil fields become main targets for sabotage because of how heavily countries rely on oil. Many countries hold strategic petroleum reserves as a buffer against the economic and political impacts of an energy crisis. All 28 members of the International Energy Agency hold a minimum of 90 days of their oil imports, for example.

The value of such reserves was demonstrated by the relative lack of disruption caused by the 2007 Russia-Belarus energy dispute, when Russia indirectly cut exports to several countries in the European Union.

Due to the theories in peak oil and need to curve demand, the United States military and Department of Defense had made significant cuts, and have been making a number of attempts to come up with more efficient ways to use oil.

Short term security: Natural gas

Compared to petroleum, reliance on imported natural gas creates significant short term vulnerabilities. Many European countries saw an immediate drop in supply when Russian gas supplies were halted during the Russia-Ukraine gas dispute in 2006.

Natural gas has been a viable source of energy in the world. Consisting of mostly methane natural gas is produced using two methods, biogenic and thermogenic. Biogenic comes from methogenic organisms located in marshes and landfills where thermogenic comes from buried material that is heated up from the earths core. Russia is the current leading country in production of natural gases. One of the biggest problems currently with natural gas is the ability to storage and transport it. With its low density it becomes harder to have pipelines in North America to transport enough natural gas as the demand increases. These pipelines are reaching near capacity and even at full capacity do not produce the amount of gas needed.

Uranium for nuclear power is mined and enriched in diverse and "stable" countries. These include Canada (about 25-30% of the world's total), Australia (21%), Kazakhstan (16%) and more than 10 other countries. Uranium is mined and fuel is manufactured significantly in advance of need. Nuclear fuel is considered by some to be a relatively-reliable power source, though a debate over the timing of peak uranium does exist. Although a very viable resource nuclear power comes under fire a lot of times because of the danger that people associate to it, nuclear power is stable but if something were to happen there are very little options that have been proposed to fix that problem.

Another big factor in the debate with nuclear power is that many people or companies do not want this high waste energy solution near them due to possible radiation leaks, nuclear runoff into streams and lakes and also the nuclear power plant ruins how appealing a city or state looks to other people in the country. Currently nuclear power powers a small fraction of the worlds electricity, but an even smaller fraction to the United States electricity. The incorporation of nuclear power can be seen through many different uses, for example there are currently nuclear powered ships that the navy uses to transport materials, soldiers and other resources.

Three of the ships names are the USS Bainbridge, USS Longbeach and the USS Enterprise. A future use for nuclear power resides in space technology, the current way of traveling through space requires a heavy consumption of fossil fuels, however in the near future there are plans to have space shuttles incorporate nuclear power generators on the shuttle which will greatly increase the distance traveled in these units and allow us to observe more of the space around us.

RENEWABLE ENERGY AND SECURITY

The deployment of renewable technologies usually increases the diversity of electricity sources and, through local generation, contributes to the flexibility of the system and its resistance to central shocks. For those countries where growing dependence on imported gas is a significant energy security issue, renewable technologies can provide alternative sources of electric power as well as displacing electricity demand through direct heat production. Renewable biofuels for transport represent a key source of diversification from petroleum products.

As the resources that have been so crucial to survival in the world to this day start declining in numbers, countries will begin to realize that the need for renewable fuel sources will be as vital as ever. With the production of new types of energy including, solar, geothermal, hydro-electric, biofuel and wind power. With the amount of sun that hits the world in one hour there is enough energy to power the world for one year. With the addition of solar panels all around the world a little less pressure is taken off the need to produce more oil.

Geothermal can potentially lead to other sources of fuel, if companies would take the heat from the inner core of the earth to heat up water sources we could essentially use the steam creating from the heated water to power machines, this option is one of the cleanest and efficient options. Hydro-electric which has been incorporated into many of the dams around the world produces a lot of energy and is very easy to produce the energy as the dams control the water that is allowed through seams which power turbines located inside of the dam. Bio-fuels have been researched using many different sources including ethanol and algae, these options are substantially cleaner than the consumption of petroleum

The environmental benefits of renewable energy technologies are widely recognised, but the contribution that they can make to energy security is less well known. Renewable technologies can enhance energy security in electricity generation, heat supply, and transportation.

ENERGY SECURITY

Access to cheap energy has become essential to the functioning of modern economies. However, the uneven distribution of fossil fuel supplies among countries, and the critical need to widely access energy resources, has led to significant vulnerabilities. Threats to global energy security include political instability of energy producing countries, manipulation of energy supplies, competition over energy sources, attacks on supply infrastructure, as well as accidents and natural disasters.

TRANSPORTATION

The International Energy Agency's *World Energy Outlook* concludes that rising oil demand, if left unchecked, would accentuate the consuming countries' vulnerability to a severe supply disruption and resulting price shock. Renewable biofuels for transport represent a key source of diversification from petroleum products. Biofuels from grain and beet in temperate regions have a part to play, but they are relatively expensive and their energy efficiency and CO_2 savings benefits, are variable. Biofuels from sugar cane and other highly productive tropical crops are much more competitive and beneficial. But all first generation biofuels ultimately compete with food production for land, water, and other resources.

Greater efforts are required to develop and commercialize second generation biofuel technologies, such as biorefineries and ligno-cellulosics, enabling the flexible production of biofuels and other products from non-edible plant materials.

According to the International Energy Agency (IEA), cellulosic ethanol commercialization could allow ethanol fuels to play a much larger role in the future than previously thought. Cellulosic ethanol can be made from plant matter composed primarily of inedible cellulose fibers that form the stems and branches of most plants. Dedicated energy crops, such as switchgrass, are also promising cellulose sources that can be produced in many regions of the United States.

HEATING

For those countries where growing dependence on imported gas is a significant energy security issue, renewable technologies can provide alternative sources of electric power as well as displacing electricity demand through direct heat production. The IEA suggests that the direct contribution that renewables can make to domestic or commercial space heating and industrial process heat deserves closer attention. Heat from solar, and geothermal sources, as well as heat pumps, is increasingly cost effective but often falls through the gap between government programmes that promote public awareness and provide incentives for renewable electricity and energy efficiency.

Solar heating systems are a well known technology and generally consist of solar thermal collectors, a fluid system to move the heat from the collector to its point of usage, and a reservoir or tank for heat storage. The systems may be used to heat domestic hot water, swimming pools, or homes and businesses. The heat can also be used for industrial process applications or as an energy input for other uses such as cooling equipment. In many warmer climates, a solar heating system can provide a very high percentage (50 to 75%) of domestic hot water energy.

ELECTRICITY GENERATION

The deployment of renewable technologies usually increases the diversity of electricity sources and, through local generation, contributes to the flexibility of the system and its resistance to central shocks. The IEA suggests that attention in this area has focused disproportionately on the issue of the variability of renewable electricity production.

However, this only applies to certain renewable technologies, mainly wind power and solar photovoltaics, and its significance depends on a range of factors which include the penetration of the renewables concerned, the balance of plant on the system, the wider connectivity of the system, and the demand side flexibility. Variability will rarely be a barrier to increased renewable energy deployment. But at high levels of penetration it requires careful analysis and management, and any additional costs that may be required for back-up or system modification must be taken into account.

COMBINED POWER PLANT

The Combined Power Plant, a project linking 36 wind, solar, biomass, and hydroelectric installations throughout Germany, has demonstrated that a combination of renewable sources and more-effective control can balance out short-term power fluctuations and provide reliable electricity with 100 percent renewable energy

FOOD SECURITY

Food security refers to the availability of food and one's access to it. A household is considered food-secure when its occupants do not live in hunger or fear of starvation. According to the World Resources Institute, global per capita food production has been increasing substantially for the past several decades. In 2006, MSNBC reported that globally, the number of people who are overweight has surpassed the number who are undernourished - the world had more than one billion people who were overweight, and an estimated 800 million who were undernourished. According to a 2004 article from the BBC, China, the world's most populous country, is suffering from an obesity epidemic. In India, the second-most populous country in the world, 30 million people have been added to the ranks of the hungry since the mid-1990s and 46% of children are underweight.

Worldwide around 852 million people are chronically hungry due to extreme poverty, while up to 2 billion people lack food security intermittently due to varying degrees of poverty (source: FAO, 2003). Six million children die of hunger every year - 17,000 every day. As of late 2007, export restrictions and panic buying, US Dollar Depreciation, increased farming for use in biofuels, world oil prices at more than $100 a barrel, global population growth, climate change, loss of agricultural land to residential and industrial development, and growing consumer demand in China and India are claimed to have pushed up the price of grain. However, the role of some of these factors is under debate. Some argue the role of biofuel has been overplayed as grain prices have come down to the levels of 2006. Nonetheless, food riots have recently taken place in many countries across the world.

It is becoming increasingly difficult to maintain food security in a world beset by a confluence of "peak" phenomena, namely peak oil, peak water, peak phosphorus, peak grain and peak fish. More than half of the planet's population, numbering approximately 3.3 billion people, live in urban areas as of November 2007. Any disruption to farm supplies may precipitate a uniquely urban food crisis in a relatively short time. The ongoing global credit crisis has affected farm credits, despite a boom in commodity prices. Food security is a complex topic, standing at the intersection of many disciplines.

A new peer-reviewed journal of *Food Security: The Science, Sociology and Economics of Food Production and Access to Food* began publishing in 2009. In developing countries, often 70% or more of the population lives in rural areas. In that context, agricultural development among smallholder farmers and landless people provides a livelihood for people allowing them the opportunity to stay in their communities. In many areas of the world, land ownership is not available, thus, people who want or need to farm to make a living have little incentive to improve the land.

In the US, there are approximately 2,000,000 farmers, less than 1% of the population. A direct relationship exists between food consumption levels and poverty. Families with the financial resources to escape extreme poverty rarely suffer from chronic hunger; while poor families not only suffer the most from chronic hunger, but are also the segment of the population most at risk during food shortages and famines.

Two commonly used definitions of food security come from the UN's Food and Agriculture Organization (FAO) and the United States Department of Agriculture (USDA):

- Food security exists when all people, at all times, have physical, social and economic access to sufficient, safe and nutritious food to meet their dietary needs and food preferences for an active and healthy life.
- Food security for a household means access by all members at all times to enough food for an active, healthy life. Food security includes at a minimum (1) the ready availability of nutritionally adequate and safe foods, and (2) an assured ability to acquire acceptable foods in socially acceptable ways (that is, without resorting to emergency food supplies, scavenging, stealing, or other coping strategies). (USDA)

The stages of food insecurity range from food secure situations to full-scale famine. "Famine and hunger are both rooted in food insecurity. Food insecurity can be categorized as either chronic or transitory. Chronic food insecurity translates into a high degree of vulnerability to famine and hunger; ensuring food security presupposes elimination of that vulnerability. [Chronic] hunger is not famine. It is similar to undernourishment and is related to poverty, existing mainly in poor countries

Many countries experience perpetual food shortages and distribution problems. These result in chronic and often widespread hunger amongst significant numbers of people. Human populations respond to chronic hunger and malnutrition by decreasing body size, known in medical terms as stunting or stunted growth. This process starts *in utero* if the mother is malnourished and continues through approximately the third year of life. It leads to higher infant and child mortality, but at rates far lower than during famines. Once stunting has occurred, improved nutritional intake later in life cannot reverse the damage. Stunting itself is viewed as a coping mechanism, designed to bring body size into alignment with the calories available during adulthood in the location where the child is born. Limiting body size as a way of adapting to low levels of energy (calories) adversely affects health in three ways:

- Premature failure of vital organs occurs during adulthood. For example a 50 year old individual might die of heart failure because his/her heart suffered structural defects during early development.
- Stunted individuals suffer a far higher rate of disease and illness than those who have not undergone stunting.
- Severe malnutrition in early childhood often leads to defects in cognitive development.

"The analysis ... points to the misleading nature of the concept of subsistence as Malthus originally used it and as it is still widely used today. Subsistence in not located at the edge of a nutritional cliff, beyond which lies demographic disaster. Rather than one level of subsistence, there are numerous levels at which a population and a food supply can be in equilibrium in the sense that they can be indefinitely sustained. However, some levels will have smaller people and higher normal mortality than others."

GLOBAL WATER CRISIS

Water deficits, which are already spurring heavy grain imports in numerous smaller countries, may soon do the same in larger countries, such as China or India. The water tables are falling in scores of countries (including Northern China, the US, and India) due to widespread overpumping using powerful diesel and electric pumps. Other countries affected include Pakistan, Afghanistan, and Iran. This will eventually lead to water scarcity and cutbacks in grain harvest. Even with the overpumping of its aquifers, China is developing a grain deficit. When this happens, it will almost certainly drive grain prices upward. Most of the 3 billion people projected to be added worldwide by mid-century will be born in countries already experiencing water shortages. After China and India, there is a second tier of smaller countries with large water deficits—Afghanistan, Algeria, Egypt, Iran, Mexico, and Pakistan. Four of these already import a large share of their grain. Only Pakistan remains self-sufficient. But with a population expanding by 4 million a year, it will also likely soon turn to the world market for grain.

Multimillion dollar investments beginning in the 1990s by the World Bank have reclaimed desert and turned the Ica Valley in Peru, one of the driest places on earth, into the largest supplier of asparagus in the world. However, the constant irrigation has caused a rapid drop in the water table, in some places as much as eight meters per year, one of the fastest rates of aquifer depletion in the world. The wells of small farmers and local people are beginning to run dry and the water supply for the main city in the valley is under threat. As a cash crop, asparagus has provided jobs for local people, but most of the money goes to the buyers, mainly the British. A recent report concluded that the industry is not sustainable and accuses investors, including the World Bank, of failing to take proper responsibility for the impact of their decisions on the water resources of poorer countries. Diverting water from the headwaters of the Ica River to asparagus fields has also led to a water shortage in the mountain region of Huancavelica, where indigenous communities make a marginal living herding.

LAND DEGRADATION

Intensive farming often leads to a vicious cycle of exhaustion of soil fertility and decline of agricultural yields. Approximately 40% of the world's agricultural land is seriously degraded. In Africa, if current trends of soil degradation continue, the continent might be able to feed just 25% of its population by 2025, according to UNU's Ghana-based Institute for Natural Resources in Africa.

LAND DEALS

Rich governments and corporations are buying up the rights to millions of hectares of agricultural land in developing countries in an effort to secure their own long-term food supplies. The head of the Food and Agriculture Organisation (FAO), Jacques Diouf, has warned that the controversial rise in land deals could create a form of "neocolonialism", with poor states producing food for the rich at the expense of their own hungry people. The South Korean firm Daewoo Logistics has secured a large piece of farmland in Madagascar to grow maize and crops for biofuels. Libya has secured 250,000 hectares of Ukrainian farmland, and China has begun to explore land deals in Southeast Asia. Oil-rich Arab investors, including the sovereign wealth funds, are looking into Sudan, Ethiopia, Ukraine, Kazakhstan, Pakistan, Cambodia and Thailand.

Some countries are using the acquisition of land for agriculture in return for other gains. Egypt is seeking land acquisition in Ukraine in exchange for access to its natural gas. Qatar has plans to lease 40,000 hectares of agricultural land along Kenya's coast to grow fruit and vegetables, in return for building a £2.4 billion port close to the Indian Ocean tourist island of Lamu.

AGRICULTURE

Approximately 2.4 billion people live in the drainage basin of the Himalayan rivers. India, China, Pakistan, Afghanistan, Bangladesh, Nepal and Myanmar could experience floods followed by severe droughts in coming decades. In India alone, the Ganges provides water for drinking and farming for more than 500 million people. The west coast of North America, which gets much of its water from glaciers in mountain ranges such as the Rocky Mountains and Sierra Nevada, also would be affected. Glaciers aren't the only worry that the developing nations have, sea level is also reported to rise as climate change progresses, reducing the amount of land available for agriculture.

In other parts of the world a big effect will be low yields of grain according to the World Food Trade Model, specifically in the low latitude regions where much of the developing world is located. From this the price of grain will rise, along with the developing nations trying to grow the grain. Due to this, every 2-2.5% price hike will increase the number of hungry people 1%. And low crop yields is just one of the problem facing farmers in the low latitudes and tropical regions. The timing and length of the growing seasons, when farmers plant their crops, are going to be changing dramatically, per the USDA, due to unknown changes in soil temperature and moisture conditions.

CHILDREN

On 2008-04-29, a UNICEF UK report found that the world's poorest and most vulnerable children are being hit the hardest by the impact of climate change. The report, "Our Climate, Our Children, Our Responsibility: The Implications of Climate Change for the World's Children," says access to clean water and food supplies will become more difficult, particularly in Africa and Asia

ENVIRONMENTAL SECURITY

Environmental security examines the threat posed by environmental events and trends to national power, as well as the impact of human conflict and international relations on the environment.

The Millennium Project did a global assessment of the definitions of environmental security and created a synthesis definition: Environmental Security is environmental viability for life support, with three sub-elements:

- preventing or repairing military damage to the environment,
- preventing or responding to environmentally caused conflicts, and
- protecting the environment due to its inherent moral value.

There is a growing understanding that environmental degradation, inequitable access to natural resources and transboundary movement of hazardous materials increase the probability of conflict and thereby pose a risk to human and even national security. For example, transboundary pollution often negatively affects negatively the relations between neighbouring states sharing the common resource base. Also health risks and involuntary migration due to e.g. water scarcity, equitable access to land resources, uncontrolled stocks of obsolete pesticides or other forms of hazardous waste have been identified as threats to stability and peace.

Ongoing disputes and disagreements over the management of natural resources shared by two or more states, can deepen divides and lead to hostilities. However, common problems regarding the use of natural resources may also bring people together in a positive manner. Communities and nations can build confidence with each other through joint efforts to improve the state and management of natural resources. Environmental co-operation can thereby act as an important tool for preventing conflicts and promoting peace between communities.

The Environment and Security Initiative (ENVSEC) seeks to facilitate a process whereby key public decision-makers in South Eastern and Eastern Europe, Central Asia and the Caucasus are able to motivate action to advance and protect peace and the environment at the same time.

COMPUTER, INFORMATION AND CYBER SECURITY[1]

Computer security, **cybersecurity** or **information technology security** (**IT security**) is the protection of computer systems from theft or damage to their hardware, software or electronic data, as well as from disruption or misdirection of the services they provide.

The field is growing in importance due to increasing reliance on computer systems, the Internet and wireless networks such as Bluetooth and Wi-Fi, and due to the growth of "smart" devices, including smartphones, televisions and the various tiny devices that constitute the Internet of things. Due to its complexity, both in terms of politics and technology, it is also one of the major challenges of the contemporary world.

INFORMATION SECURITY

Information security, sometimes shortened to **InfoSec**, is the practice of preventing unauthorized access, use, disclosure, disruption, modification, inspection, recording or destruction of information.

[1] For the information on ***Global Cybersecurity Library***, covering national cybersecyruty strategy and regulations in 90 countries, please contact Global Investment Center USA at ibpusa3@gmail.com .

The information or data may take any form, e.g. electronic or physical. Information security's primary focus is the balanced protection of the confidentiality, integrity and availability of data (also known as the CIA triad) while maintaining a focus on efficient policy implementation, all without hampering organization productivity. This is largely achieved through a multi-step risk management process that identifies assets, threat sources, vulnerabilities, potential impacts, and possible controls, followed by assessment of the effectiveness of the risk management plan.

To standardize this discipline, academics and professionals collaborate and seek to set basic guidance, policies, and industry standards on password, antivirus software, firewall, encryption software, legal liability and user/administrator training standards. This standardization may be further driven by a wide variety of laws and regulations that affect how data is accessed, processed, stored, and transferred. However, the implementation of any standards and guidance within an entity may have limited effect if a culture of continual improvement isn't adopted

Information security threats come in many different forms. Some of the most common threats today are software attacks, theft of intellectual property, identity theft, theft of equipment or information, sabotage, and information extortion. Most people have experienced software attacks of some sort. Viruses, worms, phishing attacks, and Trojan horses are a few common examples of software attacks. The theft of intellectual property has also been an extensive issue for many businesses in the IT field. Identity theft is the attempt to act as someone else usually to obtain that person's personal information or to take advantage of their access to vital information. Theft of equipment or information is becoming more prevalent today due to the fact that most devices today are mobile, are prone to theft and have also become far more desirable as the amount of data capacity increases. Sabotage usually consists of the destruction of an organization's website in an attempt to cause loss of confidence on the part of its customers. Information extortion consists of theft of a company's property or information as an attempt to receive a payment in exchange for returning the information or property back to its owner, as with ransomware. There are many ways to help protect yourself from some of these attacks but one of the most functional precautions is user carefulness.

Governments, military, corporations, financial institutions, hospitals and private businesses amass a great deal of confidential information about their employees, customers, products, research and financial status. Should confidential information about a business' customers or finances or new product line fall into the hands of a competitor or a black hat hacker, a business and its customers could suffer widespread, irreparable financial loss, as well as damage to the company's reputation. From a business perspective, information security must be balanced against cost; the Gordon-Loeb Model provides a mathematical economic approach for addressing this concern. For the individual, information security has a significant effect on privacy, which is viewed very differently in various cultures.

There are two things in this definition that may need some clarification. First, the *process* of risk management is an ongoing, iterative process. It must be repeated indefinitely. The business environment is constantly changing and new threats and vulnerabilities emerge every day. Second, the choice of countermeasures (controls) used to manage risks must strike a balance between productivity, cost, effectiveness of the countermeasure, and the value of the informational asset being protected.

Risk analysis and risk evaluation processes have their limitations since, when security incidents occur, they emerge in a context, and their rarity and uniqueness give rise to unpredictable threats. The analysis of these phenomena, which are characterized by breakdowns, surprises and side-effects, requires a theoretical approach that is able to examine and interpret subjectively the detail of each incident.

Risk is the likelihood that something bad will happen that causes harm to an informational asset (or the loss of the asset). A vulnerability is a weakness that could be used to endanger or cause harm to an informational asset. A threat is anything (man-made or act of nature) that has the potential to cause harm.

The likelihood that a threat will use a vulnerability to cause harm creates a risk. When a threat does use a vulnerability to inflict harm, it has an impact. In the context of information security, the impact is a loss of availability, integrity, and confidentiality, and possibly other losses (lost income, loss of life, loss of real property). It should be pointed out that it is not possible to identify all risks, nor is it possible to eliminate all risk. The remaining risk is called "residual risk."

A risk assessment is carried out by a team of people who have knowledge of specific areas of the business. Membership of the team may vary over time as different parts of the business are assessed. The assessment may use a subjective qualitative analysis based on informed opinion, or where reliable dollar figures and historical information is available, the analysis may use quantitative analysis.

Research has shown that the most vulnerable point in most information systems is the human user, operator, designer, or other human. The ISO/IEC 27002:2005 Code of practice for information security management recommends the following be examined during a risk assessment:

- **security policy,**
- **organization of information security,**
- **asset management,**
- **human resources security,**
- **physical and environmental security,**
- **communications and operations management,**
- **access control,**
- **information systems acquisition, development and maintenance,**
- **information security incident management,**
- **business continuity management, and**
- **regulatory compliance.**

LAWS AND REGULATIONS

Governments of many countries adopted laws and regulations that have, had, or will have, a significant effect on data processing and information security. Important industry sector regulations have also been included when they have a significant impact on information security.

The U.K. Data Protection Act 1998 makes new provisions for the regulation of the processing of information relating to individuals, including the obtaining, holding, use or disclosure of such information. The European Union Data Protection Directive (EUDPD) requires that all E.U. members adopt national regulations to standardize the protection of data privacy for citizens throughout the E.U.

The Computer Misuse Act 1990 is an Act of the U.K. Parliament making computer crime (e.g., hacking) a criminal offense. The act has become a model upon which several other countries, including Canada and the Republic of Ireland, have drawn inspiration from when subsequently drafting their own information security laws.

The E.U.'s Data Retention Directive (annulled) required internet service providers and phone companies to keep data on every electronic message sent and phone call made for between six months and two years.

The Family Educational Rights and Privacy Act (FERPA) (20 U.S.C. § 1232 g; 34 CFR Part 99) is a U.S. Federal law that protects the privacy of student education records. The law applies to all schools that receive funds under an applicable program of the U.S. Department of Education. Generally, schools must have written permission from the parent or eligible student in order to release any information from a student's education record.

The Federal Financial Institutions Examination Council's (FFIEC) security guidelines for auditors specifies requirements for online banking security.

The Health Insurance Portability and Accountability Act (HIPAA) of 1996 requires the adoption of national standards for electronic health care transactions and national identifiers for providers, health insurance plans, and employers. Additionally, it requires health care providers, insurance providers and employers to safeguard the security and privacy of health data.

The Gramm–Leach–Bliley Act of 1999 (GLBA), also known as the Financial Services Modernization Act of 1999, protects the privacy and security of private financial information that financial institutions collect, hold, and process.

Section 404 of the Sarbanes–Oxley Act of 2002 (SOX) requires publicly traded companies to assess the effectiveness of their internal controls for financial reporting in annual reports they submit at the end of each fiscal year. Chief information officers are responsible for the security, accuracy and the reliability of the systems that manage and report the financial data. The act also requires publicly traded companies to engage with independent auditors who must attest to, and report on, the validity of their assessments.

The Payment Card Industry Data Security Standard (PCI DSS) establishes comprehensive requirements for enhancing payment account data security. It was developed by the founding payment brands of the PCI Security Standards Council — including American Express, Discover Financial Services, JCB, MasterCard Worldwide and Visa International — to help facilitate the broad adoption of consistent data security measures on a global basis. The PCI DSS is a multifaceted security standard that includes requirements for security management, policies, procedures, network architecture, software design and other critical protective measures.

State security breach notification laws (California and many others) require businesses, nonprofits, and state institutions to notify consumers when unencrypted "personal information" may have been compromised, lost, or stolen.

The Personal Information Protection and Electronics Document Act (PIPEDA) of Canada supports and promotes electronic commerce by protecting personal information that is collected, used or disclosed in certain circumstances, by providing for the use of electronic means to communicate or record information or transactions and by amending the Canada Evidence Act, the Statutory Instruments Act and the Statute Revision Act.

Greece's Hellenic Authority for Communication Security and Privacy (ADAE) (Law 165/2011) establishes and describes the minimum information security controls that should be deployed by every company which provides electronic communication networks and/or services in Greece in order to protect customers' confidentiality. These include both managerial and technical controls (e.g., log records should be stored for two years).

Greece's Hellenic Authority for Communication Security and Privacy (ADAE) (Law 205/2013) concentrates around the protection of the integrity and availability of the services and data offered by Greek telecommunication companies. The law forces these and other related companies to build, deploy and test appropriate business continuity plans and redundant infrastructures.

COMPUTER SECURITY

SECURITY BY DESIGN

The technologies of computer security are based on logic. As security is not necessarily the primary goal of most computer applications, designing a program with security in mind often imposes restrictions on that program's behavior.

There are 4 approaches to security in computing, sometimes a combination of approaches is valid:

1. Trust all the software to abide by a security policy but the software is not trustworthy (this is computer insecurity).
2. Trust all the software to abide by a security policy and the software is validated as trustworthy (by tedious branch and path analysis for example).
3. Trust no software but enforce a security policy with mechanisms that are not trustworthy (again this is computer insecurity).
4. Trust no software but enforce a security policy with trustworthy hardware mechanisms.

Many systems have unintentionally resulted in the first possibility. Since approach two is expensive and non-deterministic, its use is very limited. Approaches one and three lead to failure. Because approach number four is often based on hardware mechanisms and avoids abstractions and a multiplicity of degrees of freedom, it is more practical. Combinations of approaches two and four are often used in a layered architecture with thin layers of two and thick layers of four.

There are various strategies and techniques used to design security systems. However there are few, if any, effective strategies to enhance security after design. One technique enforces the principle of least privilege to great extent, where an entity has only the privileges that are needed for its function. That way even if an attacker gains access to one part of the system, fine-grained security ensures that it is just as difficult for them to access the rest.

Furthermore, by breaking the system up into smaller components, the complexity of individual components is reduced, opening up the possibility of using techniques such as automated theorem proving to prove the correctness of crucial software subsystems. This enables a closed form solution to security that works well when only a single well-characterized property can be isolated as critical, and that property is also assessible to math. Not surprisingly, it is impractical for generalized correctness, which probably cannot even be defined, much less proven. Where formal correctness proofs are not possible, rigorous use of code review and unit testing represent a best-effort approach to make modules secure.

The design should use "defense in depth", where more than one subsystem needs to be violated to compromise the integrity of the system and the information it holds. Defense in depth works when the breaching of one security measure does not provide a platform to facilitate subverting another. Also, the cascading principle acknowledges that several low hurdles does not make a high hurdle. So cascading several weak mechanisms does not provide the safety of a single stronger mechanism.

Subsystems should default to secure settings, and wherever possible should be designed to "fail secure" rather than "fail insecure" (see fail-safe for the equivalent in safety engineering). Ideally, a secure system should require a deliberate, conscious, knowledgeable and free decision on the part of legitimate authorities in order to make it insecure.

In addition, security should not be an all or nothing issue. The designers and operators of systems should assume that security breaches are inevitable. Full audit trails should be kept of system activity, so that when a security breach occurs, the mechanism and extent of the breach can be determined. Storing audit trails remotely, where they can only be appended to, can keep intruders from covering their tracks. Finally, full disclosure helps to ensure that when bugs are found the "window of vulnerability" is kept as short as possible.

SECURITY ARCHITECTURE

Security Architecture can be defined as the design artifacts that describe how the security controls (security countermeasures) are positioned, and how they relate to the overall information technology architecture. These controls serve the purpose to maintain the system's quality attributes, among them confidentiality, integrity, availability, accountability and assurance.".

HARDWARE MECHANISMS THAT PROTECT COMPUTERS AND DATA

Hardware based or assisted computer security offers an alternative to software-only computer security. Devices such as dongles may be considered more secure due to the physical access required in order to be compromised

SECURE OPERATING SYSTEMS

One use of the term computer security refers to technology to implement a secure operating system. Much of this technology is based on science developed in the 1980s and used to produce what may be some of the most impenetrable operating systems ever. Though still valid, the technology is in limited use today, primarily because it imposes some changes to system management and also because it is not widely understood. Such ultra-strong secure operating systems are based on operating system kernel technology that can guarantee that certain security policies are absolutely enforced in an operating environment. An example of such a Computer security policy is the Bell-LaPadula model. The strategy is based on a coupling of special microprocessor hardware features, often involving the memory management unit, to a special correctly implemented operating system kernel. This forms the foundation for a secure operating system which, if certain critical parts are designed and implemented correctly, can ensure the absolute impossibility of penetration by hostile elements. This capability is enabled because the configuration not only imposes a security policy, but in theory completely protects itself from corruption. Ordinary operating systems, on the other hand, lack the features that assure this maximal level of security. The design methodology to produce such secure systems is precise, deterministic and logical.

Systems designed with such methodology represent the state of the art of computer security although products using such security are not widely known. In sharp contrast to most kinds of software, they meet specifications with verifiable certainty comparable to specifications for size, weight and power. Secure operating systems designed this way are used primarily to protect national security information, military secrets, and the data of international financial institutions. These are very powerful security tools and very few secure operating systems have been certified at the highest level

(Orange Book A-1) to operate over the range of "Top Secret" to "unclassified" (including Honeywell SCOMP, USAF SACDIN, NSA Blacker and Boeing MLS LAN.) The assurance of security depends not only on the soundness of the design strategy, but also on the assurance of correctness of the implementation, and therefore there are degrees of security strength defined for COMPUSEC. The Common Criteria quantifies security strength of products in terms of two components, security functionality and assurance level (such as EAL levels), and these are specified in a Protection Profile for requirements and a Security Target for product descriptions. None of these ultra-high assurance secure general purpose operating systems have been produced for decades or certified under the Common Criteria.

In USA parlance, the term High Assurance usually suggests the system has the right security functions that are implemented robustly enough to protect DoD and DoE classified information. Medium assurance suggests it can protect less valuable information, such as income tax information. Secure operating systems designed to meet medium robustness levels of security functionality and assurance have seen wider use within both government and commercial markets. Medium robust systems may provide the same security functions as high assurance secure operating systems but do so at a lower assurance level (such as Common Criteria levels EAL4 or EAL5). Lower levels mean we can be less certain that the security functions are implemented flawlessly, and therefore less dependable. These systems are found in use on web servers, guards, database servers, and management hosts and are used not only to protect the data stored on these systems but also to provide a high level of protection for network connections and routing services.

SECURE CODING

If the operating environment is not based on a secure operating system capable of maintaining a domain for its own execution, and capable of protecting application code from malicious subversion, and capable of protecting the system from subverted code, then high degrees of security are understandably not possible. While such secure operating systems are possible and have been implemented, most commercial systems fall in a 'low security' category because they rely on features not supported by secure operating systems (like portability, et al.). In low security operating environments, applications must be relied on to participate in their own protection. There are 'best effort' secure coding practices that can be followed to make an application more resistant to malicious subversion.

In commercial environments, the majority of software subversion vulnerabilities result from a few known kinds of coding defects. Common software defects include buffer overflows, format string vulnerabilities, integer overflow, and code/command injection. It is to be immediately noted that all of the foregoing are specific instances of a general class of attacks, where situations in which putative "data" actually contains implicit or explicit, executable instructions are cleverly exploited.

Some common languages such as C and C++ are vulnerable to all of these defects (see Seacord, *"Secure Coding in C and C++"*). Other languages, such as Java, are more resistant to some of these defects, but are still prone to code/command injection and other software defects which facilitate subversion.

Recently another bad coding practice has come under scrutiny; dangling pointers. The first known exploit for this particular problem was presented in July 2007. Before this publication the problem was known but considered to be academic and not practically exploitable.

Unfortunately, there is no theoretical model of "secure coding" practices, nor is one practically achievable, insofar as the variety of mechanisms are too wide and the manners in which they can be exploited are too variegated. It is interesting to note, however, that such vulnerabilities often arise from archaic philosophies in which computers were assumed to be narrowly disseminated entities used by a chosen few, all of whom were likely highly educated, solidly trained academics with naught but the goodness of mankind in mind. Thus, it was considered quite harmless if, for (fictitious) example, a FORMAT string in a FORTRAN program could contain the J format specifier to mean "shut down system after printing." After all, who would use such a feature but a well-intentioned system programmer? It was simply beyond conception that software could be deployed in a destructive fashion.

It is worth noting that, in some languages, the distinction between code (ideally, read-only) and data (generally read/write) is blurred. In LISP, particularly, there is no distinction whatsoever between code and data, both taking the same form: an S-expression can be code, or data, or both, and the "user" of a LISP program who manages to insert an executable LAMBDA segment into putative "data" can achieve arbitrarily general and dangerous functionality. Even something as "modern" as Perl offers the eval() function, which enables one to generate Perl code and submit it to the interpreter, disguised as string data.

CAPABILITIES AND ACCESS CONTROL LISTS

Within computer systems, two security models capable of enforcing privilege separation are access control lists (ACLs) and capability-based security. The semantics of ACLs have been proven to be insecure in many situations, e.g., the confused deputy problem. It has also been shown that the promise of ACLs of giving access to an object to only one person can never be guaranteed in practice. Both of these problems are resolved by capabilities. This does not mean practical flaws exist in all ACL-based systems, but only that the designers of certain utilities must take responsibility to ensure that they do not introduce flaws.

Capabilities have been mostly restricted to research operating systems and commercial OSs still use ACLs. Capabilities can, however, also be implemented at the language level, leading to a style of programming that is essentially a refinement of standard object-oriented design. An open source project in the area is the E language.

First the Plessey System 250 and then Cambridge CAP computer demonstrated the use of capabilities, both in hardware and software, in the 1970s. A reason for the lack of adoption of capabilities may be that ACLs appeared to offer a 'quick fix' for security without pervasive redesign of the operating system and hardware.

The most secure computers are those not connected to the Internet and shielded from any interference. In the real world, the most security comes from operating systems where security is not an add-on.

APPLICATIONS

Computer security is critical in almost any technology-driven industry which operates on computer systems. Computer security can also be referred to as computer safety. The issues of computer based systems and addressing their countless vulnerabilities are an integral part of maintaining an operational industry.

CLOUD COMPUTING SECURITY

Security in the cloud is challenging due to varied degree of security features and management schemes within the cloud entitites. In this connection one logical protocol base need to evolve so that the entire gamet of components operate synchronously and securely

AVIATION

The aviation industry is especially important when analyzing computer security because the involved risks include human life, expensive equipment, cargo, and transportation infrastructure. Security can be compromised by hardware and software malpractice, human error, and faulty operating environments. Threats that exploit computer vulnerabilities can stem from sabotage, espionage, industrial competition, terrorist attack, mechanical malfunction, and human error.

The consequences of a successful deliberate or inadvertent misuse of a computer system in the aviation industry range from loss of confidentiality to loss of system integrity, which may lead to more serious concerns such as data theft or loss, network and air traffic control outages, which in turn can lead to airport closures, loss of aircraft, loss of passenger life. Military systems that control munitions can pose an even greater risk.

A proper attack does not need to be very high tech or well funded; for a power outage at an airport alone can cause repercussions worldwide.. One of the easiest and, arguably, the most difficult to trace security vulnerabilities is achievable by transmitting unauthorized communications over specific radio frequencies. These transmissions may spoof air traffic controllers or simply disrupt communications altogether. These incidents are very common, having altered flight courses of commercial aircraft and caused panic and confusion in the past.

Controlling aircraft over oceans is especially dangerous because radar surveillance only extends 175 to 225 miles offshore. Beyond the radar's sight controllers must rely on periodic radio communications with a third party.

Lightning, power fluctuations, surges, brown-outs, blown fuses, and various other power outages instantly disable all computer systems, since they are dependent on an electrical source. Other accidental and intentional faults have caused significant disruption of safety critical systems throughout the last few decades and dependence on reliable communication and electrical power only jeopardizes computer safety.

NATIONAL SECURITY AND INTELLIGENCE AGENCIES IN SELECTED COUNTRIES

Austria	Bundesamt für Verfassungsschutz und Terrorismusbekämpfung, BVT
	Heeresnachrichtenamt, HNA
Belgium	Veiligheidsdienst van de Staat, VVDS
	Algemene Dienst Inlichting en Veiligheid, ADIV
	Service Général du Renseignement et de la Sécurité
Bulgaria	National Security Service, NSS
	National Intelligence Service, NIS
Canada	Canadian Security Intelligence Service, CSIS
	Communications Security Establishment, CSE
	Depratment of National Defense Intelligence, DNDI
	Foreing Intelligence Bureau, FIB
	Security Service Bureau, SSB
Croatia	Counter-intelligence Agency, POA
	Intelligence Agency, OA
	Military Intelligence Agency, VSA
Czech Republik	Security Information Service, BIS
	Office for Foreign Relations and Information, UZSI
	Military Intelligence, VZ
Denmark	Politiets Efterretningstjeneste, PET
	Danish Defense Intelligence Service, DDIS
Estonia	Kaitsepolitseiameti
Finland	Suojelupoliisi, SUPO
France	Les Renseignements généraux, RG
	La Direction de la Surveillance du Territoire, DST
	Direction Générale de la Sécurité Extérieure, DGSE
	Direction du Renseignement Militaire,DRM
	Direction de la Protection et de la Sécurité de la Défense, DPSD
Germany	Bundesamt für Verfassungsschutz, BfV
	Bundesnachrichtendienst, BND
	Militärischer Abschirmdienst, MAD
	Führungsstab der Streitkräfte II, FüS II
Greece	Hellenic National Intelligence Service, HNIS
Hungary	Information Office, IH
	National Security Office, NBH
	National Security Special Service, NBSZ
	Military Intelligence Office, KFH
	Military Counter-intelligence Office, KBH
Italy	Servizio per le Informazioni e la Sicurezza Democratica, SISDE
	Servizio per le Informazioni e la Sicurezza Militare, SISMI

Latvia	Valsts apsardzes dienests, VAD
Lithuania	State Security Department, VSD
	Civil Defence Office
	Communications and Information Systems Service
Luxemburg	Service de Renseignements de l´Etat Luxembourgeois, SREL
	Haut Commissariat la Securit Exterieure
	2eme Bureau de l´Arme
Netherland	Algemene Inlichtingen en Veiligheidsdienst, AIVD
	Inlichtingendienst Buitenland, IDB
	Military Intelligence Service, MID/KL
Norway	Politiets sikkerhetstjeneste
Poland	Internal Security Agency, ABW
	Intelligence Agency, AW
	Military Intelligence Service, WSI
Portugal	Servicos de Informacao e Seguranca da Republica Portuguesa, SIS
	Serviço de Informações Estratégicas de Defesa e Militares, SIEDM
Romania	Roman Information Service, SRI
	Foreign Intelligence Service, SIE
	Military Intelligence, DIM
	Military Counter-intelligence, CE
Russia	Foreign Intelligence Service, SVR
	Federal Security Service, FSB
	Federal Protective Service, FSO
	Main Intelligence Directorate, GRU
Slovenia	Slovenian Intelligence and Security Agency, SOVA
	Ministry of Defence Intelligence and Security Service,VOMO
Spain	Centro Nacional de Inteligencia, CNI
South Corea	Cchungsang Cchenbobu
	National Intelligence Service
	Defence Security Headquarters
Sweden	Säkerhetspolisen, SÄPO
	Militära Underrättelse och Säkerhetstjänsten, MUST
Switzerland	Service for Analysis and Prevention, SAP
	Strategischen Nachrichtendienstes
	Untergruppe Nachrichten Dienst und Abwehr, UNA
Turkey	Milli Instibarat Teskilati, MIT
Ukraine	Ukraine Securiry Service, SBU
	Main Intelligence Directorate, GUR
United Kingdom	Secret Intelligence Service, SIS/MI6
	Security Service, MI5
	Government Communications Headquarters, GCHQ
	Scotland Yard

	Counter-intelligence Department of the Customs Administration, Tax Office and Post Administration
	Defence Intelligence Staff, DIS
United States of America	Oficial page of the US Intelligence Community
	Central Intelligence Agency, CIA
	Federal Bureau of Investigation, FBI
	Office of Energy Intelligence, OEI
	Bureu of Intelligence and Research, INR
	Office of Intelligence Support, OIS
	Secret Service, SS
	National Counter-intelligence centre, NACIC
	National security agency, NSA
	Defense Intelligence Agency, DIA
	Office of Naval Intelligence, ONI
	National reconnaissance Office, NRO
	Air Force Intelligence, AFI
	Army Intelligence, AI
	Marine Corps Intelligence, MCI
	National Imagery and Mapping Agency, NIMA

AUSTRALIAN INTELLIGENCE AGENCIES

PARLIAMENT OF AUSTRALIA

Parliamentary Joint Committee on the
Australian Security Intelligence Organization, ASIS, and DSD
Joint Committee on the Australian Crime Commission

PARLIAMENTARY JOINT COMMITTEE ON ASIO, ASIS AND DSD

Prior to the dissolution of the House for the 2001 general election, the predecessors to this committee were known as the:

- Parliamentary Joint Committee on the Australian Security and Intelligence Organisation; and
- Joint Select Committee on the Intelligence Services.

To reflect a change in portfolio coverage following the election, these two committees were amalgamated and renamed as the Parliamentary Joint Committee on ASIO (Australian Security and Intelligence Organisation), ASIS (Australian Secret Intelligence Service) and DSD (Defence Signals Directorate).
Committee activities (inquiries and reports)
Committee establishment, role and history

The Committee Secretariat can be contacted at:
Committee Secretary
Parliamentary Joint Committee on ASIO, ASIS and DSD
Parliament House
CANBERRA ACT 2600
AUSTRALIA

Phone: (02) 6277 2360
Fax:(02) 6277 2067
email: pjcaad@aph.gov.au

EXECUTIVE GOVERNMENT

DEPARTMENT OF THE PRIME MINISTER AND CABINET

International Division
Office of National Assesments (ONA)
Department of Foreign Affairs and Trade
Australian Secret Intelligence Service (ASIS)
International Security Division
Strategic Policy and Intelligence Branch (SPI)
Intelligence and Counter-Terrorism Policy Section (ICT)
Department of Defence
Strategy and Intelligence (S&I) Program
Defense Intelligence Organisation (DIO)
Defence Security Branch (DSB)
Australian Army
Directorate of Military Intelligence
Australian Intelligence Corps (AIC)
Defence Intelligence Wing (DIW)
Defence Signals Directorate (DSD)
Royal Australian Navy
Royal Australian Air Force
Directorate of Air Force Security & Intelligence
Attorney General
Australian Security Intelligence Organization (ASIO)
Australian Protective Service (APS)
Australian Security Vetting Service (ASVS)
Protective Security Coordination Centre (PSCC)
Australian Federal Police (AFP)
National Crime Authority (NCA)
Australian Bureau of Criminal Intelligence (ABCI)
Australian Transaction Reports and Analysis Centre (AUSTRAC)
Commonwealth Law Enforcement Board
Office of Strategic Crime Assessments (OSCA)
Defence, Press and Broadcasting Committee
AUSCERT - Australian Computer Emergency Response Team
Australasian Police Ministers' Council
New South Wales Police Service
Northern Territory Police Force
Queensland Police Service
South Australian Police Department
Tasmanian Police
Victorian Police Department
Western Australian Police Service

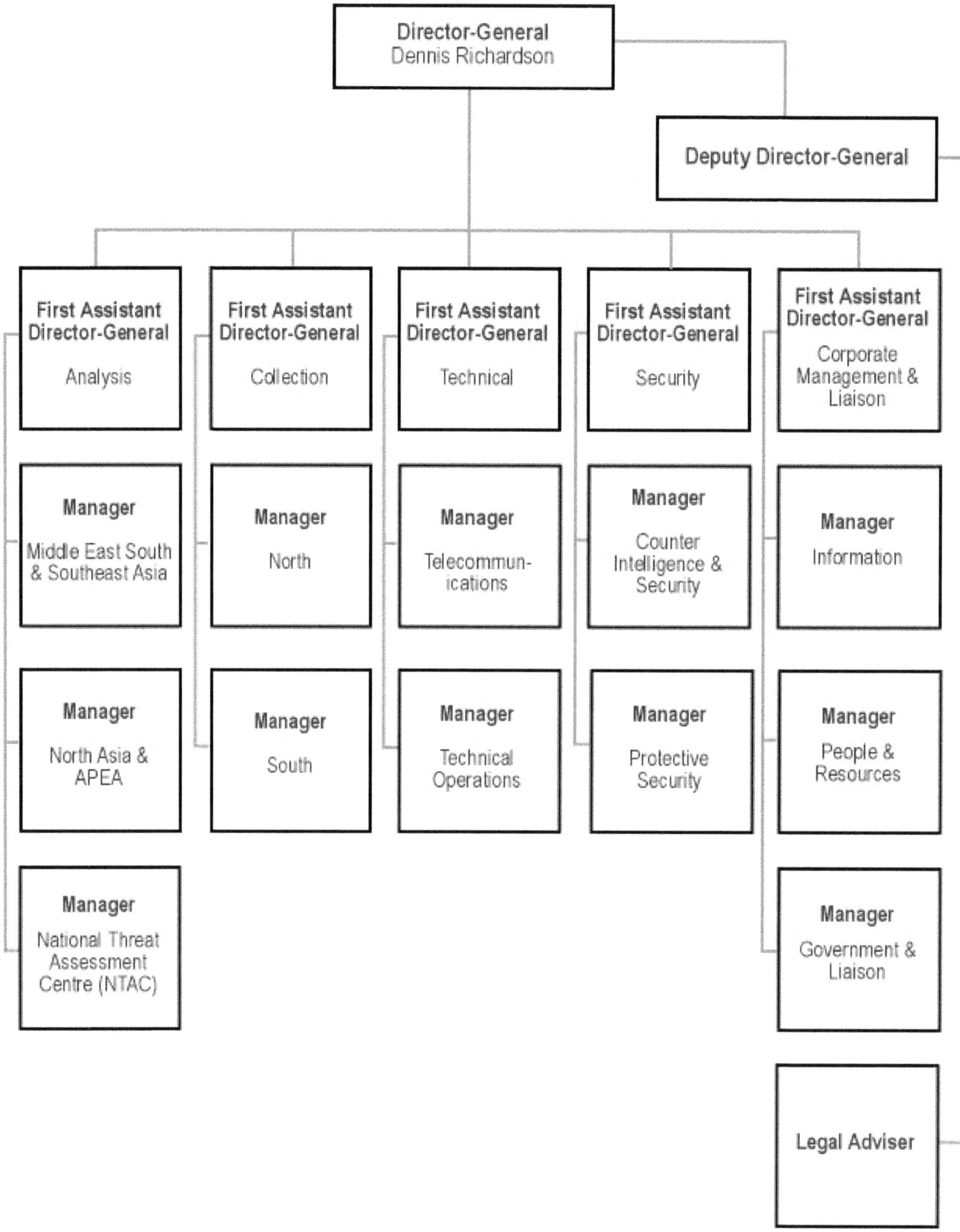
Director-General
Dennis Richardson
Deputy Director-General
First Assistant Director-General
Analysis
First Assistant Director-General
Collection
First Assistant Director-General
Technical
First Assistant Director-General
Security
First Assistant Director-General
Corporate Management & Liaison
Manager
Middle East South & Southeast Asia
Manager
North
Manager
Telecommun-ications
Manager
Counter Intelligence & Security
Manager
Information
Manager
North Asia & APEA
Manager
South
Manager
Technical Operations
Manager
Protective Security
Manager
People & Resources
Manager
National Threat Assessment Centre (NTAC)
Manager
Government & Liaison
Legal Adviser

AUSTRALIAN SECURITY INTELLIGENCE ORGANISATION

The Australian Security Intelligence Organisation (ASIO) is Australia's security service. Its functions are set out in the *Australian Security Intelligence Organisation Act 1979* (the ASIO Act).

ASIO's main role is to gather information and produce intelligence that will enable it to warn the government about activities or situations that might endanger Australia's national security. The ASIO Act defines 'security' as the protection of Australia and its people from espionage, sabotage, politically motivated violence, the promotion of communal violence, attacks on Australia's defence system, and acts of foreign interference. Some of these terms are further defined in the ASIO Act.

ASIO focuses on terrorists, people who may act violently for political reasons, and people who may clandestinely obtain sensitive government information (spies) or otherwise harm Australia's interests in order to further their own causes or the interests of foreign governments.

ASIO does not investigate lawful protest activity nor does it investigate purely criminal activities.

Other ASIO functions include providing security assessments, protective security advice and collecting foreign intelligence in Australia. In security assessments ASIO advises government agencies on the relevant backgrounds of people applying for national security clearances or visas to enter or stay in Australia. Protective security advice is given by ASIO to government agencies seeking cost-effective ways to protect their assets. Foreign intelligence is information on the capabilities, intentions and activities of foreign powers.

Under the ASIO Act, the Attorney-General, the Minister to whom ASIO is responsible, has issued guidelines on how ASIO should perform its functions relating to politically motivated violence and its functions of obtaining intelligence relevant to security.

ASIO has a staff of about 750. Its Central Office is in Canberra, and there is a local office in each mainland state and territory capital. For the financial year 2002-2003, ASIO's appropriation was $90,367 million.

MANAGEMENT AND STRUCTURE

The strategic management of the Organisation is undertaken by the Corporate Executive, comprising the Director-General, Deputy Director-General and First Assistant Directors-General, with the President of the ASIO Staff Association attending as an observer.

Various corporate committees report to this executive, covering information management, audit and evaluation, security intelligence coordination and human resource management. These committees are structured so as to draw on the range of experience available within the Organisation. Where appropriate, outside agencies also contribute - for example a Senior Executive officer from the Australian National Audit Office (ANAO) sits on ASIO's Audit and Evaluation Committee.

The ASIO Consultative Council is the principal staff-management consultative forum.

ASIO MANAGEMENT STRUCTURE

A review of ASIO's management structure, commenced in 2001-02, was completed in 2002-03 and resulted in a significant organisational restructure which took effect from 1 March 2003. The restructure - which expanded the number of divisions from three to five - takes account of new initiatives and increasing staff numbers flowing from additional counter-terrorism funding provided in the wake of the 11 September attacks and the Bali bombings.

SIO is a member of a group of Commonwealth intelligence agencies, each with distinct responsibilities. As well as ASIO they include the Office of National Assessments (ONA), the Australian Secret Intelligence Service (ASIS), the Defence Signals Directorate (DSD) Defence Intelligence Organisation (DIO) and the Defence Imagery and Geospatial Organisation (DIGO).

ACCOUNTABILITY

Due to the nature of its investigative work, ASIO does not make public details of its intelligence activities, and the identities of its officers are protected by law. However, mechanisms are in place to make sure ASIO conducts its business with legality and propriety. Some controls, such as auditing requirements, apply to all federal government agencies; others apply specifically to ASIO.

The main avenue of accountability is ASIO's relationship with its responsible Minister, the Attorney-General. ASIO briefs the Attorney-General on all major issues affecting security. The Attorney-General is also informed of ASIO's operations through his or her role in considering the grounds for warrants authorising the use of ASIO's special investigative powers. The Attorney-General issues guidelines governing ASIO's handling of sensitive aspects of its work. ASIO reports to a range of government and parliamentary committees dealing with security, legislative and financial matters. The Organisation also provides a classified annual report to the Government. An unclassified version is tabled in parliament and is publicly available.

ASIO is also subject to scrutiny by the Parliamentary Joint Committee on ASIO ASIS and DSD. Under the *ASIO Act 1979*, the Leader of the Opposition is required to be briefed on security by the Director-General. In 1986 the Parliament established the Office of the Inspector-General of Intelligence and Security to provide additional oversight of Australia's security and intelligence agencies. The Office of Inspector-General has full access to all ASIO records, has the power to inquire into public complaints, has the power to conduct inquiries referred to it by Government and has the power to initiate inquiries of its own.

FREQUENTLY ASKED QUESTIONS ABOUT ASIO

How does ASIO gather information?

Some of ASIO's information comes from publicly available sources such as news services and statistical databases or is volunteered by members of the public. Other information is collected by ASIO through interviews or covert human source operations. A good deal of useful intelligence comes from cooperating intelligence services in other countries. Part of ASIO's work - and a side which often excites public interest - involves the use of intrusive methods of investigation. If there is sufficient justification, the Attorney-General may sign a warrant allowing ASIO to employ special investigative powers to investigate whether harmful activities are being planned or carried out by people who are generally using clandestine or deceptive means to mask their true intentions. All aspects of ASIO's investigations are regulated by guidelines issued by the Attorney-General to ensure the methods used are appropriate.

What are ASIO's special investigative powers?

Legislation grants ASIO special powers to use intrusive methods of investigation. These special powers are to: intercept telecommunications, use listening devices and tracking devices, remotely access computers, enter and search premises, and examine postal articles. These powers are used under the authority of a warrant signed by the Attorney-General. Only the Director-General can seek a warrant, and the request must be accompanied by a written statement specifying the facts and other grounds on which the Director-General considers it necessary that the warrant be issued. Warrant requests are examined by a senior official of the Attorney-General's Department, who provides independent advice to the Minister on whether the relevant statutory requirements have been satisfied. Warrants are issued for specified periods only. At the expiry of each warrant ASIO must report to the Attorney-General on the extent to which the intrusive activity helped ASIO to carry out its functions.

Also the Australian Security Organisation Legislation Amendment (Terrorism Act 2002 was passed by parliament on 26 June 2003 and received Royal Assent on 22 July 2003. The legislation is designed to enhance Australia's capacity to combat terrorism by authorising ASIO to seek warrants for the questioning of persons for purpose of investigating terrorism. The warrants may authorise police officers to detain persons in limited circumstances.
In this case, ASIO is required to obtain the Attorney-General's consent before seeking a warrant from an independent issuing authority (a Federal Magistrate or Judge). Any questioning pursuant to a warrant must be undertaken in the presence of a prescribed authority (a former or serving senior Judge or the President or Deputy President of the Administrative Appeals Tribunal) under conditions determined by that authority. The Inspector-General of Intelligence and Security may attend during any questioning or detention under warrant.

Do the* Freedom of Information Act *and the* Privacy Act *apply to ASIO?
ASIO is not subject to the provisions of the *Freedom of Information Act 1982.* The *Privacy Act 1988* does not apply to the disclosure of personal information to ASIO by other agencies.

Do ASIO officers carry firearms?
ASIO officers do not carry firearms.

Is ASIO information covered by the* Archives Act*?
Under the *Archives Act 1983,* members of the public can apply to the National Archives of Australia to access information that has been held on ASIO records for more than 30 years. Many files of this age can be made available, in whole or in part. Some information may be withheld if it prejudices current investigations, reveals certain methods of investigation, identifies people as current or past sources of information or as ASIO officers, or endangers foreign liaison relationships. Applicants can request an internal reconsideration of a decision by ASIO to withhold information. If unsuccessful, they can then lodge an appeal with an external body, the Administrative Appeals Tribunal.

ASIO CONTACT INFORMATION

Written inquiries

Director-General
ASIO Central Office
GPO Box 2176
CANBERRA ACT 2601

General inquiries	Central Office switchboard	(02) 6249 6299 1800 020 648 (toll free)
Recruitment inquiries	Recruitment Officer	(02) 6257 4916
Media inquiries	Media Liaison Officer	(02) 6249 8381
State office inquiries	Australian Capital Territory	(02) 6249 7415
	Victoria	(03) 9654 8985
	New South Wales	(02) 9281 0016
	Queensland	(07) 3831 5980

	South Australia	(08) 8223 2727
	Western Australia	(08) 9221 5066
	Northern Territory	(08) 8981 2374
	Tasmanian residents can call ASIO's Central Office	1800 020 648 (toll fr

AUSTRIA

http://www.bmi.gv.at

Generaldirektion für die Öffentliche Sicherheit
General Directorate for Public Security
Postfach 100, A-1014 Wien
+43-(0)1-531 26-0

Staatspolizei
State Police
Nachrichtendienstliche Aufklärung
Army Intelligence Service
Nachrichtendienstliche Abwehr
Army Counterintelligence Service

Bundeskanzleramt
Bundeskanzler Dr. Wolfgang Schüssel
Ballhausplatz 2
1014 Wien
Tel.: ++43/1/53115-0

- **Staatssekretariate im Bundeskanzleramt**
  - **Staatssekretär Franz Morak**
    Ballhausplatz 1
    1014 Wien
    Tel.: ++43/1/53115-0
  - **Staatssekretär Mag. Karl Schweitzer**
    Ballhausplatz 1
    1014 Wien
    Tel.: ++43/1/53115-0

□ **Bundesministerien**

- Bundesministerium für soziale Sicherheit, Generationen und Konsumentenschutz
  Bundesminister Mag. Herbert Haupt
  Minoritenplatz 3
  1014 Wien
  Tel.: ++43/1/71100-0
  - Staatssekretariat im Bundesministerium für soziale Sicherheit, Generationen und Konsumentenschutz
    Staatssekretärin Ursula Haubner
    Stubenring 1
    1010 Wien
    Tel.: ++43/1/71100-0
- Bundesministerium für auswärtige Angelegenheiten
  Bundesministerin Dr. Ursula Plassnik
  Ballhausplatz 2

1014 Wien
Tel.: ++43/1/53115-0

- Österreichischer Informationsdienst in Washington
- Austria in New York

- Bundesministerium für Bildung, Wissenschaft und Kultur
  Bundesministerin Elisabeth Gehrer
  Minoritenplatz 5
  1014 Wien
  Tel.: ++43/1/53120-0

Bundesministerium für Finanzen
Bundesminister Mag. Karl-Heinz Grasser
Himmelpfortgasse 8
1015 Wien
Tel.: ++43/1/51433-0

  - Staatssekretariat im Bundesministerium für Finanzen
    Staatssekretär Dr. Alfred Finz

- Bundesministerium für Inneres
  Bundesminister Liese Prokop
  Herrengasse 7
  1010 Wien
  Tel.: ++43/1/53126-0
- Bundesministerium für Justiz
  Bundesministerin Mag. Karin Miklautsch
  Museumstrasse 7
  1070 Wien
  Tel.: ++43/1/52152-0
- Bundesministerium für Landesverteidigung
  Bundesminister Günther Platter
  Rossauerlände 1
  1090 Wien
  Tel.: ++43/1/5200-0
- Bundesministerium für Land- und Forstwirtschaft, Umwelt und Wasserwirtschaft
  Bundesminister Dipl.Ing. Josef Pröll
  Stubenring 1
  1010 Wien
  Tel.: ++43/1/71100-0
  - Umweltbundesamt
  - Umweltdatenkatalog
- Bundesministerium für Verkehr, Innovation und Technologie
  Bundesminister Hubert Gorbach
  Radetzkystrasse 2
  1030 Wien
  Tel.: ++43/1/71162-0
  - Staatssekretariat im Bundesministerium für
    Verkehr, Innovation und Technologie
    Staatssekretär Mag. Helmut Kukacka
- Bundesministerium für Wirtschaft und Arbeit
  Bundesminister Dr. Martin Bartenstein
  Stubenring 1
  1010 Wien
  Tel.: ++43/1/71100-0

- **Bundesministerium für Gesundheit und Frauen**
  Bundesministerin Maria Rauch-Kallat
  Radetzkystrasse 2
  1030 Wien
  Tel.: ++43/1/71100-0
    - Staatssekretariat im Bundesministerium für Gesundheit und Frauen
      Staatssekretär Eduard Mainoni

ARGENTINA INTELLIGENCE AGENCIES

Presidencia de la Nación
Office of the President
Secretaría de Inteligencia de Estada (SIDE)
Secretariat of State Intelligence
Central Nacional de Inteligencia (CNI)
National Intelligence Center
Escuela Nacional de Inteligencia (ENI)
National Intelligence School
Ministry of the Interior
Ministerio del Interior
Policía Federal Argentina
Federal Police of Argentina
Gendarmería Nacional Argentina

Argentine Chamber of Safety (Camara Argentina de Seguridad -CAS)
Manager: Lic. Raul A Martinez
Ayacucho 420, 3 Piso F
C1026AAB Buenos Aires
Email: camseg@cuidad.com.ar
Tel/Fax: 00 54 11 4953 7295/00 54 11 4951 0754

Argentine Chamber of Electronic Security (Camara Argentina de Seguridad Electronica - CASEL)
President: Ing. Enrique Horacio Greenberg
Av. Paseo Colon 588, Piso 5, Oficina 14
C1063ACS Buenos Aires
Email: greenberg@casel,org.ar
Tel: 00 54 11 4855 6600
Fax: 00 54 11 4856 5064
Website: www.casel.org.ar

Argentine Chamber of Security and Investigation Companies (Camara de Empresas de Seguridad e Investigaciones - CAESI)
Montevideo 666, Piso 3, Oficina 307
1019 Buenos Aires
Email: caesi@velocom.com.ar
Website: www.caesi.com

BELGIUM: INTELLIGENCE AGENCIES

MINISTRY OF JUSTICE

http://just.fgov.be/
info@just.fgov.be

http://www.policefederale.be/
Veiligheid van de Staat (SV) (Dutch) or
Surete de l'Etat (SE) (French)
(*Federal intelligence and security agency*)

MINISTRY OF DEFENSE

http://www.mil.be
Belgian Military Intelligence and Security Service
Algemene Dienst Inlichtingen en Veiligheid (ADIV) or
Service Général du Renseignement et de la Sécurité (SGRS)

BOSNIA AND HERZEGOVINA - INTELLIGENCE AGENCIES

War in Bosnia engaged three nations, Muslims, Croats and Serbs. Therefore there were three armies and three police forces; the Intelligence Community was also divided along those lines.

The Serbs had **Drzavna Bezbednost** (DB, State Security), linked with the Serbian intelligence agency of the same name.

The Muslim side had **Agencija za Informacije I Dokumentaciju** (AID, Information and Documentation Agency), reportedly linked with international Islamist organizations.

The Croat side created **Sluzba Nacionalne Sigurnosti** (SNS, National Security Service) linked with the Republic of Croatia Intelligence Community. It was officially disassembled with the constitution of Federation of Bosnia and Herzegovina (one of two entities in Bosnia). However, a number of actions suggest that the Croat Intelligence Community is still active illegally.

More than 80% of the human resources of these agencies were ex-Yugoslavia DB officers. All of these intelligence agencies were under the umbrella of the Ministry of Interior Affairs (Ministry of Police), but the current situation is different.

Bosnia and Herzegovina as a state constituted of two entities Republic of Srpska (majority Serb) and Federation of Bosnia and Herzegovina (joint entity of Muslims and Croats) has two Intelligence Agencies controlled by these Entities. As aforementioned Croat SNS is officially out of power, but since (from Croats' point of view) AID still has strong Muslim influence on agency work, Croats kept a parallel intelligence agency mainly undertaking illegal actions of surveillance over international community and local political factions.

DB in Republic of Srpska (Serb entity in Bosnia) changed its name into **Obavjestajno Bezbjedonosna Sluzba** (OBS, Intelligence and Security Agency) and is now independent from Police and other Government bodies. The AID of the Federation of Bosnia and Herzegovina kept the same name and is also independent.

It is noteworthy that an actual Joint Intelligence Community of State of Bosnia and Herzegovina does not exist. The Office of the High Representative (OHR is highest body of the International Community in Bosnia), following a number of wiretapping scandals involving actions by AID and SFOR against the still active Croat SNS, ordered the Council of Ministers (Bosnian Government) to produce legislation on Intelligence at the State level establishing a joint intelligence agency of all three nations. The Council of Ministers failed to do so and OHR announced that High Representative Paddy Ashdown will issue a Law on an Intelligence Agency of Bosnia and Herzegovina to be created by

International Community experts. This law is expected to be brought very soon in first couple of months of 2004.

BRAZIL

http://www.abin.gov.br

Agência Brasileira de Inteligência (ABIN)
Brazilian Intelligence Agency
The National Intelligence Service, 1964-90
Escola Nacional de Informações
Strategic Affairs Secretariat, 1990-94
Secretaria de Assuntos Estratégicos (SAE)

THE NATIONAL INTELLIGENCE SERVICE (SNI)

The military-dominated SNI, which the Castelo Branco government created in 1964, was intended originally as a civilian agency of the executive branch. Initially, the SNI, under retired General Golbery do Couto e Silva, freed Castelo from dependence on army and Federal Police intelligence reports. The then head of the army, General Costa e Silva, feared that the new agency would weaken the army's secret service. However, by the end of 1968, with the triumph of the hard-liners, the SNI took on a military coloration. In 1973 it secured its dominance over the so-called intelligence community with the opening of the National Intelligence School (Escola Nacional de Informações--EsNI) in Brasília. The following year, the EsNI absorbed the ESG postgraduate intelligence course. Supposedly, the EsNI did not train police agents, and it selected its own students. By 1980 some officers were saying that the EsNI would be as useful as the ESG to their careers.

Alfred Stepan observed that the SNI differed from similar agencies in other countries in that it enjoyed a near monopoly over operations and training, and that the SNI chief had ministerial rank and therefore sat in the president's cabinet. In addition, he has pointed out that the SNI had an official in every government agency, in state-owned businesses, and at one point in the universities. These officials followed the daily functioning of the administrative machinery to ensure conformity with national security goals. Moreover, the SNI was autonomous, even regarding finances.

The SNI served as the backbone of the military regime's system of control and repression. Although there have been secret police in Brazil since at least the Vargas era, military involvement reached new heights with the creation of the SNI. The SNI grew out of the Institute for Research and Social Studies (Instituto de Pesquisas e Estudos Sociais--IPES), which General Couto e Silva had established to undermine the Goulart government. The SNI provided clearances for anyone seeking a government job or requesting to conduct research in the army archives. Using an elaborate system of informants and telephone taps, the SNI accumulated and analyzed reports on a wide range of people, organizations, and topics. One study by political scientists David V. Fleischer and the late Robert Wesson suggests that there were as many as 50,000 persons in the employ of the SNI during the 1964-85 regime. Furthermore, both Presidents Médici and Figueiredo had been SNI chiefs.
In theory, the SNI supervised and coordinated the intelligence agencies of the three services. However, in practice the service agencies maintained their autonomy. The service agencies included the Army Intelligence Center (Centro de Informações do Exército--CIE); the Air Force Intelligence Center (Centro de Informações da Aeronáutica--CIA); and the Naval Intelligence Center (Centro de Informações de Marinha--Cenimar).

The chief of staff of each of the army commands supposedly was responsible for the intelligence work in that command's territory. In practice, that officer was not necessarily informed of CIE activities, which followed a parallel chain of command. Each command also had an Internal Operations Department-Internal Defense Operations Center (Departamento de Operações Internas-Centro de Operações de Defesa Interna--DOI-CODI). The DOI-CODIs became centers of dirty tricks and torture.

From the outset, there was resistance to the idea of the CIE. In 1966 President Castelo Branco rejected the idea of creating an army intelligence service annexed to the minister of army's office, because it would weaken the General Staff's influence. The next year, the new minister of army, General Aurélio de Lyra Tavares, established the CIE over the objections of the chief of staff, General Orlando Geisel. As early as 1968, the CIE was exploding bombs in theaters, wrecking bookstores, and kidnapping people. When the left began terrorist violence in late 1968, the CIE expanded to about 200 officers and became the axis of repression, eliminating all signs of leftist violence in three years.

The SNI, CIE, and other intelligence agencies were the most dubious legacy that the military regime left to the New Republic. The scars of repression and violence, including the mistreatment, torture, and murder of prisoners, will mark the officer corps for years to come. During World War II, Brazilian officers serving in Italy with the FEB (Brazilian Expeditionary Force), the first Latin American military organization in history to participate in combat in Europe, prided themselves on the correct treatment they accorded German prisoners under the Geneva Convention. Their successors, however, were taught that international law did not apply in cases of internal security. Thus, they used massive intimidation, kidnappings, beatings, secret arrests and imprisonments, psychological and physical torture, murder, and secret burial. In the past, rebels or criminals from the margins of society and working-class people could expect brutal treatment from the forces of law and order. The military regime brought that experience to the opposition in the middle and upper classes. The "repressive apparatus," as it was often referred to, cast a shadow of fear and drew an invisible pale through Brazilian society to dissuade the educated classes from crossing it. It also served to dissuade opposition within the military itself.

The creation of the DOI network beginning in 1971 formed a parallel chain of command, one that did not necessarily end with the president of the republic. President Geisel, a retired general, struggled to have his orders fulfilled by the CIE system. Consequently, the CIE sought to undermine his government and to make Minister of Army Sylvio Couto Coelho da Frota the next president. The CIE also waged a pamphlet war against General Golbery do Couto e Silva, chief of Geisel's Civilian Household, who wanted to shut down the CIE.

THE STRATEGIC AFFAIRS SECRETARIAT (SAE), 1990-94

When Collor de Mello became president in 1990, he replaced the military-dominated SNI with the civilian-led Secretaria de Assuntos Estratégicos (SAE) or Strategic Affairs Secretariat. One of his first acts as president was to dismiss 144 officers from the SNI. Under the Collor presidency, the SAE emerged as the most important actor in formulating Brazil's security policies. In part, its influence was derived from its direct access to the president. The SAE's oversight responsibilities included Brazil's nuclear, space, missile, armaments, and intelligence programs. In an example of role expansion, however, the SAE drafted the 1992 Multiyear Plan, a document formulated previously by the Ministry of the Economy's National Planning Secretariat, and continued to have a strong military presence. Such broad activities led some to refer to the SAE as a "super ministry." In addition to the SAE, there are service intelligence agencies.

Despite attempts to make the SAE more open, there was virtually no congressional oversight of SAE activities. On September 26, 1991, President Collor submitted a bill for congressional supervision of the SAE's intelligence-gathering activities. According to the bill, the secretary of the SAE would be required to submit a confidential report to Congress every six months. Congress criticized several provisions, including the exemption from congressional oversight of intelligence activities of the armed forces and Federal Police; a penalty of imprisonment for three to ten years for breaches of confidentiality by Congress; and the formation of a joint congressional committee to monitor the SAE, thereby bypassing the committees that already existed within the Chamber of Deputies (such as the Committee on National Defense) and the Senate.

By mid-1992 it was clear that the SAE had not been "demilitarized," as suggested by Collor. Reserve and active-duty military officers continued to head most of the departments and coordinating sections. Nor did the SAE effectively oversee Brazil's intelligence apparatus. There was evidence that the intelligence branches of each service did not report to the SAE. In October 1992, President Itamar Franco appointed Admiral Mário César Flores to head the SAE. Some considered this military appointment a setback for the "demilitarization" of the SAE because Flores was Collor's minister of navy and was considered a leading proponent of Brazil's nuclear-powered submarine program.

In 1995 President Fernando Henrique Cardoso, who assumed the presidency on January 1, nominated Ambassador Ronaldo Mota Sardenberg to head the SAE. A seasoned diplomat, Sardenberg was a former ambassador to Moscow and the United Nations, and was widely published on issues relating to Brazil's foreign and security policies. President Cardoso also announced the creation of the Brazilian Intelligence Agency (Agência Brasileira de Inteligência Nacional--ABIN).

BULGARIA

http://www.mvr.bg
http://www.nrs.bg

National Intelligence Service
Defence Information Service
National Security Service

CANADIAN INTELLIGENCE AGENCIES

Privy Council Office (PCO)
Security Intelligence Review Committee (SIRC)
Department of National Defence and Canadian Forces
Intelligence Branch
Communications Security Establishment (CSE)
Solicitor General
Canadian Security Intelligence Service (CSIS)
Royal Canadian Mounted Police (RCMP)
Criminal Intelligence Service Canada (CISC)
Industry Canada
Business Intelligence Express (BIX)
Competitive Intelligence E-Monitor
Security and Cryptography

ORGANIZATIONAL STRUCTURE OF CSIS - TEXT VERSION

DIRECTOR

Deputy Director (**Operations**)
Assistant Director (**Human Resources**)
Assistant Director (**Secretariat**)
Assistant Director (**Administration and Finance**)
Assistant Director (**Legal Services**)

Deputy Director (Operations)
Assistant Director (**Operations**)
Director General (**Counter Terrorism**)
Director General (**Counter Intelligence**)
Director General (**Counter Proliferation**)
Director General (**Human Sources**)
Assistant Director (**Intelligence**)

Director General (**Security Screening**)
Director General (**Research, Analysis and Production**)
Director General (**Operations Support**)
Director General (**Foreign Liaison and Visits**)
Assistant Director (**Corporate**)
Director General (**Information Management**)
Director General (**Scientific and Technical Services**)
Director General (**Internal Security**)
Directors General (**Regions**)

Assistant Director (Human Resources)
Director General (**Personnel Services**)
Director General (**Training and Development**)
Deputy Director General (**Health Services**)
Chief (**Career Management**)

Assistant Director (Secretariat)
Director General (**Communications**)
Director General (**Legislative Affairs**)
Director General (**Review**)
Deputy Director General (**External Review & Liaison**)
Deputy Director General (**Access to Information & Privacy**)

Assistant Director (Administration and Finance)
Chief **(Facilities Management)**
Comptroller
Chief **(Materiel Management)**

General Counsel (Legal Services)

CANADIAN SECURITY INTELLIGENCE SERVICE ADDRESSES AND TELEPHONE NUMBERS

H.Q. OTTAWA

CSIS
P.O.Box 9732
Postal Station T
Ottawa, Ontario K1G 4G4
(613) 993-9620
Hearing Impaired: **(613) 991-9228**

OTTAWA REGION

CSIS
P.O. Box 9732
Postal Station T
Ottawa, Ontario K1G 4G4
(613) 998-1679
Toll Free: **1-800-267-7685**
(Toll free service is only available in Ontario)

ATLANTIC REGION

CSIS
1505 Barrington St.

Suite 1901
Halifax, Nova Scotia B3J 3K5
(902) 420-5900

Atlantic Region / New Brunswick District

CSIS
Bag 6010
Waggoner's Lane
Fredericton, New Brunswick E3B 5G4
(506) 452-3786

Atlantic Region / Newfoundland District

CSIS
P.O. Box 2585
Postal Station C
St. John's, Newfoundland A1C 6J6
(709) 772-5449

B.C. Region

CSIS
P.O. Box 80629
South Burnaby, British Columbia V5H 3Y1
(604) 528-7400

Quebec Region

CSIS
P.O. Box 2000
Station A
Montreal, Quebec H3C 3A6
(514) 393-5600
Toll Free: **1-877-223-2265**
(Toll free service is only available in Quebec)

Quebec Region / Quebec City District

CSIS
P.O. Box 1172
Quebec City Terminal
Quebec City, Quebec G1K 7C3
(418) 529-8926

Toronto Region

CSIS
277 Front St. West
10th Floor
Toronto, Ontario M5V 2X4
(416) 865-1480

Prairie Region / Edmonton District

CSIS
Box 105

10011 - 109 St.
Edmonton, Alberta T5J 3S8
(780) 421-5800
Toll Free: **1-800-661-5780**
(Alberta/Saskatchewan/Manitoba/Thunder Bay)

PRAIRIE REGION / CALGARY DISTRICT

CSIS
P.O. Box 2671
Station M
Calgary, Alberta T2P 3C1
(403) 292-5255

PRAIRIE REGION / SASKATCHEWAN DISTRICT

CSIS
P.O. Box 5089
Main Postal Terminal
Regina, Saskatchewan S4P 4B2
(306) 780-5512

PRAIRIE REGION / MANITOBA DISTRICT

CSIS
P.O. Box 771
Winnipeg, Manitoba R3C 4G3
(204) 983-5405

FREQUENTLY ASKED QUESTIONS

HOW AND WHEN WAS CSIS CREATED?

CSIS was created by the passage of an Act of Parliament (Bill C-9) on June 21, 1984. The Service began its formal existence on July 16, 1984.

WHAT DOES CSIS DO?

CSIS has a mandate to collect, analyze and retain information or intelligence on activities that may on reasonable grounds be suspected of constituting threats to the security of Canada and in relation thereto, report to and advise the Government of Canada. CSIS also provides security assessments, on request, to all federal departments and agencies, with the exception of the RCMP.

WHAT ORGANIZATION COLLECTED SECURITY INTELLIGENCE BEFORE CSIS WAS CREATED?

Prior to June 21, 1984, security intelligence was collected by the Security Service of the Royal Canadian Mounted Police. CSIS was created because the Government of Canada, after intensive review and study, came to the conclusion that security intelligence investigations would be more appropriately handled by a civilian agency. CSIS has no police powers. However, CSIS works with various police forces on those investigations that have both national security and criminal implications. Although CSIS can offer assistance to the police, it has no mandate to conduct criminal investigations.

WHAT CONSTITUTES A THREAT TO THE SECURITY OF CANADA?

The complete threat definitions can be found in section 2 (a,b,c,d) of the *CSIS Act*. Simply put, terrorism (the planning or use of politically-motivated serious violence) and espionage (undeclared foreign intelligence activity in Canada and detrimental to the interests of Canada) are the two major threats which CSIS investigates. Terrorism and espionage can have criminal implications. In such cases, the RCMP investigates and can lay the appropriate criminal charges.

WHAT IS "SECURITY INTELLIGENCE" AND DOES THE GOVERNMENT REALLY NEED IT GIVEN THAT TECHNOLOGY ALLOWS NEWS BROADCASTERS TO DELIVER INFORMATION FROM AROUND THE WORLD IN A MATTER OF MINUTES?

Security intelligence is information formulated to assist government decision makers in developing policy. Regardless of the source of intelligence, it provides value in addition to what can be found in other government reports or in news stories. Intelligence conveys the story behind the story.

HOW DOES CSIS OBTAIN THIS "VALUE-ADDED" COMPONENT?

The "value-added" comes from analysis and a wide variety of investigative techniques, including the use of covert and intrusive methods such as electronic surveillance and the recruitment and tasking of human sources.

CAN THESE TECHNIQUES BE ARBITRARILY DEPLOYED?

No. All intrusive methods of investigation used by CSIS are subject to several levels of approval before they are deployed. The most intrusive methods—such as electronic surveillance, mail opening and covert searches—require a warrant issued by a judge of the Federal Court of Canada. In addition, the Security Intelligence Review Committee (SIRC) and the Inspector General closely review CSIS operations to ensure they are lawful and comply with the Service's policies and procedures.

WHAT DOES CSIS DO WITH THE SECURITY INTELLIGENCE IT COLLECTS?

CSIS reports to and advises the Government of Canada. CSIS intelligence is shared with a number of other federal government departments and agencies, including Foreign Affairs and International Trade, Immigration, the Department of National Defence and the Royal Canadian Mounted Police. As well, CSIS has arrangements to exchange security-related information with other countries. The vast majority of these arrangements deal with visa vetting. A small number deal with exchanges of information collected by CSIS in its investigation of threats to national security.

WHAT IS THE DIFFERENCE BETWEEN A SECURITY INTELLIGENCE SERVICE AND A FOREIGN INTELLIGENCE SERVICE?

A security intelligence service is restricted to investigating threats to its country's national security. A foreign intelligence service, on the other hand, conducts offensive operations for its government in foreign countries. The methods and objectives of foreign intelligence services differ from country to country.

DOES CSIS HAVE ANY FOREIGN PRESENCE AT ALL?

CSIS has liaison offices in some countries. Liaison officers are involved in the exchange of security intelligence information which concerns threats to the security of Canada.

DOES CSIS INVESTIGATE INDUSTRIAL ESPIONAGE?

CSIS does not investigate company-to-company industrial espionage. CSIS does, however, investigate the activities of foreign governments that engage in economic espionage as a means of gaining an economic advantage for themselves. Economic espionage can be defined as the use of, or facilitation of, illegal, clandestine, coercive or deceptive means by a foreign government or its surrogates to acquire economic intelligence.

What is the impact of foreign government economic espionage activity on businesses in Canada?

Foreign government economic espionage activity exposes Canadian companies to unfair disadvantage, jeopardizing Canadian jobs, Canada's competitiveness and research development investment.

Does CSIS conduct investigations on university campuses?

CSIS is very sensitive to the special role that academic institutions play in a free and democratic society and the need to preserve the free flow of ideas, therefore, investigations involving university campuses require the approval of senior officials in the Service. Furthermore, human sources and intrusive investigative techniques may only be used with the approval of the Solicitor General.

Can you name individuals or groups currently under CSIS investigation?

The CSIS Act prevents the Service from confirming or denying the existence of specific operations. To disclose such information would impede the Service's investigative capabilities which, in turn, would be injurious to national security. CSIS, however, can assure the public that it is doing everything within its mandate to ensure that Canadians are safeguarded from terrorism and foreign espionage.

Given that the Cold War is over, are there still threats with which Canadians should be concerned?

Yes. Details regarding the Service's view of the security intelligence environment can be found in its annual Public Reports.

CHILE - INTELLIGENCE AGENCIES

National Intelligence Directorate
(Dirección Nacional de Inteligencia--DINA)
replaced by the National Intelligence Agency
Agencia Nacional de Inteligencia (ANI), July 2004
Ministry of Defense
Directorate of National Defense Intelligence
(Dirección de Inteligencia de la Defensa Nacional-- DIDN)
Army
Navy
Air Force
Forces of Order and Public Security
Carabineros (Carabineros de Chile)
Investigations Police

NATIONAL INTELLIGENCE DIRECTORATE (DIRECCIÓN NACIONAL DE INTELIGENCIA--DINA)

The military authorities took power in a violent coup on 11 September 1973. The first phase of the dictatorship (1973-75) was mainly destructive, aimed at rapid demobilization, depoliticization, and stabilization. Immediately on seizing power, the military junta -- composed of the commanders in chief of the army, navy, air force, and national police -- issued a barrage of decrees to restore order on its own terms.

In the immediate aftermath of the 1973 coup, there was extensive repression, including summary executions of prisoners. During this period, the number of people who were detained so exceeded the capacities of the existing penal institutions that for a time stadiums, military grounds, and naval vessels were used as short-term prisons. Subsequently, at least five prison camps were established for political prisoners, mostly in the remote south and the far north.

In the immediate aftermath of the 1973 coup, a semiformal umbrella group, the National Intelligence Directorate (Dirección Nacional de Inteligencia--DINA), was formed, ostensibly to coordinate the activities of the intelligence services of the army, navy, air force, Carabineros, and Investigations Police. From the beginning, DINA functioned as a secret police and was engaged in the repression of dissidence within the state and the exaction of revenge on its enemies without. The National Intelligence Directorate kept secret detention centers where torture of prisoners was a routine practice [all of these places of detention had been closed down by the time of the return to civilian government in 1990]. The worst human rights abuses occurred in the first four years of the junta, when thousands of civilians were murdered, jailed, tortured, brutalized, or exiled, especially those linked with the Popular Unity parties. The DINA secret police, reporting to Pinochet), kept dissidents living in fear of arrest, torture, murder, or "disappearance." The armed forces treated the members of the UP as an enemy to be obliterated, not just as an errant political movement to be booted from office. The military commanders closed Congress, censored the media, purged the universities, burned books, declared political parties outlawed if Marxist or in recess otherwise, and banned union activities.

Col. Manuel Contreas was the organizational director of the Department of National Intelligence (DINA). During his tenure as security chief under the regime of Gen. Augusto Pinochet, Contreas organized "Operation Condor" in association with the Argentinean intelligence service (SIDE) and presided over the torture, kidnapping and "disappearance" of tens of thousands of Chilean leftists. Two DINA agents were responsible for assassinating General Carlos Prats González, who was defense minister under the Allende regime. Prats and his wife were killed by a car bomb in Buenos Aires, Argentina.

The armed forces justified the coup as necessary to stamp out Marxism, avert class warfare, restore order, and salvage the economy. They enshrined the National Security Doctrine, which defined their primary task as the defeat of domestic enemies who had infiltrated national institutions, including schools, churches, political parties, unions, and the media. Although civilians filled prominent economic posts, military officers took most government positions at the national and local levels.

NATIONAL INFORMATION CENTER (CENTRO NACIONAL DE INFORMACIÓN--CNI)

During the four-and-one-half years following the 1973 coup, Chile was officially in a state of siege and functioned under martial law. The DINA secret police reporting to Pinochet was replaced in 1977 by the National Information Center (Centro Nacional de Información--CNI). The functions of the CNI combined those functions carried out by the United States Central Intelligence Agency (CIA), FBI, and Secret Service. The military tribunals expanded their jurisdictions to include all violations (including those perpetrated by civilians) of the much more encompassing security laws enacted by the government. At the end of this period, the state of siege was replaced by a state of emergency, which restored a larger degree of authority to the civilian courts, although military tribunals continued to deal with cases involving public security. Although human rights abuses abated significantly after the abolition of DINA, its successor continued to draw criticism and was disbanded upon the return of civilian government in 1990.

Most of its approximately 2,000 operatives were absorbed either by army intelligence or by a new coordinating body for military intelligence, operating under the aegis of the National Defense Staff and known as the Directorate of National Defense Intelligence (Dirección de Inteligencia de la Defensa Nacional-- DIDN).

Throughout the second half of the 1970s, the Roman Catholic Church and international organizations concerned with human rights denounced the widespread violations of human rights in Chile. Although officially neutral, the Roman Catholic Church became the primary sanctuary for the persecuted in Chile from 1975 to 1985 and so came into increasing conflict with the junta.

The former members of Popular Unity went underground or into exile. In the early years of the dictatorship, their main goal was simply to survive. Although the Communists suffered brutal persecution, they managed to preserve their organization fairly intact. The Socialists splintered so badly that their party nearly disappeared by the end of the 1970s. Draconian repression left the Marxists with no capacity to resist or counterattack. They did, however, manage to rally world opinion against the regime and keep it diplomatically isolated. By the end of the 1970s, most Christian Democrats, after initially cooperating with the junta, had also joined the opposition, although not in any formal coalition with any coherent strategy for restoring democracy.

Pinochet soon emerged as the dominant figure and very shortly afterward as president. After a brief flirtation with corporatist ideas, the government evolved into a one-man dictatorship, with the rest of the junta acting as a sort of legislature. In 1977 Pinochet dashed the hopes of those Chileans still dreaming of an early return to democracy when he announced his intention to institutionalize an authoritarian regime to preside over a protracted return to civilian rule in a "protected" democracy.

Pinochet established iron control over the armed forces as well as the government, although insisting that they were separate entities. He made himself not only the chief executive of the state but also the commander in chief of the military. He shuffled commands to ensure that loyalists controlled all the key posts. He appointed many new generals and had others retire, so that by the 1980s all active-duty generals owed their rank to Pinochet. He also improved the pay and benefits of the services. The isolation of the armed forces from civil society had been a virtue under the democracy, inhibiting their involvement in political disputes; now that erstwhile virtue became an impediment to redemocratization, as the military remained loyal to Pinochet and resisted politicization by civilians.

Although aid and loans from the United States increased spectacularly during the first three years of the regime, while presidents Nixon and Gerald R. Ford were in office, relations soured after Jimmy Carter was elected president in 1976 on a platform promising vigorous pursuit of human rights as a major component of his foreign policy.

The former military government wrote the 1980 Constitution and amended it slightly in 1989 after General Pinochet lost a referendum to stay in office. It provides for a strong presidency and a legislative branch with more limited powers. The President has the authority to designate the "urgency" of bills and to determine time limits for Congress to consider them. In addition, the Constitution includes provisions designed to protect the interests of the military and the political right and, according to its defenders (and even some critics), to provide stability in the political process and encourage the formation of large coalitions. The center-left coalition which governed Chile in 1993 accepted the legitimacy of the 1980 Constitution but sought to amend elements characterized as "authoritarian enclaves" left over from the previous regime. These included limitations on the President's right to remove chiefs of the armed forces, an electoral system that gives the political opposition a disproportionate representation in Congress, and the existence of nonelected "institutional senators" who deprive the governing coalition of an elected majority in the Senate.

The Aylwin Administration

The former military government enacted an amnesty law in 1978, the prime beneficiaries of which were those responsible for human rights abuses committed during the first 5 years of the military government's rule. The Aylwin administration interpreted the amnesty law to mean that the courts should first determine the authors of human rights abuses before applying the amnesty. Legal reforms in 1991 remanded most human rights cases from military to civilian jurisdiction. However, when the investigation showed that a crime was committed on a military base or military personnel were accused of the crime, military tribunals reclaimed jurisdiction, and the military courts applied the amnesty law to close the cases without determining the facts or criminal responsibility. These decisions led critics to charge that Chile's Supreme Court impeded justice for victims of human rights abuses committed by the military forces.

So notorious were DINA's activities that of 957 identified "disappearances" of enemies of the Pinochet regime, DINA was blamed by the Rettig Commission on human rights abuses for perpetrating 392.

In 1995 Italian courts convicted Contreras and Raul Iturriaga, another former DINA (National Intelligence Directorate) officer, in absentia for the attempted murder of former Chilean Vice President Bernardo Leighton and his wife Anita Fresno, and sentenced each man to 18 years in prison. The Italians have requested neither their extradition nor that they serve their sentences in Chile.
The January 1995 arrest in Argentina of former Chilean intelligence agent Enrique Arancibia Clavel once again drew attention to the 1974 assassination in Buenos Aires of former Chilean army chief Carlos Prats. Prats was the army commander under President Salvador Allende and was succeeded by General Pinochet in August 1973. He left Chile for Argentina several days after the coup against Allende. The case was reopened in 1992 as a result of a petition filed by the Prats family containing new evidence.

In June 1996 the Supreme Court invoked the Amnesty Law to end all action in the 1976 murder of Carmelo Soria, a Spanish citizen employed by the United Nations. Subsequent impeachment motions against four Supreme Court justices failed in the lower house of Congress. As a result, the authorities dismissed charges against two ex-agents of the National Intelligence Center (CNI) who were indicted in June 1995 as author and accomplice in this crime; any further official investigation was terminated. This decision provoked concern and condemnation from a broad spectrum, including the embassies of the European Union states, Chilean members of congress, and political parties. In January 1997 the family of Soria announced its intention to pursue a denial of justice claim before the Inter-American Commission on Human Rights (IACHR). Proceedings against General Augusto Pinochet continue to move forward in a Spanish court for his alleged responsibility in Soria's death as well as those of the priests Joan Alsina and Antonio Llido. In November 1997 President Frei decided not to approve the promotion to brigadier general of former intelligence officer Jaime Lepe Orellana, who was reportedly involved in the murder of Soria.
Also in 1995 a military judge dismissed the case of the June 1987 deaths from "Operation Albania", in which CNI agents killed 12 people connected to the Manuel Rodriguez Patriotic Front (FPMR). This was in spite of a unanimous ruling in 1995 by the military tribunal--a higher court--that the deaths were homicides and that the cases should go to trial. At the time, the authorities claimed that all 12 died in shoot-outs with security officers, and therefore no crime was committed. The authorities implicated 28 former officers and enlisted men in this case.

Disappearance cases from before 1978 cannot be closed and the alleged perpetrator amnestied until a court determines that the victim is dead. Since the bodies of many of the disappeared have never been found, the cases were an ongoing irritant in civil-military (particularly civil-army) relations because judicial processes against officers--who would inevitably be covered by the amnesty--were both disruptive to army operations and embarrassing to the institution.

The National Reparation and Conciliation Corporation began operating in 1992 to compensate families of human rights victims. On September 30, 1993, it was paying pensions to 4,600 family members of victims who died of human rights violations committed before 1990. The Chilean State has paid $26.5 million to the victims' families, including college tuition for offspring up to the age of 35 who wish to study. Wives, children, and parents of victims are eligible for pensions, and the amount for each family member is more than double that paid under the old social security system. The Corporation also continued the work of the Rettig Commission, investigating reports of human rights abuses where victims died. In August 1995 it delivered its final report, which confirmed 899 cases in addition to those documented by the Rettig Commission, bringing the total number of victims of killings and disappearance cases to 3,197.

In September 1976, DINA agents assassinated the former Chilean ambassador to the United States Orlando Letelier and his colleague, Ronni Moffitt, in Washington DC. Letelier had been Minister of Defense in Chile in 1973, when President Salvador Allende was murdered during a CIA-supported coup. After a year in a military prison, Letelier was released and moved to the US. At the time of his assasination he was organizing against the military junta out of offices at the Institute for Policy Studies. As of 1991, the US was still seeking to extradite three suspects in the case, including former DINA head Gen. Manuel Contreras and his chief aide Col. Pedro Espinoza. Michael Townley, an American expatriate was extradited from Chile in 1978. He served a five year sentence before being released to the US witness protection program.

In April 1995 the body of former Chilean DINA agent and chemical weapons expert, Eugenio Berrios, was found on the El Pinar beach in Montevideo, Uruguay. The body had four bullet wounds in the chest and one in the back of the head, its face stripped off and its hands cut off in an attempt to prevent identification. With Michael Townley, Berrios reportedly built the bomb that killed Chilean diplomat Orlando Letelier in 1976 in Washington DC. Berrios probably produced the sarin nerve gas used to kill three human-rights victims in Chile. Berrios avoided trial in Chile by fleeing to Uruguay in April 1992, and sought protection from the Uruguayan police on 15 November 1992, saying he had been kidnapped on orders from Pinochet. The police returned him to the house of Uruguayan intelligence agent Capt. Eduardo Ravelli from whence he had supposedly escaped. He was never seen alive again.

In an important step toward ending the impunity of military officers involved in the Letelier case, Adolfo Banados, a Supreme Court justice appointed by the current Aylwin Government, sentenced retired General Manuel Contreras and Colonel Pedro Espinoza to 7- and 6-year prison terms, respectively, as intellectual authors of the 1976 murder in Washington, DC, of former Chilean Foreign Minister Orlando Letelier and his American assistant Ronni Moffitt. The Supreme Court is expected to rule early in 1994 on appeals of the sentences by all parties. This is the only case involving the now dissolved DINA--the Pinochet-era secret police--that the 1978 amnesty law specifically excluded.

In August 1993 President Aylwin reignited the censorship controversy when he requested that the national television station delay the broadcast of an interview with Michael Townley in which the former DINA agent detailed how and why he put a bomb under the car of Orlando Letelier. The President asserted that showing the interview on the government-owned station at that time was needlessly inflammatory. The program aired 10 days later, but the program's director was dismissed for adding to the debate about presidential influence over the state-owned television station and for allegedly asserting excessive independence from the board of directors.

Efforts to redress the abuses of this period are shaped by often conflicting requirements for justice and national reconciliation. The Supreme Court has been reluctant to confront the military over human rights, and one justice was impeached by Congress and removed from office for "gross neglect of duties" for his handling of a human rights case. Disputes continue over the interpretation of the 1978 amnesty law and prosecution of military personnel and their collaborators for abuses not covered by the amnesty.

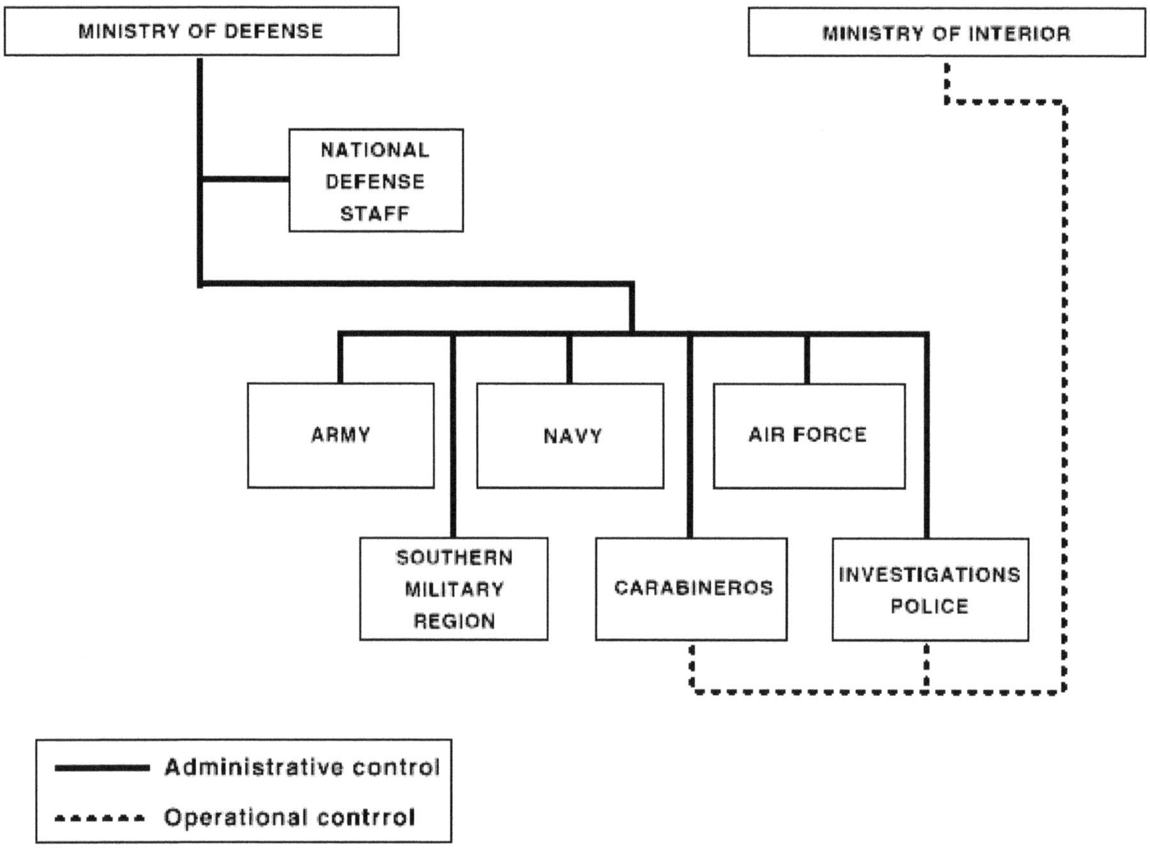

DIRECTORATE OF NATIONAL DEFENSE INTELLIGENCE (DIRECCIÓN DE INTELIGENCIA DE LA DEFENSA NACIONAL-- DIDN)

DINA was abolished in 1977 and replaced by a new organization known as the National Information Center (Centro Nacional de Informaci6n--CNI). The functions of the CNI combined those functions carried out by the United States Central Intelligence Agency (CIA), FBI, and Secret Service. Although human rights abuses abated significantly after the abolition of DINA, its successor continued to draw criticism and was disbanded upon the return of civilian government in 1990. Most of its approximately 2,000 operatives were absorbed either by army intelligence or by a new coordinating body for military intelligence, operating under the aegis of the National Defense Staff and known as the Directorate of National Defense Intelligence (Direcci6n de Inteligencia de la Defensa Nacional-- DIDN). The DIDN concerns itself primarily with defense rather than with internal intelligence.

MINISTRY OF DEFENSE

The armed forces are constitutionally subordinate to the President through an appointed Minister of Defense but enjoy a large degree of legal autonomy. Since the transition to civilian government in 1990 the president has had little actual control over the military, and the Ministry of Defense has lacked any effective control of the services and the Carabineros. Most notably, the President must have the concurrence of the National Security Council [Cosena] to remove service chiefs.
he positions of the minister of defense and the subsecretaries remained effectively unchanged under the Aylwin government. However, the Subsecretariat of the Carabineros and the Subsecretariat of Investigations are subordinate to the minister of defense rather than to the minister of interior, as was

formerly the case. However, new laws call for the Ministry of Interior to coordinate the actions of the security forces. The Carabineros (the uniformed national police) have primary responsibility for public order and safety and border security. The civilian Investigations Police are responsible for criminal investigations and immigration control. Both organizations--although formally under the jurisdiction of the Ministry of Defense, which determines their budget--are under operational control of the Ministry of Interior. Some alleged perpetrators of human rights abuses during the military regime remain on active duty in the army.

In addition to Cosena, two other bodies, whose functions are specifically limited to the advisory level, deal with matters of national defense and security: the Politico-Strategic Advisory Council (Consejo Asesor Político-Estratégico--CAPE) and the Internal Security Advisory Council (Consejo Asesor de Seguridad Interior--CASI). CAPE consists of six military and four civilian members and is entrusted with long-range planning of the defense and external security of the state. CASI, which consists of the minister of interior and seven military members, deals with internal security planning.

DIRECTORATE OF PUBLIC SECURITY AND INFORMATION (DIRECCIÓN DE SEGURIDAD PÚBLICA E INFORMACIONES)

In early 1993, the government finally enacted new legislation, after more than a year of congressional delays in approving the project, creating the Directorate of Public Security and Information (Dirección de Seguridad Pública e Informaciones). The new directorate is under the Ministry of Interior and allows the ministry to coordinate the intelligence and anticrime and antiterrorist activities of the Carabineros and Investigations Police.

PARA-STATE ADVERSARIES

Three main terrorist groups are sporadically active: pro-Cuban Movement of the Revolutionary Left (Movimiento de la Izquierda Revolucionaria), United Popular Action Movement-Lautaro (Movimiento de Acción Popular Unitario-Lautaro), Lautaro Youth Movement (Movimiento Juvenil Lautaro), Manuel Rodríguez Patriotic Front (Frente Patriótica Manuel Rodríguez), and Maoist-oriented Manuel Rodríguez Patriotic Front-Autonomous (Frente Patriótica Manuel RodríguezAutónomo). None are a serious threat to national security, but each is capable of occasional acts of terrorism.

During the first five years of the Pinochet regime (1973-78), the armed forces and security forces successfully contained leftwing resistance against the government. Many members of Chile's oldest left-wing extremist group, the Movement of the Revolutionary Left (Movimiento de la Izquierda Revolucionaria--MIR), which was founded in 1965 and had close ties to Cuba, were killed or exiled. Nevertheless, the MIR remnants, under the leadership of the late Salvador Allende's nephew, Andrés Pascal Allende, continued to operate a small underground network in Chile. The MIR's principal leader, Miguel Enríquez, returned clandestinely to Chile in 1978 to revitalize the movement and organize for armed struggle and was soon joined by newly infiltrated cadres who had been trained in Cuba and Nicaragua. The security forces kept the MIR off balance, however, and Enríquez was killed in September 1983.

Several new left-wing terrorist groups emerged in the early 1980s. One was the United Popular Action Movement-Lautaro (Movimiento de Acción Popular Unitario-Lautaro--MAPU-L), a splinter of the United Popular Action Movement (Movimiento de Acción Popular Unitario--MAPU), a party founded in 1969 by a breakaway group from the Christian Democrats. Many MAPU leaders embraced Marxist positions, but the party was not a terrorist group. In December 1982, the MAPU-L established a youth group, the Lautaro Youth Movement (Movimiento de Juventud Lautaro--MJL), and a group dedicated to the overthrow of the military government, the Lautaro Popular Rebel Forces (Fuerzas Rebeldes Popular Lautaro--FRPL).

The Manuel Rodríguez Patriotic Front (Frente Patriótica Manuel Rodríguez--FPMR), an armed group affiliated with the Communist Party of Chile (Partido Comunista de Chile--PCCh), was formed in

1983. In response to increased armed attacks, the regime promulgated the 1984 Antiterrorist Law, which greatly expanded the list of crimes that could be categorized as terrorism.

In the second half of the 1980s, the FPMR became the dominant terrorist group, emerging as a sophisticated, well-trained, and well-supported terrorist organization. Just how strong it was became evident in August 1986 when the security forces captured a huge FPMR arms cache that was traced to Cuba. That September FPMR commandos nearly succeeded in assassinating Pinochet with M-16 assault rifles and antitank rockets. In response to these two events, Pinochet declared a state of siege and mounted an offensive against the FPMR and MIR.

Intensified police and security-service pressure on the FPMR and MIR continued throughout 1987, inhibiting the groups' activities. That year the FPMR splintered as a result of the PCCh's denunciation of violence; the breakaway Maoist-oriented FPMRAutonomous (FPMR-Autónomo--FPMR-A) became the most active left-wing terrorist group, whereas the FPMR followed the PCCh's line and laid down its arms after the restoration of democracy in 1990. Mainly as a result of FPMR-A activities, terrorist attacks increased in the late 1980s.

Meanwhile, the security forces failed to apprehend any members of right-wing extremist groups, such as the Chilean Anti-Communist Action Group (Acción Chilena Anticomunista--AChA) and the Nationalist Combat Front (Frente Nacionalista de Combate--FNC). The ability of these groups to operate with apparent impunity led to speculation in the late 1980s that their actions were unofficially sanctioned by some officials in the security forces.

The rationale for continued left-wing subversion and right-wing counterterror effectively vanished with the return of civilian government in 1990. Many left-wing extremists who had fled the country following the 1973 coup were allowed to return in 1990. Nevertheless, left-wing terrorism did not disappear. Within a few months after President Aylwin's accession to power, the FPMR-A and MJL showed that they remained committed to armed struggle and were responsible for most of the increased number of terrorist incidents in the early 1990s. The total number of documented terrorist actions during the first year of the Aylwin government was 207 (including 148 attacks on buildings and other properties), compared with 465 similar actions during 1984 and 401 in 1985--two peak years for terrorist activity during the latter half of the period of military rule.

The Aylwin government's attempts to control terrorism were quite successful. In 1991 it expanded training and increased efforts by the Investigations Police and the Carabineros. Police improved their counterterrorism capabilities, surpassing the effectiveness of the military government. This was made evident by their success in arresting numerous leaders and in uncovering several safe houses and training sites used by Chilean terrorists. By early 1993, more than 200 terrorist militants were under indictment. The capture of many top leaders of the MAPU-L and FPMRA crippled these organizations, and terrorist incidents declined. The Aylwin government appointed special investigating judges to try the more serious cases of terrorism, such as the assassination of Senator Jaime Guzmán Errázuriz on April 1, 1991.

Four ringleaders of the terrorist Manuel Rodriguez Patriotic Front (FPMR) broke out of Santiago's maximum-security prison on December 30, 1996, in an elaborately orchestrated escape via helicopter. In early September, one of the escapees, Patricio Ortiz Montenegro, requested political asylum in Switzerland, claiming he could not obtain justice in Chile. (In June 1995, a military court convicted Ortiz of the 1991 murder of a police officer and sentenced him to a 10-year prison term.) Chilean authorities are seeking Ortiz' extradition from Switzerland, where he was detained at year's end.

CHINESE INTELLIGENCE AGENCIES

Communist Party Central Committee
Ministry of State Security [MSS]
Guojia Anquan Bu [Guoanbu]

Ministry of Public Security
People's Armed Police
People's Liberation Army
8341 Unit - Central Security Regiment
General Staff Department
Second Department [Intelligence]
Third Department
Fourth Department
General Political Department
International Liaison Department
[China Association for International Friendly Contacts]
PLA Navy
Naval Intelligence
PLA Air Force
Sixth Research Institute
New China News Agency (Xinhua)
COLLECTION DISCIPLINES
COLLECTION SYSTEMS

MINISTRY OF STATE SECURITY [MSS] GUOJIA ANQUAN BU [GUOANBU]

First Bureau - Domestic
Second Bureau - Foreign
Third Bureau - Hong Kong, Macao and Taiwan
Fourth Bureau - Technology
Fifth Bureau - Local Intelligence
Sixth Bureau - Counterintelligence
Seventh Bureau - Circulation
Eighth Bureau - Research [Institute of Contemporary International Relations]
Ninth Bureau - Anti-Defection and Counter-Surveillance
Tenth Bureau - Scientific and Technological Information
Eleventh Bureau - Electronic Computers
Foreign Affairs Bureau

COUNTERINTELLIGENCE BUREAU

The Sixth Bureau is the Counterintelligence Bureau. The primary task of Chinese counterintelligence activity is to work against overseas Chinese pro-democracy organizations. The bureau has been harboring all sorts of suspicions in the past few years. Investigation priorities have included Western consortiums investing in China, which were suspected of involvement in attempts to bring about peaceful evolution in China. Overseas Chinese pro-democracy organizations have been investigated under suspicions that they were sending "investors" to China who were actually engaged in anti-communist activities. However these investigations have over time declined due both to a lack of evidence and because the Bureau's activities were negatively affecting the confidence of foreign investors. Currently work is focused on surveillance, and security awareness education activities among local authorities encouraging reporting of suspicious people and activities.

MINISTRY OF PUBLIC SECURITY HEADQUARTERS

The Ministry of Public Security is headquartered in a large compound of on Eastern Changan Avenue next to the Tiananmen Square. The Ministry of State Security only has a reception office at this facility, although the signs of both the Ministry of Public Security and Ministry of State Security hang side by side at the front gate.

The Ministry of Public Security is the principal Chinese police authority. The ministry had functional departments for areas such as intelligence, police operations, prisons, and political, economic, and communications security. Subordinate to the ministry were provincial-level public security departments; public security bureaus and subbureaus at the county level (the bureaus located in the prefectures and large cities, the subbureaus in counties and municipal districts); and public security stations at the township level. While public security considerations had a strong influence at all levels of administration, the police appeared to wield progressively greater influence at the lower levels of government.

The organization of local public security stations could be inferred from the tasks with which the police were charged. Generally, each station had sections for population control, pretrial investigations, welfare, traffic control, a detention center, and other activities.

In the 1980s the public security station--the police element in closest contact with the people--was supervised by the public security subbureau as well as by local governments and procuratorates. The procuratorate could assume direct responsibility for handling any case it chose, and it supervised investigations in those cases it allowed the public security station to conduct. A great deal of coordination occurred among the public security organs, the procuratorates, and the courts, so that a trial was unlikely to produce a surprise outcome.

Police were drawn from every segment of the population without restriction as to sex or ethnic origin. Selection was based on political loyalty, intelligence, and health, as it was for the PLA. Most recruits had Communist Youth League backgrounds or were former PLA personnel. There was at least one police school in every provincial-level unit, and others were operated by municipalities.

Usually those police designated for leadership positions attended the police schools, and patrolmen were trained at the unit and on the job. Legal training was emphasized as a method of improving the quality of the police forces. In 1985 three institutions of higher learning for police personnel--the University of Public Security, the University of Police Officers, and the Institute of Criminal Police--offered more than twenty special courses. Students were recruited from senior-middle-school graduates under twenty-two years of age, with a waiver to twenty-five years of age for those having a minimum of two years' experience in public security work.

The Science and Technology Bureau, operating under the Ministry of Public Security, is in charge of national scientific and technical administration that is related to the public security. Computers are extensively used in criminal investigation, traffic control and communication. A fingerprint search system was computerized in 1986. In 1987, a special police communication network linking all the police agencies at the county level and above was established. A radio communication network at provincial level was also established in the 1980s.

The Chinese People's University of Police Officers was established in 1980 as the Institute of International Politics. It provided training for public security cadres, along with training for counterintelligence and political security cadres. When the former Central Investigation Department training institute became part of the Ministry of State Security, the Institute of International Politics, which remained part of the Ministry of Public Security, was renamed the Chinese People's University of Police Officers. Its counterintelligence department still supplies the Ministry of State Security each year with a small number of cadres, while graduates of other departments primarily work for the Ministry of Public Security.

COLOMBIAN INTELLIGENCE AND SECURITY AGENCIES

DEPARTAMENTO ADMINISTRATIVO DE SEGURIDAD (DAS)

http://www.das.gov.co/

Felipe Muñoz Gómez
Position: Director
Telephone: 4088-000
email: director@das.gov.co

Jaime Polanco Andres Barreto
Position: Assistant Director [e]
Phone: 4 088-000 Ext. 1909
email: ssubdirector@das.gov.co

Claudia Isabel González Sánchez
Position: Secretary General
Telephone: 4088-000 Ext. 1990
email: secretariageneral@das.gov.co

OBJECTIVES AND FUNCTIONS

Producing the intelligence required by the State Government and the administrative sector policies on intelligence to ensure internal and external national security of the Colombian State.

Participate in the development of policies designed by the Government security.

Obtain and process information at national and international, on matters related to national security in order to produce intelligence of State, to support the President in formulating policies and making decisions.

Participate in the preparation of the Agenda of State Intelligence requirements proposed by the President of the Republic.

Lead the strategic intelligence activities in the State nationally and internationally.

Coordinate information exchange and cooperation with other national and international compliance related functions.

Forward counterintelligence actions designed to protect the interests of the state, hostile activities against internal or external.

Perform studies on safety and reliability of national government officials.

Coordinate with the Ministry of Foreign Affairs and other state institutions setting immigration policy.

Exercising control over domestic and foreign immigration and keeping track of foreign identification.

Exercise of the Judicial Police, in coordination with the Attorney General's Office for investigation of a criminal nature, related to the nature and purpose institutions.

Criminal record keeping and national identification, and issue legal licenses, based on the domestic exchange and on the reports or notices to be timely filed the judicial authorities of the Republic.

Act as a National Central Bureau-INTERPOL NCB-information exchange, mutual assistance, in accordance with the requirements and statutes of the same.

Provide security for the President and his family, Vice President and his family, ministers and presidents of the Republic, the information related to your safety is legal reserve.

Training and specialization of officers of the Department and would, in his Academy, and other government officials, foreign governments or multilateral organizations, developing a comprehensive culture of state intelligence and international cooperation.

The other duties assigned by law.

COSTA RICA: INTELLIGENCE AGENCIES

Direcci6n de Seguridad del Estado
State Security Directorate

CROATIAN INTELLIGENCE AGENCIES

National Security Office
Ured za nacionalnu sigurnost
http://www.uvns.hr

The Office of the National Security Council is the body of the Croatian security and intelligence system which provides support in the field of national security for major state institutions.
he Office of the National Security Council performs expert and administrative tasks for the National Security Council and the Council for the Coordination of Security and Intelligence Services as well as the tasks which enable the President of the Republic and the President of the Government to have oversight of the work of security and intelligence agencies and bodies of the security and intelligence system.

UVNS, based on the security and intelligence agencies' information, creates joint and periodical reports as well as strategic assessments for the President of the Republic and the President of the Government.

UVNS is also the Croatian National Security Authority, which coordinates, harmonizes the adoption and controls the implementation of information security measures and standards in the Republic of Croatia.

At the same time UVNS will try to contribute to the national security tasks that are accomplished for the sake of freedom, prosperity and security of all our citizens, which is a pledge of secure future of the Republic of Croatia.

CZECH SECURITY INFORMATION SERVICE

The logo of the Czech Security Information Service (BIS) consists of the large version of the national coat of arms, situated on the breast of an eagle and partly covered by the eagle´s wing. The upper part is inscribed with the words "AUDI, VIDE, TACE", the lower part with the acronym "BIS". The eagle symbolizes astuteness, vigilance, tenacity, swiftness and respect - such as this species enjoys among birds. These qualities related to humankind are underlined by the Latin motto "Audi, vide, tace", meaning that an intelligence service member has to be a good listener, keen observer, and must keep silent about his or her work - in other words, must observe the essential principles of intelligence work.

MISSION

The mission of the Security Information Service (BIS), which was created as a state intelligence agency of the Czech Republic, is to protect national interests, democracy and freedom, and to defend individual citizens and the state vis-a-vis the most serious forms of crime. Unlike the police, who enter the scene when a criminal offence is perpetrated, seek to find the facts and apprehend the culprit, BIS identifies, describes and assesses threats and dangers in areas within its purview as defined by law. In this preventive role its activities and existence are irreplaceable. And this involves by far not only defence against potential threats to the foundations of the democratic system and the sovereignty of the Czech Republic alone. In collaboration with other intelligence agencies of our state and partner services of all democratic countries, BIS fulfils the task of anticipating, blunting and eliminating threats which put in jeopardy the entire human civilization. The global anti-civilization threats include international terrorism and organized crime, particularly the spread of technologies and components for the production of nuclear, chemical and biological weapons; transfers of classical weapons to neuralgic places in different parts of the world; and attempts of organized crime to inflitrate the government, economic and political structures of states.

The main goals and objectives are defined for the Security Information Service by the Act on Intelligence Services, while the Government and President of the Republic may charge it with quite specific tasks. In all its activities BIS respects and strictly adheres to the unchallengeable principles of its work: it observes human rights, and if it is compelled to infringe upon them, it does so solely in keeping with rules set by law. It is non-partisan, its internal structure is clearly organized, and observance of human rights in the execution of intelligence work is overseen by a special parliamentary body.

The Service must not have any repressive powers - contrary to the secret services of totalitarian states, it is not for instance allowed to arrest, interrogate and bring charges against people - and it must not collect information beyond the frame of the defined task. The creed of the Service is to serve national interests and to protect the society against serious threats. It accepts this commitment in the spirit of loyalty to the democratic values, the Constitution and other legislation, while preserving human dignity and integrity, respecting and observing laws to the maximum possible degree. The Security Information Service serves the state - not political parties - and it strives to develop a high level of ethical conduct and professionality.

The Security Information Service, whose existence is in the interest of the Czech Republic and its citizens, was set up as a secret service because only as such it can effectively fulfil the tasks defined for it by law. Even though it mostly has to work covertly, it should be remembered that it is funded by the state, that means with money collected from taxpayers who therefore have the right to know how it works and what it does. It pursues a policy of maximum possible openness in relation to the public which, however, is connected also with the declaration of the government policy as an open one, and clearly proves that BIS is an institution of a democratic state.

In fulfilling its mission, the intelligence service cannot do without the support of the public. All who believe that they possess useful and relevant information concerning the areas of BIS activities can directly contact the Service. The Security Information Service relies on the support of citizens and is grateful to anybody who has helped or has been assisting it in the protection of the nation's security, democracy and freedom.

Aside from the Security Information Service (BIS), which is responsible for counterintelligence, the principal Czech foreign intelligence agency is the Office for Foreign Relations and Information (UZSI) (Úrad pro zahranicní styky a informace). Its director answers to the Minister of Interior.
There is a separate "Military Intelligence Service" and an office of "Military Defense Intelligence." The "National Security Authority" (Národní bezpeènostní úøad) is responsible for protection of classified information and related security policies.

CUBA

Communist Party of Cuba
Departmento America (DA)
America Department

Ministry of the Interior
Dirección General de Inteligencia (DGI)
General Intelligence Directorate

Ministry of Revolutionary Armed Forces
Dirección de Contra-Inteligencia Militar
Military Counterintelligence Department
Dirección de Inteligencia Militar

Military Intelligence Directorate

DIRECTORATE GENERAL OF INTELLIGENCE (DGI) MINISTRY OF THE INTERIOR

The principal intelligence collection arms of the Cuban government are the Directorate General of Intelligence (DGI) of Ministry of the Interior, and the Military Counterintelligence Department of the Ministry of Revolutionary Armed Forces. Both have been closely associated with the Soviet and Russian intelligence services. The relationship between these services is likely to continue based upon the June 14, 1993 agreement on military cooperation between Russia and Cuba.

The General Directorate of Intelligence (DGI) was established under the Ministry of the Interior (MININT) in late 1961. The new agency included three Liberation Committees - for the Caribbean, Central America, and South America - collectively known as the Liberation Directorate (DL). In the early 1960's, the DL also was responsible for supporting liberation movements in Africa, including those who overthrew the government of Zanzibar in 1963. However Soviet economic pressure on Cuba in 1967-68 forced Castro to develope a more selective revolutionary strategy, and subordinate the DGI to the KGB. The KGB compelled Castro to replace its chief, Manuel Piñeiro, with José Méndez Cominches in 1969. The DGI thereafter focused its efforts on collecting military, political and economic intelligence, with responsibility for supporting national liberation movements shifting to the new National Liberation Directorate (DLN), which was independent of the MININT. The DLN was subsequently reorganized into the America Department (DA).

The DGI is responsible for foreign intelligence collection. The DGI has six divisions divided into two categories of roughly equal size: the Operational Divisions and the Support Divisions.

The operational divisions include the Political/Economic Intelligence Division, the External Counterintelligence Division, and the Military Intelligence Division. The Political Economic Intelligence Division consists of four sections: Eastern Europe, North America, Western Europe, and Africa-Asia-

Latin America. The External Counterintelligence Division is responsible for penetrating foreign intelligence services and the surveillance of exiles.

The support divisions include the Technical Support Division, the Information Division, and the Preparation Division. The Technical Support Division is responsible for production of false documents, communications systems supporting clandestine operations, and development of clandestine message capabilities. The Information and Preparation Divisions are responsible for intelligence analysis functions.

On November 15, 1982, four close aides to Castro were convicted on charges of smuggling drugs into the United States. The four included René Rodríguez-Cruz, a senior official of the DGI (Cuban Intelligence Service). On February 7, 1983, a former member of the DGI testified in the District Court for the Southern District of Florida, that Cuban involvement in international drug operations was a multifaceted, methodical campaign aimed at undermining the United States and its international stature. And in 1988 testimony from José Blandón Castillo, a former intelligence aid to Panamanian leader Manuel Noriega, provided further evidence concerning Cuba's role in the drug flow of the United States.

The Cuban mission to the United Nations is the third largest UN delegation, and it has been alleged that almost half the personnel assigned to the mission are DGI officers. The DGI actively recruits within the Cuban emigre community and has used refugee flows into the United States to place agents. The DGI collects political, economic, and military information within the United States. More recently, the DGI has started to conduct operations to gain access to technologies required to improve the Cuban economy. Cuba is considered by the United States to be a sponsor of international terrorism and has worked closely with Puerto Rican separatist and Latin American terrorist groups. Much of this activity has been handled through the DGI.

AMERICA DEPARTMENT (DA) CENTRAL COMMITTEE COMMUNIST PARTY OF CUBA

In December 1974 the independent National Liberation Directorate [DLN] was reorganized into the America Department (DA) under the Communist Party of Cuba Centra Committee. The DA centralized control over covert Cuban activities for supporting national liberation movements and the efforts of regimes such as those of Nicaragua and Grenada. This DA was responsible for planning and coordinating Cuba's secret guerrilla and terrorist training camps, networks for the covert movement of personnel and material from Cuba, and a propaganda apparatus. DA agents also operated in Europe and other regions in support of operations in the Americas.

The DA is organized into four regional sections - Central America, South America, the Caribbean, and North America - as well as a Center for Latin American Studies (CEAL) and a Center for North American Studies (CEA). Covers used by DA staff include diplomats, Cuba's Prensa Latina news agency, Cubana Airlines, the Institute for Friendship With the Peoples (ICAP), and Cuban-front companies.

Although usually overlooked by most analysts, the DA is reportedly the most powerful branch of the Cuban security apparatus. DA personnel regard themselves as the elite of the various Cuban security agencies. In 1983 the DA had between 200 and 300 members. The DA draws on the expertise and support of the DGI, sharing manpower to conduct specific operations.

MILITARY COUNTERINTELLIGENCE DEPARTMENT MINISTRY OF REVOLUTIONARY ARMED FORCES

The principal intelligence collection arms of the Cuban government are the Directorate General of Intelligence (DGI) of Ministry of the Interior, and the Military Counterintelligence Department of the Ministry of Revolutionary Armed Forces. Both have been closely associated with the Soviet and Russian intelligence services. The relationship between these services is likely to continue based upon the June 14, 1993 agreement on military cooperation between Russia and Cuba.

The Military Intelligence Department is focused on collecting information on the U.S. Armed Forces and coordinates SIGINT operations with the Russians at Lourdes. The Military Counterintelligence Department is responsible for conducting counterintelligence, SIGINT, and electronic warfare activities against the United States.

DENMARK

http://www.pet.dk/

Danish Security Intelligence Service
Politiets Efterretningstjeneste, PET
Defense Intelligence Service
Forsvarets Efterretningstjeneste, FET

DANISH SECURITY INTELLIGENCE SERVICE *POLITIETS EFTERRETNINGSTJENESTE, PET*

Rigspolitiets afd. G/Politiets Efterretningstjeneste
Klausdalsbrovej 1
2860 Søborg
Telefon: +45 33148888
Fax: +45 33430190
Pressekontakt: +45 33148888 lokal 9085 eller 9005
Webmaster: webmaster@pet.dk

In its capacity as the national security and intelligence service of Denmark, PET must prevent, investigate and counter operations and activities that pose or may pose a threat to the preservation of Denmark as a free, democratic and safe country. Therefore the main objective of the Service is to counter and fight threats against the national security and the safety of the population.

To preserve the national security is, however, not the only task of an intelligence service. An efficient and permanent preservation of the national security and order requires permanent, wide-ranging and co-ordinated efforts by a number of authorities.

As the national security authority, PET obviously plays an important part in the efforts to ensure the direction and substance of the joint efforts in relation to the contributions from the individual bodies and authorities.

The main task of PET's intelligence activity is to prevent and investigate actions and undertakings that may jeopardise the independence, security and legal order of the State, and to prevent these actions or undertakings from being implemented or developed.

The actions that, in this connection, fall within PET's area of responsibility are primarily the actions as defined in accordance with Chapter 12 and 13 of the Danish Penal Code. Such actions include attacks on the Constitution, terrorism, and proliferation of weapons of mass destruction, extremism and espionage. PET must provide the basis for handling such threats as early in the process and as appropriately as possible. (The Provisions of the Minister of Justice regarding the Service include a description of the tasks of PET).

PET's actions are essentially preventive. From the information gathered, processed and analysed by PET, the objective is to procure as much information as possible on the capacity, determination and ability of PET's target persons and target groups to commit any such action as mentioned above.

On this basis, the Service prepares assessments and risk analyses that again provide the basis for an evaluation of what action that must be implemented to prevent any threats from developing further. Such actions may, among other things, consist of surveillance of target persons or target groups with the aim of assessing whether an identified and potential threat may develop further. By doing so the actions of PET differ from the investigations carried out by the rest of the police, where the police often find themselves in a situation where they have no knowledge of a criminal offence until it is already committed.

Consequently, it is a characteristic of most of the matters that PET deals with that they do not develop into actual criminal cases. This also means that the results of the work carried out by the Service traditionally have not been made known to or shall not be brought to the knowledge of the public in the same way as the work of the rest of the Danish police. This situation may change slightly, as the new Danish legislation on terrorism expands the scope of the Intelligence Service so that PET's investigations, to a higher degree than previously, may provide the basis of actual criminal cases or other more offensive initiatives.

Furthermore, the intelligence activities of the Service provide the basis for PET to act as adviser to the government, to a number of public authorities and to private enterprises regarding issues of importance to the security of the Danish society and its citizens. The same applies to matters in relation to the rest of the Danish police, airport authorities and the many other authorities involved in the general preparation of civil emergency in Denmark.

In this respect, PET also prepares risk analyses that are included in determining the specific level of preparedness in Denmark. PET does not determine the actual preparedness initiatives to be implemented by the individual authorities but will only provide some recommendations based on the assessments made.

Similarly, PET makes threat assessments concerning official foreign missions in Denmark, visits by heads of state and international conferences etc. held in Denmark.

In addition to this, PET plays an important part in connection with the protection of members of the Royal Family and the Government etc. as well as having an advisory function regarding the security responsibilities of the civil administration.

EGYPT: INTELLIGENCE AGENCIES

Mukhabarat al-Aama Al-Mukhabarat al-'Ammah
(General Intelligence and Security Service)

Mukhabarat el-Khabeya
(Military Intelligence Service)

Mubahath el-Dawla
(General Directorate of State Security Investigations)

Jihaz Amn al Daoula
(State Security Service)

Internal security was the responsibility of three intelligence organizations: General Intelligence, attached to the presidency; Military Intelligence, attached to the Ministry of Defense; and the General Directorate for State Security Investigations (GDSSI), under direct control of the minister of interior. Any of these agencies could undertake investigations of matters pertaining to national security, but the GDSSI was the main organization for domestic security matters. After the Sadat era, the tendency of military intelligence to encroach on civilian security functions had been curbed.

Nasser established a pervasive and oppressive internal security apparatus. The security police detained as many as 20,000 political prisoners at a time and discouraged public discussions or meetings that could be construed as unfriendly to the government. The security police recruited local informants to report on the activities and political views of their neighbors. Under Sadat intelligence forces were less obtrusive but still managed to be well informed and effective in monitoring subversives, opposition politicians, and foreigners. The security police's failure to uncover the plot leading to Sadat's assassination tarnished the reputation of the force. The security police also seemed to be taken by surprise by the CSF riots and failed to prevent other disorders such as a series of assassination attempts by radical Islamists in the late 1980s.

The authorities have never revealed the personnel strength of the GDSSI, which played an important role in government by influencing policy decisions and personnel matters. The GDSSI engaged routinely in surveillance of opposition politicians, journalists, political activists, foreign diplomats, and suspected subversives. The GDSSI focused on monitoring underground networks of radical Islamists and probably planted agents in those organizations. According to some sources, the GDSSI had informants in all government departments and public-sector companies, labor unions, political parties, and the news media. The organization was also believed to monitor telephone calls and correspondence by the political opposition and by suspected subversives.

In the past, the regime had given the GDSSI considerable leeway in maintaining political control and using emergency laws to intimidate people suspected of subversion. The GDSSI remained in 1990 the primary organ for combatting political subversion even after Mubarak and the judiciary took several steps to limit the organization's power.

The GDSSI was accused of torturing Islamic extremists to extract confessions. In 1986 forty GDSSI officers went on trial for 422 charges of torture that were brought by Al Jihad defendants. After lengthy legal wrangling, the court absolved all the GDSSI officers in mid-1988. The judgment concluded that the GDSSI had indeed tortured Al Jihad members but said there was insufficient evidence to link the particular GDSSI officers on trial with the torture.

ESTONIA: INTELLIGENCE

http://www.kapo.ee
Kaitsepolitseiamet Security Police Board

Estonia is a small country with the territory of 45.200 square kilometres and the population of 1.5 million. The official language is Estonian and the capital is Tallinn. Tallinn was first mentioned in old chronicles in 1154. Estonia is situated on the crossroad of different worlds, between the East and the West, not talking about the North. Our neighbours are Russia from the East, Latvia from the South; Sweden from the West and Finland from the North across the Baltic Sea. That causes the significant role of the Security Police Board on defending the sovereignty of the Republic of Estonia in its sphere of administration.

The Security Police gained the status of an independent institution on June 18, 1993 and has been constantly developing and improving from the very first moments of its establishment, having by now developed into a security service and law enforcement institution appropriate to a democratic legal country. One of the principal elements of the strength of statehood is the law abiding behaviour (loyalty) of its citizens. The main task of the Security Police Board is supporting independent statehood; prevention, obstruction and detection of certain crimes and pre-trial proceeding of criminal cases having initiated on such basis. To create a safe living environment in the country, the aim of the Security Police Board is to operate according to justified expectations of the public, perfectly and correctly performing the tasks imposed on the board. I hope our previous and prospective mutual attempts at law enforcement will bear better fruits at the beginning of the new millennium.

THE SECURITY POLICE BOARD: CONTACTS

Toompuiestee 3, Tallinn 10142
Secretary +372 612 1400
kapo@kapo.ee
Press Representative +372 612 1406 press@kapo.ee
Orderly Officer +372 612 1455
The headquarters of the Security Police and the Tallinn Department **The South-Estonian Department: The Virumaa Department:**

Tartu
51006
Lutsu Street 17
phone +372 7 441 981
Võru
Karja Street 18a
phone +372 78 20 180
Valga
Puiestee 4
phone +372 76 61 008

Kohtla-Järve
30328
Järveküla tee 36
phone +372 33 72 360
Sillamäe
Pavlovi 4
phone +372 39 24 131
Narva
1.mai Street 7
phone +372 35 60 311
Rakvere
Koidula 12
phone +372 32 22 790 **The Pärnu Department: The Tallinn Department:**

Pärnu
80013
Pikk 18
phone +372 44 31 072
Viljandi
Pargi 2
phone +372 43 49 404
Saaremaa
Lossi 7
phone +372 45 33 048

Tallinn
10142
Toompuiestee 3
phone +372 612 1400
Haapsalu
Lossiplats 4
phone +372 47 34 505

FINLAND: INTELLIGENCE

Central function areas of the Finnish Security Police is a) to avert espionage and illegal reconnaissance activities against Finland, b) to avert activities which might endanger interior security of Finland and international relations, c) to act against terrorism, d) security guarding and e) preventive work for security. The Finnish Security Police has three operational units, which are divided by their purpose into 1) the Unit of Counter-Espionage, 2) the Security Unit, and 3) the Unit of Development and Supportive Activities.

Suojelupoliisi (SUPO) is the Finnish security police. As a police unit that specializes in the prevention of security threats of the State, the Security Police participates with other authorities in the protection of parliamentary democracy and the security interests of the society.

During the year 2003 the Finnish Security Police has invested the most of its resources in terrorism prevention. Above all the turbulent situation in Iraq and the continuing hostilities between Israel and Palestinians have contributed to the growth of terrorism in Middle-East, Asia and Europe. Many extreme Islamic groups have taken advantage of the situation by recruiting new members to join their rows.

The main tasks of the Security Police are
- counterespionage
- counterterrorism
- preventing threats to internal security
- preventive security work
- protection
- participation in fighting international organised crime.

The basic values of the Security Police are legality, reliability and quality.

The headquarters of the Security Police is in Helsinki and the Service operates in the whole country. From October 1st 1996, the Director of the Security Police is Mr Seppo Nevala. Approximately 200 people work at the Security Police. The Service has three lines: operational, preventive and strategic line. They are further divided into separate units.

FINNISH SECURITY & INTELLIGENCE SERVICES

http://www2.poliisi.fi
Suojelupoliisi
PL 151
00121 HELSINKI
Finland
Puhelin 09-134471

FINLAND HAS A MILITARY AND A CIVILIAN INTELLIGENCE SERVICE.

The military intelligence service (*Pääesikunnan Tiedusteluosasto* – 'General Staff Intelligence Division'), which is accountable to the Defence Minister, has no separate legal basis. It is responsible for ensuring the territorial integrity of the country and to that end it monitors the national territory, in cooperation with other authorities, by land, sea and air. It also carries out signals intelligence via the Communications Experience Facility (VKL).

The civilian intelligence service (*Suojelupoliisi* – SUPO – Security Police) has been described as a Finnish counterpart of the FBI. It is accountable to the Interior Minister. Its tasks comprise counter-espionage and the prevention of activities which might pose a threat to Finland's internal security and its international relations, as well as combating terrorism.

The Central function areas of the Finnish Security Police are a) to avert espionage and illegal reconnaissance activities against Finland, b) to avert activities which might endanger interior security of Finland and international relations, c) to act against terrorism, d) security guarding and e) preventive work for security. The Finnish Security Police has three operational units, which are divided by their purpose into 1) the Unit of Counter-Espionage, 2) the Security Unit, and 3) the Unit of Development and Supportive Activities.

FRANCE

MINISTRY OF DEFENCE
14, rue Saint-Dominique
00452 ARMEES (France)
Telephone : (33) 01 42 19 30 11
http://www.defense.gouv.fr
Contact : webmestre@dicod.defense.gouv.fr

INTELLIGENCE AGENCIES

http://www.defense.gouv.fr

54th Air Intelligence Wing
54 ème Escadron de Renseignement Air
Air Combat Command
CFAC Commandement de la Force Aérienne de Combat
Air Force
L'Armée De L'Air
Analysis and Forecasting Center
BRGE - Intelligence and Electronic Warfare Brigade
Brigade de Renseignement et de Guerre Electronique
CNCIS - National Commission for the Control of Security Interceptions
Commission Nationale de Controle des Interceptions de Securite
CRS - Companies for Republican Security
Compagnies Républicaines de Sécurité
DCPJ - Judicial Police
Direction Centrale Police Judiciaire
DGSE - General Directorate for External Security
Direction Generale de la Securite Exterieure
DPSD - Directorate for Defense Protection and Security
Direction de la Protection et de la Securite de la Defense
DRM - Directorate of Military Intelligence
Direction du Renseignement Militaire
DST - Directorate of Territorial Security
Direction de la Surveillance du Territoire
Foreign Ministry
Ministry of the Interior

RG - General Information Service
Direction Centrale Renseignement Generaux
SCSSI - Central Service for Information System Security
Service central de la sécurité des systèmes d'informations
DISSI - Interministerial Office for Information Systems Security Service
Delegation Interministerielle a la Securite des Systemes d'Information
SGDN - National Defense General Secretariat
Secrétariat général de la défense nationale (SGDN)
Strategic Affairs Delegation

DGSE - GENERAL DIRECTORATE FOR EXTERNAL SECURITY DIRECTION GENERALE DE LA SECURITE EXTERIEURE

General Directorate for External Security, subordinate to the Ministry of the Defense, is responsible for military intelligence as well as for strategic information, electronic intelligence, and it is also responsible for the counterespionage outside the borders of the national territory.

The DGSE was formed through the the integration of the diverse agencies of French intelligence from the Second World War. The Free French forces in 1942 created the Central Bureau of Information and Action (BCRA), which in November 1943 relocated to Algiers as the General Directorate of Special Services (DGSS). On 06 November 1944 the intelligence networks of the French Resistance were integrated to the DGSS, which was redesignated the Directorate of Studies and Research (DGER). This merger incorporated a limited number of communist networks, which was not entirely satisfactory in the post-War environment. Consequently in 1946 the government of the Fourth Republic created the External Documentation and Counterespionage Service (SDECE) subordinated to the prime minister.

After abolition of the French Indochina opium monopoly in 1950, SDECE imposed centralized, covert controls over the illicit drug traffic that linked the Hmong poppy fields of Laos with the opium dens operating in Saigon. This generated profits that funded French covert operations in their Vietnam war.

With the advent of the Fifth Republic, and through 1962, the SDECE was used as a strategic intelligence service by the prime minister Michel Debre, and was particularly efficient in the struggle against the rebellion in Algeria. In 1962, following the Ben Barka affair, General De Gaulle decided to subordinate the SDECE to the minister of the defense, and the institution adapted to the military environment.

Charles De Gaulle undertook covert operations in Quebec using nationalist and separatist movements in Quebec, under the rubric of "Assistance et Cooperation Technique" or "Operation Ascot." Jacques Foccart dispatched SDECE agents to Quebec to develope and foment the growth of separatist movements. In 1968 Foccart and SDECE tried to wrest control of Nigerian oil from Britain and the US by arming and supplying secessionists in Nigeria's oil-rich Biafra region. The revolt was crushed at a cost of 500,000 lives.

The "Common Program" established by the Socialist and Communist partiess in 1972 included the demand of Communists for the dissolution of the SDECE. This measure was not supported by socialist camp, and intentions of President François Mitterand were unknown at the time of his election in May 1981. In fact, the arrival of the Socialists marked the attempt to "civilize" the SDECE. In June 1981, Stone Marion, a civilian who was the former Director of the Paris Airport, was named to the head of the SDECE. Perceived as a "man of the socialists" and a civilian among soldiers, Marion encountered internal opposition from SDECE.

On 04 April 1982 the SDECE was replaced by the Directorate of the External Security (DGSE). Based on his experience as an enterprise manager, Stone Marion consolidated the structure and the cohesion of the service by the creation of a General Directorate that controls Directorates of Searches, Counterespionage, Personnel and the mythical Division Action. This stimulated the coordinate computerization of service. Furthermore, the DGSE was no longer permitted to operate on French territory.

The contested personality of Marion, and the absence of success in the campaign against terrorism, led to the naming of Admiral Lacoste as the head of the DGSE in 1982. But the "militarization" of the DGSE had slowed, and since the early 1980s the top DGSE military management was gradually replaced by civilians. The proportion of civilians has risen from 45% in 1989 to 60% in 1993. Jacques Dewatre has been the Director of the DGSE since 07 June 1996.

In 1996 the total staff of 2,500 included 1,700 civilians, with an official budget of FF 1,350,000,000. About half these resources were devoted to political and diplomatic intelligence, with the remainder equally divided between military and economic intelligence.

DRM - DIRECTORATE OF MILITARY INTELLIGENCE DIRECTION DU RENSEIGNEMENT MILITAIRE

The DRM was created to solve intelligence shortcomings observed during the Gulf War at the instigation of the then-Interior Minister Pierre Joxe. The DRM was formed from the Military Intelligence Exploitation Center [CERM - Centre d'Exploitation du Renseignement Militaire], the Center for Information on Electromagnetic Radiation (CIREM - Centre d'Information sur les rayonnements Electrotmagnétiques), [Centre l'Interprétation Interarmées de l'Imagerie], the Inter-Army HELIOS Unit [l'Unité Interarmées HELIOS], the Inter-Army Imagery Interpretation Center and the Second Bureau of the Army and Air Force. Naval Intelligence was not absorbed by the DRM remaining under the Foreign Affairs Bureau (BRE) subordinate to the Operating Staff of the Navy in order better to follow naval developments around the world.

The CERM was a tactical intelligence unit subordinated to the chief of staff of the Armed (CEMA). CERM was the smallest and the most secretive unit of French tactical intelligence. It coordinated the intelligence units of the three armed forces, and was responsible for operational and strategic intelligence, while the three Armed Forces were responsible for tactical intelligence. CERM was located at the Inter-Army Intelligence Center (CIFR - Centre de Formation Interarmées du Renseignement (CIFR)) at Strasbourg. Created in 1974, CIFR was also integrated into the DRM.

The DRM's founding decree of 16 June 1992 tasks the Directorate with "planning, coordinating, and leading investigations and the use of military intelligence." But over time the Directorates's responsibilities have gradually evolved from purely military intelligence to intelligence of military interest to the political and strategic intelligence that is the primary resonsibility of the DGSE. The DRM is not a secret service, it is not responsible for internal security, and its employees are not spies, and the DRM has no "operations" branch comparable to the DGSE "action" department. The Directorate's activities include analyzing satellite and other electromagnetic imagery, and it is largely dependent on the collection resources of the Armed Forces, such as the BRGE - Intelligence and Electronic Warfare Regiment.

Its headquarters and activities devoted to administration and current intelligence are located in Paris, while technical and processing Sub-Directorates are located in Creil (Oise).

Since 1992 the DRM has been one of the few defense agencies to recruit new staff. The staff of 1,600 in 1995 is anticipated to grow to 1,900 by the year 2000. In 1995 its staff composition was 50% Army, 23% Aviation, 12%e Navy, 2% General Delegation for Armament, l% Police and 12% civil service. Initially it was headed by General John HEINRICH, former Director of Operations of DGSE, who was replaced on 22 November 1995 by General Bruno ELECTS. The 1994 DRM budget was FF 243,000,000.

The DRM director reports directly to the Defense Ministry, rather than through the Armed Forces chiefs of staff to which the Directorate is attached.

- The Research Sub-Directorate is responsible for human and electronic collection activities at the operational level. For this purpose, it utilizes the services of the Intelligence and Electronic Warfare Brigade (BRGE), created 1st September 1993 which is an element of the Headquarters of the Army.
- The Exploitation Sub-Directorate is composed essentially the former CERM and the Inter-Army Imagery Interpretation Center. It is responsible the production and dissemination of intelligence.
- The Proliferation and Armament Sub-Directorateis responsible for study and analysis of threats from nuclear technology proliferation, chemical weapons, and other armaments.
- The Technical Sub-Directorate is responsible for providing technical support to the other elements of the Directorate.
- The Human Allowances and Administration Sub-Directorate is responsible for the recruitment, management and training of personnel. It has resumed prerogatives of the CERM for the formation of the personnel of military information, notably with School Interarmées of the Information and Linguistic Studies (EIRL) to Strasbourg.

Its activities include liaison with the Directorate of the National Police (DGGN) and the Directorate of Defense Protection and Security (DPSD), the Headquarters of the Armed Forces, and to the General Delegation for the Armament (DGA).

DPSD - DIRECTORATE FOR DEFENSE PROTECTION AND SECURITY DIRECTION DE LA PROTECTION ET DE LA SECURITE DE LA DEFENSE

The Directorate for Defense Protection and Security (formerly *Securite Militaire - SM* - Military Security) is responsible for military counterintelligence operations, as well as political surveillance of the military, ensuring the political reliability of the armed forces, and other military security duties.

In December 1995 DPSD Director Roland Guillaume was promoted to a full general, and his mandate as DPSD chief was renewed. The move was seen as reflecting approval of his renovation and modernization of the "old-fashioned" SM into a modern counter-intelligence and security service. The planned 1997-2002 military budget left the DPSD stable with 1,620 personnel.

The DPSD has carried out some surveys, particularly in order to assess the impact of the far Right in the barracks. The DPSD survey shows that 10 percent of the military vote for [FN Leader] Le Pen, some 5 percent less than the national average. Rather than about the FN vote, the DPSD is worried about the growing influence of traditional Catholic circles among officers.

BRGE - INTELLIGENCE AND ELECTRONIC WARFARE BRIGADE BRIGADE DE RENSEIGNEMENT ET DE GUERRE ELECTRONIQUE

The Intelligence and Electronic Warfare Brigade (BRGE) was created 1st September 1993, to solve intelligence shortcomings observed during the Gulf War at the instigation of the then-Interior Minister Pierre Joxe. It provides the Defense Ministry and military commands with signals intelligence (SIGINT) support. The BRGE derives signal intelligence by monitoring a variety of communications and other signals, such as radars. For this purpose it controls and administers facilities which operates from a number of locations. In addition to providing signals intelligence, the BRGE also provides advice and assistance to the Armed Forces on the security of their communications and information technology systems.

DCSSI - CENTRAL INFORMATION SYSTEMS SECURITY DIVISION

The DCSSI (Central Information Systems Security Division) has succeeded the Central Information Systems Security Division, the State's focal centre for Information Systems Security, and was instituted by decree on 31 July 2001. It is under the authority of the General Secretary for National Defence.

GERMANY

INTELLIGENCE AGENCIES

Federal Chancellor's Office
Federal Intelligence Service [BND]
Bundesnachrichtendienst

DEFENSE MINISTRY
Office of Intelligence of the Federal Armed Forces [ANBw]
Amt für Nachrichtenwesen der Bundeswehr
Office for Radio Monitoring of the Federal Armed Forces [AFMBw]
Amt für Fernmeldwesen Bundeswehr
Military Security Service [MAD]
Militaerischer Abschirmdienst

INTERIOR MINISTRY
Federal Office for the Protection of the Constitution [BfV]
Bundesamt für Verfassungsschutz
State Office for the Protection of the Constitution [LfV]
Landesamt für Verfassungsschutz
Federal Office for Information Technology Security [BSI]
Bundesamt für Sicherheit in der Informationstechnik

FEDERAL INTELLIGENCE SERVICE [BND] BUNDESNACHRICHTENDIENST

http://www.bundesnachrichtendienst.de/index1.htm
Bundesnachrichtendienst
- Zentrale-
Heilmannstrasse 30
82049 Pullach
E -Mail: zentrale@bundesnachrichtendienst.de
Pressestelle@bundesnachrichtendienst.
Federal Information Service
Press Officed
Welfare man route 30
82049 Pullach

TASKS OF THE FEDERAL INTELLIGENCE SERVICE

The Federal Government needs at any time as exact, reliable and comprehensive an information about developments in other states as possible. This applies in particular to foreign affairs and national security.

The end of the cold war changed nothing. Rather:

The different interests of states, which had to be frequently subordinated to those of the respective power bloc in the past, stand out substantially more clearly in today's multi-polar global arena. Seen this way the world became less clear, less predictable, which means, in addition, that the need grows for reports. More and more reliable background information is needed promptly than before on the increased significance and responsibility of united Germany.
The interest situations of other states are an important variables to be evaluated for foreign and national security actions of the Federal Government:

- The search for common interests is the basis of a strengthened bi- and multi-lateral cooperation.

- Knowledge of opposing interests improves our own negotiating position, by making suitable preventive strategies possible.

- Early recognition of separate current interests - direct threat potential of a state aimed at us - can help to defuse unfolding conflicts in time to ease them.

The need for information of the Federal Government covered by a range of information providers, as e.g. by national institutions as Ministries and authorities, and, in addition, by private mechanisms and media. These cover a broad spectrum. However, for some countries and topics the information is not sufficient. Here the Federal Intelligence Service acts as the only foreign intelligence service of Germany.

It procures among other things with its specific intelligence capabilities secret communications and supplements that with other information sources. It can be replaced therefore by no other institution. Without the Federal Intelligence Service important information for foreign affairs and national security decisions would be lacking to the Federal Government.

OPERATIONS

Nearly the entire world is of interest to the BND, which has operatives in more than 100 countries concerned with obtaining information. More often than not, they are disguised as embassy staffers and have their own address under the cover of "second political officer." Approximately 1,000 "cruising monitors" comb the airwaves around the clock and transcribe telephone and radio conversations and telex and fax traffic. Important priorities, beyond current crisis reporting, include weapons and the drugs trade, plutonium smuggling, armament or terrorist organizations and threats to international traffic routes.
The BND regularly exchanges information with other security agencies, including the Federal Criminal Police Office, Customs and Federal Border Protection. In addition to daily current reporting to Bonn, in crisis situations the BND provides additional overview and situation assessment derived from its own sources or from the services of other countries.
The BND has been involved in a coordinated European effort to stop arms deals and smuggling. The BND has deployed agents among Islamic activists in various German cities, and has intensified its surveillance of activities in Central Europe.
In August 1994 three small-time crooks smuggled some 363 grams of plutonium from Moscow to Munich on a Lufthansa aircraft. After they were apprehended at the Munich Airport by officers of the Bavarian Land Office of Criminal Investigations, it was revealed that two BND agents, Karsten Uwe Schnell (cover name: "Roberto") and Rafael Ferreras Fernandez ("Rafa"), encouraged the plutonium deal, code named Operation Hades, in a meeting with the perpetrators in Madrid. There has been an enormous amount of controversy, and a fair amount of disinformation, surrounding the Munich incident.
The BND has an agreement with the Russian FSK covering cooperation in area of contending with nuclear contraband.

BND ORGANIZATION

Administratively the BND is part of the Federal Chancellor's Office, where it reports to the intelligence coordinator in the Chancellor's Office. Some have suggested placing the BND with the Defense Ministry.

DEPARTMENT 1 (OPERATIONAL PROCUREMENT)

DEPARTMENT 2 (TECHNICAL SURVEILLANCE)

Department 2A of the BND, quartered in the high security building No 109 in Pullach, is responsible for counternarcotics and countering money-laundering activities. It was also involved in the *Operation Hades* Plutonium incident.

DEPARTMENT 3 (INTERPRETATION)

Department 3 includes 750 officials for assessing information.

DEPARTMENT 4 (ADMINISTRATION)

Department Four activities include the maintenance of the BND its Central File for Persons (PEZD). The centerpiece of the intelligence service and one of the most closely protected files in Germany, the PEZD contains all findings on persons with contacts with the intelligence services.

DEPARTMENT 5 (SECURITY AND DEFENSE)

DEPARTMENT 6 (CENTRAL TASKS)

MILITARY SECURITY SERVICE [MAD] MILITAERISCHER ABSCHIRMDIENST

Military counterintelligence (MAD) is part of the main military offices of the German armed forces. It is one of three Federal German intelligence agencies, along with the German Intelligence Service (BND) and the Federal Office for the Protection of the Constitution (BfV). Established in 1956, until 1984 it was known as the Office for Security of the German Armed Forces (Amt für Sicherheit der Bundeswehr - ASBw). As directed in the law on military counterintelligence [of 20 December 1990], MAD responsibilities include the collection and analysis of information about anticonstitutional efforts and adversary secret service activities, the interpretation of information for the assessment of the security situation of German and allied armed forces and allied, and providing security evaluations and technical safety precautions for classified material protection.

In fullfilment of its functions MAD maintains close contacts with security representatives and agency managers of the German Federal Armed Forces and advises them in security affairs. Though organizationally part of the armed forces, officially it is technically subordinated to the Deputy of the General Inspector of the German Federal Armed Forces for military security. Its competence is basically limited to the division of the BMVg. The functions are assumed in the Office for Military Conterintelligence, located Cologne, and in subordinate agencies at other locations.

The total of some 1,950 staff members consists of about 500 at the MAD main office, 1,000 at MAD Groups and some 500 elsewhere.

ORGANIZATION

- Headquarters Departments of the MAD office
  - ZA head office functions
  - I personnel security
  - II defense of anticonstitutional forces
  - III defense of gegenerischer intelligence services
  - IV technical support
- MAD groups:

- S-Group (for BMVg, NATO staffs etc..)
  Military District Command Groups
    - Kiel
    - Hanover
    - Duesseldorf
    - Mainz
    - Stuttgart
    - Munich

School for Intelligence of the German Federal Armed Forces (SNBw), Bad Ems
The training activities of the School for intelligence of the German Federal Armed Forces in Bad Ems are being transfered to the Office for Intelligence of the German Federal Armed Forces or by the military guard service. The school and facility at Bad Ems is being closed.

GREECE

NATIONAL INTELLIGENCE SERVICE

webmaster@nis.gr
http://www.nis.gr
Adress
4, Panagioti Kanelopoulou Street
10177 Athens
Telephone Numbers
+30 210 6973100

The Hellenic National Intelligence Service has recently been reorganized in response to a new Presidential Decree.
The mission of the National Intelligence Service, as defined in Article 2 of Law 1645/86, includes the following:

- The collection, processing and dissemination, to the competent Authorities, of information pertaining to the Country's National Security.
- Counterintelligence activities focusing on foreign Intelligence Officers acting against the country.
- The security of national communications.

In time of war or mobilisation the NIS, in parallel with its above mentioned powers, also becomes the country's intelligence staff.

MISSION

The mission of EYP is the security of Greece. The agency fulfills its mission by:

- Information collecting, processing, evaluating and distribution. This information may be of a political, economic or military nature.
- Confronting spying activities by foreign agents.
- Securing national communications.

PERSONNEL

The director general of EYP is *Pavlos Apostolides* (alternative spelling: *Pavlos Apostolidis*).
The agency is directly responsible to the *Minister of Public Order*, who can appoint or dismiss the director general.
EYP employs the following categories of personnel:

- Permanent civilian personnel.
- Scientific civilian personnel, serving on the basis of private contracts of employment.
- A number of officers on active service of the Armed Forces, the Harbour Guard or the Hellenic Police.

HISTORY

The agency had the name *Central Intelligence Service* (KYP, Greek: ΚΥΠ) from 1953 until 1986, when its name changed to *National Intelligence Service* .
EYP was established by law 1645/86 on August 28, 1986

Service is monitored by:

1. The Special Committee for the Protection of Communication Privacy(Law 2225/1994) of Parliament.

This particular Committee whose term ends with the parliamentary term, consists of one Vice-President of Parliament who is the President of the Committee assigned by the President of Parliament, of a member of Parliament from each political party which is represented in Parliament and has a parliamentary group according to the regulation of Parliament and of an individual of prominent reputation who has specific knowledge on communication issues (assigned by the President of Parliament).

Does The N.I.S. Co-operate with other Intelligence Services?

The N.I.S. cooperates with other Greek and foreign intelligence and Security Agencies:

- The Directorate of State Security under the Minister of Public Order.
- The Intelligence Offices and General Staff of the Armed Forces. They deal with military information and the security of the Armed Forces.
- The D.A.E.E.B. (Directorate for coping with Special Crimes of Violence) under the Chief of the Hellenic Police.
- The SDOE (Economic Crime Prosecution Agency) on issues of exchanging information related to its subject.
- Foreign intelligence Services

Who Is Responsible for the Activities of the N.I.S.?
The N.I.S.'s task, as it is outlined by its mission and as it is clearly laid down in the Article 2 of the Law 1645/86 includes the following: the collection, processing and dissemination to the competent Authorities of information pertaining to the Country's National Security.
The N.I.S.'s political superior is the Minister of Public Order.
The KYSEA (Foreign Affairs and Defence Government Council) provides guidelines of the strategic importance on the General Security and Public Policy Matters as well as guidelines on the implementation of decisions in the Ministries.

HUNGARY

INTELLIGENCE AGENCIES

Nemzetbiztonsági Hivatal (NBH) National Security Office
Információs Hivatal (IH)
Information Agency
Katonai Biztonsági Hivatal (KBH)

Military Security Agency
Katonai Felderito Hivatal (KFH)
Military Detection Agency
Nemzetbiztonsági SzakSzolgálat (NBSzSz)
National Security Services

NEMZETBIZTONSÁGI HIVATAL (NBH) NATIONAL SECURITY OFFICE

nbh@nbh.hu
Telephone number: (+36 1) 485-2300
Postal address: 1391 Hungary, Budapest 62. Pf. 217.
E-mail address: nbh@nbh.hu
Information on employment: (+36 1) 484-3950, (1) 484-3953
humanpolitika@nbh.hu

Legality is one of the most important principles of secret service activity, the most significant elements of which were defined by the Act on National Security and other regulations. Its scope, however, cannot be limited to the observance of normative controls. Since legality is the main concern, the NBH must always adhere to the limitation of civil rights guaranteed by law, if the security interests of the Republic of Hungary demand so. At the same time, special means and methods of secret information gathering can only be applied if the data required for the successful accomplishment of the tasks defined by law cannot be acquired in any other way. The legality of the operations of the NBH is also guaranteed by the constitutional supervision of the Security Committee of the National Assembly. Parliamentary supervision does not only provide a guarantee of legality, but also ensures that the government cannot monopolise the security services to act in its own interests.
The National Security Office is engaged in the assessment of risks jeopardising the security of the nation and in the elimination of the sources of danger. It acts to meet the expectations of the government in power. It will continue accomplishing these objectives in 2004.

The Office had to face a wide range of challenges in 2003, too. To measure what effect the Iraqi military operations of the coalition forces had on Hungary and to co-ordinate the operational assurance of the training of the Iraqi nationals in Taszár were honourable, and, at the same time, responsible tasks. Our efforts demanded co-operation with our sister- and partner services and with law enforcement organs, in the course of which we gained accurate and authentic information, suitable for substantiating governmental decisions. When taking action we tried not to affect the everyday life of our fellow-countrymen in the slightest degree.

With keeping international events in view we paid special attention to the struggle against terrorism. On the basis of the knowledge at our disposal we can establish that although the risks have potentially grown, Hungary is still not a target of international terrorism. Events of 2003, nevertheless, point out that there are people living in Hungary who aid organisations that can be evaluated as terrorist. The judicial decision brought in case of the participant of one of the widely publicised cases reinforced us in the conviction that professional work should only be carried out on the basis of facts, with the exclusion of subjective feelings.

INDIA

INTELLIGENCE AND SECURITY AGENCIES

Joint Intelligence Committee (JIC)
Research and Analysis Wing [RAW]
Intelligence Bureau (IB)

Ministry of External Affairs

National Technical Facilities Organisation
Defense Ministry
Joint Cipher Bureau

Army
Directorate of Military Intelligence
Defence Security Corps
Special Frontier Force
National Security Guards (NSG)
Special Security Bureau

Air Force
Directorate of Air Intelligence

Navy
Directorate of Naval Intelligence
Coast Guard
Minister of State for Home Affairs
Central Bureau of Investigation (CBI)

Department of Internal Security
Central Reserve Police Force (CRPF)
Rapid Action Force (RAF)
Special Protection Group (SPG)
Central Industrial Security Force
Border Security Force (BSF)
Home Guards
Ministry of Finance
Economic Intelligence Council

Department of Revenue
Central Economic Intelligence Bureau
Directorate General of Revenue Intelligence (DGRI)
Directorate of Enforcement
Directorate General of Anti-Evasion
Directorate General of Income Tax Investigation
Narcotics Control Bureau (NCB)
Collection Systems

MILITARY CONTACTS

DEPARTMENT OF DEFENCE

SL. NO.	NAME	DESIGNATION	DEPARTMENT	TEL NO.(O)	OFFICE ADDRESS
1.	Shri Ajai Vikram Singh	Defence Secretary	Defence	23012380	101, South Block, New Delhi
2.	Vacant	Special Secretary (Acquisition)	Defence	23014219	5-A, South Block, New Delhi
3.	Dr. (Smt) Rekha Bhargava	Additional Secretary (B)	Defence	23011775	199-A, South Block. New

					Delhi
4	Shri Ranjit Issar	Additional Secretary (I)	Defence	23017678	199-B, South Block, New Delhi
5	Shri Bimal Julka	Joint Secretary. (G/Air)	Defence	23011410	108-A, South Block, New Delhi
6.	Shri C.R. Mohapatra	Joint Secretary & Acquisition Manager (Air)	Defence	23014944	198-A, South Block, New Delhi
7.	Shri Gautam Chatterjee	Joint Secretary (Navy/Ordnance)	Defence	23014222	8-B, South Block, New Delhi
8.	Shri Gautam Mukhopadhaya	Joint Secretary (Planning and International Cooperation)	Defence	23011752	109-B, South Block, New Delhi
9	Shri Harcharanjit Singh	Joint Secretary (Pension) and Secretary Border Road Development Board	Defence	23015884	418 'B' Wing Sena Bhawan, New Delhi
10	Shri P.K. Anand	Joint Secretary & Acquisition Manager (Land Systems)	Defence	23015952	198-B, South Block, New Delhi
11.	Shri P.K. Rastogi	Joint Secretary (Trg) & Chief Administrative Officer	Defence	23018201	155, E-Block, New Delhi
12.	Shri Ranjan Chatterjee	Joint Secretary (Estt) & Public Grievances & Chief Vigilance Officer	Defence	23011553	108-B, South Block, New Delhi
13.	Shri S.K. Sharma	Joint Secretary (Ex-Servicemen Welfare)	Defence	23011804	109-A, South Block, New Delhi
14.	Dr. Thomas Mathew	Joint Secretary & Acquisition Manager (Maritime & Systems)	Defence	23016447	110, South Block, New Delhi
15.	Maj. Gen HS Sehgal	Technical Manager (Land Systems)	Defence	23019609	306, North Hutments, Kashmir House, Rajaji Marg
16.	Rear Admiral RM Kshetrapal, AVSM	Technical Manager (Maritime & Systems)	Defence	23792903	Room No 50, 'A' Block Hutments, Dalhousie Marg
17.	AVM Rajesh Lal	Technical Manager (Air)	Defence	23012068	Room No 469, Vayu Bhawan

JOINT INTELLIGENCE COMMITTEE (JIC)

The Joint Intelligence Committee (JIC) of the government of India analyzes intelligence data from the Intelligence Bureau and the RAW, Directorate of Military Intelligence, Directorate of Naval Intelligence, Directorate of Air Intelligence. JIC has its own secretariat that is under the Cabinet Secretariat,

The National Security Council (NSC), established on 24 August 1990, includes the Prime Minister as Chairman, and the Home Minister, External Affairs Minister, Defence Minister and Finance Minister as members. Since its inception the Council has met just once, on 05 October 1990.

RESEARCH AND ANALYSIS WING [RAW]

The Research and Analysis Wing [RAW] is India's foreign intelligence agency. RAW has become an effective instrument of Indian national power, and has assumed a significant role in carrying out India's domestic and foreign policies. RAW has engaged in espionage against Pakistan and other neighboring countries. It has enjoyed the backing of successive Indian governments in these efforts. Working directly under the Prime Minister, the structure and operations of the Research & Analysis Wing are kept secret from Parliament.
Founded in 1968, RAW focused largely on Pakistan. Its formation was initially motivated by reports of Pakistan supplying weapons to Sikh militants, and providing shelter and training to guerrillas in Pakistan.

Numerous missions were assigned to RAW upon its creation. These included monitoring political and military developments in neighboring countries that affects Indian national security. Consequently, considerable attention is paid by RAW to Pakistan and China, countries that are traditional rivals of India.

RAW has evolved from its origins as a part of the Intelligence Bureau to develop into India's predominant intelligence organization. In 1968, RAW had 250 agents and a budget of Rs. 2 crore. This has expanded to the present day total of an estimated eight to ten thousand agents and a budget that experts place at Rs. 1500 crore, alternately estimated at $145 million.

Pakistan has accused the Research and Analysis Wing of sponsoring sabotage in Punjab, where RAW is alleged to have supported the Seraiki movement, providing financial support to promote its activities in Pakistan and organizing an International Seraiki Conference in Delhi in November-December 1993. RAW has an extensive network of agents and anti-government elements within Pakistan, including dissident elements from various sectarian and ethnic groups of Sindh and Punjab. Published reports in Pakistan allege that as many as 35,000 RAW agents entered Pakistan between 1983-93, with 12,000 working in Sindh, 10,000 in Punjab, 8,000 in North West Frontier Province and 5000 in Balochistan.

RAW has a long history of activity in Bangladesh, supporting both secular forces and the area's Hindu minority. The involvement of RAW in East Pakistan is said to date from the 1960s, when RAW supported Mujibur Rahman, leading up to his general election victory in 1970. RAW also provided training and arms to the Bangladeshi freedom fighters known as Mukti Bahini. RAW's aid was instrumental in Bangladesh's gaining independence from Pakistan in 1971.

During the course of its investigation the Jain Commission received testimony on the official Indian support to the various Sri Lankan Tamil armed groups in Tamil Nadu. From 1981, RAW and the Intelligence Bureau established a network of as many as 30 training bases for these groups in India. Centers were also established at the high-security military installation of Chakrata, near Dehra Dun, and in the Ramakrishna Puram area of New Delhi. This clandestine support to the Liberation Tigers of Tamil Eelam (LTTE), some of whom were on the payroll of RAW, was later suspended. Starting in late 1986 the Research and Analysis Wing focused surveillance on the LTTE which was expanding ties with Tamil Nadu separatist groups. Rajiv Gandhi sought to establish good relations with the LTTE, even after the Indian Peace Keeping Force [IPKF] experience in Sri Lanka. But the Indian intelligence community failed to accurately assess the character of the LTTE and its orientation India and its political leaders. The LTTE assassination of Rajiv Gandhi was apparently motivated by fears of a possible re-induction of the Indian Peace Keeping Force (IPKF) in Sri Lanka and a crackdown on the LTTE network in Tamil Nadu.

RAW was heavily criticized in 1999, following the Pakistani incursions at Kargil. Critics accused RAW of failing to provide intelligence that could have prevented the ensuing ten-week conflict that brought India and Pakistan to the brink of full-scale war. While the army has been critical of the lack of information they received, RAW has pointed the finger at the politicians, claiming they had provided all the necessary information. Most Indian officials believe that in order to prevent another such occurrence, communication needs to be increased between the intelligence agencies, which would require structural reform.

Most recently, RAW has gained attention for providing the US with intelligence on Al-Qaeda and Taliban targets for the war on terrorism in Afghanistan. Maps and photographs of terrorist training camps in Afghanistan and Pakistan, along with other evidence implicating Osama bin Laden in terrorist attacks, were given to US intelligence officials.

INTELLIGENCE BUREAU (IB)

The Intelligence Bureau (IB) is the Indian government's domestic intelligence agency, and reputedly the world's oldest intelligence agency. It is rather difficult to ascertain what the IB does, since its operations are outside the purview of audit or inquiry. In addition to domestic intelligence responsibilities, the IB is particularly tasked with intelligence collection in border areas, following the 1951 recommendations of the Himmatsinhji Committee (also known as the North and North-East Border Committee), a task entrusted to military intelligence organizations prior to independence in 1947. The IB was also tasked with other external intelligence responsibilities as of 1951.

The Indian Telegraph Act authorizes the surveillance of communications, including monitoring telephone conversations and intercepting personal mail, in case of public emergency or "in the interest of the public safety or tranquility." These powers have been used by every state government. It has been reported that as many as 5,000 letters from abroad are intercepted every day by the Intelligence Bureau under the provisions of the Indian Post Office Act. Indian courts do not issue warrants or accept wiretaps as evidence, giving the police little incentive to intercept. Many wiretaps are conducted "informally" by agencies such as the Intelligence Bureau, and the targets are frequently opposition politicians. From time to time a few such cases have come to light, been furiously debated in Parliament, and declared illegal.

The IB has also employed officers, who submit letters and opinion pieces under assumed names, to ensure that newspapers carry the government's point of view. The Intelligence Bureau (IB) procures information which is more often than not related to the security of the current Government rather than of the nation.

The DMK government led by M. Karunanidhi in Tamil Nadu was dismissed in 1990 on grounds of having encouraged the Liberation Tigers of Tamil Eelam (LTTE) movement in the state. karunanidhi had portrayed the fellow Tamils' cause in Sri Lanka as just and noble. Imposition of central rule in Tamil Nadu, a political step taken under pressure from the Congress (I) Party, was taken following a series of reports filed by the Intelligence Bureau (IB) that reveale the growing informal relationship between the followers of the DMK and the LTTE. Although the IB had established Karunanidhi's sympathy towards the LTTE, it was unaware of the group's plan to assasinate Rajiv Gandhi.

MINISTRY OF DEFENSE

The Minister of Defense is the highest authority over the Indian armed forces and is its link to civilian political authorities, responsible for budgetary, administrative, industrial, and policy matters affecting the military.

JOINT CIPHER BUREAU

The inter-services Joint Cipher Bureau has primary responsibility for cryptology and SIGINT, providing coordination and direction to the other military service organisations with similar mission. Most current equipment providing tactical intelligence is of Russian origin, including specialised direction finding and monitoring equipment.

The Joint Cipher Bureau is also responsible for issues relating to public and private key managment. The cryptographic situation in India is in the early stages of development. Cryptographic products are export-controlled licenced items, and licences to India are not generally available for products of key length of more than 56 bits. The domestic Indian computer industry primrily produces PCs, and PC-compatible cryptographic products have been developed and are being used commercially. More robust cryptologic systems are not commercially produced in India, and progress of in this field has been slow due to the general inavailability of technology and know-how. Customised cryptographic products have been designed and produced by organisations in the defense sector are engaged in the implementation of cryptographic techniques, protocols and the products.

ARMY DIRECTORATE OF MILITARY INTELLIGENCE

India's military intelligence traces its origins to the appointment in 1885 of Maj. Gen. Sir Charles MacGregor as head of the Intelligence Department of the British Indian Army. Headquartered in Simla, the Department was primarily tasked collection and analysis of intelligence relating to Russian troop dispositions in Central Asia. The departure of the British in 1947 marked the low point, as the British left behind very little in the way of assets or infractructure for the Intelligence Corps of the newly independent India.

Through the 1960s Military Intelligence was largely focused on field security services rather than external intelligence collection. Responsibilities primarily consisted of policing the army, rooting out corruption and misuse of facilities and equipment by Army personnel. Subsequently the increasing deployment of Army units in support of civil authorities has led Military Intelligence to focus on counter-insurgency operations.

DEFENCE SECURITY CORPS

The Defence Security Corps, with 31,000 personnel, provides security at Defence Ministry sites

SPECIAL FRONTIER FORCE

The Special Frontier Force has around 10,000 personnel, includeing a large number Tibetans. It was formed with the help of the CIA and the Research & Analysis Wing (RAW), India's foreign intelligence gathering espionage service. Their main objective is the disruption of logistics and other tasks, including disruption of the enemy behind its lines.

NATIONAL SECURITY GUARDS BLACK CAT COMMANDOS

The National Security Guards [NSG], established under the National Security Guard Act of 1986 (Act 47 of 1986), is India's premier counter-terrorist force. The NSG provides security to VIP's, conducts anti-sabotage checks, and is responsible for neutralizing terrorist threats to vital installations. Its

missions include engaging terrorists in specific situations, responding to piracy in the air and on the land, and rescuing hostages in kidnap situations.
The NSG strength of around 7500 personnel is evenly divided between the Special Action Group (SAG) and the Special Rangers Group (SRG). The SAG is the offensive wing, with the members drawn from the Indian Army. The SRG, with members from central police organizations, supports the SAF in isolating target areas.

NSG was established following the 1984 Operational Bluestar that caused widespread damage in the Golden Temple complex. Shortcomings in that operational indicated the need for a special force for executing such operations with greater precision. The NSG has been deployed on only a few occasions, including Operation Black Thunder I & II in the Amritsar Golden Temple complex in 1988, and the Operation Ashwamedh storming of a hijacked Indian Airlines aircraft at Amritsar airport on 24 April 1994.
As part of its occupation of Kashmir, the Indian Government has deployed more than half a million soldiers and a quarter of a million paramilitary forces, including significant elements of the National Security Guards. While Indian forces have allegedly committed excesses, including torture, extrajudicial executions, disappearances, willful destruction of property and forced displacement in Kashmir, NSG personnel have not been prominently implicated in these activities.

Special Security Bureau

The Special Security Bureau is unique, as it is both an intelligence agency and also a specialized commando organization for behind enemy line operations. Its strength is currently about two battalions.

Directorate of Air Intelligence

Air Force intelligence responsibilities include imagery intelligence collection MiG-25R and Jaguar recconnaissance aircraft. During the 1971 war with Pakistan, Russian satellite imagery provided India with information on Chinese force deployments. And with advances in the Indian space program, the Indian Air Force will be acquiring independent space-based imagery intelligence capabilities.

Naval Intelligence

The Navy Directorate of Signal Intelligence can intercept signals by means of communication equipment. Intercepts are routed through the Director of Naval Operations/Director of Naval Signals as part of operational tasking.

INDONESIA

INTELLIGENCE AND SECURITY AGENCIES

Badan Intelijen Negara (BIN) State Intelligence Agency

Iran Intelligence Agencies
Introduction
Ministry of Security [SAVAK]
Joint Committee for Special Operations
Ministry of Intelligence and Security [MOIS]
Ministry of Information
Vezarat-e Ettela'at va Amniat-e Keshvar VEVAK
Military Intelligence

Jerusalem Force, Guardians of the Islamic Revolution
Qods, Pasdaran- e Enghelab-e Islami,

BADAN INTELIJEN NEGARA (BIN) STATE INTELLIGENCE AGENCY

http://www.bin.go.id
info@bin.go.id

Since 1980, the State Intelligence Agency has maintained its headquarters at Pejaten in South Jakarta. Within this site, headquarters personnel are split among nearly a dozen buildings; surrounding this are training facilities, a pistol range, and living quarters for senior personnel.

On 22 August 2002, the Pejaten headquarters was officially christened the Sukarno-Hatta State Intelligence Unit (Kesatuan Intelijen Negara Soekarno-Hatta) in honor of the nation's founding fathers. The following year, renowned Indonesian sculptor Nyoman Nuarta was commissioned to produce statues of Sukarno and Hatta for placement at the entrance to the complex; these will be officially dedicated by the president during the second quarter of 2004.

Pejaten is also home to a population of more than 100 deer. The original stock was presented as a gift from the King of Nepal to then President Sukarno in the sixties; their prodigy can now be found at the presidential palace in Bogor, Monas park in downtown Jakarta, and BIN headquarters.

ABDULLAH MAHMUD HENDROPRIYONO was born in Yogyakarta on 7 May 1945. His undergraduate university education includes degrees in Public Administration, Law, Economics, and Industrial Engineering. He earned a Masters in *Business Administration* from the University of the City of Manila in the Philippines.

Hendropriyono is a graduate of the National Military Academy's Class of 1967. He attended the *Australian National Intelligence Course* in Woodside in 1971, the *U.S. Army General Staff College* at Fort Leavenworth in 1980, the Indonesian Command and Staff College in 1989, and graduated top of his class at the *National Resilience Institute* in 1995.

Hendropriyono's military qualifications include completion of the para-commando and military freefall courses. Among his military assignments, he served as Intelligence Assistant for the Jakarta Metropolitan Military Region in 1985, commander of the Black Garuda 043 Military District in Lampung during 1987, a director at the Armed Forces Strategic Intelligence Agency in 1990, commanding general of the Jakarta Metropolitan Military Region in 1993, commandant of the Army Training and Education Command in 1994, and secretary for the Management of Operational Development in 1996. He served as Minister of Transmigration and Resettlement in 1997, and concurrently as Minister of Manpower in 1999. Since 2001, he has been Head of the State Intelligence Agency with ministerial rank.

In 1986, Hendropriyono was named the chairman of the Association of Alumni from the State Administration Institute. In 1997, he was named the chairman of the Association of Alumni from the *National Resilience Institute.*

Hendropriyono has been awarded numerous awards for excellence in service, including the Bintang Mahaputra Indonesia Adipradana, the Bintang Kartika Eka Paksi Naraya-prestasi, the Bintang Dharma, and the Setya Lencana Bakti for injuries sustained in the field of battle. He holds black belts in several martial arts, including a sixth degree in Goju Kai Karate.

What is BIN doing in the war on terrorism?
BIN was the first Indonesian government agency to recognize the threat of international terrorism. Its first operations against Jemaah Islamiyah, a Southeast Asian affiliate of al-Qaeda, predate the 11 September 2001 attacks in the United States.

Following those U.S. attacks, BIN quickly moved into the forefront of continued operations against Jemaah Islamiyah. It also operated against several other domestic extremist groups operating in places like the Malukus and Central Sulawesi.

BIN also focused against international terrorists on Indonesian soil. Media reports indicate that BIN officers were instrumental in the apprehension of at least persons linked to al-Qaeda during 2002.

BIN, in concert with the national police and other government bodies, remains committed to the war on terrorism. It continues to score notable successes, the details of which can not be revealed at this time.

To whom does BIN report?
The head of the State Intelligence Agency reports to the president of the Republic of Indonesia and holds ministerial status. He briefs relevant cabinet members on pertinent intelligence topics during weekly cabinet meetings. He is frequently requested to brief members of the legislative branch.

According to an October 2002 presidential decree, the head of BIN is charged with coordinating all intelligence operations within the republic.

How has BIN's mandate changed during reformasi?
BIN's intelligence collection and analysis mandate has not changed in a significant manner since 1998.

That said, political reforms in Indonesia have made it paramount that all government bodies act in a responsible and open manner. To the extent that this is possible in intelligence operations, BIN is committed to transparency. The existence of this website is part of this effort.

Does BIN have the power of arrest?
BIN does not currently have the legal power to detain suspects.

Why does BIN have a presence in provinces across Indonesia?
Since the seventies, Bakin (BIN's forerunner) had at least a small official presence in virtually every Indonesian province. This presence has been maintained through the present time. Recent media controversy about the plan to establish BIN provincial posts is ill-founded: these have been in existence for more than three decades.

IRELAND

INTELLIGENCE AGENCIES

The Irish Intelligence Services are comprised of the following:
Two dedicated units are within the Irish Defence Forces - Óglaigh na h-Éireann.

Contact with the Department can be made in a number of ways:

- By email archives@ucd.ie
- By telephone +353-1-716 7555 during Research Room opening hours

- By fax +353-1-716 1146
- By letter Archives Department,

University College Dublin
Belfield, Dublin 4
Ireland

1. **The G-2 Military Intelligence Branch** of the Irish Defence Forces Military Intelligence. The most secretive unit, it is known to have a liaison relationship with Britain's SIS and MI5 and the United States' FBI and CIA.
2. **The Army Ranger Wing**. This Unit is officially designated 'Sciathán Fianóglach an Airm'. The missions of this unit are multiple, including long range patrolling, training of other units, VIP security, anti-hijacking, hostage rescue, and counterterrorism (CT). These duties, specifically as they related to CT, are considered supplemental to Ireland's primary response unit, the Garda Siochana.

An Garda Siochana. This is Ireland's National Police Service which has primary responsibility for law and order, including the protection of the internal security of the State.
The Deputy Commissioner of Operations is responsible for the following units:

- Special Services
- Security & Intelligence
- Special Branch C3 Section (dealing with terrorism and subversion)

ISRAEL

INTELLIGENCE AGENCIES

Mossad - Institute for Intelligence and Special Tasks
ha-Mossad le-Modiin ule-Tafkidim Meyuhadim
Shabak - Israel Security Service
Sherut ha-Bitachon ha-Klali
Aman - Military Intelligence
Agaf ha-Modi'in
Lekem -Bureau of Scientific Relations
Leshkat Kesher Madai
Center for Political Research
Ministry of Foreign Affairs

MOSSAD THE INSTITUTE FOR INTELLIGENCE AND SPECIAL TASKS *[HA-MOSSAD LE-MODIIN ULE-TAFKIDIM MEYUHADIM]*

1-800-363-003;
Israeli Intelligence Agency (IIA)
DCI/Director: Yitzhak M. Shamir
Tel Aviv, Israel
European office:
***Kidon Agency* (Merkazi Intelligence Belgique)**
(Bruxelles-Hoofdstad, Belgium, Europe)
manulam@host23.de

Mossad [Hebrew for "institute"] has responsibility for human intelligence collection, covert action, and counterterrorism. Its focus is on Arab nations and organizations throughout the world. Mossad also is responsible for the clandestine movement of Jewish refugees out of Syria, Iran, and Ethiopia. Mossad agents are active in the former communist countries, in the West, and at the UN.

Mossad is headquartered in Tel Aviv. The staff of Mossad was estimated during the late 1980s to number between 1,500 to 2,000 personnel, with more recent estimates placing the staff at an estimated 1,200 personnel. The identity of the director of Mossad was traditionally a state secret, or at least not widely publicized, but in March 1996 the Government announced the appointment of Major General Danny Yatom as the replacement for Shabtai Shavit, who resigned in early 1996. In September 2002, Meir Dagan was designated the new Mossad director.

Formerly known as the Central Institute for Coordination and the Central Institute for Intelligence and Security, Mossad was formed on 01 April 1951. Mossad was established by then Prime Minister David Ben Gurion, who gave as Mossad's primary directive: "For our state which since its creation has been under siege by its enemies. Intelligence constitutes the first line of defence...we must learn well how to recognise what is going on around us."

Mossad has a total of eight departments, though some details of the internal organization of the agency remain obscure.

- **Collections Department** is the largest, with responsibility for espionage operations, with offices abroad under both diplomatic and unofficial cover. The department consists of a number of desks which are responsible for specific geographical regions, directing case officers based at "stations" around the world, and the agents they control. Beginning in 2000, the Mossad undertook an advertising campaign to promote recruitment of collection officers. See a June 2001 recruiting poster here. A flash version of the recruiting ad, published September 2002, may be viewed here.
- **Political Action and Liaison Department** conducts political activities and liaison with friendly foreign intelligence services and with nations with which Israel does not have normal diplomatic relations. In larger stations, such as Paris, Mossad customarily had under embassy cover two regional controllers: one to serve the Collections Department and the other the Political Action and Liaison Department.
- **Special Operations Division**, also known as **Metsada**, conducts highly sensitive assassination, sabotage, paramilitary, and psychological warfare projects.
- **LAP (Lohamah Psichologit) Department** is responsible for psychological warfare, propaganda and deception operations.
- **Research Department** is responsible for intelligence production, including daily situation reports, weekly summaries and detailed monthly reports. The Department is organized into 15 geographically specialized sections or "desks", including the USA, Canada and Western Europe, Latin America, Former Soviet Union, China, Africa, the Maghreb (Morocco, Algeria, Tunisia), Libya, Iraq, Jordan, Syria, Saudi Arabia, the United Arab Emirates and Iran. A "nuclear" desk is focused on special weapons related issues.
- **Technology Department** is responsible for development of advanced technologies for support of Mossad operations. In April 2001, the Mossad published a "help wanted" ad in the Israeli press seeking electronics engineers and computer scientists for the Mossad technology unit.

HABAK SHIN BET ISRAEL SECURITY SERVICE SHERUT HA-BITACHON HA-KLALI (SHABAK)

Shabak, or Shin Bet, the Israeli counter-intelligence and internal security service, is believed to have three operational departments and five support departments. The current director (2003) is Avi Dichter.

- **Arab Affairs Department** is responsibile for antiterrorist operations, political subversion, and maintenance of an index on Arab terrorists. Shabak detachments worked with Aman undercover detachments [known as *Mist'aravim*] to counter the uprising. This Department has also been active in countering the military wing of Hamas.

- **Non-Arab Affairs Department**, formerly divided into communist and noncommunist sections, concerned itself with all other countries, including penetrating foreign intelligence services and diplomatic missions in Israel and interrogating immigrants from the Former Soviet Union and Eastern Europe.
- **Protective Security Department** is responsibile for protecting Israeli government buildings and embassies, defense industries, scientific installations, industrial plants, and the *El Al* national airline.

Shabak monitors the activities of and personalities in domestic right-wing fringe groups and subversive leftist movements. It is believed to have infiltrated agents into the ranks of the parties of the far left and had uncovered a number of foreign technicians spying for neighboring Arab countries or the Soviet Union. All foreigners, regardless of religion or nationality, are liable to come under surveillance through an extensive network of informants who regularly came into contact with visitors to Israel. Shabak's network of agents and informers in the occupied territories destroyed the PLO's effectiveness there after 1967, forcing the PLO to withdraw to bases in Jordan.

Shabak's reputation as a highly proficient internal security agency was tarnished severely by two public scandals in the mid-1980s. In April 1984, Israeli troops stormed a bus hijacked by four Palestinians in the Gaza Strip. Although two of the hijackers survived, they were later beaten to death by Shabak agents. It appeared that the agents were acting under orders of Avraham Shalom, the head of Shabak. Shalom falsified evidence and instructed Shabak witnesses to lie to investigators to cover up Shabak's role. In the ensuing controversy, the attorney general was removed from his post for refusing to abandon his investigation. The president granted pardons to Shalom, his deputies who had joined in the cover-up (but who aided its exposure), and the agents implicated in the killings.

In 1987 Izat Nafsu, a former IDF army lieutenant and member of the Circassian minority, was released after his 1980 conviction for treason (espionage on behalf of Syria) was overturned by the Supreme Court. The court ruled that Shabak had used unethical interrogation methods to obtain Nafsu's confession and that Shabak officers had presented false testimony to the military tribunal that had convicted him. A judicial commission set up to report on the methods and practices of Shabak found that for the previous seventeen years it had been the accepted norm for Shabak interrogators to lie to the courts about their interrogation.

In 1987 the Israeli government-appointed Landau Judicial Commission condemned torture but allowed for the use of "moderate physical and psychological pressure" to secure confessions and obtain information. In addition, although the Israeli Penal Code prohibits the use of force or violence by a public official to obtain information, the GSS chief is permitted by law to allow interrogators to employ "special measures" that exceed the use of "moderate physical and psychological pressure" when it is deemed necessary to obtain information that could potentially save Israeli lives in certain "ticking bomb" cases. The GSS first permitted interrogators "greater flexibility" in applying the guidelines shortly after a bus bombing in Tel Aviv in October 1994 that killed 22 Israelis. The Government has not defined the meaning of "greater flexibility" or what might constitute a "ticking bomb" case. At roughly quarterly intervals, the Government has approved the continued use of "special measures." On August 22, Israel's ministerial committee on GSS interrogations authorized the continued use of "special measures," including shaking.

The International Committee of the Red Cross (ICRC) declared in 1992 that such practices violate the Geneva Convention. Human rights groups and attorneys challenged the use of "special measures," especially shaking, before the Israeli High Court a number of times. Israeli authorities maintain that torture is not condoned but acknowledge that abuses sometimes occur and are investigated. However, the Government does not generally make public the results of such investigations. Israel conducted two official investigations into the 35 complaints received in 1997. In 2000, the Israeli Supreme Court ruled against the use of torture by the Shabak, although the use of informants as proxies is rumored to serve as a loophole.

Shabak's reputation was further compromised by the assassination of Prime Minister Yitzhak Rabin in November 1995 by a right-wing Israeli extremist.
Shabak was known as the General Security Service until 2002, when it was renamed the Israel Security Service.

AMAN MILITARY INTELLIGENCE - *AGAF HA-MODI'IN*

Military intelligence, or *Aman*, produces comprehensive national intelligence estimates for the prime minister and cabinet, daily intelligence reports, risk of war estimates, target studies on nearby Arab countries, and communications intercepts. Aman also conducts across-border agent operations. *Aman* is an independent service, co-equal with the army, navy and air force and has an estimated staff of perhaps 7,000 personnel. It is currently (2003) led by Major General Aharon Ze'evi.
Aman's **Foreign Relations Department** is responsible for liaison with foreign intelligence services and the activities of Israeli military attachés abroad. The **Sayeret Maktal** General Staff Deep Reconnaissance Unit is Israel's primary counter-terrorism and intelligence-gathering entity.

Small air force and naval intelligence units operated as semi-autonomous branches of Aman. Air force intelligence primarily uses aerial reconnaissance and radio intercepts to collect information on strength levels of Arab air forces and for target compilation. In addition to reconnaissance aircraft, pilotless drones are used extensively to observe enemy installations. Naval intelligence collects data on Arab and Soviet naval activities in the Mediterranean and prepares coastal studies for naval gunfire missions and beach assaults.
A number of electronic intelligence collection and observation facilities are located on the Golan Heights, including a facility at Har Avital which monitors Syria, and another at Mount Hermon which monitors both Lebanon and Syria.

Aman was held responsible for the failure to obtain adequate warning of the Egyptian-Syrian attack that launched the October 1973 War. Many indications of the attack were received but faulty assessments at higher levels permitted major Arab gains before the IDF could mobilize and stabilize the situation.

During preparations for the invasion of Lebanon in 1982, Aman correctly assessed the weaknesses of the Christian militia on which Israel was depending and correctly predicted that a clash with the Syrian garrison in Lebanon was inevitable. The chief of intelligence, Major General Saguy, made these points to the general staff and privately to the prime minister. But, although he was present at cabinet meetings, he failed to make his doubts known to avoid differing openly with Begin and Sharon. Saguy was forced to retire after the Kahan Commission found that he had been delinquent in his duties regarding the massacres at the Sabra and Shatila Palestinian refugee camps.

LEKEM BUREAU OF SCIENTIFIC RELATIONS *LESHKAT KESHER MADAI*

Until officially disbanded in 1986, the Bureau of Scientific Relations (*Leshkat Kesher Madai*--Lekem) collected scientific and technical intelligence abroad from both open and covert sources. Lekem was dismantled following the scandal aroused in the United States by the arrest of Jonathan Jay Pollard for espionage on behalf of Israel. Pollard, a United States naval intelligence employee in Washington, received considerable sums for delivering vast quantities of classified documents to the scientific officers (Lekem agents) at the Israeli embassy. Pollard was sentenced to life imprisonment. Although the Israeli government asserted that the operation was an unauthorized deviation from its policy of not conducting espionage against the United States, statements by the Israeli participants and by Pollard himself cast doubt on these claims.

Some sources assert that open and covert collection of scientific and technical information formerly conducted by Lekem is now conducted by a unit of the Ministry of Foreign Affairs.

CENTER FOR POLITICAL RESEARCH MINISTRY OF FOREIGN AFFAIRS

The Foreign Ministry formulates, implements and presents the foreign policy of the Government of Israel. It represents the state vis-a-vis foreign governments and international organizations, explains its positions and problems throughout the world, endeavors to promote its economic, cultural, and scientific relations, and fosters cooperation with developing countries. Israel currently maintains diplomatic relations with 160 countries. The Ministry promotes relations with Diaspora communities and safeguards the rights of Israeli citizens abroad.
The Center for Political Research, which has ten departments, monitors events, developments, and political processes, mainly in the Middle East, including international involvement therein. The Center's main tasks include gathering, analyzing and evaluating political information, as required by the Ministry; regular political briefings and guidance to Israel's missions throughout the world; and assisting the political information network, in Israel and overseas, with its expertise in Middle East affairs.

ITALY

INTELLIGENCE SERVICES

Segreteria Generale del CESIS
Servizio per le Informazioni e la Sicurezza Democratica
Intelligence and Democratic Security Service
Per aspera ad veritatem, Revista di intelligence e di cultura professionale
Servizi di Informazione e Sicurezza della Repubblica Italiana
Intelligence and Security Services of the Republic of Italy
I Servizi di Informazione e Sicurezza
Ministry of Interior Intelligence and Security Services

JAPAN

INTELLIGENCE AND SECURITY AGENCIES

Security Council
Cabinet Research Office [Naicho]
Defense Agency / Japan Self-Defense Force (Bôeichô)
Defence Intelligence Office DIO [Jouhou Honbu]
Defense Intelligence Headquarters DIH
Chobetsu
Ground Self-Defense Force [Nihon Rikujyo Jieitai]
Intelligence Office
Maritime Self-Defense Force [Nihon Kaijyo Jieitai]
Fleet Intelligence Command
Air Self-Defense Force [Nihon Koku Jieitai]
Intelligence Division
Tactical Reconnaissance Group
National Police Safety Commission (NPSC)
National Police Agency [NPA - Keisatsuchô]
Security Bureau
Ministry of Foreign Affairs [MOFA - Gaimusho]
Intelligence and Analysis Bureau
Ministry of Justice (Homusho)
Public Security Investigation Agency [Koancho]
(former) Ministry of International Trade and Industry [MITI - Tsûsanshô] (now METI)
Japanese External Trade Organization [JETRO]
Collection Programs

RF-4EJ Phantom
U-125 Peace Krypton / Paekdu
Information Gathering Satellites

SECURITY COUNCIL

The Security Council was established in July 1986. The council is presided over by the prime minister and includes the ministers of state specified in advance in Article 9 of the Cabinet Law; the foreign minister, the finance minister, the chief cabinet secretary, the chairman of the National Public Safety Commission, the director general of the Defense Agency, and the director general of the Economic Planning Agency.

The chairman of the Security Council also can invite the chairman of the Joint Staff Council and any other relevant state minister or official to attend. Replacing the National Defense Council, which had acted as an advisory group on defense-related matters since 1956, the Security Council addresses a wider range of military and nonmilitary security issues, including basic national defense policy, the National Defense Program Outline, the outline on coordinating industrial production and other matters related to the National Defense Program Outline, and decisions on diplomatic initiatives and defense operations.
In the postwar political system, executive power has been vested in the cabinet. The cabinet head is the prime minister, responsible for appointing and dismissing other cabinet members. Cabinet ministers include those appointed to head the twelve ministries, and the ministers of state placed in charge of the agencies and commissions of the Office of the Prime Minister, which itself has the status of a ministry. They include the director general of the Defense Agency, equivalent to a minister of defense but lacking ministerial status (a reflection of the Article 9 renunciation of war). Also among the ministers of state are the chief cabinet secretary, who coordinates the activities of the ministries and agencies, conducts policy research, and prepares materials to be discussed at cabinet meetings, and the director of the Cabinet Legislative Bureau, who advises cabinet members on drafting the legislation to be proposed to the Diet. Although the chief cabinet secretary does not have ministerial rank, the position is influential within the cabinet because of its coordination role.

CABINET RESEARCH OFFICE [NAICHO - NAIKAKU CHOSASHITSU BETSUSHITSU]

Japan's central intelligence agency is the Naicho, a small section of the Prime Minister's Office staffed by some 80 personnel who analyze information from abroad. It is supposed to act as a coordinating agency for other groups in the government, but critics say it does not. Critics suggest that this office is rather ineffectual, spending most of its effort on outside researchers and professors translating newspaper articles and official documents from abroad. Other critics, from a different perspective, have charged [not entirely credibly] that the office is being strengthened to conduct surveillance on citizen activists.

JAPAN DEFENSE AGENCY (BÔEICHÔ) JAPAN SELF-DEFENSE FORCE

http://www.jda.go.jp
info@jda.go.jp

Japan is a major world economic and political power, with an aggressive military tradition, resisting the development of strong armed forces. A military proscription is included as Article 9 of the 1947 constitution stating, "The Japanese people forever renounce war as a sovereign right of the nation and the threat or use of force as a means of settling international disputes." That article, along with the rest of the "Peace Constitution," retains strong government and citizen support and is interpreted as permitting the Self-Defense Forces (SDF), but prohibiting those forces from possessing nuclear weapons or other offensive arms or being deployed outside of Japan.

The Defense Agency and the SDF both comprise the same defense organization. However, the term Defense Agency is used to denote an administrative organization responsible for the management, operation, etc., of the GSDF, MSDF and ASDF, while the term SDF is used to mean armed organizations that conduct unit activities for the defense of the nation and for other purposes. The SDF are under control of the civilian Defense Agency, subordinate to the prime minister. Although highly trained and fully qualified to perform the limited missions assigned to them, the SDF are small, understaffed, and underequipped for more extensive military operations. Its activities are confined to disaster relief and limited UN peacekeeping efforts.

Following World War II Japan's Imperial Army and Navy were dissolved, and the old regime was replaced with a democratic government. Article 9 of the new Constitution of Japan renounced war or even possessing combat potential. However, the Cold War and the Korean War forced Japan to reestablish defensive capabilities. A constitutional interpretation of Article 9 grants Japan the inherent right of self-defense and the possession of the minimum armed strength needed to exercise that right. Having renounced war, the possession of war potential, the right of belligerency, and the possession of nuclear weaponry, Japan held the view that it should possess only the minimum defense necessary to face external threats. Within those limits, the Self-Defense Forces Law of 1954 provides the basis from which various formulations of SDF missions have been derived. The law states that ground, maritime, and air forces are to preserve the peace and independence of the nation and to maintain national security by conducting operations on land, at sea, and in the air to defend the nation against direct and indirect aggression.

To avoid the appearance of a revival of militarism, Japan's leaders emphasized constitutional guarantees of civilian control of the government and armed forces and used nonmilitary terms for the organization and functions of the forces. The overall organization was called the Defense Agency rather than the Ministry of Defense. The armed forces were designated the Ground Self-Defense Force (GSDF), the Maritime Self-Defense Force (MSDF), and the Air Self-Defense Force (ASDF), instead of the army, navy, and air force.
Based on the Self-Defense Forces Law of 1954, the nation's defense establishment is organized to ensure civilian control of the armed forces. The result has been a unique military system. All SDF personnel are technically civilians: those in uniform are classified as special civil servants and are subordinate to the ordinary civil servants who run the Defense Agency. There is no military secrets law, and offenses committed by military personnel- -whether on base or off base, on duty or off duty, of military or nonmilitary nature--are all adjudicated under normal procedures by civil courts in appropriate jurisdictions.

The general framework through which these missions are to be accomplished is set forth in the Basic Policy for National Defense adopted by the cabinet in 1957; it remains in force. According to this document, the nation's security would be achieved by supporting the United Nations (UN) and promoting international cooperation, by stabilizing domestic affairs and enhancing public welfare, by gradually developing an effective self-defense capability, and by dealing with external aggression on the basis of Japan-United States security arrangements, pending the effective functioning of the UN.

Japan's national defense policy has been based on maintaining the 1960 Treaty of Mutual Cooperation and Security with the United States, under which Japan assumed unilateral responsibility for its own internal security and the United States agreed to join in Japan's defense in the event that Japan or its territories were attacked. Although the size and capability of the SDF have always limited their role, until 1976 defense planning focused on developing forces adequate to deal with the conventional capabilities of potential regional adversaries. Beginning in 1976, government policy held that the SDF would be developed only to repel a small-scale, limited invasion and that the nation would depend on the United States to come to its aid in the event of a more serious incursion.

The Soviet invasion of Afghanistan in 1979 and the buildup of military forces in the Soviet Far East, including a group of islands to the north of Hokkaido, which were occupied by the Soviet Union but claimed by Japan, led Japan to develop a program to modernize and improve the SDF in the 1980s, especially in air defense and antisubmarine warfare. In the early 1990s, the government was reevaluating its security policy based on reduced East-West tensions.

The very general terms in which military missions are couched left specifics open to wide interpretation and prompted the criticism that the nation did not possess a military strategy. In the 1976 National Defense Program Outline, the cabinet sought to define missions more specifically by setting guidelines for the nation's readiness, including specific criteria for the maintenance and operation of the SDF. Under these guidelines, in cases of limited and small-scale attack, Japanese forces would respond promptly to control the situation. If enemy forces attacked in greater strength than Japan could counter alone, the SDF would engage the attacker until the United States could come to its aid. Against nuclear threat, Japan would rely on the nuclear deterrence of the United States. To accomplish its missions, the SDF would maintain surveillance, be prepared to respond to direct and indirect attacks, be capable of providing command, communication, logistics, and training support, and be available to aid in disaster relief.

The outline specified quotas of personnel and equipment for each force that were deemed necessary to meet its tasks. Particular elements of each force's mission were also identified. The GSDF was to defend against ground invasion and threats to internal security, be able to deploy to any part of the nation, and protect the bases of all three services of the Self-Defense Forces. The MSDF was to meet invasion by sea, sweep mines, patrol and survey the surrounding waters, and guard and defend coastal waters, ports, bays, and major straits. The ASDF was to render aircraft and missile interceptor capability, provide support fighter units for maritime and ground operations, supply air reconnaissance and air transport for all forces, and maintain airborne and stationary early warning units.

The Mid-Term Defense Estimate for FY 1986 through FY 1990 envisioned a modernized SDF with an expanded role. While maintaining Japan-United States security arrangements and the exclusively defensive policy mandated by the constitution, this program undertook moderate improvements in Japanese defense capabilities. Among its specific objectives were bettering air defense by improving and modernizing interceptor-fighter aircraft and surface-to-air missiles, improving antisubmarine warfare capability with additional destroyers and fixed-wing antisubmarine patrol aircraft, and upgrading intelligence, reconnaissance, and command, control, and communications. Most of the goals of this program were met, and the goals of the Mid-Term Defense Estimate for FY 1991 through FY 1995, although building on the early progam, were considerably scaled back.

The SDF disaster relief role is defined in Article 83 of the Self-Defense Forces Law of 1954, requiring units to respond to calls for assistance from prefectural governors to aid in fire fighting, earthquake disasters, searches for missing persons, rescues, and reinforcement of embankments and levees in the event of flooding. The SDF has not been used in police actions, nor is it likely to be assigned any internal security tasks in the future.

In June 1992, the National Diet passed a UN Peacekeeping Cooperation Law which permitted the SDF to participate in UN medical, refugee aid, transportation, infrastructural repair, election-monitoring, and policing operations under strictly limited conditions. This law was used in 1992- 93 to authorize the deployment of 600 SDF and seventy-five police personnel for UN engineering and election-monitoring projects in Cambodia and again in the spring of 1993 to send fifty-three persons to participate in peacekeeping operations in Mozambique.

The Defense Agency, aware that it could not accomplish its programs without popular support, paid close attention to public opinion. Although the Japanese people retained a lingering suspicion of the armed services, in the late 1980s antimilitarism had moderated, compared with its form in the early 1950s when the SDF was established.

At that time, fresh from the terrible defeat of World War II, most people had ceased to believe that the military could maintain peace or serve the national interest. By the mid-1970s, memories of World War II had faded, and a growing number of people believed that Japan's military and diplomatic roles should reflect its rapidly growing economic strength. At the same time, United States-Soviet strategic contention in the area around Japan had increased. In 1976 Defense Agency director general Sakata Michita called upon the cabinet to adopt the National Defense Program Outline to improve the quality of the armed forces and more clearly define their strictly defensive role. For this program to gain acceptance, Sakata had to agree to a ceiling on military expenditures of 1 percent of the gross national product and a prohibition on exporting weapons and military technology.

The outline was adopted by the cabinet and, according to public opinion polls, was approved by approximately 60 percent of the people. Throughout the remainder of the 1970s and into the 1980s, the quality of the SDF improved and public approval of the improved forces went up.

In November 1982, when the Defense Agency's former director general, Nakasone Yasuhiro, became prime minister, he was under strong pressure from the United States and other Western nations to move toward a more assertive defense policy in line with Japan's status as a major world economic and political power.

Strong antimilitarist sentiment remained in Japanese public opinion, however, especially in the opposition parties. Nakasone chose a compromise solution, gradually building up the SDF and steadily increasing defense spending while guarding against being drawn beyond self-defense into collective security. In 1985 he developed the Mid-Term Defense Estimate. Although that program had general public backing, its goals could not be met while retaining the ceiling of 1 percent of GNP on military spending, which still had strong public support. At first the government tried to get around the problem by deferring payment, budgeting only the initial costs of major military hardware. But by late 1986, it had become obvious that the 1 percent ceiling had to be superseded. Thus, on January 24, 1987, in an extraordinary night meeting, the cabinet abandoned this ceiling. A March 1987 Asahi Shimbun [Tokyo] poll indicated that this move was made in defiance of public opinion: only 15 percent approved the removal of the ceiling and 61 percent disapproved. But a January 1988 poll conducted by the Office of the Prime Minister reported that 58 percent approved the defense budget of 1.004 percent of GNP for fiscal year 1987.

During 1987 the Japanese government reviewed ways in which it could assist friendly forces in protecting shipping in the Persian Gulf. Several possibilities were seriously considered, including sending minesweepers to the gulf. But, in the end, the government determined that sending any military forces to the gulf would be unacceptable to the Japanese people. Instead, the Japanese government agreed to fund the installation of radio navigation guides for gulf shipping.

Appreciation of the SDF continued to grow in the 1980s, with over half of the respondents in a 1988 survey voicing an interest in the SDF and over 76 percent indicating that they were favorably impressed.

Although the majority (63.5 percent) of respondents were aware that the primary purpose of the SDF was maintenance of national security, an even greater number (77 percent) saw disaster relief as the most useful SDF function. The SDF therefore continued to devote much of its time and resources to disaster relief and other civic action. Between 1984 and 1988, at the request of prefectural governors, the SDF assisted in approximately 3,100 disaster relief operations, involving about 138,000 personnel, 16,000 vehicles, 5,300 aircraft, and 120 ships and small craft. In addition, the SDF participated in earthquake disaster prevention operations and disposed of a large quantity of World War II explosive ordnance, especially in Okinawa. The forces also participated in public works projects, cooperated in managing athletic events, took part in annual Antarctic expeditions, and conducted aerial surveys to report on ice conditions for fishermen and on geographic formations for construction projects. Especially sensitive to maintaining harmonious relations with communities close to defense bases, the SDF built new roads, irrigation networks, and schools in those areas. Soundproofing was installed in homes and public buildings near airfields. Despite these measures, local resistance to military installations remained strong in some areas.

On 24 May 1999, the Japanese Diet (parliament) passed, with partial amendments, a set of government-sponsored bills and a Japan-U.S. agreement, designed to ensure effective implementation of the Guidelines for Japan-U.S. Defense Cooperation (the Guidelines legislation for short). The Guidelines legislation consists of the Law Concerning Measures to Ensure the Peace and Security of Japan in Situations in Areas Surrounding Japan (the Law Ensuring Peace and Security in Situations in Areas Surrounding Japan for short), which went into force on 25 August 1999; the Agreement to Amend the Acquisition and Cross- Servicing Agreement, which went into force on 25 September 1999; and the Amendment to Article 100-8 of the Self-Defense Forces Law, which went into force on 28 May 1999. The passage of the Guidelines legislation has put the final touches to the process of building a new framework of cooperation under the Japan-U.S. security arrangements after the end of the Cold War, a process that had been initiated by the Japan-U.S. Joint Declaration on Security of 1996.

With the passage of the Guidelines legislation, it has become possible for Japan to support, under the Japan-U.S. Security Treaty, the activities of the U.S. forces in “situations in areas surrounding Japan that have an important influence on Japan’s peace and security” (situations in areas surrounding Japan), situations short of a direct armed attack on Japan. In coming years, a Japan-U.S. bilateral planning and work for building a “bilateral coordination mechanism,” which are currently under way, will be carried out. Meanwhile, reactions and fears expressed by East Asian countries regarding the new framework of cooperation from the time the Japan-U.S. Joint Declaration on Security was issued and to the passage of the Guidelines legislation suggest the growing importance of promoting bilateral and multilateral security dialogue and cooperation with these countries.

The Defense Agency, as part of the Office of the Prime Minister, is required by Article 66 of the constitution to be completely subordinate to civilian authority. Its head, the director general, has the rank of minister of state. He is assisted by two vice directors general (vice ministers), one parliamentary and one administrative; the Defense Facilities Administration Agency; and the internal bureaus. The highest figure in the command structure is the prime minister, who is responsible directly to the Diet. In a national emergency, the prime minister is authorized to order the various components of the SDF into action, subject to the consent of the Diet. In times of extreme emergency, that approval might be obtained after the fact.

The internal bureaus, especially the Bureau of Defense Policy, Bureau of Finance, and the Bureau of Equipment, are often headed by officials from other ministries and are the main centers of power and instruments of civilian control in the Defense Agency. The Bureau of Defense Policy is responsible for drafting defense policy and programs, for determining day-to-day operational activities, and for information gathering and analysis in the SDF. The Bureau of Finance is instrumental in developing the Defense Agency budget and in establishing spending priorities for the Defense Agency and the SDF. The Bureau of Equipment, organized into subunits for each of the military services, focuses on equipment procurement. Before any major purchase is recommended to the Diet by the Defense Agency, it has to be reviewed by each of these bureaus.

Below these civilian groups is the uniformed SDF. Its senior officer is the chairman of the Joint Staff Council, a body that included the chiefs of staff of the ground, maritime, and air arms of the Self-Defense Forces. Its principal functions are to advise the director general and to plan and execute joint exercises. The three branches maintain staff offices to manage operations in their branches. Although rank establishes echelons of command within the SDF, all three branches are immediately responsible to the director general and are coequal bodies with the Joint Staff Council and the three staff offices.

This structure precludes the concentration of power of the pre1945 general staffs, but it impedes interservice coordination, and there are few formal exchanges among commanders from various branches. Moreover, some dissatisfaction has been reported by highranking officers who feel they have little power compared with younger civilian officials in the bureaus, who most often have no military experience. To rectify this situation and to increase input by the SDF in policy matters, in the early 1980s the Joint Staff Council was enlarged to establish better lines of communication between the internal bureaus and the three staff offices. A computerized central command and communications system and various tactical command and communications systems were established, linking service and field headquarters with general headquarters at the Defense Agency and with one another.

In the 1980s, efforts were also under way to facilitate a clear and efficient command policy in the event of a crisis. The government stood by the principle that military action was permitted only under civilian control, but in recognition that delay for consultation might prove dangerous, ships of the MSDF began to be armed with live torpedoes, and fighter-interceptors were allowed to carry missiles at all times. Although aircraft had long been allowed to force down intruders without waiting for permission from the prime minister, ships were still required to receive specific orders before interdicting invading vessels. The Defense Agency had recommended drawing up more complete guidelines to clarify what action SDF combat units could take in emergencies.

Cooperation between the SDF and other civilian agencies in contingency planning is limited. No plans exists to ensure the support of civilian aircraft and merchant fleets in times of crisis, even though the SDF transportation capabilities are generally judged inadequate. In 1990 legislation was being studied to provide the SDF with the ability to respond in emergency situations not specifically covered by Article 76 of the Self Defense Forces Law.
SDF training includes instilling a sense of mission. Personnel are provided with the scientific and technical education to operate and maintain modern equipment and with the physical training necessary to accomplish their missions. Modern equipment is gradually replacing obsolescent matériel in the SDF. In 1987 the Defense Agency replaced its communications system (which formerly had relied on telephone lines of the Nippon Telegraph and Telephone Corporation) with a microwave network incorporating a three-dimensional transmission system using a communications satellite. Despite efforts to increase stocks, however, supplies of ammunition and maintenance and repair parts in 1990 remained at less than satisfactory levels.

The Defense Agency relocated its main offices on 08 May 2000, leaving the entertainment district of Roppongi for a 247.3 billion yen complex on the fromer site of the Japanese Imperial Army's Imperial Headquarters in Ichigaya, near Shinjuku. At least 7,000 agency personnel with eight organizations e moved from the 40-year-old Minato-ku facility to the traditional Shinjuku-ku home of the military. The 23-hectare site is home to a daytime work force of 8,500. The new complex has five wings.

- A-Wing is the home of the military's central nervous system, hosting the Joint Staff Council and the Staff Offices for each of the three branches of the Self-Defense Forces (SDF) - Ground, Maritime and Air. The wing has 23 floors, 19 of which are above ground. The four basement floors house the central coordination center. Atop the wing are two heliports where large helicopters can land.
- B-Wing hosts the SDF's communications corps and contains a massive, 220-meter-high communications tower.
- C-Wing is home to intelligence divisions. The two buildings each have eight floors and four basements.
- D-Wing houses the Defense Facilities Administration Agency and the Defense Agency's Central Procurement Office.

The Defense Agency had used the Roppongi complex as its headquarters since 1960, when the US military transferred buildings it constructed on the site to Japan. With the agency's departure, control of the Roppongi site reverted to the Ministry of Finance.
The new building of Defense Agency were completed at the old military academy's site on top of Ichigaya Hill (the site where Mishima Yukio committed suicide in 1971). The Military Academy of the Japanese Imperial Army located on Ichigaya Heights trained many cadets for about 60 years from the first year of the Meiji Era. Following the start of war between Japan and the United States, the Ministry of War, the General Staff Headquarters, the Department of Military Education, and the army's Central Government Agency all moved from Miyakezaka to Ichigayadai. The "Tokyo trial" was held at this site to prosecute major war criminals. A limited part of old military academy building is preserved as a building for archives. A historical hall where the international war criminal trials in Far East were held after the war was restored in the building.

DEFENCE INTELLIGENCE OFFICE DIO [JOUHOU HONBU]

The Bureau of Defense Policy is responsible for drafting defense policy and programs, for determining day-to-day operational activities, and for information gathering and analysis in the SDF. A research office in the DA's Bureau of Defense Policy was created in July 1998, responsible for making recommendations on security and defense policy. Although there is also a section in MOFA in charge of security policy, this new office reflected a change in the previous formula under which MOFA was in charge of policy, while the DA dealt with the operational backup. Previously, the DA was preoccupied with managing the SDF. The intent was that the DA will develop into a policymaking organ through its involvement with policy research.

Within the Bureau of Defense Policy, the First Intelligence Division in charge of domestic intelligence recently changed its name to the Intelligence Division, and the Second Division in charge of foreign intelligence changed its name to the International Planning Division.

DEFENCE INTELLIGENCE HEADQUARTERS (DIH)

Under the former organizational structure of the Defense Agency, intelligence-related divisions and sections were internal bureaus, such as the first and the second intelligence division, the intelligence department for each of the chiefs of staff for the Ground, Maritime, and Air Self-Defense Forces [GSDF, MSDF, and ASDF], the Central Data Command Unit, the Joint Staff Council's Second Office, and each unit's information division. Each of these units separately mobilized communications posts, naval vessels, and airplanes to collect and analyze military intelligence pertaining to the Soviet Union, China, and North Korea. Each unit was trying to collect information independently from images and published sources, as well as from its "own" officers stationed abroad.

A plan to centralize intelligence-gathering activities by consolidating the intelligence departments of the three SDFs was proposed around 1988, when Seiki Nishihiro became the vice-minister. Thwarted by the lack of cooperation and subordination from the uniformed officers, centralization had to be postponed.

The National Defense Program Outline which determines Japan's defense capabilities, was reviewed and newly established in December 1995. According to this review:

> "Japan's defense structure must be capable of conducting warning and surveillance on a continuous basis to detect any changes in circumstances as soon as possible, so as to utilize this information for quick decision-making. It must be capable of high-level intelligence gathering and analysis, including strategic intelligence, through possession of diversified intelligence-gathering means and mechanisms, and highly able intelligence specialists. Additionally, it must possess a sophisticated command

and communication capability and be able to quickly and effectively conduct integrated defense operations from a joint perspective."

In May 1996 Japan's parliament passed a law authorizing creation of a central military intelligence agency, the first of its kind since the country's WWII defeat. The Defence Intelligence Headquarters (DIH) collects, processes and analyses information from remote listening devices operated by Japanese defence forces in the air, on the ground and at sea, as well as satellite images, intelligence supplied by friendly countries and public information such as foreign media reports.

The establishment of DIH in January 1997 was expected to enable the country to deal with the rising uncertainties of the Asia-Pacific region in the post-Cold War era. Information demand has been shifting from tactical information like movements of the Soviet Far Eastern Army to high-quality strategic information. Because the director of the headquarters can report directly to the prime minister's secretary, the risk management capability of the Prime Minister's Office will be improved.

The first director was Army General Masahiro Kunimi, who was promoted from the commanding general of the 10th Division. A 1965 graduate of the Defense Academy, he worked in the intelligence field at the GSDF for many years. He served as a resident defense officer at the Japanese Embassy in Beijing for three years from 1983.

The intelligence headquarters is placed under the Joint Staff Council and is controlled by the "Defense Intelligence Committee," which consists of the permanent vice-minister, the director of the Defense Bureau, the chairman of the Joint Staff Council, and the chiefs of the GSDF, the MSDF, and the ASDF. The committee determines the overall framework of international military intelligence to be collected, and based on this basic plan, each division of the intelligence headquarters will collect, analyze, and assess information gathered from radio waves, images, and publications.

The Defence Intelligence Headquarters (DIH), the Japanese version of the US Defence Intelligence Agency (DIA), integrates the five intelligence elements from its three services, the Japan Defence Agency (JDA) and the Joint Staff Council. Based in the new JDA headquarters in Tokyo's Ichigaya district, the organisation reports to the Joint Staff Council and is the armed forces' first fully integrated unit. At the time of its formation DIH strength was 1,580, both military and civilian, although this could rise to 2,000 [according to some reports, the total staffing level was eventually expected to reach 5,000 or even 6,000 personnel, half of whom would be field staff].

The organisation has five directorates:

- The Administration / General Headquarters Division carries out administrative functions and provides logistic support.
- The Planning Division is probably concerned with human intelligence collection. Over 40 SDF officers seconded from the Defense Agency to the Foreign Ministry and assigned to 33 overseas diplomatic missions as defense attaches are conducting related activities, such as collecting military information. The DIH draws on intelligence from a range of sources, including Japan's overseas defence attaché network and foreign intelligence organisations. While intelligence liason is an important part of the Japan-US alliance, the DIH plans to develop bilateral relationships with a broader range of partners, although actively exchanging intelligence with other countries has only just started.
- The Imagery Division has 50 staff members. It was created by consolidating the Satellite Image Analysis Divisions of the three SDFs. It assumes a leading role in the newly created organization. For the time being, it buys images from commercial satellites in the United States, and primarily receives and analyzes [visual data] at the GSDF's Central Geographical Command (in Tachikawa, Tokyo). In order to enhance the capability of analyzing the information obtained by the reconnaissance satellite, Japan plans to increase the staff of the

image information processing center from the initially planned 200 to 321 people. As of late 1998 Japan only had about 30 satellite data analysts.

- The Signals Intelligence (SIGINT) has 10 sections with 350 staff members, and is the largest division at the intelligence headquarters. The electronic intelligence unit at the GSDF facility in Ichigaya, with a staff of over 100, has three separate sections for monitoring North Korean communications. In addition to those working in Ichigaya, it oversees 970 staff members working at the two CDAA "elephant cages," as well as six other communications offices in Kobunato (in Niigata Prefecture), Oi (in Saitama Prefecture), Tachiarai (in Fukushima Prefecture), and Kikaijima (in Kagoshima Prefecture). Initially the SIGINT directorate provided most of intelligence collection, although in the future the Imagery Directorate would gain importance when Japan introduces its own reconnaissance satellites.
- The Analysis [Assessment] Division is responsible for summarizing and assessing information, plus reports from resident defense officers in 40-some countries and information from the United States and other allies, as well as HUMINT from collaborators. It has eight sections and 120 specialists to analyze the meaning and value of information and determine the overall significance to the Defense Agency. The "Defense Secrets Registration Manual" supposedly contains crucial data on armaments and military affairs around the world. The Assessment Directorate, responsible for analysis, is intended to achieve improvement over the previous de-centralized system.

Although a large new organization was created, there has been almost no consolidation or unification of the internal bureaus or the former organizations and units under the SDFs. As the new organization was formed, the three SDFs consolidated their first and second intelligence divisions into a single intelligence division. But, only a handful of individuals from these SDFs had been transferred to the intelligence headquarters. Each SDF's intelligence division still continues to work on data analysis at the tactical level as before. The intelligence units other than the communications offices have also remained almost intact, still being kept under control of the director of each SDF.

CHOBETSU (CHOSA BESSHITSU)

The Chosa Besshitsu (or Chobetsu), which analyzes radio and other transmissions in and around Japan, was established in 1958. Chobetsu makes use of facilities built in Japan by the various arms of the NSA, including the affiliated Naval Security Group, Army Security Agency, and Air Force Intelligence operations. The Chobetsu, is part of the Self-Defense Forces, so its main focus is on military intelligence. This unit, operating under the highest level of secrecy, engages in the interception and decryption of North Korean communications. Digital pattern recognition technology is used to identify the voices of North Korean military commanders. Initiallly focused on the Soviet Far East, China and North Korea, the expansion of collection capabilities extended its area of interest to Taiwan, Southeast Asia and the South China Sea.

By the early 1980s it was believed to operate nine signals intelligence ground stations with an estimated staff of nearly 1,000. A circularly distributed and arranged antenna (CDAA), the same model as the "elephant cage" that became famous at the communications office in Sobe in Okinawa, stands in Higashi Chitose in Hokkaido and another in Miho in Tottori Prefecture (they both belong to the GSDF). Chobetsu embarked on a major expansion in the early 1980s, and by the early 1990s operated a total of 18 or 19 ground stations with some 1,100 personnel.

While under the Joint Chiefs of Staff, the Chobetsu reported directly to the Cabinet Research Office. Although this "special intelligence unit" was organizationally attached to the GSDF, its chief had been successively assigned from the National Police Agency. Therefore, most of the collected information was reported directly to the Cabinet's Office of Intelligence. According to some accounts, Chobetsu is directed domestically at US installations and US companies in Japan, and at domestic Japanese companies.

The communications office in Tachiarai in Fukuoka Prefecture -- a detached force from the "special intelligence unit" on China-related information -- had the information on former Chinese Communist Party Vice Chairman Lin Biao's decision to defect aboard a Trident airplane and his subsequent demise due to the plane crash. Another success happened when the Korean Airlines' airplane was shot down. A detached force in Wakkanai from the special office of the second intelligence division of the GSDF's intelligence department, also known as the "special intelligence unit," was able to intercept and record the communications between the pilot of the Soviet fighter plane and the air strike control center in Sakhalin, capturing the first-rate classified information pertaining to the incident. Through voice analysis, it even identified the name of the pilot, proving that its daily accumulation of data was useful.

Japan's current intelligence system involves compiling, collating, analyzing, and evaluating data from satellites, radio transmissions, and telecommunications gathered from both US and Japanese sources. Japan is a signatory to the UK-USA intelligence sharing agreement, but only at the level of a "Third Party", with substantial limitations on what information is shared and the timeliness of its delivery. And allthough Japan and the United States are bound by a defense alliance, this does not mean the United States is required to provide all of its reconnaissance information to Japan.

This interaction with the US was illustrated when on 21 March 1998 the radio monitoring facility of the Self Defense Agency (SDA) in Tottori Prefecture detected an unidentified code transmitted from ships in the Sea of Japan. The activity of the two North Korean intelligence collection boats was detected by a US intelligence satellite. Based on this detection, an American EP-3 electronic intelligence aircraft identified the location of the two Morth Korean boats, and on 23 March Japanese SDA patrol planes found the two boats. The information from the US satellite was transmitted to DIA and CINCPAC. CINCPAC sent the information to the US base in Yokota City in Tokyo, and Japan's SDA Intelligence Office received it from the US base. The US Army Headquarter Office has three intelligence officers with liaison offices in SDA offices, and the SDA has counterpart officers at the US base in Yokota City.

JAPAN GROUND SELF DEFENCE FORCE NIHON RIKUJYO JIEITAI

http://www.jda.go.jp

The largest of the three services, the Ground Self-Defense Force (GSDF), operates under the command of the chief of the ground staff, based in the city of Ichikawa, east of Tokyo.
Strategy is determined by the nation's elongated insular geography, its mountainous terrain, and the nearness of the Asian mainland. The terrain favors local defense against invasion by ground forces, but protection of the approximately 15,800-kilometer coastline of the four main islands would present unique problems in the event of a large-scale invasion. Potentially hostile aircraft and missile bases are so close that timely warning even by radar facilities might be difficult to obtain. Maneuver space is limited to such an extent that ground defenses would have to be virtually in place at the onset of hostilities. No point of the country is more than 150 kilometers from the sea. Moreover, the straits separating Honshu from the other main islands restrict the rapid movement of troops from one island to another, even though all major islands are now connected by bridges and tunnels. Within each island, mountain barriers and narrow roads restrict troop and supply movements. The key strategic region is densely populated and highly industrialized central Honshu, particularly the area from Tokyo to Kobe.

Japan has many places suited for landing operations and is geographically located close to neighboring countries on the continent. It is expected that an aggressor will attempt to assure the safety of its landing forces by concentrating its naval and air assets to secure overwhelming combat power at the time and on the point they choose. It is extremely difficult, or practically impossible, for Japan to have enough defense capability to repel all troops of an aggressor on the sea. It would incur enormous and unbearable costs to build up such defense capability. Consequently, we need to preserve an adequate ground defense capability to destroy those aggressor troops on the ground who have succeeded in their landing operation. A robust ground defense capability to repel an aggressor, which might succeed in breaking through our maritime defense, will enable us to maintain solid defense posture required for effective deterrence against an aggression.

Intended to deter attack, repulse a small invasion, or provide a holding action until reinforced by United States armed forces, the ground element is neither equipped nor staffed to offer more than a show of conventional defense by itself. Antitank artillery, ground-to-sea firepower, and mobility were improved and surface-to- ship missiles were acquired in the Mid-Term Defense Estimate completed in FY 1990. The number of uniformed personnel is insufficient to enable an immediate shift onto emergency footing. Instead, the ratio of officers to enlisted personnel is high, requiring augmentation by reserves or volunteers in times of crisis. In 1992, however, GSDF reserve personnel, numbering 46,000, had received little professional training.

Although allotted 180,000 slots for uniformed personnel, in 1992 the force was maintained at about 86 percent of that level (with approximately 156,000 personnel) because of funding constraints. The GSDF consists of one armored division, twelve infantry divisions, one airborne brigade, two combined brigades, four training brigades, one artillery brigade with two groups, two air defense brigades with three groups, one helicopter brigade with twenty-four squadrons, and two antitank helicopter platoons.

	Classification	1976 NDPO	Current NDPO
GSDF	SDF Personnel	180,000	160,000
	Major Units		
	Regionally Deployed		
	Divisions	12	8
	Brigades	2	6
	Mobile Operation		
	Armored Division	1	1
	Airborne Brigade	1	1
	Helicopter Brigade	1	1
	Ground-to-Air Missile		
	Anti-aircraft Groups	8	8
	Main Equipment		
	Tanks (Approx.)	1,200	900
	Artillery (Approx.)	1,000	900

The GSDF is divided into five regional armies, each containing two to four divisions, antiaircraft artillery units, and support units. The largest, the Northern Army, is headquartered on Hokkaido, where population and geographic constraints are less limiting than elsewhere. It has four divisions and artillery, antiaircraft artillery, and engineering brigades. The Northeastern Army and the Eastern Army, headquartered in Sendai and Ichikawa, respectively, each has two divisions. The Central Army, headquartered in Itami, has three divisions in addition to a combined brigade located on Shikoku. The Western Army, with two divisions, is headquartered at Kengun and maintains a combined brigade on Okinawa.

The National Defense Program Outline which determines Japan's defense capabilities, was reviewed and newly established in December 1995. Through a review of the troop structure, the Self-Defense Personnel of the GSDF was reduced from the current 180,000 to 160,000. Some units may be staffed by new Self-Defense Force Reserve Personnel (Ready Reserve Personnel) capable of being quickly mobilized and to create a high-quality and effective system, will be established by 15,000 Ready Reserve Personnel, and 145,000 Regular Personnel. A fundamental review of the troop structure, previously consisting of 13 divisions and 2 combined brigades stationed nationwide, resulted in a balanced deployment of divisions and brigades uniquely suited to the local circumstances of the area where each unit is deployed. Present 4 divisions and 2 combined brigades will be reorganized into new brigades. According to the Outline, the GSDF planned to reduce the four divisions belonging to the Northern Army (two divisions), the Northeastern Army (one division), and the Middle Army (one division) into brigade size and mobilize them, while maintaining the two divisions belonging to the Western Army as they are and turning the First Mixed Group into a brigade.

The previous Outline adopted the concept that Ground Self-Defense Force units to be deployed in peacetime should be deployed in conformity with Japan's geographical characteristics in a well-balanced way so that they can implement systematic defense operations from the outset of aggression in any part of Japan. Specifically, based on the concept that Japanese territory can be divided into 14 districts in light of Japan's geographical characteristics such as mountain ranges, rivers and straits, one division of the Ground Self-Defense Force was deployed in principle in each district while one combined brigade each was deployed in Shikoku and Okinawa. Accordingly, unit structure was of 12 divisions and two combined brigades.

The new Outline sets forth the deployment of eight divisions and six brigades based on the concept that divisions are deployed in districts which are of great importance from the viewpoint of defense and brigades are deployed in districts of relative importance so that divisions and brigades are deployed in an appropriate combination. This setup continues to be the previous Outline's concept that the GSDF units are deployed in conformity with Japan's geographical and other characteristics in order to be capable of implementing rapid and effective systematic defense operations from the outset of aggression, by taking into account the characteristics of each region, such as its proximity to other countries and its political and economic importance, and thereby leaving no room for regional or functional deficiencies.

Specifically, the new Outline sets forth the following deployment:

- Regions where divisions are deployed
  - Region located close to other countries and embracing important straits (Soya, Tsugaru and Tsushima straits): northern Hokkaido, northern part of the Tohoku district and northern part of Kyushu
  - Politically and economically pivotal region (Kanto and Kansai districts)
  - Region that serves as base for conducting mobile reinforcement operations for the above-mentioned regions which is important from the viewpoint of defense: southern part of the Tohoku district, the Tokai and Hokuriku district and southern part of Kyushu
- Regions where brigades are deployed
  - Regions considered of relative importance compared with above-mentioned regions from the viewpoint of defense (Eastern and central parts of Hokkaido and Okinawa)
  - Other regions (Koshinetsu and Chugoku districts, and Shikoku)

A brigade is a unit combined with various types of forces, including combat units, such as infantry, armored and artillery units, combat support units and logistical support units. It is a regionally independent and permanent entity. Though its function is similar to a division in that it possesses the capability to engage in operations on one front, it is smaller than a division in scale and has limited capability. (A division in principle consists of 6,000 to 9,000 personnel, whereas a brigade in principle consists of 3,000 to 4,000 personnel.)

To enable regionally deployed units and other units to exercise their defense capability effectively, they should be supplemented, whenever necessary, by the mobile striking capability possessed by tank units, the airborne transport mobility possessed by helicopter units and various airborne operation capabilities. Accordingly, the GSDF, just as it did previously, must possess at least one tactical unit of each of various types of forces used mainly for mobile operation so that it will leave no room for functional deficiencies. Specifically, the GSDF must possess one tank-based armored division, one helicopter brigade equipped with a large type of transport helicopter and one airborne (parachute) brigade.

The ground-to-air missile units of the GSDF engages in air defense operations for units in aggression fronts, as well as for strategical mobile divisions. It also engages in air defense for politically and economically pivotal areas. The GSDF will continue to possess eight anti-aircraft artillery groups as the ground-to-air unit.

From the viewpoint of indicating the basic framework of ground defense capability, the new Outline gives in an annexed table the organized strength of Self-Defense Forces personnel needed to maintain the GSDF defense posture at 160,000. This organized strength is required to maintain major units including divisions, brigades and other main units, as well as supply depots and other logistic support units. Compared with the previous ceiling of 180,000, the new strength has been determined through reorganization of divisions into brigades and other means.

The GSDF units under the new structure are organized in principle by regular Self-Defense Forces personnel in order to maintain a high level of proficiency and to rapidly counter aggressions and other situations. However, from the viewpoint of maintaining personnel in an efficient manner in peacetime and ensuring the flexibility of smooth response to changes in situations, some units will be staffed mainly by high readiness Self-Defense Force Reservists (Ready Reserve Personnel). For example, three of four regiments of a division may be staffed by regular personnel which one regiment may be staffed mainly by Ready Reserve Personnel. Based on such a concept, 145,000 of the 160,000 members of the GSDF will be regular personnel and 15,000 will be Ready Reserve Personnel.

In regard to equipment of the GSDF, the new Outline, from the viewpoint of specifically showing the framework of ground-defense capability, describes in the Annexed Table the number of battle tanks and main artillery (howitzers rockets and SSM launchers), which are main equipment for the GSDF, in addition to the number of main units. Through reorganization of divisions into brigades and other measures, the quota of tanks was set at about 900, compared with 1,200 set in the previous Outline, and that of main artillery at 900, compared with 1,000 in the previous Outline.

In 1989 basic training for lower-secondary and upper-secondary school graduates began in the training brigade and lasted approximately three months. Specialized enlisted and noncommissioned officer (NCO) candidate courses were available in branch schools, and qualified NCOs could enter an eight-to-twelve- week second lieutenant candidate program. Senior NCOs and graduates of an eighty-week NCO pilot course were eligible to enter officer candidate schools, as were graduates of the National Defense Academy at Yokosuka and graduates of four-year universities. Advanced technical, flight, medical, and command staff officer courses were also run by the GSDF. Like the maritime and air forces, the GSDF ran a youth cadet program offering technical training to lower-secondary school graduates below military age in return for a promise of enlistment.

Because of population density on the Japanese islands, only limited areas were available for large-scale training, and, even in these areas, noise restrictions were a problem. The GSDF tried to adapt to these conditions by conducting command post exercises and map maneuvers and by using simulators and other training devices. In live firing during training, propellants were reduced to shorten shell ranges. Such restrictions diminished the value of combat training and troop morale.

JAPAN GROUND SELF DEFENCE FORCE INTELLIGENCE

Ground Self-Defense Forces intelligence units include the Nibetsu Investigation Division, the Second Section, and the 101st Survey Battalion.

JAPAN MARITIME SELF DEFENCE FORCE NIHON KAIJYO JIEITAI

http://www.tk.airnet.ne.jp
http://www.jda.go.jp
info@jda.go.jp

Two kinds of operations are conducted by the Japan Maritime Self Defence Force [JMSDF] for the purpose of defending Japan: securing maritime traffic and securing Japanese territory. For Japan, which relies on foreign countries for the supply of almost all energy and food, the influence to national life is quite serious in case that maritime traffic is cut off. It can also be said that the impact to the world economy is significant in such case. Therefore, the JMSDF must be able to secure maritime traffic against attack by enemy submarines, surface ships and aircraft by effectively combining each operation such as surveillance, escort and defense of ports and straits. In case of aggression which aims at territorial occupation, it is necessary to stop it at sea in order to prevent direct damage to our territory. For that purpose, the JMSDF, in cooperation with the JGSDF and the JASDF, contributes defense of Japan by destroying enemy surface ships aircraft and, according to the situation, laying mines around the expected landing place.

The nation is vitally dependent on maintaining access to regional and worldwide shipping lanes and fishing areas, but it is incapable of defending the sea routes on which it relied. Its energy supplies came primarily from Middle Eastern sources, and its tankers had to pass through the Indian Ocean, the Strait of Malacca, and the South China Sea, making them vulnerable to hostilities in Southeast Asia. Vulnerability to interception of oceangoing trade remained the country's greatest strategic weakness. Efforts to overcome this weakness, beginning with Prime Minister Suzuki Zenko's statement in May 1981 that Japan would attempt to defend its sea lines of communication (SLOC) to a distance of 1,000 nautical miles, met with controversy. Within the Defense Agency itself, some viewed a role for the MSDF in defending the SLOC as "unrealistic, unauthorized, and impossible." Even the strongest supporters of this program allowed that constitutional and other legal restrictions would limit active participation of the MSDF to cases where Japan was under direct attack. Japan could, however, provide surveillance assistance, intelligence sharing, and search-and-rescue support to United States naval forces.

The large volume of coastal commercial fishing and maritime traffic limits in-service sea training, especially in the relatively shallow waters required for mine laying, mine sweeping, and submarine rescue practice. Training days are scheduled around slack fishing seasons in winter and summer--providing about ten days during the year. The MSDF maintains two oceangoing training ships and conducted annual long-distance on-the-job training for graduates of the one-year officer candidate school.

The naval force's capacity to perform its defense missions varies according to the task. MSDF training emphasizes antisubmarine and antiaircraft warfare. Defense planners believe the most effective approach to combating submarines entails mobilizing all available weapons, including surface combatants, submarines, aircraft, and helicopters, and the numbers and armament of these weapons were increased in the Mid-Term Defense Estimate. A critical weakness remains, however, in the ability to defend such weapons against air attack. Because most of the MSDF's air arm is detailed to antisubmarine warfare, the ASDF has to be relied on to provide air cover, an objective that competes unsuccessfully with the ASDF's primary mission of air defense of the home islands. Extended patrols over sea lanes are also beyond the ASDF's capabilities. The fleet's capacity to provide ship-based anti-air- attack protection is limited by the absence of aircraft carriers and the inadequate number of shipborne long-range surface-to-air missiles and close-range weapons. The fleet is also short of underway replenishment ships and seriously deficient in all areas of logistic

support. These weaknesses seriously compromise the ability of the MSDF to fulfill its mission and to operate independently of the United States Air Force and the United States Seventh Fleet.
When two North Korean spy boats were later discovered in Japanese territorial waters, Japanese Naval Forces fired their guns in anger for the first time in 54 years.
The MSDF is commanded by the chief of the maritime staff and includes the maritime staff office, the self-defense fleet, five regional district commands, the air-training squadron, and various support units, such as hospitals and schools. The maritime staff office, located in Tokyo, serves the chief of staff in command and supervision of the force. The self-defense fleet, headquartered at Yokosuka, is charged with defense of all waters around the Japanese Archipelago. It commands four escort flotillas (two based in Yokosuka and one each in Sasebo and Maizuru), the fleet air force headquartered at Atsugi, two submarine flotillas based at Kure and Yokosuka, two mine-sweeping flotillas based at Kure and Yokosuka, and the fleet training command at Yokosuka.
Five district units act in concert with the fleet to guard the waters of their jurisdictions and provide shore-based support. District headquarters are located in Ominato, Maizuru, Yokosuka, Kure, and Sasebo.

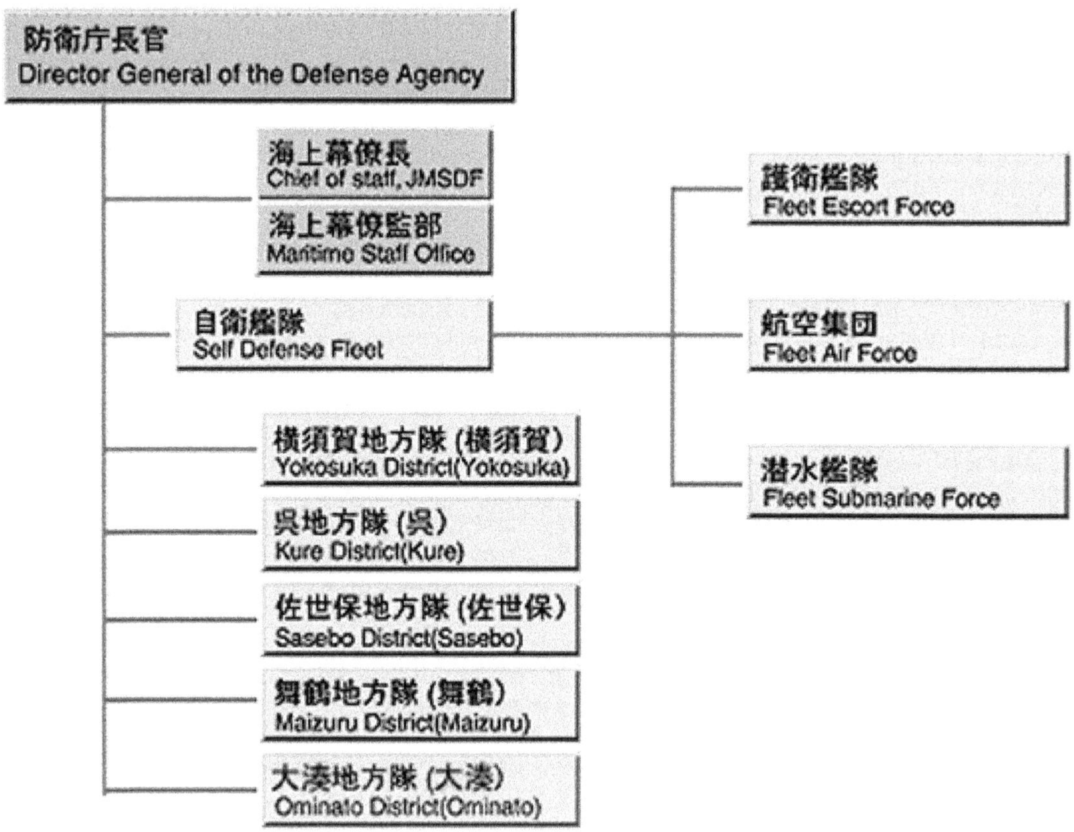

Maritime Staff Office (Tokyo), Self Defense Fleet Headquarters (Yokosuka), main bases (Yokosuka, Kure, Sasebo, Maizuru and Ominato), other bases (Yoichi, Hakodate, Kobe, Shimonoseki, and Katsuren) and air bases (Hachinohe, Ominato, Simofusa, Tateyama, Atsugi, Komatsujima, Tokushima, Iwakuni, Ozuki, Omura, Kanoya, Naha).

MSDF recruits receive three months of basic training followed by courses in patrol, gunnery, mine sweeping, convoy operations, and maritime transportation. Flight students, all upper-secondary school graduates, enter a two-year course. Officer candidate schools offer six-month courses to qualified enlisted personnel and those who have completed flight school. Graduates of four-year universities, the four-year National Defense Academy, and particularly outstanding enlisted personnel undergo a one-year officer course at the Officer Candidate School at Eta Jima (site of the former Imperial Naval Academy). Special advanced courses for officers are also available in such fields as submarine duty and flight training. The MSDF operates its own staff college in Tokyo for senior officers.

The Maritime Self-Defense Force (MSDF) had an authorized strength in 1992 of 46,000 and maintained some 44,400 personnel and operated 155 major combatants, including thirteen submarines, sixty-four destroyers and frigates, forty-three mine warfare ships and boats, eleven patrol craft, and six amphibious ships. It also flew some 205 fixed-wing aircraft and 134 helicopters. Most of these aircraft were used in antisubmarine and mine warfare operations. The MSDF's former unit structure emphasized anti-submarine and mine warfare.

The National Defense Program Outline which determines Japan's defense capabilities, was reviewed and newly established in December 1995. After reorganization, the MSDF will become a more functionally balanced force capable of conducting a variety of operations ranging from surveillance and patrol in surrounding sea areas to such public welfare support as disaster relief activities. Through a review of the balance between rear and forward units, the MSDF determined the following organizational changes are necessary in order to maximize force effectiveness while optimizing limited resources. First, the number of destroyer units of Regional Districts will be adjusted from ten to seven. Second, two Minesweeper Flotillas will be consolidated into one flotilla and last, the number of land-based patrol aircraft units will be adjusted from 16 to 13.

Classification		1976 NDPO	Current NDPO
MSDF			
	Major Units		
	Destroyer Flotillas (For Mobile Operations)	4	4
	Destroyer Divisions (Regional District Units)	10	7
	Submarine Divisions	6	6
	Minesweeping Flotillas	2	1
	Land-based Patrol Aircraft Squadrons	16	13
	Main Equipment		
	Destroyers (Approx.)	60	50
	Submarines	16	16
	Combat Aircraft (Approx.)	220	170
	Artillery (Approx.)	1,000	900

In order to ensure the safety of Japan's maritime transportation when an emergency such as aggression at sea takes place, the MSDF must constantly keep at least one escort flotilla as a mobile operating ship unit so that it can be dispatched to sea areas where armed attacks take place. However, four escort flotillas will be needed in order to constantly keep at least one escort flotilla on a rapid response posture. This is because a considerable period of time is needed for basic training of personnel following relief of crew members of ships, as well as for repair of ships, and the period of time for an escort flotilla to maintain a high level of proficiency in performing duties under difficult conditions is limited. Consequently, the MSDF will maintain four escort flotillas. "Anti-submarine surface ship units" mentioned in the previous Outline were renamed "destroyer units" in the new Outline, because all patrol chasers (PC) exclusively engaged in mission of anti-submarine warfare were removed from service.

The previous Outline divided Japan's sea areas into five districts (defense districts) in conformity with the nation's geographic characteristics, for the purpose of coastal surveillance and defense. Two destroyer divisions were assigned to each regional defense district for surveillance and defense so that at least one destroyer division was always on a combat ready basis. Accordingly, the MSDF possessed a total of 10 destroyer divisions. Under the new structure of the MSDF, from the viewpoint that the MSDF must ensure such a posture at least to leave no room for deficiencies in our regions, it will possess seven destroyer divisions in order to be ready to deploy one each destroyer division in the five defense districts, as well as in the Tsugaru and Tsushima straits. Accordingly, the number of destroyers assigned to destroyer units (for mobile operations and regional districts units) will be reduced to about 50 compared with about 60 under the previous Outline.
Submarine units engage in surveillance and defense in major straits. In order to ensure the safety of Japan's maritime transportation, the MSDF needs to maintain the posture capable of deploying two submarines each in the three straits of Soya, Tsugaru and Tsushima, where necessary. In order to maintain such capability, it will be necessary to possess six divisions with 16 submarines, taking into account geographical relations between submarine bases and sea areas where submarines engage in surveillance and defense. The MSDF will maintain six divisions with 16 submarines.

Under the previous Outline, minesweeping units, as ship units which engage in, as necessary, removal and disposal of mines laid in main harbors and straits, were maintained with two minesweeping flotillas one each assigned to the East Japan and West Japan Sea areas, in conformity with Japan's geographical characteristics. Under the new structure of the MSDF, the two flotillas will be unified into one from the viewpoint of maintaining minimum functions.

Under the new Outline, the number of land-based patrol aircraft units was set at 13 squadrons, compared with 16 set in the previous Outline. Broken down into details, 1) fixed-wing patrol aircraft units engaging in surveillance in nearby seas will be reduced to eight squadrons from 10, and 2) land-based patrol helicopter units engaging in surveillance and defense in main harbors and straits will be reduced to five squadrons from six. Aircraft previously called "anti-submarine aircraft" are referred to as "patrol aircraft" in the new Outline because anti-submarine aircraft will engage in extensive surveillance patrols over the sea, not limited to anti-submarine missions.

As to fixed-wing patrol aircraft units, the MSDF previously possessed eight squadrons with 80 aircraft needed to conduct patrols at least once a day in Japan's nearby seas where necessary, and two squadrons with 20 aircraft capable of escorting ships. Under the new MSDF structure, the two squadrons with 20 aircraft engaging in the latter mission will be abolished because assignment of patrol aircraft for the escort of ships will no longer be considered from the viewpoint of defense buildup.

As to land-based patrol helicopter units, the MSDF previously possessed six squadrons, one each assigned to the two straits of Tsugaru and Tsushima, as well as four regions of Keihan, Hanshin, Japan Sea and Okinawa, to provide defense for straits and harbors. Under the new structure, MSDF will possess five squadrons, one each to five defense districts, from the viewpoint of ensuring the minimum posture and not creating a lack of regional capability.

Due to the MSDF structural changes, the number of combat aircraft will be reduced to about 170 from about 220 possessed under the previous Outline.

Fleet Intelligence Command

The Japan Maritime Self Defense Force Fleet Intelligence Command is headquartered at Yokosuka base. As the home of the U.S. Navy's Seventh Fleet, the Base, often referred to as CFAY (Commander Fleet Activities Yokosuka), hosts 13 afloat commands and more than 50 other shore commands and tennant activities. The Imperial Japanese Navy had four principal navy yards – Kure, Sasebo, Maizuru, and Yokosuka. During World War II, activities at the Yokosuka Navy Yard reached their peak. By 1944, the Yard covered 280 acres and employed over 40,000 workers. In addition to the shipbuilding plant, the yard also had a gun factory, ordnance and supply depots, a fuel storage facility, a seaplane base and a naval air station.

JAPAN AIR SELF DEFENCE FORCE NIHON KOKU JIEITAI

Japan has a long configuration from the north to the south with its population and industrial centers concentrated in particular regions. In addition, as the Japanese government maintains an exclusively defense-oriented policy, Japan is forced to take a passive position at the early stage of the air incursions in which invaders take the initiative. In order to defend the life and the property of the Japanese people from invading aircraft and missiles under Japan's geographical characteristics and defense-oriented policy, the Air Self-Defense Force should detect invading aircrafts and missiles as soon as possible and destroy them as far from Japan as possible.

So the ASDF should have capability for vigilance and surveillance and for a quick counterattack to fight against invading aircrafts and missiles. The ASDF must possess aircraft control and warning units that consist of a network of radar sites and airborne early warning capable of vigilance and surveillance throughout the air space in and around Japan on a continuous basis, fighter units and ground-to-air missile units to take immediate and appropriate steps against violations of Japan's territorial airspace and air incursions, units capable of engaging in the interdiction of airborne or amphibious landing invasions and air-support for land forces as necessary, and units capable of effective operational supports including air reconnaissance, air transportation and other operations as necessary.

Major units of the ASDF are the Air Defense Command, Flight Support Command, Flying Training Command, Air Developing and Proving Command, and Air Matériel Command. The Flight Support Command is responsible for direct support of operational forces in rescue, transportation, control, weather monitoring, and inspection. The Flying Training Command is responsible for basic flying and technical training. The Air Developing and Proving Command, in addition to overseeing equipment research and development, is also responsible for research and development in such areas as flight medicine. The Air Defense Command has northern, central, and western regional headquarters located at Misawa, Iruma, and Kasuga, respectively, and the Southwestern Composite Air Division based at Naha on Okinawa. All four regional headquarters control surface-to-air missile units of both the ASDF and the GSDF located in their respective areas.

The ASDF maintains an integrated network of radar installations and air defense direction centers throughout the country known as the Basic Air Defense Ground Environment. In the late 1980s, the system was modernized and augmented with E-2C airborne earlywarning aircraft.

The nation relies on fighter-interceptor aircraft and surface-to -air missiles to intercept hostile aircraft. Both of these systems were improved beginning in the late 1980s. Outmoded aircraft were being replaced in the early 1990s with more sophisticated models, and Nike-J missiles were being replaced with new Patriot systems. Essentially, however, the nation relies on United States forces to provide interceptor capability.

The ASDF also provides air support for ground and sea operations of the GSDF and the MSDF and air defense for bases of all the forces. Although support fighter squadrons started being modernized in 1989, they lack precision-guided weapons for support of ground operations and attacks on hostile ships, and ASDF pilots receive little flight training over oceans to prepare for maritime operations.

The ASDF has an inadequate poor base defense capability, consisting mainly of outmoded antiaircraft guns and portable shelters to house aircraft. Base defenses were being upgraded in the late 1980s with new surface-to-air missiles, modern antiaircraft artillery, and new fixed and mobile aircraft shelters.

The Air Self-Defense Force (ASDF) is the major aviation arm of the SDF. It had an authorized strength of 47,000 and maintained some 46,000 personnel and approximately 330 combat aircraft in 1992. Front-line formations include three ground-attack squadrons, nine fighter squadrons, one reconnaissance squadron, and five transport squadrons.

The National Defense Program Outline which determines Japan's defense capabilities, was reviewed and newly established in December 1995. Aircraft Warning and Control system will be made more efficient and functional: for instance, as regards the aircraft warning and control units at radar sites throughout the country, 20 aircraft control and warning groups out of 28 shall be reorganized into the warning squadrons while the AWACS aircraft shall be introduced. One squadron of the fighter units shall be disbanded, with the remaining 12 fighter squadrons forming a more efficient and flexible system.

Classification	1976 NDPO	Current NDPO
ASDF		
Major Units		
Aircraft Control and Warning Groups	28	8 + 20 Squadrons
Airborne Early Warning Squadron	1	1
Interceptor Squadrons	10	9
Support Fighter Squadrons	3	3
Air Recon Squadron	1	1
Air Transport Squadrons	3	3
Ground-to-Air Missile Groups	6	6
Main Equipment		
Fighter/Combat Aircraft (Approx.)	430	400
(Fighter Aircraft only) (Approx.)	350	300

The Air Self-Defense Force must possess 28 fixed ground radar sites in 28 locations throughout the nation in conformity with its geographical characteristics so that it can maintain vigilance and surveillance throughout Japanese airspace on a continuous basis. Thus, the ASDF has possessed 28 groups of aircraft control and warning units. In addition, since there is a limit to the surveillance and detection capability of fixed ground radar sites against aircraft intruding at low altitude, the ASDF has also possessed one airborne early-warning squadron to engage in early-warning missions against aircraft intruding at low altitude.

Under the new Outline, however, the ASDF will reorganize 20 of the 28 early-warning groups into smaller early-warning squadrons by enhancing the efficiency of control and warning mission considering the introduction of AWACS (airborne warning and control system) aircraft. Thus the ASDF will now possess eight early-warning groups and 20 early-warning squadrons. In addition, one squadron of airborne early-warning aircraft will be maintained in order to supplement the limited capability of fixed ground radar against aircraft intruding at low altitude, and to maintain early-warning capabilities over ocean areas remote from the mainland.

Under the previous Outline, the ASDF has possessed 13 fighter squadrons in order to maintain constant and continuous capability for scrambles and other appropriate responses against violations of territorial airspace and air incursions, in conformity to Japan's geographical characteristics. This posture was based on the idea that, while a total of 14 fighter squadrons -- two each in seven districts throughout the nation -- are needed, one squadron larger in size than other squadrons can be assigned to the district over Southwestern Islands.

In view of recent changes in the international military situation, however, partial reductions in the posture of the ASDF is considered to be possible. Accordingly, under the new structure, the ASDF will reduce one fighter squadron and possess a total of 12 fighter squadrons.
The 12 fighter squadrons consist of nine interceptor units and three support fighter units. The main mission of interceptor units is to intercept intruding aircraft, while that of support fighter units is to counter landing invasions, and to support from the air the GSDF and MSDF units fighting against invading forces as necessary.

The ground-to-air missile units of the ASDF counter air invasion together with the fighter squadrons. The ASDF will maintain six ground-to-air missile groups for the air defense of each area of political, economic and strategic importance _ central part of Hokkaido, area around Tsugaru Strait, Kanto district, Keihanshin district, northern part of Kyushu, and Okinawa.

The ASDF must possess air reconnaissance and air transport units in order to provide effective support for air operations through air reconnaissance and air transport operations as necessary. The ASDF will maintain one air reconnaissance squadron to engage in air reconnaissance in case of aggression and other eventualities. At the same time, the ASDF will continue to possess three air transport squadrons to support mobile operations of fighter units and parachute operations of airborne units, as necessary, and to engage in transportation between main bases in peacetime.

Combat aircraft are the main equipment of the ASDF. About 430 combat aircraft were to be possessed under the previous Outline, but following the changes in the structure of the ASDF as mentioned so far, the number of combat aircraft will be reduced to about 400. The number of interceptors will be reduced to about 300 from about 350.
The Defense Agency has been seeking to introduce in-flight refueling aircraft. In December 1999, the Security Council of Japan (SCJ) recommended that Japan introduce air tankers without delay in the next defense plan. The agency will therefore work out details about when and how many to introduce.

After passing an entrance examination, recruits can enter several training programs. Lower-secondary school graduates are eligible to enter the MSDF's four-year youth cadet program to earn upper-secondary school equivalency and NCO status, or they can undergo twelve-week recruit training courses followed by technical training lasting from five to fifty weeks. Upper-secondary school graduates can also enter either two-year NCO or four-year flight courses. Specialized training is available for all NCOs, as are opportunities to enroll in officer and flight officer candidate courses. Graduates of the four-year National Defense Academy or four-year universities receive thirty to forty weeks of instruction in officer candidate schools. Advanced technical, flight, and command staff officer programs are available for officers.

DIRECTOR GENERAL OF DEFENSE AGENCY(MINISTER OF STATE FOR DEFENSE)

Chief of Staff, ASDF
Air Staff Office
Air Defense Command
Northern Air Defense Force

- Headquarters,Northern Air Defense Force (Misawa)
- 2nd Air Wing(Chitose)
- 3rd Air Wing(Misawa)
- Northern Aircraft Control & Warning Wing(Misawa)
- 3rd Air Defense Missile Group(Chitose)
- 6th Air Defense Missile Group(Misawa)
- 1st Base Air Defense Group(Chitose)
- Others

CENTRAL AIR DEFENSE FORCE

- Headquarters,Central Air Defense Force(Iruma)
- 6th Air Wing(Komatsu)
- 7th Air Wing(Hyakuri)
- Central Aircraft Control & Warning Wing(Iruma)
- 1st Air Defense Missile Group(Iruma)
- 4th Air Defense Missile Group(Gifu)
- Others

WESTERN AIR DEFENSE FORCE

- Headquarters,Western Air Defense Force(Kasuga)
- 5th Air Wing(Nyutabaru)
- 8th Air Wing(Tsuiki)
- Western Aircraft Control & Warning Wing(Kasuga)
- 2nd Air Defense Missile Group(Kasuga)
- Others

SOUTHWESTERN COMPOSITE AIR DIVISION

- Headquarters,Southwestern Composite Air Division(Naha)
- 83rd Air Wing(Naha)
- Southwestern Aircraft Control and Warning Wing(Naha)
- 5th Air Defense Missile Group(Naha)
- Others

INTELLIGENCE DIVISION TACTICAL RECONNAISSANCE GROUP

The Intelligence Division of the Air Self-Defense Forces is Japan's primary imagery and imagery analysis organization. The ASDF possesses air reconnaissance units in order to provide effective support for air operations through air reconnaissance operations as necessary. The ASDF maintains one air reconnaissance squadron, based in Hyakuri, to engage in air reconnaissance in case of aggression and other eventualities.
A total of 17 F-14EJ Kais will be converted to the reconnaissance role, all being assigned to the 501st Hikotai [Squadron] "Teisatsu Kokutai" based at Hyakuri. This unit also uses the 12 remaining RF-4Es, ten of which are to Kai standards.

NATIONAL POLICE SAFETY COMMISSION (NPSC)

The national level police organizations are the National Police Safety Commission (NPSC) and the National Police Agency (NPA). Since the NPSC makes basic policy and the NPA administers police affairs, the NPSC has control over the NPA.

The NPSC is a governmental body responsible mainly for the administrative supervision of the police and coordination of police administration. It also oversees matters relating to police education, communication, criminal identification, criminal statistics and police equipment. To ensure its independence and neutrality, not even the Prime Minister is empowered to direct and give orders to the NPSC.

The mission of the National Police Safety Commission is to guarantee the neutrality of the police by insulating the force from political pressure and to ensure the maintenance of democratic methods in police administration. The commission's primary function is to supervise the National Police Agency, and it has the authority to appoint or dismiss senior police officers. The commission consists of a chairman, who holds the rank of minister of state, and five members appointed by the prime minister with the consent of both houses of the Diet. The commission operates independently of the cabinet, but liaison and coordination with it are facilitated by the chairman's being a member of that body.

Japan's police are an apolitical body under the general supervision of independent agencies, free of direct central government executive control. They are checked by an independent judiciary and monitored by a free and active press. The police are generally well respected and can rely on considerable public cooperation in their work. Officials involved in the criminal justice system are usually highly trained professionals interested in preventing crime and rehabilitating offenders. They are allowed considerable discretion in dealing with legal infractions and appear to deserve the trust and respect accorded to them by the general public.
Conditions of public order compare favorably with those in other industrialized countries. The overall crime rate is low by North American and West European standards and has shown a general decline since the mid-1960s. The incidence of violent crime is especially low, owing in part to effective enforcement of stringent firearms control laws. Problems of particular concern are those associated with a modern industralized nation, including juvenile delinquency, traffic control, and white-collar crime.

Civil disorders occurred beginning in the early 1950s, chiefly in Tokyo, but did not seriously threaten the internal security of the state. Far less frequent after the early 1970s, they were in all cases effectively countered by efficient and well-trained police units employing the most sophisticated techniques of riot control.

NATIONAL POLICE AGENCY (NPA) (KEISATSUCHÔ)

The Police Law, enacted in 1945, in conforming with principles such as rule of law and local autonomy, aims at providing an efficient police structure on a democratic base. The police structure consists of the national police and the prefectural police. Formerly, most police agencies functioned as guards for the imperial family. Now, there is a mix of centralization and decentralization in that police administration is the responsibility of prefectural governments.

The national level police organizations are the National Police Safety Commission (NPSC) and the National Police Agency (NPA). Since the NPSC makes basic policy and the NPA administers police affairs, the NPSC has control over the NPA.

As the central coordinating body for the entire police system, the National Police Agency determines general standards and policies; detailed direction of operations is left to the lower echelons. In a national emergency or large-scale disaster, the agency is authorized to take command of prefectural police forces. In 1989 the agency was composed of about 1,100 national civil servants, empowered to collect information and to formulate and execute national policies. The agency is headed by a commissioner general who is appointed by the National Public Safety Commission with the approval of the prime minister. The central office includes the Secretariat, with divisions for general operations, planning, information, finance, management, and procurement and distribution of police equipment, and five bureaus. The Administration Bureau is concerned with police personnel, education, welfare, training, and unit inspections. The Criminal Investigation Bureau is in charge of research statistics and the investigation of nationally important and international cases. This bureau's Safety Department is responsible for crime prevention, combating juvenile delinquency, and pollution control. In addition, the Criminal Investigation Bureau surveyes, formulates, and recommends legislation on firearms, explosives, food, drugs, and narcotics. The Communications Bureau supervises police communications systems.

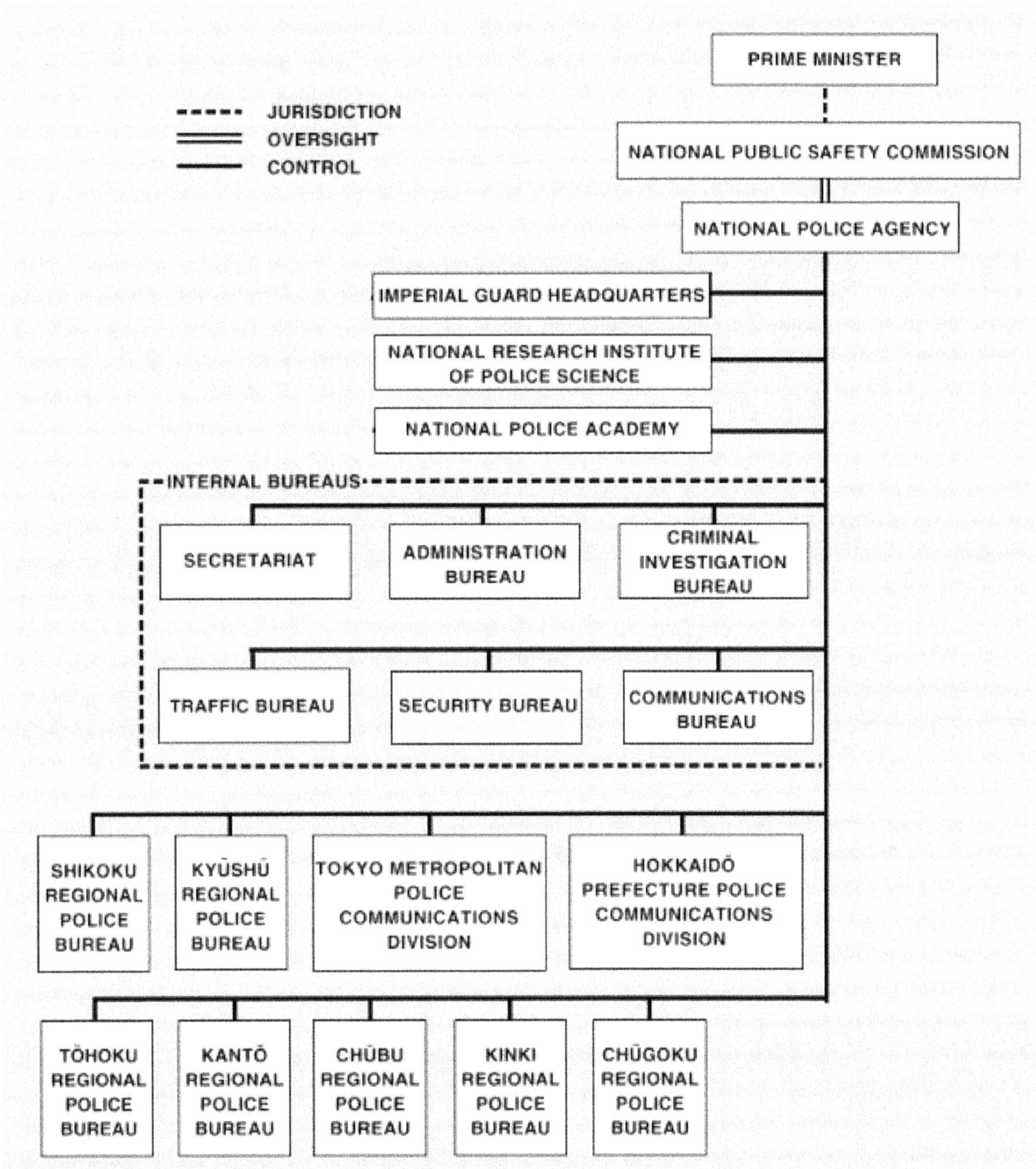

The NPA maintains Regional Police Bureaus as its local agencies throughout the country. There are seven bureaus in the major cities, excluding Tokyo and the northern island of Hokkaido. Police law stipulates that each prefectural government, which is a local entity, shall have its own Prefectural Police (PP). The PP is supervised by the Prefectural Public Safety Commission, which carries out all police duties within the boundaries of the prefecture. In practice, the PP forces are located in each of the 47 prefectures. The National Police Academy, the National Research Institute of Police Science and the Imperial Guard Headquarters are also organizations affiliated with the NPA.

The National Police Agency has seven regional police bureaus, each responsible for a number of prefectures. Metropolitan Tokyo and the island of Hokkaido are excluded from these regional

jurisdictions and are run more autonomously than other local forces, in the case of Tokyo, because of its special urban situation, and of Hokkaido, because of its distinctive geography. The National Police Agency maintains police communications divisions in these two areas to handle any coordination needed between national and local forces.
The Koban system provides local residents with safety and peace through daily contacts of police officers with residents in the area. Its success depends on the human relationship between the police officers and the community people. At times, there is an excess of intervention by police. The Koban system rests on approximately 15,000 police boxes (Hasshusho) and residential police boxes (Chuzaisho) located throughout the country.

The NPA and the PP personnel forces are composed of police officers, officers of the Imperial Guard Headquarters, and civilian employees such as clerical workers and technical engineers. In 1990, there were about 258,800 authorized full-time police personnel. The ratio of police to population is about one officer to 556 citizens. The NPA is comprised of approximately 7,600 personnel, of whom 1,200 are police officers, 900 are Imperial Guards and 5,500 are civilian personnel. The 47 PP forces have a total strength of approximately 250,000, of whom 220,000 are police officers and 30,000 are civilians.

There are two types of police budgets: the national budget and the prefectural budget. The national police budget covers the expenditures of the NPA relevant to the execution of duties under its jurisdiction, including personnel costs, expenses incurred by the prefectural police which are shouldered by the state, and subsidies to the PP. Expenditures needed by the PP to carry out their duties are appropriated in the budget of each prefecture. In 1992, the NPA budget totalled 213,464 billion yen and the PP budget totalled 2,992,454 million yen (270 billion USD). The total National Police Agency Budget for the 1990 fiscal year was 198,420 billion yen, of which 41.5% (82,282 billion yen) went toward personnel expenses, 14.5% (28,870 billion yen) went toward equipment, communications, and facilities, 18.2% (36,149 billion yen) were allocated toward other expenses, and 25.8% (51,119 billion yen) went toward subsidies for Prefectural Police. In all, 74.2% of the total (147,301 billion yen) went toward NPA expenses.

The Japanese government established a European-style civil police system in 1874, under the centralized control of the Police Bureau within the Home Ministry, to put down internal disturbances and maintain order during the Meiji Restoration. By the 1880s, the police had developed into a nationwide instrument of government control, providing support for local leaders and enforcing public morality.

They acted as general civil administrators, implementing official policies and thereby facilitating unification and modernization. In rural areas especially, the police had great authority and were accorded the same mixture of fear and respect as the village head. Their increasing involvement in political affairs was one of the foundations of the authoritarian state in Japan in the first half of the twentieth century.

The centralized police system steadily acquired responsibilities, until it controlled almost all aspects of daily life, including fire prevention and mediation of labor disputes. The system regulated public health, business, factories, and construction, and it issued permits and licenses. The Peace Preservation Law of 1925 gave police the authority to arrest people for "wrong thoughts." Special Higher Police were created to regulate the content of motion pictures, political meetings, and election campaigns. Military police operating under the army and navy and the justice and home ministries aided the civilian police in limiting proscribed political activity. After the Manchurian Incident of 1931, military police assumed greater authority, leading to friction with their civilian counterparts. After 1937 police directed business activities for the war effort, mobilized labor, and controlled transportation. During the Pacific War (1941-45), the government created the Order Maintenance Law and the Special Police Force to control thought and religion. A considerable number of non-conformists including Individualists and Communists was put into jail until the end of the war.

After Japan's surrender in 1945, occupation authorities retained the prewar police structure until a new system was implemented and the Diet passed the 1947 Police Law. Contrary to Japanese proposals for a strong, centralized force to deal with postwar unrest, the police system was decentralized. About 1,600 independent municipal forces were established in cities, towns, and villages with 5,000 inhabitants or more, and a National Rural Police was organized by prefecture. Civilian control was to be ensured by placing the police under the jurisdiction of public safety commissions controlled by the National Public Safety Commission in the Office of the Prime Minister. The Home Ministry was abolished and replaced by the less powerful Ministry of Home Affairs, and the police were stripped of their responsibility for fire protection, public health, and other administrative duties.

When most of the occupation forces were transferred to Korea in 1950-51, the 75,000 strong National Police Reserve was formed to back up the ordinary police during civil disturbances, and pressure mounted for a centralized system more compatible with Japanese political preferences. The 1947 Police Law was amended in 1951 to allow the municipal police of smaller communities to merge with the National Rural Police. Most chose this arrangement, and by 1954 only about 400 cities, towns, and villages still had their own police forces. Under the 1954 amended Police Law, a final restructuring created an even more centralized system in which local forces were organized by prefectures under a National Police Agency.

The revised Police Law of 1954, still in effect in the 1990s, preserves some strong points of the postwar system, particularly measures ensuring civilian control and political neutrality, while allowing for increased centralization. The National Public Safety Commission system has been retained. State responsibility for maintaining public order has been clarified to include coordination of national and local efforts; centralization of police information, communications, and recordkeeping facilities; and national standards for training, uniforms, pay, rank, and promotion. Rural and municipal forces were abolished and integrated into prefectural forces, which handled basic police matters. Officials and inspectors in various ministries and agencies continue to exercise special police functions assigned to them in the 1947 Police Law.

Security Bureau

The National Police Agency's Security Bureau formulates and supervises the execution of security policies. It conducts research on equipment and tactics for suppressing riots and oversaw and coordinates activities of the riot police. The Security Bureau is also responsible for security intelligence on foreigners and radical political groups, including investigation of violations of the Alien Registration Law and administration of the Entry and Exit Control Law. The bureau also implements security policies during national emergencies and natural disasters. The National Police Agency's First Public Safety Division investigates radical leftists.

A secret unit in the Japanese National Police Agency was set up to deal with contingencies related to North Korea. It has recruited and trained North Koreans to gather intelligence on Japan's behalf. According to some reports, high-ranking members of Chosen Soren, the North Korean residents' organization in Japan, have been recruited to work for Japan, performing such tasks as exposing North Korean agents.

MINISTRY OF FOREIGN AFFAIRS [GAIMUSHO]

2-1,Kasumigaseki 2 chome, Chiyoda-ku, Tokyo
Tel. 03-3580-3311

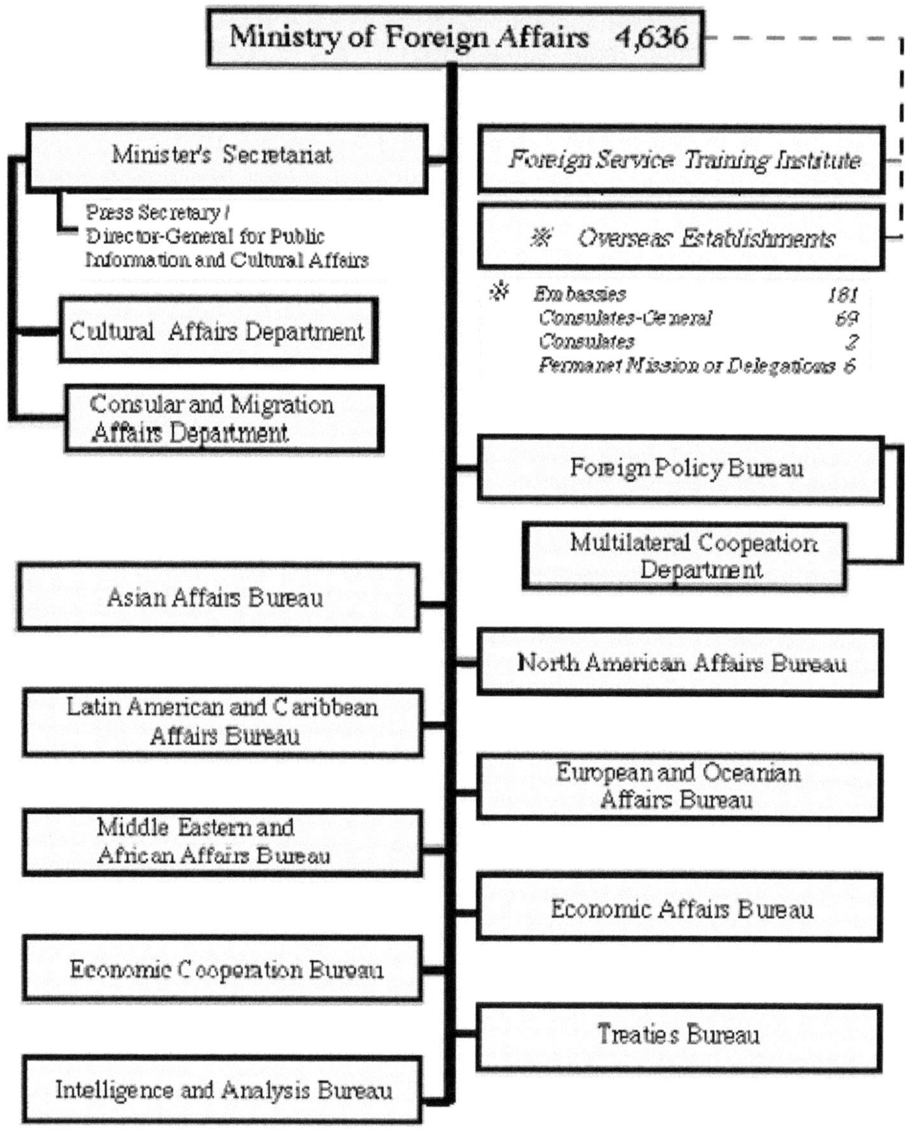

The Ministry of Foreign Affairs takes charge of the planning of basic and middle- or long-term foreign policy from wider points of view and the coordination of policies formulated by other bureaus. Special emphasis is put on national security issues and issues related to the United Nations. It also plays a leading part in a serious emergency. It also takes charge of the following matters: arms control and disarmament; non-proliferation; nuclear energy, and; science cooperation and other scientific affairs.

When increasing its personnel, the Ministry has placed priority on strengthening its crisis-management and security systems, which must enable the government to respond immediately. In spite of tight budgetary and recruitment restraints, the Ministry increased its staff by 72 during FY1998: 22 at the Ministry itself and 50 at overseas diplomatic and consular establishments. This brought staff totals to 5,169: 2,010 at the Ministry itself and 3,159 at overseas establishments. At the same time, the Ministry not only increased staff numbers but also made efforts to utilize its staff more effectively and to streamline administration, and in addition has implemented reforms to enhance staff recruitment and training.

INTELLIGENCE AND ANALYSIS BUREAU [INFORMATION ANALYSIS, RESEARCH AND PLANNING BUREAU]

http://www.moj.go.jp

The Intelligence and Analysis Bureau takes charge of the following matters: general management of information on the international situation; general administration of research affairs; research and surveys on foreign countries (except matters under the charge of other bureaus), and; general analysis of the international situation and collection of necessary information. The Intelligence and Analysis Bureau is divided into the General Management Division, the First Analysis Division and the Second Analysis Division.

In accordance with the rising international status of Japan, the volume of activities of the Ministry of Foreign Affairs had been sharply increasing even before the end of the Cold War, and this trend has become even more pronounced in recent years. For example, during the 15 years between 1976 and 1992, the number of diplomatic cables, the principal means of communication between the Ministry of Foreign Affairs and Japan's overseas establishments, increased by about eight times. The Ministry made efforts in 1993 to strengthen its organization, personnel and budget.

The Information Analysis, Research and Planning Bureau was reorganized into the Intelligence and Analysis Bureau, which specializes in information and analysis, in order to strengthen and improve the intelligence function of the Ministry. The reorganized Bureau plans and formulates a comprehensive policy on how the Ministry as a whole collects, analyzes, manages and provides information. The analysis system has also been further improved: to meet the increasingly complex and volatile international situation, the functions of regional analysis and item-wise analysis such as analysis of security situations are being strengthened.

MINISTRY OF JUSTICE (HOMUSHO)

The Ministry of Justice is in charge of a broad area of legal affairs, which include civil, criminal, immigration and other matters. In particular, it takes charge of nationality, family registration and registration of real estate, prosecution of criminal cases, correction and rehabilitation of offenders, litigations involving the interests of the State, immigration control and registration of foreign residents, and the protection of the rights of citizens in general. Thus the Ministry of Justice is primarily responsible for maintaining the legal order of the country in which the rule of law is ensured.

While in the pre-war days the Ministry of Justice (called as "Shihosho") had jurisdiction over all matters of judicial administration including supervision over the court operation, after the end of World WarII, with the enforcement of the New Constitution and the Court Organization Law as from May 3, 1947, the matters pertaining to courts, including their administration, have been transferred to the jurisdiction of the Supreme Court independent of the Ministry of Justice.

With the enforcement of the Law for Establishment of the Attorney General's Office as from February 15, 1948, the Attorney General's Office (called as "Homucho") was established as the Supreme Legal Advisor to the Prime Minister in charge of the administration of justice,replacing the Ministry of Justice (Shihosho).

The new Office, in addition to the work of the Ministry of Justice (Shihosho), was them entrusted with the work of the examination of drafting of laws and regulations and international treaties which had been under the jurisdiction of the Legislative Bureau of the Cabinet, research and study of judicial and legal systems of other countries as well as matters pertaining to civil and administrative suits, and the work of the protection of human rights.

Through a number of subsequent administrative reforms starting from the one of June 1, 1949 to that of August 1, 1952, the Attorney General's Office was abolished and the new Ministry of Justice (called "Homusho") was born,accompanied with considerable organizational reforms, which included the abolition of the Attorney General and Assistants system and the introduction of the system of placing the Minister of Justice as head of the Ministry and Vice Minister of Justice under him as in the case of other Ministries of the Government.

Now, the Ministry is equipped with the Minister's Secretariat, and seven bureaus such as the Civil Affairs Bureau, the Criminal Affairs Bureau, the Correction Bureau, the Rehabilitation Bureau, the Litigation Bureau, the Civil Liberties Bureau and the Immigration Bureau. Although there have since been some changes, basically this is the organizational structure of the Ministry of Justice as it is today.

PUBLIC SECURITY INVESTIGATION AGENCY [KOANCHO]

http://www.moj.go.jp/ENGLISH/PSIA/psia-01.html

The Public Security Intelligence Agency was established on July 21, 1952, when the Subversive Activities Prevention Act came into force, to carry out the comprehensive tasks of intelligence activity and investigation and request for control to be imposed on subversive organizations as by the act enacted.

The Act Regarding the Control of Organizations Which Committed Indiscriminate Mass Murder, which was enforced on December 27, 1999, granted the Agency additional duty to conduct intelligence activity and investigation and apply for controlling and regulating those organizations which committed indiscriminate mass murder.

Subversive Activities Prevention Act

The Subversive Activities Prevention Act aims to ensure the public safety by preventing disruption of the constitutional order that underlies democracy from happenings by violent activities. Under the Japanese Constitution, which regards the democracy as its basic principle, one's political position and claims should be expressed through speech and writing. But at times, we see some subversive organizations attempting to use violent means to achieve their own political goals without an avenue of speech. The Act provides for such necessary measures against those organizations as restricting particular organizational activities, disbanding them and penalizing individuals who resort to act of violence.

The Act Regarding the Control of Organizations Which Committed Indiscriminate Mass Murder

The Act Regarding the Control of Organizations Which Committed Indiscriminate Mass Murder aims to enhance the public security by revealing the activities of those organizations which have committed indiscriminate mass murder in the past and are still considered to have dangerous nature and by determining control measures against such organizations necessary to prevent the recurrence of the act of indiscriminate mass murder. The Act provides for surveillance action which requires such organizations to submit reports and receive on-the-spot inspections, for regulations such as banning such organizations from obtaining or using facilities or accepting money and goods as donation, and for appropriate punishment to be imposed on those members who committed prohibited acts or refused on-the-spot inspection.

ORGANIZATION

The Public Security Intelligence Agency is formed with internal departments, an institute and regional bureaus. The internal departments comprise the General Affairs Department, the First Intelligence Department and the Second Intelligence Department. The institute is called the Training Institute, and the Regional Bureaus consist of 8 Public Security Intelligence Bureaus and 14 Public Security Intelligence Offices located nationwide.

FUNCTIONS

(1) Duties

The Public Security Intelligence Agency perform its duties based on the Subversive Activities Prevention Act, which allows the Agency to conduct intelligence activity and investigation to those organizations which are likely to commit subversive activities by means of act of violence and to place a request with the Public Security Examination Commission for the implementation of any control measure such as imposing the restriction on such organizations' activities or disbanding them, when considered to be necessary as a result of the intelligence activity and investigations.

Also, under the Act Regarding the Control of Organizations Which Committed Indiscriminate Mass Murder, the Agency may request the Public Security Examination Commission for the decision to take the surveillance action on those organizations which have committed indiscriminate mass murder in the past and are still considered to have dangerous nature or for the measure to prevent the recurrence. The surveillance action qualifies the Agency to conduct on-the-spot inspections to the facilities that belong to the organization.

As for the implementation of the investigations, it is ruled that such investigations should always be conducted with the consent of the organization in question. Any compulsory investigations such as forcible seizure of evidence or forced domiciliary search are beyond the scope of the Agency's duties.

(2) Providing Information to Relevant Organizations

Public Security Intelligence Agency, as one of the governmental organizations, contributes to the government's policy making process by sharing with other governmental organizations concerned the information at any time, which was obtained through its intelligence activity and investigations to the subversive organizations and other organizations which have committed indiscriminate mass murder.

The Agency's effort to utilize collected information also takes the form of the publication of a report. The report named "Review and Prospect of Internal and External Situations" is released annually by the end of each year, and "Reviewing the International Terrorism" is released on a regular basis.

THE PUBLIC SECURITY EXAMINATION COMMISSION

The Public Security Examination Commission is an independent administrative board, which, upon receiving the request from the Agency for disposition concerning organizations, conducts examinations requested from the impartial as well as objective point of view and determine whether or not requested measures are necessary or what measures should apply.

The Commission consists of a chairman and six members, who are appointed, with the approval of both Houses of the Diet, by the Prime Minister from among men of learning and experience.

MINISTRY OF INTERNATIONAL TRADE AND INDUSTRY (MITI)

Historical Background: Japan's Ministry of International Trade and Industry (MITI) was formed in 1949 from the union of the Trade Agency and the Ministry of Commerce and Industry in an effort to curb postwar inflation and provide government leadership and assistance for the restoration of industrial productivity and employment. MITI held primary responsibility for formulating and implementing international trade policy, although it did so by seeking a consensus among interested parties, including the Ministry of Foreign Affairs and the Ministry of Finance. MITI also coordinated trade policy, on issues affecting their interests, with the Economic Planning Agency, the Bank of Japan, and the ministries of agriculture, construction, forestry and fisheries, health and welfare, posts and telecommunications, and transportation.

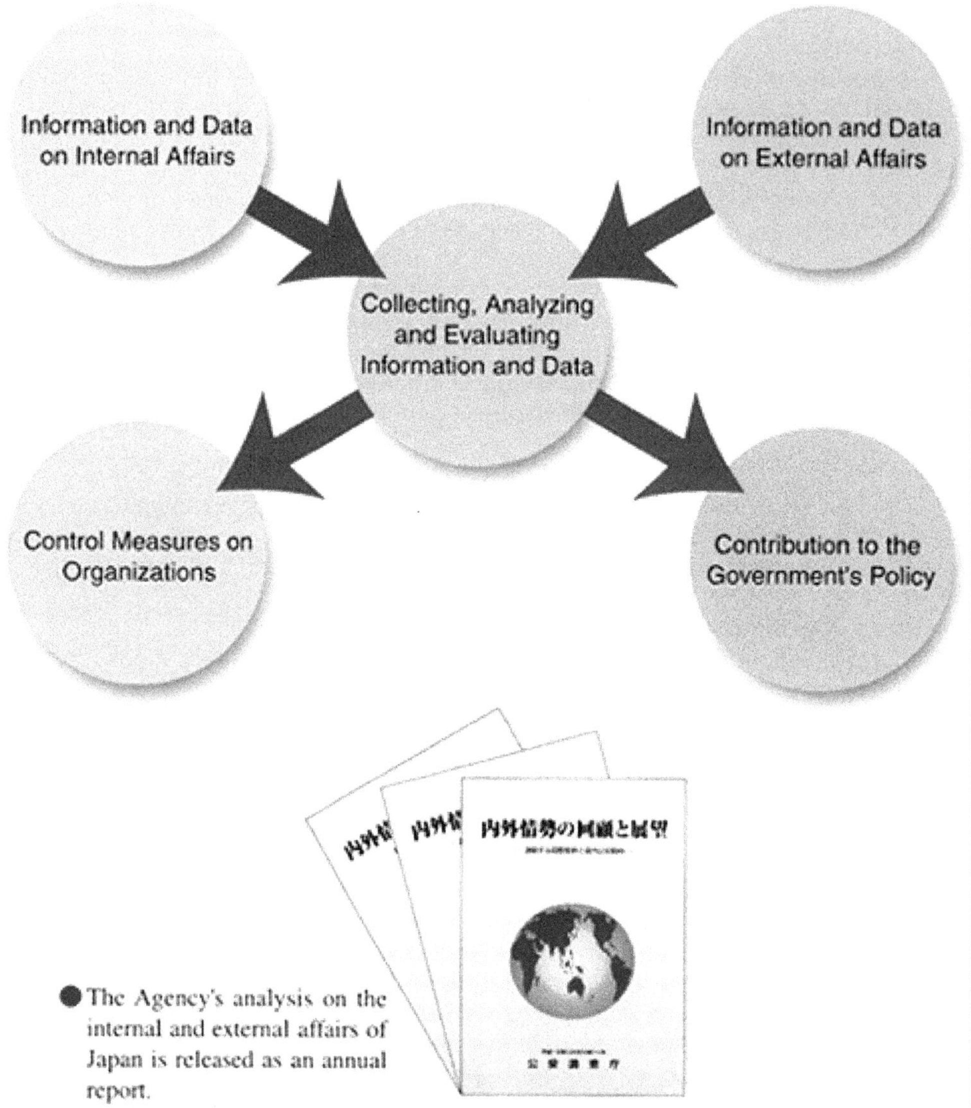

● The Agency's analysis on the internal and external affairs of Japan is released as an annual report.

As trade issues broadened in scope, these other ministries became more important in international negotiating, so that in the late 1980s MITI had less control in formulating international trade policy than it had had in the 1950s and 1960s. The prime minister, the National Diet (Japan's legislature), and the Fair Trade Commission also circumscribed MITI's operations.

MITI was responsible not only in the areas of exports and imports but also for all domestic industries and businesses not specifically covered by other ministries in the areas of investment in plant and equipment, pollution control, energy and power, some aspects of foreign economic assistance, and consumer complaints. This span has allowed MITI to integrate conflicting policies, such as those on pollution control and export competitiveness, to minimize damage to export industries.

MITI served as an architect of industrial policy, an arbiter on industrial problems and disputes, and a regulator. A major objective of the ministry was to strengthen the country's industrial base. It did not managed Japanese trade and industry along the lines of a centrally planned economy, but it did provide industries with administrative guidance and other direction, both formal and informal, on modernization, technology, investments in new plants and equipment, and domestic and foreign competition.

The close relationship between MITI and Japanese industry led to foreign trade policy that often complemented the ministry's efforts to strengthen domestic manufacturing interests. MITI facilitated the early development of nearly all major industries by providing protection from import competition, technological intelligence, help in licensing foreign technology, access to foreign exchange, and assistance in mergers.

These policies to promote domestic industry and to protect it from international competition were strongest in the 1950s and 1960s. As industry became stronger and as MITI lost some of its policy tools, such as control over allocation of foreign exchange, MITI's policies also changed. The success of Japanese exports and the tension it has caused in other countries led MITI to provide guidance on limiting exports of particular products to various countries. Starting in 1981, MITI presided over the establishment of voluntary restraints on automobile exports to the United States to allay criticism from American manufacturers and their unions.

Similarly, MITI was forced to liberalize import policies, despite its traditional protectionist focus. During the 1980s, the ministry helped to craft a number of market-opening and importpromoting measures, including the creation of an import promotion office within the ministry. The close relationship between MITI and industry allowed the ministry to play such a role in fostering more open markets, but conflict remained between the need to open markets and the desire to continue promoting new and growing domestic industries.

JAPAN EXTERNAL TRADE ORGANIZATION (JETRO)

http://www.jetro.go.jp

JETRO Atlanta
245 Peachtree Center Avenue
Suite 2208
Marquis One Tower
Atlanta, GA 30303
tel: 404.681.0600
fax: 404.681.0713

JETRO Chicago
401 North Michigan Avenue
Suite 660
Chicago, IL 60611
tel: 312.832.6000
fax: 312.832.6066

JETRO Denver
1200 Seventeenth Street
Suite 1110
Denver, CO 80202
tel: 303.629.0404
fax: 303.893.9522

JETRO Houston
1221 McKinney
Suite 4141
Houston, TX 77010
tel: 713.759.9595
fax: 713.759.9210

JETRO Los Angeles
777 South Figueroa Street
Suite 4900
Los Angeles, CA 90017
tel: 213.624.8855
fax: 213.629.8127

JETRO New York
1221 Avenue of the Americas
McGraw Hill Building, 42nd Floor
New York, NY 10020-1079
tel: 212.997.0400
fax: 212.997.0464

JETRO San Francisco
235 Pine Street
Suite 1700
San Francisco, CA 94104
tel: 415.392.1333
fa

The Japan External Trade Organization (JETRO) is a Japanese government organization that promotes mutually beneficial investment and trade relations between Japan and other nations.

JETRO was established in 1958, and has a worldwide network of 38 offices in Japan and 79 offices overseas.

The Trade Tie-up Promotion Program (TTPP) is a web-based matching service for companies seeking partners for international trade and investment. By registering online, the user may browse through business proposals from companies in Japan. This service is free of charge.
The Invest Japan! Website provides information for companies interested in starting or expanding business activities in Japan. Invest Japan! resources include national and regional surveys, tax and law information and a cost simulation program.

The Japan External Trade Organization (JETRO) was established by MITI in 1958 to consolidate Japan's efforts in export promotion. The government has provided more than half of JETRO's annual operating budget. As of 1989, JETRO maintained seventy-eight offices in fifty-seven countries, as well as thirty offices in Japan, with a total staff of 1,200. Initially, JETRO's activities focused mainly on promoting exports to other countries. As exporters established themselves in world markets and the balance of trade turned from deficit to surplus, however, JETRO's role shifted to encompass more varied activities. These have included the furtherance of mutual understanding with trading partners, import promotion, liaison between small businesses in Japan and their overseas counterparts, and data dissemination. Import promotion services have included publications, promotion of trade fairs, seminars, and trade missions.

JETRO has attracted attention because of the larger focus given to economic intelligence, and the fact that JETRO's activities are mostly focused on Japan's nominal allies in the US and Western Europe. During the early 20th century and in the prewar and wartime periods, it is well documented that Japanese trading companies were valuable sources of information to government agencies. Nor can it be said that such relationships no longer exist.

JETRO is one of the best examples of a true Japanese commercial intelligence organization. JETRO, aware of scrutiny from the FBI as well as the Central Intelligence Agency, is almost certainly complying with American law. It is engaged in the collection of business intelligence, the collection of business and competitive information through legal and ethical methods. As much as 80% to 90% of this information may be obtained through open sources, such as newspaper articles, trade journals, Security & Exchange Commission (SEC) filings, specialized databases and trade show material. JETRO makes that information available to a range of Japanese trading companies, big manufacturers and smaller companies, who then attempt to license it or form relationships of some sort.

As of 1994 JETRO had 84 domestic offices composed of 33 trade information centers and 51 economic internationalization centers in Japan. Internationally, JETRO had 48 overseas offices and operates 28 specialized JETRO Centers. JETRO had a total staff of approximately 1200 people which was equally divided between the Japan domestic (600 Japanese staff members) and overseas offices (300 Japanese and 300 local country staff members). By 1997 JETRO's US operations -- with an annual budget of at least $30 million and 160 employees -- were the linchpin of a pervasive information-gathering effort.

JORDAN

DAIRAT AL MUKHABARAT GENERAL INTELLIGENCE DEPARTMENT

gid@gid.gov.jo

Director of the National Security Council

General Sa'ad Kheir
Advisor to His Majesty King Abdullah on Security Affairs,
Director of the General Intelligence Dept., &
Director of the National Security Council

The General Intelligence Department [GID] is tasked with collecting and analyzing information to assist the government in political decision making. It is also responsible for countering illegal organizations whose goals are to spread havoc within the country through means of sabotage or psychological warfare, as well as to counter espionage. Additional duties include combating corruption, the smuggling of arms and drugs, and counterfeiting operations. The focus of its efforts are intelligence gathering and analysis on issues concerning Jordan and the Middle East. Its intelligence reports disseminated to key decision makers in the government. GID also assists other government agencies in maintaining awareness of security and strategic issues.

GID intensifies its efforts for the continuous protection of the Jordanian National Security in its political, social, security, and economic dimensions.

GID draws its vision from the moderate approach that the Hashimate Leadership in Jordan is characterized with, and dedicated it as one of the firm Jordanian polices, with strong beliefs in democracy, political pluralism and respect for human rights, dignity and basic freedoms.

GID within the framework of the Jordanian vision, is aware of the importance of cooperation regionally and internationally in enhancing international security and stability, through non - interference of the internal affairs of others and fighting terrorism no matter its target or source.

Interpreting this vision through our daily work, requires extraordinary efforts and capabilities that depend on the continuous development of performance, self-education and exchanging expertise with others, to reach a qualitative intelligence performance that can confront challenges and developments, executed by qualified officers and non-officers from both genders, guided by just, rightness and law abiding principles.

GID's objective is to defend Jordan's national security and protect its interests. **GID** maneuvers to defend Jordan from internal and external currents which may target its political stability, violate its sovereignty, or threaten the security of its people for the purpose of destabilizing its political pillars, slowing down its economic growth or hindering its untarnished international image.
The **GID** is committed to preserving the power of the Jordanian constitution when executing its duties. In addition, Jordan and the **GID** fully recognize and enforce the International Declaration of Human rights in addition to many other International documents.

The **GID** must work very diligently to keep up to speed on all the issues which may effect Jordan. The Department is continuously developing the capabilities of its staff for the purpose of achieving the highest standard of professionalism in order to meet the many challenges of today.

The **GID** is also a leader in the national fight against corruption in all its forms. **GID** is convinced that the phenomenon of corruption is a major obstacle to the nations political, social, and economical development.

The **GID** role is to collect various forms of information on political issues, economical indicators, progress and mind set of the social factor, as well as in-depth and complex security concerns, for the purpose of analysis and prediction. The conclusions are summed up in detailed reports that are dispatched to decision-makers for utilization and knowledge.

The detainment quarters of the **GID** meet internationally approved standards. As a result of the "Jordanian Prison Administration laws," the Ministry of Interior recognizes the **GID's** detainment center as an official state prison making it accessible for inspection and review. Detainees, who are detained as a result of memorandums signed by the Attorney General and various courts, are provided with three nutritious meals a day, clean quarters and are allowed visits from defense lawyers. In addition, the International Red Cross Organization is granted access to the departments detainment quarters upon an approved

G.I.D's Duites

GID's strategy is manifested in accordance with its Law and acting legislation in the Kingdom to protect the National Security from any targeting through executing the following duties:

- Collecting and analyzing information and presenting it to the decision-maker.
- Countering ideological sabotage which, in turn, generates material sabotage, in addition to encountering any attempts to infiltrate the Jordan society.
- Countering physical sabotage, and terrorism in all its kinds, targets and sources.
- Countering espionage.
- Following-up corruption and ill-legal trade through specialized Anti-Corruption

Directorate established in 1996.
Jordan witnessed two major changes during the 1990's:
Resumption of Paramilitary activities, political pluralism.
and signing peace treaty with Israel.

GID and the resumption of democracy:
Jordanian democracy is targeted by external and internal powers and sides to undermine it, so one of the **GID** major duties is protecting it.

GID and the peace era :
Peace with Israel is a strategic Arabian choice. The Jordanian-Israeli peace treaty achieved a numerous gains for Jordan, Palestinians and Arabs. There are internal and external opposition for the peace process trying to derail it by all means, especially through terrorist acts, the thing which made protecting the peace process and contributing in providing suitable conditions of peace and stability for the peace building stage (investments, tourism, etc.) , one of the major objectives of **GID**.

IMPORTANT WEBSITES

His Majesty King Abdullah II web site	www.kingabdullah.gov.jo
-Her Majesty Queen Rania Al-Abdullah	www.queenrania.jo/
-His Majesty King Hussein web site	www.kinghussein.gov.jo
-Her Majesty Queen Noor	www.noor.gov.jo
-Special Operations Forces Exhibition and Conference	www.sofexjordan.com

-Ministry of Tourism and Antiquities	www.mota.gov.jo
-Ministry of Industry and Trade	www.mit.gov.jo
-National Information Center	www.nic.gov.jo
-Jordan Embassy in US	www.jordanembassyus.org
-Jordan Embassy in UK	www.jordanembassyuk.org
-Amman Financial Market	www.ammanstockex.com
-Investment Promotions Corporation	www.jordaninvestment.com
-Civil – Passport Department	
-Royal Jordanian	www.rja.com.jo
-Petra News Agency	www.petra.gov.jo
-Addustour Newspaper	www.Addustour.com
-Star	www.star.com.jo
-Al Rai Newpaper	www.alrai.com
-Jordan Times	www.jordantimes.com
-Jordan Television	www.jrtv.jo

KENYA

KENYAN NATIONAL SECURITY INTELLIGENCE SERVICE (NSIS)

In 1998, a new act of Parliament in Kenya established the National Security Intelligence Service (NSIS) to replace the former Directorate of Security Intelligence which was commonly known as the "Special Branch" and which was part of the Kenya Police Department.
The NSIS brief, like all other intelligence organisations, is to gather and exploit secret information. It identifies conditions that threaten Kenya's political, economic and social stability. It subsequently develops opportunities and strategies to neutralise such threats.

In May 1999, President Daniel arap Moi appointed retired Brig. Wilson Bonett to head NSIS whose intelligence gathering work includes: internal, external and strategic intelligence. NSIS is divided into seven sections:

1. Administration
2. Information technology
3. Internal intelligence
4. External intelligence
5. Economic affairs
6. Operations
7. National Intelligence Academy

It changed name and relocated from its notorious Nyati House offices to new headquarters on the outskirts of the city, near the Windsor Golf and Country Hotel. As the Director general of NSIS, Retired Brig. Boinet is the principle advisor of the President on matters relating to national security. In April 1999, the Moi government appointed Mrs Pamela Mboya, the former Permanent representative to the Habitat, to head a Committee that was charged with formulating a scheme of service for NSIS officers.

Security of tenure given the director of NSIS is designed to protect him from such abuse by members of the governing elite. He has the opportunity to say 'no' to any unlawful or sectarian instructions from his bosses without fear of losing his job.
The position of intelligence boss is, therefore, crucial in maintaining democratic balance and, in Kenya's case, from taking it back to the torture chambers.
Officials of the new Intelligence body are:

- Mr. Stephen Kimani Muhu - Director of operations,
- Mr. Petkay Shen Miriti - Director of external intelligence,
- Mr. Shukri Baramadi - Director of internal intelligence,
- Mr. Alloys Meltus Okindah, Director of National Intelligence Academy,
- Mr. Joseph Murei Mangira - Director of administration,
- Mr. Fidel Mumia - Director of economic affairs
- Mr. Kibwon Sergon - Director of information technology.

SOUTH KOREA

INTELLIGENCE & SECURITY AGENCIES

National Security Council (NSC)
Ministry of National Defense
Defense Security Command
Army
Navy
Marine Corps
Air Force
Homeland Reserve Force
National Intelligence Service
Agency for National Security Planning (ANSP)
Korean Central Intelligence Agency (KCIA)
National Police Agency
Presidential Security Service (PSS)

From the end of the Korean War to 1990, South Korea had evolved from a country dependent on other nations for its national security to a strong and growing nation, increasingly capable of meeting its own defense needs. Civilian industries maintained military assembly lines as a separate, and generally small, part of their corporate activities.

By deploying main forces such as mechanized and self-propelled artillery units, attack weapons and equipment in the forward area, the North has a combat posture that would allow it to launch surprise attacks at any time. Under such circumstances, Pyongyang may launch provocations against the South as a way of resolving the sense of crisis or dissatisfaction within its system, or to gain international attention. Conflicts deriving from food shortages or from decision-making processes could also result in an emergency within the North Korean regime.

Korean participation in the Vietnam War that provided an opportunity for the modernization of ROK armed forces. In 1966 when combat divisions were actively deployed in Vietnam after the initial expedition in 1965, ROK force improvement, though limited, was initiated through the US Brown Memorandum which promised to support a ROK force modernization plan. This memorandum, howevert did not clearly specify any effect, characteristics or time limit. As a result, the memorandum led only to modest improvements such as provision of old-model tanks and M-16 rifles to the ROK forces in Vietnam. In the meantime, a series of North Korean provocations occurred, with a North Korean guerrilla attempt to infiltrate the Blue House on January 21, 1968, and two days later the hijacking of the USS Pueblo, an American reconnaissance ship, on the East Sea. In April 1969, a US EC-121 reconnaissance aircraft was also shot down.

In response to these events and upon ROK request, the US government decided to hold cabinet-level annual conferences on security issues with the ROK government. Korea was promised military assistance of one hundred million dollars as well as the construction of an M-16 manufacturing facility. President Park Chung Hee, however, decided to proceed further to realize the goal of a self-reliant defense posture in preparation for the future possibility of a national crisis. The need for self-reliant defense was all the more strengthened by the international environment at that time. In March 1971, the Seventh Division of the US Forces in Korea (USFK) withdrew from the peninsula following the Nixon Doctrine of July 1969, which champions the importance of the self-reliant defense responsibility for all nations.

The US government declared a $1,596 million aid program during 1971-1975 to support the Five-Year Modernization Plan of ROK forces. This was agreed as compensation for participation in the Vietnam War as well as for the decrease in the size of the USFK. This program, however, did not reach all its initial goals as the aid period was delayed to 1977. Nevertheless, it did result in upgrading a part of ROK forces' equipment for the first time since the truce of the Korean War. The equipment used by ROK troops in Vietnam also contributed to the partial modernization of ROK forces.

On April 19, 1973, President Park Chung Hee gave an instruction during an inspection of the 1973 Ulchi Exercise, to establish independent military strategies for self-reliant defense and to develop a force improvement plan. In response, the Joint Chiefs of Staff drew up Joint Basic Military Strategies in July 1973, delivered the Guidelines for Military Equipment Modernization Program to each service and integrated plans of the three services. The result was the Eight-Year National Defense Plan (1974-1981), the first self-reliant force improvement plan for the ROK, which was subsequently approved by the president on February 25, 1974.

In order to respond more quickly to the North's provocations, the ROK military tracks and surveys not only its major military trends, but also its non-military trends. Also, the ROK military is reflecting detailed military countermeasures to be taken immediately in various plans and is developing them against predicted provocations from the North. In order to survey the activities of North Korean aircraft, a monitor control and reporting center (MCRC) operation system is run 24 hours a day. If North Korean military activities seem suspicious, the movement must be thoroughly tracked and surveyed until it becomes clear; if necessary, the ROK military can receive support from US military intelligence satellites.

In case a war breaks out on the Korean peninsula, the first two to three days of combat will play a decisive role in winning or losing the war. One comes to such a conclusion after summarizing and analyzing the following: North Korea's military strategy toward the South and its military capability including preemptive surprise attacks and short-term blitkrieg using WMDs, artillery units and high-speed in-depth task forces; the current level of ROK-US allied force capability; and the deployment plan of the US augmentation forces.

Under the terms of the 1954 Republic of Korea-United States of America Mutual Defense Treaty, the United States and South Korea agreed to cooperate in defending the security and strategic interests of both countries. South Korea's deployment of army and marine units to South Vietnam in the 1960s and 1970s demonstrated its commitment to meeting its obligations under the treaty. By 1990 the United States had stationed 44,500 military personnel in South Korea--a signal to North Korea and other countries in the region that Washington would meet its security commitments to Seoul under the Mutual Defense Treaty.
In the confusion of the early days of the Korean War, Seoul placed its armed forces under the command of General Douglas MacArthur as United Nations (UN) commander. This arrangement

continued after the armistice. For some twenty-five years, the United Nations Command headquarters, which had no South Korean officers in it, was responsible for the defense of South Korea, with operational control over a majority of the units in the South Korean military. The command was the primary peacetime planning organization for allied response to a North Korean invasion of South Korea and the principal wartime command organization for all South Korean and United States forces involved in defending South Korea.

In 1968 the United States and South Korea held their first annual Security Consultative Meeting. This meeting provided highlevel defense experts from the two countries with an official forum for reassessing the nature of the North Korean threat to South Korea, for agreeing on an overall defense strategy for South Korea, and for outlining the roles of both countries in deterring a North Korean invasion.

In 1978 a binational headquarters, the South Korea-United States Combined Forces Command (CFC), was created, and the South Korean military units with front-line missions were transferred from the UN Command to the CFC's operational control. The commander in chief of the CFC, a United States military officer, answered ultimately to the national command authorities of the United States and the Republic of Korea.

Historically, operational control of South Korea's tactical armed forces has made the United States commander vulnerable to the politics of association. United States commanders have rigidly avoided commentary on South Korean party politics, confining public statements to purely military matters on such issues as arms buildups and threats from North Korea. However, in the complex politics of the Korean Peninsula, the United States commander's military opinions often have been publicly manipulated as support for Seoul's authoritarianism.

In May 1961 and December 1979, the command structure was breached by South Korean troops participating in military coups. A more complex set of circumstances occurred in May 1980, when troops were withdrawn from the CFC under existing procedures and dispatched to Kwangju to respond to the student uprising. Confusion in the South Korean public over the particular circumstances of the incident, the United States position, and the limits of the CFC's control led many South Koreans to believe that the United States fully supported the violent suppression of the uprising. The lack of an accurate historical record for nearly ten years generated widespread misunderstanding, and it has been credited with the rise of anti-Americanism in South Korea, a movement which continues.

Only after President Chun stepped down at the end of 1987, and the opposition in the National Assembly grew stronger, did the United States begin answering the questions concerning United States involvement in Kwangju. On June 19, 1989, Washington issued the "United States Government Statement on Events in Kwangju, Republic of Korea, in May 1980," in response to formal requests from the National Assembly. The statement addressed a series of questions related to the rise to power of then Lieutenant General Chun Doo Hwan. The statement noted no prior knowledge of the assassination of President Park Chung Hee, nor warning of the December 12, 1979, incident, in which a group of South Korean army officers led by Major General Chun seized control of the military. It was revealed that Washington repeatedly protested to the government and the military leadership about the misuse of forces under the Combined Forces Command. The report also stated that South Korean authorities gave the United States two hours advanced warning of the extension of martial law on May 18, 1980, and no prior warning of the military's intention to arrest political leaders or to close both the National Assembly and the universities.

The statement clearly noted that none of the South Korean forces deployed at Kwangju were, during that time, under either the operational control of the CFC or the control of any United States authorities. Additionally, the United States had neither prior knowledge of the deployment of special forces to Kwangju nor responsibility for their actions there. The report addressed the use of the Twentieth Division, CFC, and clarified that the CFC agreement allowed both the United States and South Korea to assert control over its forces at any time without the consent of the other. According to the statement, the United States was informed in advance of intentions to use elements of the Twentieth Division to reenter Kwangju, that United States officials, after cautioning against the use of military force to solve a political crisis, accepted that it would be preferable to use the Twentieth Division rather than Special Forces units (but the latter were also involved). The report further documented that the United States repeatedly protested public distortions of Washington's actions and policy by Seoul and the South Korean press, namely allegations that the United States knew either of the December 12 incident in advance or of the extension of martial law, or that Washington approved of the Special Forces actions in Kwangju.

While the report rebutted most of the myths of American culpability for events in 1979 and 1980, the ten-year delay in issuing the report did little to resolve the misgivings held by many South Koreans, who still persisted in believing that the United States was in some way a party to the military takeover in May 1980, and the harsh suppression of the Kwangju demonstrations that followed.

During the 1989 Security Consultative Meeting in Washington (the meetings were held in alternate years in Seoul and Washington), the two nations agreed that the Moscow-assisted modernization of P'yongyang's air force and army indicated that the military situation in Northeast Asia remained tense and unpredictable. Soviet leader Mikhail Gorbachev's Korean policy, focused on promoting unofficial contacts with Seoul though Moscow, continued to bolster P'yongyang's military establishment.

South Korean and United States leaders who attended the 1989 Security Consultative Meeting considered it unlikely that the Soviet Union would initiate a military conflict targeting South Korea. They believed, however, that increasing Soviet military support for North Korea made it highly probable that the Soviet Union would continue to assist North Korea if war broke out. For this reason, United States secretary of defense Richard B. Cheney and South Korean minister of national defense Yi Sang-hun agreed to strengthen strategic planning through existing organizations, such as the CFC.

In 1990 a few hundred United States military personnel were assigned to the United Nations Command headquarters in P'anmunjom, in the DMZ, and were responsible for representing the United States at meetings of the Military Armistice Commission. Because the Seoul and P'yongyang governments had never negotiated a peace agreement after the Korean War, the sometimes shaky 1953 armistice concluded between the United Nations Command, North Korea, and China remained the only formal channel for handling complaints about violations of the truce.

There were 32,000 United States Army personnel in South Korea in 1990; most were assigned to the Eighth Army, which included the Second Infantry Division, the Seventeenth Aviation Brigade, and other detachments deployed north of Seoul as part of the joint South Korean-United States forward defense strategy. If a conflict were to occur, the Second Infantry Division would be expected to serve as a reserve force for the South Korean army on one of the main invasion routes between the DMZ and Seoul. United States Army personnel with command or planning responsibilities for combat units also were assigned to the headquarters of the CFC and to the headquarters of the Republic of Korea-United States Combined Field Army, of which the Second Infantry Division was the main American component. The remaining United States Army personnel were assigned to support the missions of selected United States and South Korean combat units, serving primarily in communications, logistics, and training positions.

There were 12,000 United States Air Force personnel in South Korea in 1990. They were assigned to units responsible for early warning, air interception, close air support of United States and South Korean ground forces, combat support, aircraft maintenance, and the transportation of personnel and supplies from the United States, Japan, and other United States military installations in the Pacific. The Seventh Air Force, headquartered at Osan Air Base, was the command element for all United States Air Force organizations in South Korea. United States Lockheed U-2 high- altitude reconnaissance and South Korean Grumman E-2C early warning aircraft patrolled the North Korean border and monitored the Soviet Union's air and naval activities in the Sea of Japan area. Advanced F-16 fighter aircraft were used by tactical fighter squadrons based at Osan and Kunsan. These squadrons operated alongside South Korean air force tactical squadrons in both air interception and close air support roles. South Korea and the United States jointly managed the South Korean tactical air control system, which had wartime responsibility for North Korean airspace and the entire South Korean coastline. The United States Military Airlift Command was responsible for transporting United States military personnel, weapons, and supplies from the United States and locations in the Pacific to South Korea.

United States Navy and United States Marine Corps personnel in South Korea consisted of about 500 officers and enlisted personnel who occupied critical staff and liaison positions in the CFC. The United States Pacific Command in Hawaii frequently deployed units of the United States Pacific Fleet, based in Japan, and units of the marine corps, based in Okinawa and other locations in the Pacific, to South Korea for joint training exercises, particularly Team Spirit, held every spring to promote South Korean-United States military cooperation and readiness. During the 1988 Seoul Olympics, the United States Seventh Fleet operated in the Sea of Japan and was assigned specific missions to assist units of the CFC in discouraging P'yongyang from attempting to disrupt the Olympic Games.

To execute the US "win-win strategy" and support the United Nations Command (UNC) and ROK-US Combined Forces Command (CFC) operation plans, the US augementation forces deployment plan on the Korean peninsula is set at all times. This plan mainly includes in-Korea forces, pre-planned time-phased deployment forces, augmentation forces, and foreign support forces. The plan centers on the forces under the US Pacific Command, and part of the forces from the US and other theaters are included as well. The size of the US augmentation forces, which include ground, naval, air and marine forces, will amount to at least 640 thousand troops, and these forces possess fighters, support aircraft, and aircraft carrier battle groups and amphibious flotillas equipped with the latest fighters. If a crisis does occur on the Korean peninsula, the US augmentation forces units will be deployed after the approval of the National Supreme Command and under the command of the US Joint Chiefs of Staff. After deployment, the augmentation forces will go through the process of unit integration, and then be committed to specific operations.

MINISTRY OF NATIONAL DEFENSE

General Song, Young Keun
http://www.dsc.or.kr/

Korean armed forces modified their command system on October 1, 1990, from a trilateral system of three services to the joint force system, and reformed the organizations and functions of the Ministry of National Defense, the JCS and the headquarters of three services in April 1995 to enhance the capabilities of crisis management and to complete the self-reliant systems of the joint planning and integrated operations. Meanwhile, unit structure is under improvement towards qualified unit structure focused on efficiency of operations and on a balance of three services so that integrated combat capabilities are maximized. The Ministry of National Defense is organized into bureaus responsible for force development, budget, personnel, reserve forces, logistics, military installations, medical affairs, the defense industry, and the military education system.

Annual defense budgets are proposed by the Ministry of National Defense and approved by the president following consultations with the National Assembly. Beginning in fiscal year 1979, the Ministry of National Defense adopted a budget management system based on the United States Department of Defense project planning budget system. The South Korean system focused on force modernization and the maintenance of military organizations in peacetime at 70 percent of their wartime strength. The government's mobilization and resource management plans for support of the military were designed to bring the armed forces up to full strength quickly and to maintain the country's capability to supply the military during wartime. Under the 1987 Constitution, the National Assembly was accorded more responsibility to review the defense budget and to recommend appropriate levels of spending. In 1990, however, the president continued to have the final say on budget matters.

Seoul's defense budget increased in proportion to the growth of the national economy throughout the 1970s and 1980, demonstrating how strongly national leaders felt about improving the armed forces (see fig. 16). Between 1971 and 1975, defense spending increased from US$411 million to US$719 million. Defense expenditures averaged about 4.5 percent of the country's gross national product (GNP--see Glossary). In 1976, the first year that the government included proceeds from the defense tax in published figures for military expenditures, the budget for the armed forces and defense industries increased 100 percent over the 1975 figure to US$1.5 billion. The costs involved in initiating weapons production and the loss of military grant aid from the United States were the major reasons for the gradual increase of defense spending from 5.2 percent of GNP in 1979 to 6.2 percent of GNP in 1982. By 1990 defense spending had increased to almost US$10 billion a year, but because of the dramatic growth in the country's economy, this figure was below 30 percent of the government's budget and less than 5 percent of GNP for the first time since 1975.

The rank and grade structure of the three services correspond, with minor exceptions, to that of the United States forces, as did the correlation between rank and responsibility. In peacetime, the army and air force were each commanded by a four-star general; a lieutenant general commanded the marines, and an admiral commanded the navy. Service uniforms also resembled those of the United States forces in color and style. Service personnel wore a summer uniform of denim and a winter uniform of wool. Troops in forward areas wore a more expensive padded winter uniform. Noncommissioned officers of the army and air force wore a tunic buttoned to the top; navy noncommissioned officers wore the United States-type seaman's blouse. Officers' uniforms were similar to those worn by officers of the United States.

Until mid 1960's the procurement of military materiel for the Republic of Korea largely relied upon military aid from the United States. However, with the goal of modernizing and developing domestic weapon production capability, the Defense Procurement Agency (DPA) was established in Jan 1, 1971 by integrating the Defense Construction Agency, procurement organizations of each service, and the Laboratory of Army Research and Development Command under the 5402nd order of the president. DPA has continued to carry out its functions, undergoing ten reorganization processes in its history. In 1990 South Korean industries provided about 70 percent of the weapons, ammunition, communications and other types of equipment, vehicles, clothing, and other supplies needed by the military.

U.S. decryption of codified Japanese transmissions proved to be a critical element to bringing victory during the Midway Battle, which marked a major turning point in the course of the Pacific War. This aptly illustrates that preserving military secrets is a decisive element that can determine the outcome of wars. The DSC carries out functions of protecting military secrets and preventing security breaches, so that the highest level of military readiness can be maintained. In addition, the DSC is putting particular emphasis on becoming an "Open DSC" that proactively publicizes matters in which the public has a right to know, so long as military security is not compromised.

COUNTERINTELLIGENCE

The DSC protects the people and the military from various exogenous threats by arresting spies and radical leftist activists, and by supporting counter-espionage, counter-terrorism, and psychological warfare operations. To take an analogy, the DSC would be the equivalent of the white blood cells within our bodies that protect us from harmful exogenous microbes. Accounting for 43% of the total arrest of spies by security agencies, the DSC stands committed at the forefront of our nation to safeguard peace and prosperity.

In a knowledge and information-based society, competition is determined by the ability to collect and analyze information with speed and accuracy, and the military is no exception. The DSC contributes to ensuring optimum combat capability by preemptive detection and removal of elements hampering military readiness, and by guaranteeing that grievances in the ranks are addressed in policy. Furthermore, using various means of intelligence gathering, the DSC closely scrutinizes North Korean movements and international developments to ensure constant readiness against contingencies engendered by North Korean provocation.

NATIONAL SECURITY COUNCIL

http://www.dsc.or.kr/

The National Security Council and the Ministry of National Defense were the primary executive bodies responsible for military affairs. The former, comprising the prime minister, the director of the Agency for National Security Planning (ANSP), and the ministers of national defense, foreign affairs, home affairs, and finance, was responsible for advising the president on security issues and was convened at the pleasure of the president. The Ministry of National Defense was organized into bureaus responsible for force development, budget, personnel, reserve forces, logistics, military installations, medical affairs, the defense industry, and the military education system

DEFENSE SECURITY COMMAND

http://www.dsc.or.kr/

Defense Security Command (DSC) was originally founded as "Army Counter-Intelligence Corps" on October 21, 1950, and it worked as the forerunning anti-Communist force on shattering the attempts by the North Korean regime to disintegrate the Korean Military, as well as strengthening the military power and establishing an independent national defense. Ever since it changed its official title to Defense Security Command on 01 January 1991, in order to comply with the era of change and reform, it has been enforcing necessary changes for the command while maintaining its main objective of upkeeping military confidentiality and counterintelligence activities as a pure "military intelligence and investigation organization".

The DSC (and its predecessors) was created to deal with the real question of loyalty within a military on a divided peninsula. It was inspired by the Guomindang model, in which political officers monitored the military services for subversion or disloyalty. The DSC was responsible for monitoring the military for loyalty; safeguarding military information; monitoring domestic political, economic, and social activities that might jeopardize military capabilities and national unity; maintaining defense industrial security--both physically and in terms of counterespionage; countering North Korean infiltration; detecting espionage and anticommunist law violations; and conducting special investigations at the direction of the president.

It was Syngman Rhee, not the military, who initiated the political involvement of the military in intelligence activities. The turning point came in 1952 when Rhee proclaimed martial law-- and the presence of military police in the chamber of the National Assembly guaranteed passage of the constitutional amendment he sought over the objections of a recalcitrant legislative branch and still-independent judicial branch. Throughout Rhee's administration, two military units--the Joint Military Provost Marshal and the army Counterintelligence Corps (CIC)--engaged in extralegal and violent political tactics, apparently not excluding the outright murder of politically undesirable people. Although the details never were disclosed fully, more than a few minor political figures' disappearances were connected to the two units.

Under Park, the provost marshal's political role declined, while the CIC and its successor, the Army Security Command (ASC), concentrated on internal military security. The CIC/ASC, which was under Park's direct control, maintained strict surveillance over all high-ranking officers. It acted as a deterrent to wouldbe coup leaders. It tried, less successfully, to prevent the rise of disruptive factions within the military.

The Defense Security Command was formally activated in October 1977. This merger of the Army Security Command, the Navy Security Unit, and the Air Force Office of Special Investigations produced a single, integrated unit under the direct command and operational control of the minister of national defense. Although technically subordinate to the minister, the DSC commander operated semiautonomously and typically had personal, direct access to the president. Given the disparity in service size, the old ASC predominated within the DSC. The strength of the DSC varied over time within a probable range of 5,000 to 7,000 people during the 1980s.

The DSC assigned small elements to all major military units to monitor security and loyalty. These elements operated outside the unit's chain of command and performed a highly effective independent audit function. The DSC representatives never rivaled unit commanders as political officers occasionally had in communist military units. Their input into officer evaluations, however, often played a decisive role in career progression, giving DSC members influence far beyond their rank and producing friction between them and the "regular" military. Corruption within the DSC was difficult to verify, but political manipulations, misappropriation of operating funds, and undue influencing of promotions certainly occurred and were particularly rampant in the mid- to late 1970s.

For most of the Park regime, the ASC/DSC remained concerned primarily with internal military matters and was involved in the Yun P'il-yong incident in 1972 and removing the army chief of staff, General Yi Se-ho, in 1979 for corruption. Yun P'il-yong, head of the Capital Garrison Command, was court martialed, along with several close followers, on charges of bribery and corruption. His "real" offense, however, was creating a faction among the classes of the four-year graduates of the Korea Military Academy. Yun's faction did not disappear when he was purged. The group of young officers, who called themselves the "Hanahoe," (One Mind Society), had its origins in an alumni group, the Taegu Seven Stars, of seven young officers, including Chun Doo Hwan and Roh Tae Woo, from the first graduating class of the Academy (Class 11). The Hanahoe evolved into a group of some 200 members through ten graduating classes. In 1979 and 1980, Chun drew on the Hanahoe in his ascent to power. The irony of Park's death at the hands of his KCIA chief in 1979, however, was compounded by the rise to power of the commander of the DSC, then Major General Chun Doo Hwan, who used the military's anticoup apparatus to ensure the success of his own coup .

During and following Chun's rise to power, the DSC greatly expanded its charter into domestic politics and during the early 1980s was, perhaps, the dominant domestic intelligence service. The DSC was "credited" with masterminding the media reorganization of 1980 and with being the midwife for the first political parties of the Fifth Republic. Many former DSC members played prominent roles in Chun's administration and in the ruling Democratic Justice Party.

The end of the Fifth Republic brought the DSC under even more pressure than the ANSP to cut back on its domestic political activities. Both the DSC and the ANSP withdrew from the National Assembly at the same time in 1988. In October 1988, Minister of National Defense O Cha-bok reported to the National Assembly that the DSC would concentrate on counterespionage activities, preventing the spread of communism, conducting "relevant research," major restructuring, and would discontinue the investigation of civilians. Subsequently, the DSC eliminated the Office of Information that had been charged with collecting information on civilians, whose members had been active in local government offices. As a result of this move, 116 small detachments were disbanded, and the DSC announced plans to cut 860 personnel, or 14 percent of its 1990 strength. Additionally, the DSC curtailed its involvement in security screening of nonmilitary government personnel. An official of the DSC claimed that surveillance of politicians was turned over to "another agency." Given the historically broad interpretation of national security threats espoused by DSC personnel, however, many analysts doubted that the DSC had totally disengaged from domestic political surveillance. Despite the democratic trends of the late 1980s, intelligence and security agencies still were populated by individuals who were both institutionally and personally loyal to the president and ready to use any means at their disposal to support him.

DSC welcomes all reports and inquiries in order to search out North Korean spies who are threatening the national security and peace by engaging in secret maneuvers within our society, as well as pro-North leftists who, following the directions of the North Korean regime, infiltrate into the Korean military and try to obstruct operations. People to be reported include those:

- Keeping in touch with someone who voluntarily has been to North Korea in the past
- Unintentionally using peculiar North Korean words in speech, or secretly burying objects at well-marked places such as near cemetries and around big trees
- Hiding walkie-talkies or firearms, wearing a Korean military uniform while bearing an M-16 rifle, or taking photographs of military facilities and airports
- Propagandizing the ideology of the North Korean regime such as "juche" and instigating servicemen to form factions inside military

Each case is promptly handled on the scene by DSC's branches all around the nation. Swift arrests are possible since the troops are quickly put into operation upon the outbreak of each situation As a

special agency against spies and pro-North leftists, DSC makes sure to thoroughly verify the substance in order to reach a satisfying conclusion for each report, and the knowledgeable experts are available for helpful advice.
Additional areas of responsibility include:

- Matters related to improving or impeding morale of soldiers and battle capability
- Matters related to soldiers and troops who give good or bad impression to people
- Matters related to reports about persons who have or let out military secrets
- Matters related to reports for environmental preservation, such as discharging polluted water or illegally burying wastes from constructions and hospitals
- Matters related to construction and placement of military facilities, such as reports about unlawfulness and unreasonableness of the overseeing managers in military construction work or illegal infringement of lands for military use
- Matters related to munition supply, such as reports about bribery in connection with certain munition companies or illegal carry-out of goods for military use
- Other kinds of matters related to military

NATIONAL INTELLIGENCE SERVICE

DIRECTOR OF NIS KO YOUNG KOO

http://www.nis.go.kr

The Korea Central Intelligence Agency (KCIA) was created in 1961, and in 1981 the agency changed its name to the Agency for National Security Planning (NSP). In 1994, the NSP had its law revised following the agreement between Korea's ruling and opposition parties and established an "Information Committee" in the Assembly to lay a foundation for political neutrality. The NSP also launched operations against international crime and terrorism to protect the Korean people from international organized crime.

The Korean Central Intelligence Agency (KCIA) was originally established on June 19, 1961 as the directly under the Supreme Council for National Reconstruction in the immediate aftermath of the May 16, 1961, military coup. Its duties were to "supervise and coordinate both international and domestic intelligence activities and criminal investigation by all government intelligence agencies, including that of the military." Its mission was akin to that of a combined United States Central Intelligence Agency and Federal Bureau of Investigation.

The first head of the KCIA was Kim Chong-p'il. Kim, utilizing the existing Army Counterintelligence Corps, built a 3,000-member organization--the most powerful intelligence and investigatory agency in the republic. The KCIA maintained a complex set of interlocking institutional links with almost all of the government's key decision-making bodies. The KCIA had a nearmonopoly over crucial information concerning national security under the charter of the Act Concerning Protection of Military Secrets and, more importantly, possessed considerable veto power over other agencies through its supervisory and coordination functions.

The KCIA's practically unlimited power to investigate and to detain any person accused of antistate behavior severely restricted the right to dissent or to criticize the regime. The frequent questioning, detention, or even prosecution of dissidents, opposition figures, and reporters seriously jeopardized basic freedoms and created an atmosphere of political repression.

Under Park, the lack of advancement in civil liberties continued to be justified by referring to the threat from North Korea. The political influence of the Ministry of Home Affairs and the police declined in the face of the KCIA's power. The relationship between the police and general public, however, was not significantly altered. As Se-Jin Kim wrote in 1971: "The former still act with arbitrary arrogance; the latter respond with fear but not respect."

The government often used martial law or garrison decree in response to political unrest. From 1961 to 1979, martial law or a variant was evoked eight times. The October 15, 1971, garrison decree, for example, was triggered by student protests and resulted in the arrest of almost 2,000 students. A year later, on October 17, 1972, Park proclaimed martial law, disbanded the National Assembly, and placed many opposition leaders under arrest. In November the yusin constitution (yusin means revitalization), which greatly increased presidential power, was ratified by referendum under martial law.

The government grew even more authoritarian, governing by presidential emergency decrees in the immediate aftermath of the establishment of the yusin constitution; nine emergency decrees were declared between January 1974 and May 1975. The Park regime strengthened the originally draconian National Security Act of 1960 and added an even more prohibitive Anticommunism Law. Under those two laws and Emergency Measure Number Nine, any kind of antigovernment activity, including critical speeches and writings, was open to interpretation as a criminal act of "sympathizing with communism or communists" or "aiding antigovernment organizations." Political intimidation, arbitrary arrests, preventive detention, and brutal treatment of prisoners were not uncommon.

Opposition to the government and its harsh measures increased as the economy worsened in 1979. Scattered labor unrest and the government's repressive reactions sparked widespread public dissent: mass resignation of the opposition membership in the National Assembly and student and labor riots in Pusan, Masan, and Ch'angwon. The government declared martial law in the cities. In this charged atmosphere, under circumstances that appeared related to dissatisfaction with Park's handling of the unrest, on October 26, 1979, KCIA chief Kim Chae-gyu killed Park and the chief of the Presidential Security Force, Ch'a Chi-ch'ol, and then was himself arrested. Emergency martial law was immediately declared to deal with the crisis, placing the head of the Defense Security Command, Major General Chun Doo Hwan, in a position of considerable military and political power.

After the 1979 assassination of President Park Chung Hee by the KCIA director, the KCIA was purged and temporarily lost much of its power. Chun Doo Hwan used his tenure as acting director of the KCIA from April to July 1980 to expand his power base beyond the military.

The slow pace of reform led to growing popular unrest. In early May 1980, student demonstrators protested a variety of political and social issues, including the government's failure to lift emergency martial law imposed following Park's assassination. The student protests spilled into the streets, reaching their peak during May 13 to 16, at which time the student leaders obtained a promise that the government would attempt to speed up reform. The military's response, however, was political intervention led by Lieutenant General Chun Doo Hwan, then KCIA chief and army chief of staff. Chun, who had forced the resignation of Ch'oe's cabinet, banned political activities, assemblies, and rallies, and arrested many ruling and opposition politicians. In Kwangju, demonstrations to protest the extension of martial law and the arrest of Kim Dae Jung turned into rebellion as demonstrators reacted to the brutal tactics of the Special Forces sent to the city. The government did not regain control of the city for nine days, after some 200 deaths.

The KCIA was renamed the Agency for National Security Planning, and its powers were redefined in presidential orders and legislation. The ANSP, like its predecessor, was a cabinet-level agency directly accountable to the president. The director of the ANSP continued to have direct presidential access. In March 1981, the ANSP was redesignated as the principal agency for collecting and processing all intelligence. The requirement for all other agencies with intelligence-gathering and analysis functions in their charters to coordinate their activities with the ANSP was reaffirmed.

Legislation passed at the end of 1981 further redefined the ANSP's legally mandated functions to include the collection, compilation, and distribution of foreign and domestic information regarding public safety against communists and plots to overthrow the government. The maintenance of public safety with regard to documents, materials, facilities, and districts designated as secrets of the state was the purview of the ANSP as was the investigation of crimes of insurrection and foreign aggression, crimes of rebellion, aiding and abetting the enemy, disclosure of military secrets, and crimes provided for in the Act Concerning Protection of Military Secrets and the National Security Act.

The investigation of crimes related to duties of intelligence personnel, the supervision of information collection, and the compilation and distribution of information on other agencies' activities designed to maintain public safety also were undertaken by the ANSP. By 1983 the ANSP had rebounded and again was the preeminent foreign and domestic intelligence organization.

Discontent was kept under control until 1987 by the regime's extensive security services--particularly the Agency for National Security Planning, the Defense Security Command (DSC), and the Combat Police of the Korean National Police (KNP). Both the civilian ANSP and the military DSC not only collected domestic intelligence but also continued "intelligence politics."
The Act Concerning Assembly and Demonstration was used to limit the expression of political opposition by prohibiting assemblies likely to "undermine" public order. Advanced police notification of all demonstrations was required. Violation carried a maximum sentence of seven years' imprisonment or a fine. Most peaceful nonpolitical assemblies took place without government interference. However, the act was the most frequently used tool to control political activity in the Fifth Republic, and the Chun regime was responsible for over 84 percent of the 6,701 investigations pursued under the act.

The security presence in city centers, near university campuses, government and party offices, and media centers was heavy. Citizens, particularly students and young people, were subject to being stopped, questioned, and searched without due process. The typical response to demonstrations was disruption by large numbers of Combat Police, short-term mass detention of demonstrators, and selective prosecution of the organizers. Arrest warrants--required by law--were not always produced at the time of arrest in political cases.

The National Security Act increasingly was used after 1985 to suppress domestic dissent. Intended to restrict "antistate activities endangering the safety of the state and the lives and freedom of the citizenry," the act also was used to control and punish nonviolent domestic dissent. Its broad definition of offenses allowed enforcement over the widest range, wider than that of any other politically relevant law in South Korea. Along with other politically relevant laws such as the Social Safety Act and the Act Concerning Crimes Against the State, it weakened or removed procedural protection available to defendants in nonpolitical cases.

Questioning by the security services often involved not only psychological or physical abuse, but outright torture. The 1987 torture and death of Pak Chong-ch'ol, a student at Seoul National University being questioned as to the whereabouts of a classmate, played a decisive role in galvanizing public opposition to the government's repressive tactics.

The security services not only detained those accused of violating laws governing political dissent, but also put under various lesser forms of detention--including house arrest--those people, including opposition politicians, who they thought intended to violate the laws. Many political, religious, and other dissidents were subjected to surveillance by government agents. Opposition assembly members later charged in the National Assembly that telephone tapping and the interception of correspondence were prevalent. Ruling party assembly members, government officials, and senior military officials probably also were subjected to this interferencal though they did not openly complain.

Listening to North Korean radio stations remained illegal in 1990 if it were judged to be for the purpose of "benefiting the antistate organization" (North Korea). Similarly, books or other literature considered subversive, procommunist, or pro-North Korean were illegal; authors, publishers, printers, and distributors of such material were subject to arrest.

Use of tear gas by the police (over 260,000 tear gas shells were used in 1987 to quell demonstrations) increasingly was criticized; the criticism eventually resulted in legal restrictions on tear gas use in 1989. The government continued, however, to block many "illegal" gatherings organized by dissidents that were judged to incite "social unrest." In 1988 government statistics noted 6,552 rallies involving 1.7 million people. There were 2.2 million people who had particiated in 6,791 demonstrations in 1989.

As of 1990, the organizational structure of the ANSP, was considered classified by Seoul, although earlier organizational information was public knowledge. Despite the social and political changes that came with the Sixth Republic, the ANSP apparently still considered the support and maintenance of the president in power to be one of its most important roles. In April 1990, for example, ruling Democratic Liberal Party (DLP) coleader Kim Young Sam complained that he and members of his faction within the DLP had been subjected to "intelligence maneuvering in politics" that included wiretapping, surveillance, and financial investigations.

Nevertheless, the ANSP's domestic powers were indeed curtailed under the Sixth Republic. Prior to the change, the ANSP had free access to all government offices and files. The ANSP, Defense Security Command, Office of the Prosecutor General, Korean National Police, and the Ministry of Justice had stationed their agents in the National Assembly to collect information on the activities of politicians. In May 1988, however, overt ANSP agents, along with agents of other intelligence agencies, were withdrawn from the National Assembly building.

The ANSP's budget was not made public, nor apparently was it made available in any useful manner to the National Assembly in closed sessions. In July 1989, pressured by opposition parties and public opinion, the ANSP was subjected to inspection and audit by the National Assembly for the first time in eighteen years. The ANSP removed its agents from the chambers of the Seoul Criminal Court and the Supreme Court in 1988.

As of 1990, however, the ANSP remained deeply involved in domestic politics and was not prepared to relinquish the power to prevent radical South Korean ideas--much less North Korean ideas- -from circulating in South Korean society. Despite an agreement in September 1989 by the chief policymakers of the ruling and opposition parties to strip the ANSP of its power to investigate pro-North Korean activity (a crime under the National Security Act), the ANSP continued enforcing this aspect of the law rather than limiting itself to countering internal and external attempts to overthrow the government. The ANSP continued to pick up radical student and dissident leaders for questioning without explanation.

In another move to limit the potential for the ANSP to engage in "intelligence politics," the ANSP Information Coordination Committee was disbanded because of its history of unduly influencing other investigating authorities, such as the Office of the Prosecutor General. Additionally, the ANSP, responding to widespread criticism of its alleged human rights violations, set up a "watchdog" office to supervise its domestic investigations and to prevent agents from abusing their powers while interrogating suspects.

Aside from its controversial internal security mission, the ANSP also was known for its foreign intelligence gathering and analysis and for its investigation of offenses involving external subversion and military secrets. The National Unification Board and the ANSP (and the KCIA before it) were the primary sources of government analysis and policy direction for South Korea's reunification strategy and contacts with North Korea. The intelligence service's reputation in pursuing counterespionage cases also was excellent.

The ANSP monitored visitors, particularly from communist and East European countries, to prevent industrial and military espionage. Following the diplomatic successes of the late 1980s-- the establishment of diplomatic relations with the Soviet Union and the countries of Eastern Europe, and the increased informal contacts with China, Mongolia, and Vietnam--this mission grew in importance. The security watch list contained 162 out of 3,808 visitors from communist nations in 1988 and 226 out of 6,444 visitors in 1989.

In 1995, by relocating to a new intelligence building equipped with up-to-date facilities in Naegok-dong, southern Seoul, from its 34-year-old site in Mt. Nam in downtown Seoul and Imun-dong, eastern Seoul, the NSP laid the cornerstone to becoming a 21st century, advanced intelligence agency. With the inauguration of the People's Government, on 22 January 1999 the agency was renamed the National Intelligence Service (NIS). The former Minister of Defense Chun Yong-taek took office as the 23rd Director General of the National Intelligence Service on 26 May 1999. He had served as National Assemblyman, Party member of the Government of the People, Minister of Defense, and Lieutenant-general in the armed forces reserve.

National Intelligence Service missions and functions include:

- Collection, coordination, and distribution of information on the nation's strategy and security
- Investigation of crimes affecting national security, including crimes that violate the Military Secrecy Protection Law, the National Security Law, which prohibit the incitement of civil war, foreign troubles, and insurrection
- Investigation of crimes related to the missions of NIS staff
- Maintenance of documents, materials, and facilities related to the nation's classified information
- Planning and coordination of information and classified information

SECRET INTELLIGENCE SERVICE OF THE LATE CHOSUN DYNASTY

The roots of modern intelligence gathering in Korea can be traced back almost 100 years, when King Kojong of the late Chosun Dynasty operated a clandestine intelligence agency, according to facts revealed by a recently-discovered text entitled, "the Je kook Ik Moon Sa Bee Bo Jang Jung(Secret Code of Imperial Press)".

Disguised as a news agency, the intelligence organization was founded in 1902 under the official title, "the Je Kook Ik Moon Sa(the Imperial Press)". This secret service was the first organization in Korea, with the attributes of a modern intelligence agency, with its own tightly-knit organization and strict codes of conduct for its operatives.

At that time, stability on the Korean Peninsula was affected by both domestic and foreign threats, primarily political rifts formed between factions of incompetent officials and power struggles by foreign powers -- Japan, China's Quing Dynasty, and Russia.

In an attempt to save the kingdom from the danger of collapse, King Kojong decided to establish a secret intelligence agency.

The old text is essentially a code book that outlines the purpose, organization, major intelligence objectives, briefing methods, and operating guidelines that were utilized by the intelligence agency.

Headquartered in Seoul, the agency "gathered and reported intelligence information to the king on a daily basis, so that he could be well informed and prepared to make the right decisions," according to the text.

Under the leadership of a supervisor, three officials were put in charge of piecing together, writing, and delivering secret information. Also, 61 agents posing as reporters, were dispatched to Seoul, each of the kingdom's provinces, major port cities, as well as Japan, China and Russia.

These agents were divided into five categories according to their mission -- 16 permanent correspondents covered government ministries and provincial government branches, 15 regular correspondents covered each district of Seoul, 21 special correspondents covered foreign diplomatic missions, Japanese military installations and port facilities, while nine foreign correspondents resided in Japan, China and Russia.

Another category of agents were the so-called "temporary correspondents," whose number the agency either increased or decreased depending on the situation. These agents were dispatched to the various provinces of Korea, as well as to foreign countries, thereby adding flexibility in the number of operatives that could be dispatched to a certain location, according to varying situations.

Perhaps one of the most striking aspects of the agency is that its intelligence-gathering activities were conducted on foreign soil. The agency dispatched two agents to Tokyo and Shanghai, and one agent to Osaka, Nagasaki, Beijing, Vladivostok and Yesun. At their respective areas of operation, Korean agents gathered intelligence information on policies affecting Korea, the political climate of the host country, and monitored ethnic Koreans there who were either fugitives from Korean laws or had been classified as hostile to the interests of Korea.

These overseas agents gathered 72 different categories of intelligence information-- 30 in Seoul, 18 in the various provinces of Korea, 12 in major port facilities and 12 in foreign countries.

Agents gathered 16 different categories of intelligence data on Japanese activities in Korea in the areas of troop movements, and the activities of Japanese police, politicians, merchants, religious figures, employees of railway firms, academics and underworld figures.

To mask its true identity, the Imperial Press Agency published a daily newspaper which featured praiseworthy episodes in Korea, misdeeds of Koreans and foreigners, instances of royal benevolence, and articles for sounding out public opinion. The agency also published important books.

To protect classified information, confidential reports were written using a special chemical, visible to agents only after a secret curing method was applied to the paper.

Financing for the agency was provided through monthly payments each government ministry submitted, and the funding system appears to have been a prudent method which ensures a stable and continuous life span of the agency.

Documents detailing the specific activities of Imperial Press Agency operatives have yet to be discovered, possibly due to strict levels of security that were practiced.

Judging from these facts, it appears that there has been a full-fledged effort by future-oriented thinkers to change the fate of the threatened kingdom through the use of an advanced intelligence agency.

DEALING WITH TERRORIST ACTIVITIES

In accordance with the guidelines above, the military, the police and other related government organizations are performing counter-terrorism activities in their given capacity. In particular, thorough

inspections of travelers and goods brought into Korea at airports and harbors are performed in order to prevent the entry of international terrorists and goods to be used for terrorism.
In addition, to prepare for possible terrorist activities such as the abduction of hostages, the military and the police command counter-terrorism troops assembled as an elite special attack unit. They have strengthened their combat tactics through training simulations of actual scenarios, and are therefore fully prepared to immediately go into action to protect lives and property in the event of an emergency situation.

- Prevention of terrorist activities

In the wake of increased global terrorist threats that have surfaced surrounding large-scale international events such as the World Cup Games in Korea and the 2004 Olympics in Athens, the Security Measures Control Center has formulated and implemented counter-terrorism and security measures at the government level, and through such efforts, the World Cup Games concluded without incident. Moreover, through cooperation with intelligence agencies around the world, the activities and whereabouts of international terrorists and criminals were continually monitored to prevent their entry into Korea. Additionally, through monitoring activities at airports and harbors, a list of international terrorists and criminals was compiled and measures were taken to block their entry or infiltration.

- Counter-Terrorism activities of the National Intelligence Service (NIS)

The NIS carefully analyzes terrorism-related information and terrorist attacks occurring around the world to look for signs of terrorist activities in order to protect people and property. Such information is then communicated to relevant units, and the NIS is cooperating with related institutions overseas.

Korea has taken on a greater role in the international community after the successful completion of the World Cup Games in 2002, the Busan Asian Games and other major international events. Korea also participates in a continually increasing number of global activities due to its improved national strength and the frequent occurrence of terrorist activities in Southeastern Asia. The expectation is that there will be an increased number of terrorist threats from rebellious forces at home and abroad. Thus, the Korean government will augment its counter-terrorism activities to protect lives and property.

NATIONAL POLICE AGENCY

http://www.npa.go.kr

The Korean National Police Agency system consists of, from the top: one National Police Headquarters located in Seoul; 5 special task police agencies, including Marine Police; 13 provincial police headquarters; 220 police stations; and 3,389 police branch offices across the country. The Korean Police has its own chain of command independent of the Army. There are no local municipal police systems or state police departments like those in many western nations.

During the Japanese Occupation Period. (1910 - 1945) Japan established the Police Administration Bureau (1910) under the Governnor-general in Choson. This had forced discontinuation of the Korean police system and caused the people's hatred and mistrust about the police. With the end of World War II, Korea restored its independence on August 15, 1945. However, Korea was suffering from disorder and chaos without any countermeasure or systematic organization to ensure public peace and order. On 17 August 1945 an autonomy organization was established by the Preparatory Committee for the Establishment of the Republic of Korea (Chairman: Yeo Woonyoung) This contributed to the public peace and order until the US Army was stationed in Korea on September 9. Various organizations formed, such as the Public Peace Corps., Student Organizations, Youth Organizations, Guards Corps., Self-Defence Organization, and Choson Student Group.
The Police Administration Office was established under the U.S. Miliatary Government on October 21, 1945, with Police Administration Departments in each province.

On 01 January 1946 the Police Administration Bureau was elevated to the Police Administration Department by Military Government Order No.23104 [Subject of Police Administration Bureau and Police Administration Department] . Subsequently the Provincial Police Departments were reorganized to District Police Bureaus (9 districts nationwide).
The new government that had declared the establishment of the Republic of Korea on August 15, 1948, took over administrative power from U.S. Military Government on September 13. However, the policy system did not remain as a department but was downgraded as an office within the Ministry of Home Affairs. The July 17, 1948 Law of Government Organizations Article 15 (Korean Law No. 1) stated that the Minister of Home Affairs shall govern the affairs on local administration, election, security, fire fighting, road, bridge, rivers, water service, construction and statistics and supervise the local organization for public peace and order to provide the basis of subordination to the Ministry of Home Affairs. On 03 September 1948 the Police Administration Department became subordinate to the Security Bureau in the Ministry of Home Affairs; local the police headquaters became subordinate to provincial Governors.

As the National Assembly was dismissed by emergency martial law, on 17 October 1972 the government suddenly decided upon the so called "October Revitalization"style of Korean democracy. In 1974, the government started to study the police system to revive the proper functionality of the police. The Security Bureau was upgraded to the Security Headquarters and the Head of the Security Bureau was promoted to chief of Security Headquarter at the vice-minister level. The Security Bureau of the Ministry of Home Affairs was reorganized on 24 December 1974 into the Security Headquarters with three departments. The Personnel Education Department was established within the Department NO.1 and the Computer Center was established within Department NO.3. In the 1990s the Police searched for the political neutralization of the police.

The efforts for this neutralization, such as the introduction of a bill based on the committee type that organized the national police committee belonging to the Prime Minister on March, 1989, and enlisted the police agency under the banner of the committee, has been continued. On May 31, 1991, the Police Law was established and promulgated. On July 31, 1991, the Police Committee of the Ministry of Home Affairs was inaugurated. The matter for the main policy about personnel management, budget, equipment, communications etc. and the development of police affairs, the matter for the management and improvement of police related to safeguard the human rights, the matter for the cooperation of affairs from the other national organization except police affairs, and the matter that is presented to a committee by recognition of the Ministry of Internal Affairs and NPA Commissoner General are deliberated and decided.

On 01 August 1991 the NPA was inaugurated as an independent government organization which is not a subordinate organization of the Ministry of Home Affairs. It was reorganized to one Deputy Commissoner General, nine major staffs, and 41 sections, with reenforced management through the planning, readjustment and control. The NPA was reorganized into large departments and large sections by considering specialization and efficiency.
The police box is a first-line organization of the police and served as a base for anti-crime activities for maintaining the security of an area in consideration of the population, area, administrative district, frequency of crime. The total number of nationwide police boxes is 3,422, manned by 38,000 policeman; 43% of the entire police force work day and night in protecting the population from crime.

The NPA performs various surveillance activities to guard against the appearance of anarchistic ideology struggle; reappearance of anti-democratic and anti-government violence. It also monitors increased labor circle meetings and demonstrations due to the IMF impact. Activities include watching various events such as ceremonial meetings, athletic events, and guarding the people visiting hometowns or parent's graves. The NPA utilizes its own order keeping guardians as well as guardians from security guard service company, allocating a minimum number of policemen when keeping order is required. It is also responsible for checking the protection status of important facilities and paying guidance visits to protect them from various dangerous activities. The chief of the facility takes primary responsibility for protection; the police takes responsibility for guidance and supervision. Protection of candidate activities include pre-investigate and present disrupting activities to the election speech sites, voting place and ballot counting locations.

PRESIDENTIAL SECURITY SERVICE (PSS)

http://www.cwd.go.kr

The Presidential Security Service (PSS) is charged with providing security for the President, his immediate family and the Blue House, the presidential residence. The PSS is also authorized to protect former Presidents, their spouses and minor children for seven years after leaving office. PSS is also charged with protecting security for visiting heads of foreign states, their accompanying spouse and family, and other visiting dignataries when deemed necessary for national interest.

The Kyong Mu Dae Presidential Security Police (predecessor to the present Presidential Security Service) was established in 1949, and was renamed Blue House Presidential Police in 1960. In 1961 the Security Force to protect Park Chung Hee, National Revolution Leader, was established. The PSS was established in 1963 after PSS Law 157 was enacted, with Hong Jong Chul as its first Chief. After the 1968attack against the Blue House by North Korean guirillas, PSS responsibilities are increased. After the First Lady was fatally shot in a 1974 failed attempt to assassinate President Park Chung Hee by Moon Sei Kwang, acting under orders from the North Korean government, PSS was given sigificantly greater authority over presidential security operations including mobilization of military, police, etc. These measures included enactment of Security Committee for presidential protection (Executive Order 7246) and of Security Control Unit for presidential protection (Executive Order 7246).

A reduction of PSS responsibilities came after the assassination of President Park Jung Hee in 1979. This included abolishment of Security Committe for presidential protection (Executive Order 9692) and abolishment of Security Control Unit for presidential protection (Executive Order 9692). The 1981 revision of Presidential Security Law (PSL) included enactment of the Protection Law for former presidents and their families. The PSS began protecting the President-elect and his family, along with a revision of Security Committee for presidential protection. After North Korean agents commit a terrorist bombing attack in Myanmar in 1983, PSS responsibilities were broadened and intensified for the presidential entourge.

NORTH KOREA

INTELLIGENCE AGENCIES

Central Committee Korean Workers Party
Cabinet General Intelligence Bureau
Liaison Department
Research Department for External Intelligence (RDEI)
General Association of Korean Residents in Japan (Chosen Soren)

General Staff Department
Reconnaissance Bureau
State Safety & Security Agency
State Security Department
Ministry of Public Security

THE PUBLIC SECURITY APPARATUS

http://www.korea-dpr.com/
korea@korea-dpr.com.

The Ministry of Public Security and the State Security Department are responsible for internal security. Although both are government organs, they are tightly controlled by the party apparatus through the Justice and Security Commission and the penetration of their structures by the party apparatus at all levels. The formal public security structure is augmented by a pervasive system of informers throughout the society. Surveillance of citizens, both physical and electronic, also is routine.

The Ministry of Public Security, responsible for internal security, social control, and basic police functions, is one of the most powerful organizations in North Korea and controls an estimated 144,000 public security personnel. It maintains law and order; investigates common criminal cases; manages the prison system and traffic control; monitors citizens' political attitudes; conducts background investigations, census, and civil registrations; controls individual travel; manages the government's classified documents; protects government and party officials; and patrols government buildings and some government and party construction activities.

The ministry has vice ministers for personnel, political affairs, legal counselling, security, surveillance, internal affairs, rear services, and engineering. There are approximately twenty-seven bureaus, but the functional responsibilities of only some of the bureaus are known. The Security Bureau is responsible for ordinary law enforcement and most police functions. The Investigation Bureau handles investigations of criminal and economic crimes. The Protection Bureau is responsible for fire protection, traffic control, public health, and customs. The Registration Bureau issues citizen identification cards and maintains public records on births, deaths, marriages, residence registration, and passports.

Below the ministry level, there are public security bureaus for each province and directly administered city. These bureaus are headed by either a senior colonel or a lieutenant colonel of police, depending on the size of the population. Public security departments at each city or county and smaller substations through the country are staffed by about 100 personnel. They are organized roughly parallel to the ministry itself and have several divisions responsible for carrying out various functions.

In 1973 political security responsibilities were transferred from the Ministry of Public Security to the State Security Department, an autonomous agency reporting directly to Kim Il Sung. The State Security Department carries out a wide range of counterintelligence and internal security functions normally associated with "secret police." It is charged with searching out antistate criminals--a general category that includes those accused of antigovernment and dissident activities, economic crimes, and slander of the political leadership. Camps for political prisoners are under its jurisdiction. It has counterintelligence responsibilities at home and abroad, and runs overseas intelligence collection operations. It monitors political attitudes and maintains surveillance of returnees. Ministry personnel escort high-ranking officials. The ministry also guards national borders and monitors international entry points. The degree of control it exercises over the Political Security Bureaus of the KPA--which has representatives at all levels of command--is unclear.

The Border Guards are the paramilitary force of the Ministry of Public Security. They are primarily concerned with monitoring the border and with internal security. The latter activities include physical protection of government buildings and facilities. During a conflict, they would probably be used in border and rear area security missions.

MINISTRY OF PUBLIC SECURITY SOCIAL SAFETY MINISTRY

The Ministry of Public Security [also termed the Social Safety Ministry] and the State Security Department are responsible for internal security. Although both are government organs, they are tightly controlled by the party apparatus through the Justice and Security Commission and the penetration of their structures by the party apparatus at all levels. The formal public security structure is augmented by a pervasive system of informers throughout the society. Surveillance of citizens, both physical and electronic, also is routine. In 1973 political security responsibilities were transferred from the Ministry of Public Security to the State Security Department, an autonomous agency reporting directly to the President.

The Ministry of Public Security, responsible for internal security, social control, and basic police functions, is one of the most powerful organizations in North Korea. It controlled an estimated 144,000 public security personnel in the early 1990s, and by the end of the decade the total staff was estimated to number some 180,000 persons. It maintains law and order; investigates common criminal cases; manages the prison system and traffic control; monitors citizens' political attitudes; conducts background investigations, census, and civil registrations; controls individual travel; manages the government's classified documents; protects government and party officials; and patrols government buildings and some government and party construction activities.

The ministry has vice ministers for personnel, political affairs, legal counselling, security, surveillance, internal affairs, rear services, and engineering. There are approximately twenty-seven bureaus, but the functional responsibilities of only some of the bureaus are known. The Security Bureau is responsible for ordinary law enforcement and most police functions. The Investigation Bureau handles investigations of criminal and economic crimes. The Protection Bureau is responsible for fire protection, traffic control, public health, and customs. The Registration Bureau issues citizen identification cards and maintains public records on births, deaths, marriages, residence registration, and passports.
Below the ministry level, there are public security bureaus for each province and directly administered city. These bureaus are headed by either a senior colonel or a lieutenant colonel of police, depending on the size of the population. Public security departments at each city or county and smaller substations through the country are staffed by about 100 personnel. They are organized roughly parallel to the ministry itself and have several divisions responsible for carrying out various functions.

The Public Security Bureau is North Korea's equivalent of a police force, and its duties are to maintain public security and investigate crime, issue citizen registration cards to monitor movement of the populace, and provide security for various facilities.

Every thirty to forty North Korean households are organized into a managed by a Unit Supervisor, Chief of Heads of Households, and Sanitation Chief. The heads handle all day-to-day administration and work in cooperation with the Public Security Bureau to monitor members of the unit. Individual party committees have been installed at every level of the military and government, and all major economic and social organizations. This binds all the organizations to the party and makes for a more effective control mechanism.

The Border Guards are the paramilitary force of the Ministry of Public Security. They are primarily concerned with monitoring the border and with internal security. The latter activities include physical protection of government buildings and facilities. During a conflict, they would probably be used in border and rear area security missions.

Special Custody Areas, Political Prisoners Custody Zones, or Political Prisoners Concentration camps are some of the synonyms for approximately ten detention camps for political prisoners located in Yodock, Hoeryong, or other mountainous areas in North Korea. The total estimated number of prisoners, most of whom are interned without due process of law, stands at 200000, representing 0.8% of the population, or one prisoner for every 115 North Koreans. Internees include anyone declared "threats to the regime," usually a wide array of people designated "enemies of the state" such as purged "sectarians", counterrevolutionaries and anti-party elements; former landlords, Japanese collaborators, religious clergy, and families of defectors to the south. Residents repatriated from Japan accused of criticizing the system constituted the greater percentage of the internees in the past. They are being replaced by cadres who have been defeated in frequent political struggles and their families, whose numbers have been on the rise since the establishment of the North's cult of personality, for obvious reasons.

Tight security measures check all escape attempts and possible disturbances. At the perimeter of the camps are four to six fences, each ten to thirteen feet high. Points along the perimeter deemed easy escape routes are fortified by electrical fences, minefields, and booby traps, in addition to guards posted in 20-feet-high guard posts located every two kilometers. Anyone attempting escape is shot dead immediately upon discovery, and those lucky enough to survive become living targets in training exercises for the special forces.

Neither political nor human rights exist in the camps, and prisoners exist as instruments of labor and production. Registration cards are confiscated upon arrival, and internees cannot vote. Rations are kept to a minimum, and marriage and childbirth are banned, as well as letters, visits, and other means of contact with the outside world. The daily schedule of the prisoners depends on the season and the type of work assignment. Teams assigned to farm work usually rise at five or six AM, with their work ending at eight. They go to bed at ten PM following two hours of roll-call and re-education. Prisoners in the mines work in three shifts, regardless of seasons.

The diet consist of corn, potatoes, wheat, and barley supplied once every harvest season. Up to 600 grams were alloted per mineworker per day, with 500 grams for other prisoners. The rations have been reduced to 100 to 200 grams following the food crisis. No condiments, side dishes, or vegetables are provided, and garlic and pepper for seasoning have to be grown within the premises. The prisoners are collecting anything from wild herbs, plant roots, even frog eggs, or undigested beans in the cow dung, out of sheer desperation for anything with nutritional value. Living quarters are usually fashioned from plyboards or straw mats, and diseases like pellagra, tuberculosis, and hepatitis are endemic due to poor living conditions and malnutrition.

CABINET GENERAL INTELLIGENCE BUREAU

The majority of the North Korean intelligence agencies are within the Cabinet General Intelligence Bureau of the Korean Worker's Party Central Committee.

The Liaison Department is responsible for conducting intelligence operations in South Korea and Japan. Its agents are used to undermine the South Korean government by supporting internal subversion and to gather information on U.S. forces in Korea.

The Research Department for External Intelligence (RDEI) is the primary agency responsible for foreign intelligence collection. The RDEI is composed of four geographic subsections, one of which is North America.

GENERAL ASSOCIATION OF KOREAN RESIDENTS IN JAPAN (CHOSEN SOREN)

Chosen Soren (the General Association of Korean Residents in Japan - *Zainichi Chosenjin Sorengokai*), the association of Korean residents in Japan, is North Korea's *de facto* embassy in Tokyo. Since *Chosen* was the formal name of Korea when Japan ruled the peninsula, and Japan does not have diplomatic relations with the North, Korean nationals who do not change their nationality to South Korea remain Chosen nationals. The *Chosen Soren* (in Japanese), or *Chongryon* (in Korean), was founded on May 25, 1955. The number of members has declined from 290,000 in 1975 to 200,000 today. Its organizational structure includes the headquarters in Tokyo, prefectural and regional head offices and branches with eighteen mass propaganda bodies and twenty-three business enterprises. Nearly one-third of the Japanese *pachinko* [pinball] industry is controlled by *Chosen* affiliates or supporters. *Chosen* remittences in hard currencies to Pyongyang have been variously estimated at between $600 million and $1.9 billion each year, with the most likely value in the lower to middle of this range. In recent years the amount has substantially decreased. In 1994, Japanese police testified that some $600 million was being sent to North Korea, though this amount has recently declined to $100 million a year or less.

Gakushu-gumi is *Chosen*'s underground organization, which is a quasi-formal body of the North Korean Workers' Party.

Gakushu-gumi , with a membership estimated at 5,000, engages in intelligence activities and political maneuverings against South Korea. The *Chosen Soren* supports intelligence operations in Japan, assists in the infiltration of agents into South Korea, collects open source information, and diverts advanced technology for use by North Korea. North Korea uses several methods to acquire technology related to nuclear, biological, or chemical warfare and missiles. The *Chosen Soren* has among other activities an ongoing effort to acquire and export advanced technology to North Korea.

RECONNAISSANCE BUREAU

The Reconnaissance Bureau of the General Staff Department is responsible for collecting strategic, operational, and tactical intelligence for the Ministry of the People's Armed Forces. It is also responsible for infiltrating intelligence personnel into South Korea though tunnels under the demilitarized zone and seaborne insertion.

By any consideration North Korea has one of the world's largest special operations forces. Estimates of the size of the army's special operations forces ranged from 60,000 persons to over 100,000 persons. The uncertainty over the number derives from both the lack of information and the varying definitions of special operations forces. Organized into twenty-two brigades and at least seven independent battalions, the special operations forces are believed to be the best trained and to have the highest morale of all North Korean ground forces.

Special operations forces were developed to meet three basic requirements: to breach the flankless fixed defense of South Korea; to create a "second front" in the enemy's rear area, disrupting in-depth South Korean or United States reinforcements and logistical support during a conflict; and to conduct battlefield and strategic reconnaissance. The ultimate goal was to create strategic dislocation. The additional missions of countering opposing forces and internal security were added over time.

The Ministry of the People's Armed Forces controls the bulk of the special operations forces through one of two commands, the Reconnaissance Bureau and the Light Infantry Training Guidance Bureau. The Reconnaissance Bureau is the primary organization within the Ministry of People's Armed Forces for the collection of strategic and tactical intelligence. It also exercises operational control over agents engaged in collecting military intelligence and in the training and dispatch of unconventional warfare teams. The Light Infantry Training Guidance Bureau is directly subordinate to the General Staff Department. The party directly controls approximately 1,500 agents.

Operations are categorized on the basis of the echelon supported. Strategic special operations forces support national or Ministry of People's Armed Forces objectives, operationalsupported corps operations, and tactical-supported maneuver divisions and brigades. Strategic missions of special operations forces in support of national and Ministry of People's Armed Forces objectives involve reconnaissance, sniper, and agent operations, but not light infantry operations, which primarily are tactical operations. The main objectives of these units are to secure information that cannot be achieved by other means, neutralize targets, and disrupt rear areas. In executing these operations, special operations troops may be disguised either as South Korean military personnel or as civilians.

Strategic missions require deep insertions either in advance of hostilities or in the initial stages by naval or air platforms. Based on available insertion platforms, North Korea has a one-time lift capability of 12,000 persons by sea and 6,000 persons by air. Most North Korea special operations forces infiltrate overland and are dedicated to operational and tactical missions, that is, reconnaissance and combat operations in concert with conventional operations in the forward corps. Although it is unknown how forces will be allocated, limits on North Korea's insertion capabilities constrain operational flexibility and determine the allocation of strategic, operational, and tactical missions.

North Korean army special operations forces units are broken down into three categories based on mission and mode of operation: agent operations, reconnaissance, and light infantry and sniper. The Reconnaissance Bureau has four sniper brigades and at least seven independent reconnaissance battalions. The Light Infantry Training Guidance Bureau controls fourteen light infantry/sniper brigades: six "straight-leg" brigades, six airborne brigades, and two amphibious brigades. Four light infantry brigades of unknown subordination are under the operational control of the forward corps. In addition, each regular infantry division and mechanized brigade has an special operations forces battalion.
Reconnaissance units are employed in rear area, strategic intelligence collection, and target information acquisition. Light infantry units operate in company- or battalion-sized units against military, political, or economic targets. Sniper units are distinguished from light infantry units in that their basic operational unit is the team, rather than the larger company or battalion of the light infantry unit.

A reconnaissance brigade consists of between 3,600 and 4,200 personnel. It is organized into a headquarters, rear support units, a communications company, and ten reconnaissance battalions. The basic unit of operation is the reconnaissance team, which has from two to ten men. A light infantry brigade has between 3,300 and 3,600 personnel organized into between five and ten battalions. The brigade can fight as a unit or disperse its battalions for independent operations. A sniper brigade's organization parallels that of the light infantry brigade.

The unique special operations forces dedicated to strategic operations are the two amphibious light infantry/sniper brigades subordinate to the Light Infantry Guidance Bureau. These brigades are believed deployed to Wonsan on the east coast and Namp'o and Tasa-ri on the west coast. In organization and manpower, they are reduced versions of the regular light infantry brigades. The two brigades have a total strength of approximately 5,000 men in ten battalions. Each battalion has about 400 men organized into five companies each. Some amphibious brigade personnel are trained as frogmen.

In the 1970s, in support of overland insertion, North Korea began clandestine tunneling operations along the entire DMZ, with two tunnels per forward division. By 1990 four tunnels dug on historical invasion routes from the north had been discovered by South Korean and United States tunnel neutralization teams: three in the mid-1970s and the fourth in March 1990. The South Koreans suspect there were as many as twenty-five tunnels in the early 1990s, but the level of ongoing tunneling is unknown.

At the operational and tactical level, infiltration tactics are designed for the leading special operations forces brigades to probe and penetrate the weak points of the defense; disrupt the command, control, and communications nodes; and threaten lines of communication and supply. To achieve its goal of nearterm distraction and dislocation of the defender, at least one special operations forces brigade is assigned to each of the four regular army corps deployed along the DMZ.

STATE SAFETY & SECURITY AGENCY STATE SECURITY DEPARTMENT

The Ministry of Public Security and the State Security Department are responsible for internal security. Although both are government organs, they are tightly controlled by the party apparatus through the Justice and Security Commission and the penetration of their structures by the party apparatus at all levels. The formal public security structure is augmented by a pervasive system of informers throughout the society. Surveillance of citizens, both physical and electronic, also is routine.

The State Safety & Security Agency is the supreme public security apparatus. In 1973 political security responsibilities were transferred from the Ministry of Public Security to the State Security Department [also known as the State Political Security Agency], an autonomous agency reporting directly to the President. The Ministry of State Political Security was separated from the State

Administration Council altogether in April, 1982 and renamed the State Security Agency. It was renamed the State Safety & Security Agency in early 1993.

The State Safety & Security Agency carries out a wide range of counterintelligence and internal security functions normally associated with "secret police." The Agency carries out duties to ensure the safety and maintenance of the system such as search for and management of anti-system criminals, immigration control, activities for searching out spies and impure and anti-social elements, collection of overseas information, and supervision over ideological tendencies of residents. It is charged with searching out antistate criminals--a general category that includes those accused of antigovernment and dissident activities, economic crimes, and slander of the political leadership. Camps for political prisoners are under its jurisdiction. It has counterintelligence responsibilities at home and abroad, and runs overseas intelligence collection operations. It monitors political attitudes and maintains surveillance of returnees. Agency personnel escort high-ranking officials. The Agency also guards national borders and monitors international entry points. The degree of control it exercises over the Political Security Bureaus of the KPA--which has representatives at all levels of command--is unclear.

Total personnel number some 50,000 persons. The State Safety & Security Agency is supervised by the director, and there are several deputy directors for organization, investigation, censorship, and other specialized responsibilities. There are state security bureaus in each province (or metropolitan area) and city (or county). Security staffers are stationed in the smallest municipalities, and are dispatched even to individual institutions and public corporations. The agency is likely under direct control of Kim Jong-il, as no one was selected to succeed the late director Lee Jin-soo after his death in Oct. 1987.

LUXEMBOURG

INTELLIGENCE AGENCIES

CONTACTS

Service Information et Presse
33, boulevard Roosevelt
L-2450 Luxembourg
Europe

Tél: +352 478 2181
Fax: +352 47 02 85
E-mail: info@sip.etat.lu

MINISTRY OF STATE

Service de Renseignements de l'Etat (SRDE) (French)
(*National intelligence agency*)
Haute Commissariat de la Securite Exterieure (HCSE) (French)
(*High commission for foreign security*)

MINISTRY OF DEFENSE

http://www.gouvernement.lu/gouv/fr/gouv/minist/aececd.html
2ieme Bureau de l'Armee (French)
(*Military intelligence and security agency*)

THE NETHERLANDS

MINISTRY OF HOME AFFAIRS

Algemene Inlichtingen- en Veiligheidsdienst (AIVD)
(*General Intelligence and Security Service*)
(formerly the BVD)

MINISTRY OF DEFENSE

Militaire Inlichtingen- en Veiligheidsdienst (MIVD)
(*Military Intelligence and Security Service*)
Koninklijke Marechaussee, Bijzondere Dienst en Veiligheid (Kmar/BD&V)
(*Military police, Special section for intelligence and security*)
Bijzondere Bijstands Eenheid
(*Special Help Union* Anti-Terrorist Service)

Landmachtstaf Prinses Julianakazerne
Thérèse Schwartzestraat 15
Postbus 90711
2509 LS Den Haag
Tel 070 316 91 11

Marinestaf Frederikkazerne
Admiraliteit Van der Burchlaan 31
Postbus 20702
2500 ES Den Haag
Tel 070 3169111

Luchtmachtstaf Binckhorsthof
Binckhorstlaan 135
Postbus 20703
2500 ES Den Haag
Tel 070 339 6911

Staf Koninklijke Marechaussee Koningin Beatrixkazerne
Van Alkemadelaan 85
Postbus 90615
2509 LP Den Haag
tel 070 441 40 00

Dienstverlenende organisaties zijn samengebracht :
Commando DienstenCentra
Koningin Marialaan 17
Postbus 20701
2500 ES Den Haag
Tel 070 318 7900

MINISTRY OF JUSTICE

Ministerie van Binnenlandse Zaken en Koninkrijksrelaties
Postbus 20010
2500 EA Den Haag
Telefoon en fax

Telefoon: 070 - 3178610
Fax: 070 - 3200733

Korps landelijke politiediensten (KLPD)
(Commission of National Police Services)

NEW ZEALAND

INTELLIGENCE AGENCIES

Parliament
Intelligence and Security Committee (I&SC)
Security Intelligence Service (SIS)
Government Communications Security Bureau [GCSB]
New Zealand Police
Criminal Intelligence Bureau [CIB]
Financial Intelligence Unit [FIU]

CABINET STRATEGY SUBCOMMITTEE ON INTELLIGENCE AND SECURITY

The Cabinet Strategy Subcommittee on Intelligence and Security, chaired by the Prime Minister, considers issues of oversight, organisation and priorities for the New Zealand intelligence community and any issues which, because of their security or intelligence implications, the Prime Minister directs be considered by the committee. This Committee has power to act where security considerations so require, subject to any decisions requiring the consideration of the allocation of additional resources being referred to the Cabinet Strategy Subcommittee on Expenditure Control and Government Administration and Cabinet.

GOVERNMENT COMMUNICATIONS SECURITY BUREAU [GCSB]

The mandate of the Government Communications Security Bureau [GCSB] is to satisfy the foreign intelligence requirements of the NZ Government. The focus of its intelligence activities is restricted to foreign intelligence. GCSB collects, assesses, produces reports and disseminates foreign intelligence to meet the national foreign intelligence requirements of the New Zealand Government and its agencies. It also has subsidiary functions which assist its collection capability by signals research identification and analysis of signal sources and devices.

Collection is made from electronic communication transmitted through satellite, radio waves or other open means. GCSB does not intercept private or other communication transmitted by telephone land lines. GCSB operates a satellite monitoring station at Waihopai near Blenheim and a radio receiving station at Tangimoana near Foxton. These are both capable of receiving and collecting foreign intelligence. The equipment is equally capable of receiving signals transmitted by radio and satellite which do not include foreign intelligence and which are domestic concerning and involving NZ citizens.

Government initiatives announced in 1997 to enhance the foreign signals intelligence collection capability of the GCSB include constructing a second antenna at Waihopai and to extend the authority of the GCSB to collect foreign voice communications. The latter was attended to by the making of the Crimes (Exemption of Listening Device) Order 1997. That exempted the GCSB's station at Waihopai from the provisions of Part IX.A of the Crimes Act 1961 for the purpose only of intercepting foreign voice communications containing foreign intelligence.

Through the UK-USA agreements, GCSB has links with the National Security Agency US, Communications Security Establishment Canada, Defence Signals Directorate Australia and the Government Communications Headquarters United Kingdom.

FINANCIAL INTELLIGENCE UNIT

New Zealand's Police Financial Intelligence Unit is a member of the Egmont Group. At present there is no evidence of any significant money laundering activities taking place in New Zealand. As a member of FATF, New Zealand has criminalized money laundering and has a range of anti-money laundering measures in place.

MEXICO

INTELLIGENCE AGENCIES

Office of Coordination of the Presidency
Centro de Información de Seguridad Nacional
Center for Research on National Security (CISEN) [1989-]
Secretaría de la Defensa Nacional
Secretariat of National Defense (SEDENA)
S-2 Second Section (Military Intelligence)
General Transmissions Directorate (DGT)
Federal Military Judicial Police
Secretaría de Marina
Secretariat of the Navy (SM)
Secretaría de Relaciones Exteriores
Secretariat of Foreign Relations (SRE)
Secretaría de Seguridad Pública y Servicios a la Justicia
Secretariat of Public Security (SSP)
Procuraduría General de la República
Attorney General of the Republic (PGR)
Special Prosecutor's Office for Crimes Against Health (FEADS)
National Institute for Combating Drugs (INCD)
Center for Drug Control Planning (CENDRO)
Policía Judicial Federal
Federal Judicial Police (PJF)
Policía Judicial del Distrito Federal
Federal District Judicial Police (PJDF)
Policía Judicial Estatal
State Judicial Police (PJE)

MOROCCO

DIRECTION DE LA SURVEILLANCE DU TERRITOIRE (DST)

Colonel-Major Hamidou Laanigri is Director General of the "Direction de la Surveillance du Territoire" (DST) - Moroccan Secret Service
Col. Driss Basri was appointed head of the counter-intelligence unit (Direction generale de la Surveillance du territoire - DST) in the late 70s.

NIGERIA

INTELLIGENCE AGENCIES

http://www.aivd.nl/

Provisional Ruling Council (PRC)
Nigerian Security Organisation (NSO)
National Intelligence Agency (NIA)
State Security Service (SSS)

National Guard
Special Bodyguard Unit
Defence Intelligence Agency (DIA)
Ministry of Internal Affairs
Nigeria Police Force (NPF)
Federal Investigation and Intelligence Bureau (FIIB)
National Drug Law Enforcement Agency

NORWAY

INTELLIGENCE AGENCIES

Control Committee for the Intelligence and Security Services Kontrollutvalget for overvåkings- og sikkerhetstjenesten

National Police Security Service Politiets sikkerhetstjeneste
http://www.pst.politiet.no/
post@pst.politiet.no
22 66 81 22

Joint Defense Security Service Forsvarets sikkerhetstjeneste

NORWEGIAN INTELLIGENCE SERVICE ETTERRETNINGSTJENESTEN

http://www.mil.no
PO Box 193
Alnabru bedriftssenter
N-0614 Oslo
NORWAY
Phone: +47 23 09 40 00
Fax: +47 23 09 44 00
E-mail: post@foe.mil.no

The Norwegian Intelligence Service (NIS) is Norway's only foreign intelligence service. The NIS Director General is directly subordinated the Chief of Defence Norway.

The NIS provides information on developments outside of Norwegian territory and contributes to maintaining Norway's sovereignty. The Norwegian Intelligence Service collects, processes and analyses information relevant to Norwegian interests; information on other states, organisations and individuals. The NIS keeps close track on events and global developments and provides relevant information to the Norwegian authorities within its area of responsibility.

On behalf of the Chief of Defence Norway, the Director General shoulders the responsibility for co-ordinating and providing advice on all intelligence-related activities within the Norwegian Armed Forces.

Following the end of the Cold War, the NIS has been presented with a number of new challenges. The Intelligence Act was passed in 1998, and the Regulations to the Act were presented in 2001. International terrorism, proliferation of weapons of mass destruction and supranational environmental issues are new key areas for the Norwegian Intelligence Service.

The NIS has a number of land-based collection sites and has for many years made use of a vessel for monitoring of military activities, collection of intelligence information and military research in the Northern region, the "F/S Marjata".

PAKISTAN

The separation in 1947 of British India into the Muslim state of Pakistan (with two sections West and East) and largely Hindu India was never satisfactorily resolved. A third war between these countries in 1971 resulted in East Pakistan seceding and becoming the separate nation of Bangladesh. A dispute over the state of Kashmir is ongoing. In response to Indian nuclear weapons testing, Pakistan conducted its own tests in 1998. The Kashmir dispute is now again threatening the "peace" between the two nations.

GENERAL

Pakistan is located between Iran and Afghanistan on the west and India on the east and China in the north.
The official name of the country is Islamic Republic of Pakistan - "Pakistan" in short.
Pakistan is a federal republic with capital Islamabad.

ADMINISTRATIVE DIVISIONS

4 provinces (Balochistan, North-West Frontier Province, Punjab, Sindh), 1 territory (Federally Administered Tribal Areas) and 1 capital territory (Islamabad Capital Territory).
Note: the Pakistani-administered portion of the disputed Jammu and Kashmir region includes Azad Kashmir and the Northern Areas.

MILITARY BRANCHES

Army, Navy, Air Force, Civil Armed Forces, National Guard.

INTELLIGENCE AND SECURITY

- Ministry of Interior
- Federal Investigation Authority (FIA)
- Narcotics Control Division
- Intelligence Bureau (IB)
- Directorate of Inter-Services Intelligence (ISI)
- Directorate of Inter-Services Public Relations
- Military Intelligence (MI)

From 1958 to 1970, the USA maintained one of the largest SIGINT stations in the world at Bada Bier in Pakistan. The base was located on a strategic place near Afghanistan and only 240 km from the Soviet border. Ideal to eavesdrop on Soviet and Chinese communications. In the early 1980's the USA was permitted to re-establish the Bada Bier station. The US needed a new facility because they had to abandon the Iran facility in 1979 and reportedly moved back to Bada Bier. The station was now useful to monitor the Soviet/Afghan war.
Russian SIGINT posts were (still are?) established in the Russian consulate in Karachi and the embassy in Islamabad.

MINISTRY OF INTERIOR

The Ministry of Interior is responsible for two agencies: the Federal Investigative Agency and the Narcotics Control Division. In addition to these agencies, the government has control over a number of specialized police forces and paramilitary organisations:

NATIONAL GUARD

The National Guard has the following branches: Janbaz Force, Mujahid Force, National Cadet Corps and the Women Guards

FRONTIER CORPS

The Frontier Corps are subordinate to the Ministry of Interior.

PAKISTAN RANGERS

Pakistan Rangers are also subordinate to the Ministry of Interior.

OTHER ORGANISATIONS

- Anti-corruption Task Force
- Railroad and Airport Police Forces
- Maritime Security Agency
- Coast Guard

FEDERAL INVESTIGATIVE AGENCY (FIA)

The duties of the security forces in the British days were mainly the maintenance of law and order, not very different from their current duties.

The FIA reportedly has contacts with the Israeli Mossad to investigate Islamist terrorists. In the past the agency clashed with the ISI when the FIA launched a secret war against the Islamists.

NARCOTICS CONTROL DIVISION (NCD)

The Narcotics Control Division was formed in April, 1989. Prior to that date, the Ministry of Interior and the PNCB -Pakistan Narcotics Control Board- handled these matters.

PNCB and the ANTF -Anti Narcotics Task Force- are the two main branches of the NCD, where PNCB is in charge of the coordinating, controlling and supervisory functions, and the ANTF investigates everything that has to do with drugs (smuggling, production, transportation, etc, etc.)

INTELLIGENCE BUREAU (IB)

IB is one of the most important security agencies in Pakistan that reports directly to the Prime Minister's office. The agency is mainly focussed on domestic political activities. It monitors politicians, political activists, suspected terrorists, and suspected foreign intelligence agents and politicians.

DIRECTORATE FOR INTER-SERVICES INTELLIGENCE (ISI)

Together with the Intelligence Bureau and Military Intelligence, ISI is one of the main intelligence agencies of Pakistan. It was founded in 1948 and is charged with safeguarding Pakistan's interests, monitoring opposition politicians, and sustaining military rule in Pakistan.

The ISI is a very powerful agency that reportedly answers to nobody; not to the government and not to the military. According to various sources no-one seems to be in total control over the ISI. Their actions are often dubious; rumor has it that the war in Kashmir is financed with drugs money generated by the ISI.

The tasks of the ISI include:

- SIGINT activities.
- collection of intelligence, both domestic and international.
- surveillance of foreigners, embassy and consulate personnel in Pakistan and Pakistani diplomats in other countries.

The ISI has a number of divisions, including:

- Joint Counter Intelligence Bureau (JCIB). JCIB is responsible for surveillance of Pakistani diplomats abroad, as well as for conducting intelligence operations in the Middle East, Afghanistan, South Asia, China and the Muslim republics of the former Soviet Union.
- Joint Intelligence Miscellaneous (JIM) conducts espionage and covert activities in foreign countries.
- Joint Intelligence X (JIX) is the administrative division of the ISI.
- Joint Intelligence Bureau (JIB). This division is responsible for political intelligence.
- Joint Signal Intelligence Bureau (JSIB) operates a chain of SIGINT collection stations along the border with India, and provides communication support to militants operating in Kashmir.
- Joint Intelligence North (JIN) is responsible for operations in Jammu, Kashmir and Afghanistan.
- Joint Intelligence Technical (JIT) is tasked with the collection of technical intelligence.

Like the ISPR, the ISI is also affiliated with the Joint Chiefs of Staff Committee. This committee deals with the military aspects of state security.
When the Soviets invaded Afghanistan, the CIA provided ISI a large quantity of espionage equipment and information. Throughout the years of Soviet occupation of Afghanistan and recently during the war against terrorism in Afghanistan, governmental relations between the USA and Pakistan were close, although forces within the ISI sided with Al Qaida and supplied them with weapons and information. Not surprising of course as the ISI supported the Taliban and trained some 83,000 Afghan Mujahideen warriors during the Soviet occupation of Afghanistan. Now they support Kashmiri Mujahideen in their fight against the Indian authorities in Kashmir. The ISI is not only involved in the politics in Kashmir and Afghanistan, but also plays an important role in domestic politics. It is widely believed that the 1990 elections were fixed by the ISI.
Like Al Qaida, the ISI is reported to operate training camps where terrorist groups, separatist or freedom fighters (or whatever they like to call themselves) are trained. The following groups are mentioned in this respect:

- Liberation Tigers
- United Liberation Front Of Seven Sisters [ULFOSS]
- National Security Council of Nagaland [NSCN]
- People's Liberation Army [PLA]
- United Liberation Front of Assam [ULFA]
- North East Students Organisation [NESO]

OFFICE OF INTER-SERVICES PUBLIC RELATIONS (ISPR)

The ISPR controls and coordinates the release of military news and access to military sources. The agency censors the news coverage with regards to the armed forces, intelligence and certain political sensitive matters.

MILITARY INTELLIGENCE (MI)

MI's activities include operations in Sindh against the Indian intelligence operatives. This organization also monitors the activities of the leaders of political opposition groups.

INTELLIGENCE AND SECURITY

- Ministry of Interior
- Federal Investigation Authority (FIA)
- Narcotics Control Division

- Intelligence Bureau (IB)
- Directorate of Inter-Services Intelligence (ISI)
- Directorate of Inter-Services Public Relations
- Military Intelligence (MI)

SECURITY THREATS

Pakistan came into existence on August 14, 1947 with the Partition and independence of British India. The creation of a separate Muslim nation was accomplished largely through the efforts of Mohammed Ali Jinnah (known as the QuaidiAzam or "great leader"). Jinnah served as Pakistan's first Governor-General until his death in 1948; his picture graces virtually every official Pakistani office. Pakistan initially consisted of two areas, East Pakistan and West Pakistan, separated by 1,000 miles of Indian territory. In 194748, Pakistan and India fought the first of their three wars involving the Muslimmajority territory of Kashmir, which both claimed and whose Hindu maharajah opted for India at Partition. The conflict ended in stalemate and Kashmir remains disputed territory divided by a heavilydefended Line of Control where since 1948 UN observers have investigated reported violations.
As Pakistan passed its first half-century of existence, its security problems had changed yet were in many ways the same.

The global setting has altered radically, but the enmity with India remains a constant, although it has gained in predictability and, probably, stability. Subversion is still a potential rather than an active threat. Problems of law and order are more acute, but the means of dealing with them has not changed greatly. Rather, Pakistan's security problems are rooted in its own polity and society. Repeated political collapse, corruption, inability to define its ethnic and religious identities, and failure to meet the needs of the people are challenges that could eviscerate a state even with the most capable military machine and efficient security apparatus.

Poverty remains a serious problem in Pakistan. Average per capita income was only $495 in 1995-96, and income and wealth are not equitably distributed. The population of 135 million is growing at almost 3 percent per year. Domestic political instability throughout the Bhutto administration and continuing ethnic and sectarian violence under the caretakers and the government of Nawaz Sharif who was elected February 3, 1997, has stunted foreign investment.

Internal threats to Pakistan come from several sources. The greatest danger to the democratic constitutional structure is posed by the recurrent intervention in the government of the Pakistani military and, since the Zia years, by the president who, under the controversial Eighth Amendment to the constitution, is empowered to arbitrarily dismiss the prime minister and National Assembly as well as the provisional governors. It could be argued that the military has only intervened when the political situation has deteriorated hopelessly and that the threat is in fact from much more deepseated problems.
Another danger is the problem of ethnic unrest. Punjab, with almost 60 percent of the population, dominates almost all aspects of national life. This fact is resented by smaller ethnic groups, all of whom have at one time been actively dissident.

For the most part, with the exception of Sindh, the situation was quiet in the early 1990s. Sparsely settled Balochistan required an extensive pacification campaign by the army from 1973 to 1977, and both Afghan and Soviet involvement was alleged.

After the war in Afghanistan, however, there was no source of outside support and no significant violence. The potential for unrest remains, however, because Baloch feel threatened by the growing numbers of non-Baloch moving into the province. The North-West Frontier Province has long been restive and subject to Kabul's blandishments on the basis of shared Pakhtun identity, but Afghanistan no longer offers a feasible alternative, and the Afghan Pakhtun tribal groups have participated rather well in Pakistan's modest prosperity. Some Kashmiris in Pakistani-held Azad (Free) Kashmir probably envision a future independent of Pakistan, but their attentions have been absorbed by the problems of Indian-held Kashmir.

In the early 1990s, the principal challenge in civil unrest came from Sindh, Pakistan's second most populous province, where the indigenous population was under increasing pressure from non-Sindhis who had migrated there. Based on their ethnic identity, Sindhis have formed several political movements, notably the Jaye Sindh, which the government perceived as threatening to Pakistan's unity. Islamabad also claimed that these groups were receiving help from India in their quest to establish a "Sindhudesh," or independent homeland for Sindhis. The muhajir (immigrants from India and their descendants) minority in Sindh, which dominated Karachi and the other cities, have been in sharp conflict with the Sindhis and other ethnic groups. Further, large numbers of kidnapping and bombings in Sindh--the virtual breakdown of law and order--necessitated the imposition of army rule in 1992.

An additional source of unrest has been the rampant gun culture and spread of narcotics-based corruption, particularly since the war in Afghanistan. Pakistanis have always been well armed, but the availability of cheap, modern weapons has meant that criminals and private citizens have significant firepower at their disposal. Because most violence is criminal or anomic, it does not pose a direct threat to the state, but should the crisis of governability in Sindh spread more broadly, it could place unbearable stress on the nation.

In the early 1990s, foreign-sponsored subversion in Pakistan appeared to be insignificant. The Afghans were too preoccupied with their own concerns to agitate along the frontier, and the Soviet Union, which had long had adversarial relations with Pakistan, had fragmented into a number of self-absorbed states occupied by the struggle for survival in a new postcommunist world.

India has ties to dissident groups in Sindh and perhaps elsewhere; these, however, are probably maintained in order to remind Pakistan that its involvement with Punjabi Sikh and Kashmiri Muslim insurgents in India was not cost-free. In its more youthfully exuberant days, the Islamic regime in Iran was involved in subversive support of Shia elements in Pakistan, but such activity was no longer a significant factor.

During the Zia period, a group called Al-Zulfiqar, operating from Damascus and Kabul and seeking to destabilize the government through terrorist actions hijacked, an aircraft in 1981. Murtaza Bhutto, a son of Zulfiqar Ali Bhutto, was involved, and AlZulfiqar claimed to have some relationship to the Pakistan People's Party (PPP), which was totally denied by the PPP. Although authorities have reported continued activity by AlZulfiqar , its existence is shadowy at best, and with the return of democratic rule, its activities have been insignificant. There are no other known, organized subversive groups that threaten the government in any serious way.

Pakistan's attitude toward terrorism is somewhat more ambivalent than that of most other countries. On the one hand, Al-Zulfiqar demonstrated to Pakistan the importance of international cooperation in combatting international terrorism as manifested in airplane hijackings and bombings. On the other hand, however, Pakistan has had no qualms about supporting insurgents in India, some of whom were engaged in activities that can only be described as terrorist.

In January 1993, the United States warned Pakistan that it was under "active continuing review" for possible inclusion on the Department of State list of terrorist countries for its alleged support of terrorist activities in the Indian states of Punjab and Kashmir. By July, however, the United States had withdrawn its threat, having determined that Pakistan had implemented "a policy for ending official support for terrorism in India."

PAKISTAN INTELLIGENCE - BACKGROUND

Pakistan's foreign policy stance shifted significantly in 1953 when it accepted the United States offer of military and economic assistance in return for membership in an alliance system designed to contain international communism. When the administration of Dwight D. Eisenhower sought a series of alliances in the "Northern Tier"--Pakistan, Iran, and Turkey--and in East Asia, Pakistan became a candidate for membership in each. In 1954 Pakistan signed a Mutual Defense Agreement with the United States and became a member of the Southeast Asia Treaty Organization (SEATO). The following year, Pakistan joined Iran, Iraq, and Turkey in the Baghdad Pact, later converted into the Central Treaty Organization (CENTO) after Iraq's withdrawal in 1959. Pakistan also leased bases to the United States for intelligence -gathering and communications facilities. Pakistan saw these agreements not as bulwarks against Soviet or Chinese aggression, but as a means to bolster itself against India.

During the regime of General Ziaul Haq, CIA provided ISI a large quantity of espionage equipment along with training and other information. Initially Pakistani intelligence was trained along British lines, but subsequently CIA, trained 200 ISI officers in improved intelligence methods.

Throughout the years of Soviet occupation of Afghanistan, relations between the United States and Pakistan were best characterized by close cooperation. Still, United States policy makers became increasingly concerned that Zia and his associates- -most notably, General Akhtar Abdur Rahman, then head of the Directorate for Inter-Services Intelligence --appeared to give preferential treatment to the Islamic fundamentalists, especially mujahidin leader Gulbaddin Hikmatyar.

INTELLIGENCE BUREAU

The three main intelligence agencies in Pakistan are ISI, Military Intelligence [MI] and the Intelligence Bureau [IB]. Each agency has its own specific responsibilities, but all share the common goal of preserving Paksitan's national security. Since any significant domestic or foreign political activity impinges on national security, there has traditinally been considerable overlap in the activities of these three agencies. The ISI and MI have generally focused on matters of immediate military interest, and the IB concentrated on domestic political activities.

Prior to the imposition of Martial Law in 1958, the IB reported directly to the Prime Minister and the two military agencies to the Commander-in-Chief of the Army (C-in-C). When martial Law was promulgated in 1958 all the intelligence agencies fell under the direct control of the President and Chief Martial Law Administrator, and the three intelligence agencies began competing to demonstrate their loyalty to Ayub Khan and his government.
The Intelligence Bureau monitors politicians, political activists, suspected terrorists, and suspected foreign intelligence agents.The IB keeps tabs on political operatives from countries it considers hostile to Pakistan's interests, and it is responsible for harassing domestic opposition parties. Credible reports indicate that the authorities commonly resort to wiretapping and occasionally intercept and open mail.

The Intelligence Bureau is under the Prime Minister's cabinet division. A total of Rs. 25.8 million was spent on the IB in 1976-77. The Intelligence Bureau grew in importance with the re-election of Benazir Bhutto in 1993. One of her most controversial appointments to government posts was that of Masood Sharif as Director General Intelligence Bureau. Sharif was believed to have played an active role in toppling the Shabir Shah government in the North West Frontier Province (NWFP). His appointment precipitated a major crisis in the Pakistani state apparatus, because Benazir then began using the IB chief to erode the once all powerful ISI's base. Benazir's attempts to root out the influence of military intelligence in the country's internal affairs mirrored the failed efforts of her father in the 1970s. This was the last straw as far as the military was concerned.

In his order dismissing Prime Minister Bhutto on 05 November 1996, President Leghari accused the Government of massive illegal wiretapping, including the telephone conversations of judges, political party leaders, and military and civilian officials. One of the first acts of President Leghari after dismissing Benazir was to imprison Masood Sharif, head of Intelligence Bureau under Prime Minister Benazir Bhutto. He was arrested and imprisoned, not on corruption charges but as part of a murder investigation.

On 15 December 1996, the caretaker government announced that effective immediately all foreign and domestic mail was to be subject to censorship by the Special Branch and the Intelligence Bureau.

EHTESAB [ACCOUNTABILITY] BUREAU

The Government has sometimes used the "accountability" process--by which the present Government hopes to expose previous wrongdoing, recoup ill-gotten gains, and restore public confidence in government institutions--for political purposes by arresting a number of prominent politicians and bureaucrats connected with the main opposition party. Few of those arrested and questioned have been put on trial.

The Accountability Commission established by the caretaker government and headed by a retired judge has been overshadowed by an "accountability cell" headed by a close associate of the Prime Minister. This cell has been accused of conducting politically-motivated investigations of politicians, senior civil servants, and business figures, designed to extract evidence and in some cases, televised confessions of alleged wrongdoers. Some examples of televised confessions included Salman Farooqi, Secretary of Commerce under Benazir Bhutto; Ahmed Sadiq, Benazir Bhutto's principal secretary; and Zafar Iqbal, chairman of the Capital Development Authority.

Corruption is prevalent in both public and private sectors in Pakistan. Early in 1997, the government initiated an accountability process aimed at identifying corrupt individuals. An Accountability and Coordination Cell was established in the Prime Ministerns Secretariat, tasked with monitoring and coordinating the accountability process. The Federal Investigation Authority (FIA), conducts the investigations on receiving reports of corruption, either through the Accountability and Coordination Cell or directly from the public. After the investigations, the cases are referred to the Chief Ehtesab Commissioner for trial by the Ehtesab courts. However, the Chief Ehtesab Commissioner, Mr Mujaddad Ali Mirza, has complained that the Federal Investigation Authority and the Anti-Corruption Police have failed to cooperate with the Commission.

To date, the government has booked over 250 cases of corruption against senior civil servants and bureaucrats working in both the federal and provincial ministries and corporations like WAPDA, OGDC, Pakistan Steel, National Highways Authority, PIA, Railways, etc. The government has suspended 87 officials in its anticorruption drive including 16 high officials of the Oil and Gas Development Corporation.

Those involved in the corruption charges are prominent politicians, bankers, bureaucrats, members of judiciary (judges and lawyers) and business magnates. Some of them have been dismissed from service, a few arrested, while investigations are under way against some very high officials. The corruption charges include : non-payment of huge loans taken from the nationalized commercial banks and financial institutions, massive financial irregularities, frauds committed in the purchase of project equipment, award of large project and service contracts in violation of the prescribed rules and regulations, selling of state lands on throw away prices, allotment of residential lands to favorites. According to some estimates, 30 percent to 40 percent of the original cost of many projects end up in the pockets of contractors and officials in the shape of kickbacks and commissions.

The point which is causing the most concern to common people is the purpose behind setting up a chain of Ehtesab Committees across the country. Even more disconcerting is the move to repeat the follies of the past by reinvesting politicians with a new clout that empower them to nominate their agents of doubtful integrity to a chain of divisional, district and sub-divisional Ehtesab Committees. The choice of the people to be targeted is arbitrary. The Ehtesab Cell starts a media trial of the accused even before their cases are sent to the courts, using the APP and radio and TV for their character assassination while they are yet to be proved guilty. As if this was not enough to discredit the process of accountability, the chief of the Accountability Cell is making deals with various business houses in a way that can only be termed as murky.

In order to made the whole process of accountability both even-handed and transparent, the Accountability Cell must not target only the people whom the government has reasons to dislike. Further, the government must fix criteria for making deals with the parties accused of owing money to the state or to the banks. All deals should be open to public scrutiny.

MINISTRY OF DEFENSE

Tel: 9248439, Fax:9248426

Deals with all policy and administrative matters pertaining to all the armed forces engaged in the defence of the country. The Ministry of Defence has two Divisions : Defence Division and Defence Production Division.

The defence Division is responsible for policy and administrative matters pertaining to the Defence of the Federation and three Armed Forces. It also deals with various administrative & financial matters pertaining to Aviation side and cases relating to meteorological, Civil Aviation Authority, Air Force, Security Force, Pakistan International Airlines Planning and Development matters side. The responsibility in respect of Inter-national negotiation, agreements and purchases of defence equipment along with allied accessories are also being handled by this Division.

The Defence Production Division is charged with the responsibility of providing the three Services with arms, ammunition and weapon systems through manufacturing or purchases. Besides providing the overall, re-build and upgrade services for major equipment like aircraft, tanks and sub marines etc. The Defence Production Division was created in 1972 after the experience of 1965 &1971 wars when all types of US military aid was suspended and it was felt necessary to strive towards achieving self-reliance in production of military equipments along with research based modifications, as per day to day requirements of the military and Para-military Forces.

DIRECTORATE FOR INTER-SERVICES INTELLIGENCE [ISI]

The Directorate for Inter-Services Intelligence [ISI] was founded in 1948 by a British army officer, Maj Gen R Cawthome, then Deputy Chief of Staff in Pakistan Army. Field Marshal Ayub Khan, the president of Pakistan in the 1950s, expanded the role of ISI in safeguarding Pakistan's interests, monitoring opposition politicians, and sustaining military rule in Pakistan.

The ISI is tasked with collection of foreign and domestic intelligence; co-ordination of intelligence functions of the three military services; surveillance over its cadre, foreigners, the media, politically active segments of Pakistani society, diplomats of other countries accredited to Pakistan and Pakistani diplomats serving outside the country; the interception and monitoring of communications; and the conduct of covert offensive operations.

Critics of the ISI say that it has become a state within a state, answerable neither to the leadership of the army, nor to the President or the Prime Minister. The result is there has been no real supervision of the ISI, and corruption, narcotics, and big money have all come into play, further complicating the political scenario. Drug money was used by ISI to finance not only the Afghanistan war, but also the ongoing proxy war against India in Kashmir and Northeast India.

The Joint Chiefs of Staff Committee deals with all problems bearing on the military aspects of state security and is charged with integrating and coordinating the three services. Affiliated with the committee are the offices of the engineer in chief, the director general of medical service, the Director of Inter-Services Public Relations, and the Director of Inter-Services Intelligence.

Staffed by hundreds of civilian and military officers, and thousands of other workers, the agency's headquarters is located in Islamabad. The ISI reportedly has a total of about 10,000 officers and staff members, a number which does not include informants and assets. It is reportedly organized into between six and eight divisions:

- **Joint Intelligence X (JIX)** serves as the secretariat which co-ordinates and provides administrative support to the other ISI wings and field organisations. It also prepares intelligence estimates and threat assessments.
-
- The **Joint Intelligence Bureau (JIB)**, responsible for political intelligence, was the most powerful component of the organisation during the late 1980s. The JIB consists of three subsections, with one subsection devoted to operations against India.
-
- The **Joint Counter Intelligence Bureau (JCIB)** is responsible for field surveillance of Pakistani diplomats stationed abroad, as well as for conducting intelligence operations in the Middle East, South Asia, China, Afghanistan and the Muslim republics of the former Soviet Union.
-
- **Joint Intelligence / North (JIN)** is responsible for Jammu and Kashmir operations, including infiltration, exfilteration, propaganda and other clandestine operations.
- **Joint Intelligence Miscellaneous (JIM)** conducts espionage in foreign countries, including offensive intelligence operations.
- The **Joint Signal Intelligence Bureau (JSIB)**, which includes Deputy Directors for Wireless, Monitoring and Photos, operates a chain of signals intelligence collection stations along the border with India, and provide communication support to militants operating in Kashmir.
- **Joint Intelligence Technical**

In addition to these main elements, ISI also includes a separate explosives section and a chemical warfare section. Published reports provide contradictory indications as to the relative size of these organizational elements, suggesting that either JIX is the largest, or that the Joint Intelligence Bureau is the largest with some sixty percent of the total staff.
The Directorate for Inter-Services Intelligence is of particular importance at the joint services level. The directorate's importance derives from the fact that the agency is charged with managing covert operations outside of Pakistan. The ISI supplies weapons, training, advice and planning assistance to terrorists in Kashmir and the the Northeast frontier areas of India.

The 1965 war in Kashmir provoked a major crisis in intelligence. When the war started there was a complete collapse of the operations of all the intelligence agencies, which had been largely devoted to domestic investigative work such as tapping telephone conversations and chasing political suspects. The ISI after the commencement of the 1965 Indo-Pakistan war was apparently unable to locate an Indian armoured division due to its preoccupation with political affairs. Ayub Khan set up a committee headed by General Yahya Khan to examine the working of the agencies.

The ISI has been deeply involved in domestic politics and, has kept track of the incumbent regime's opponents. Prior to the imposition of Martial Law in 1958, ISI reported to the Commander-in-Chief of the Army (C-in-C). When martial Law was promulgated in 1958 all the intelligence agencies fell under the direct control of the President and Chief Martial Law Administrator, and the three intelligence agencies began competing to demonstrate their loyalty to Ayub Khan and his government.

The ISI became even more deeply involved in domestic politics under General Yahya Khan, notably in East Pakistan, where operations were mounted to ensure that no political party should get an overall majority in the general election. An amount of Rs 29 lak was expended for this purpose, and attempts were made to infiltrate the inner circles of the Awami League. The operation was a complete disaster.

Mr. Bhutto promoted General Zia-Ul-Haq in part because the Director of ISI, General Gulam Jilani Khan, was actively promoting him. General Zia, in return, retained General Jilani as head of ISI after his scheduled retirement.

The ISI became much more effective under the leadership of Hameed Gul. The 1990 elections are widely believed to have been rigged. The Islami Jamhoori Ittehad [IJI] party was a conglomerate formed of nine mainly rightist parties by the ISI under Lt General Hameed Gul to ensure the defeat of Bhutto's Pakistan People's Party (PPP) in the polls. Gul denies this, claiming that the ISI's political cell created by Z.A. Bhutto only 'monitored' the elections.

The Soviet invasion of Afghanistan made Pakistan a country of paramount geostrategic importance. In a matter of days, the United States declared Pakistan a "frontline state" against Soviet aggression and offered to reopen aid and military assistance deliveries. Pakistan's top national security agency, the Army's Directorate for Inter-Services Intelligence, monitored the activities of and provided advice and support to the mujahidin, and commandos from the Army's Special Services Group helped guide the operations inside Afghanistan. The ISI trained about 83,000 Afghan Mujahideen between 1983 to 1997 and dispatched them to Afghanistan. Pakistan paid a price for its activities, as Afghan and Soviet forces conducted raids against mujahidin bases inside Pakistan.

The ISI continued to actively participate in Afghan Civil War, supporting the Taliban in their fight against the Rabbani government. Backing of the Taliban would officially end after the terrorist attacks of September 11, 2001; however, there are suspicions that sympathetic elements of the ISI continue to aid Taliban fighters.

ISI has been engaged in covertly supporting the Kashmiri Mujahideen in their fight against the Indian authorities in Kashmir. Reportedly "Operation Tupac" was the designation of the three part action plan for the capture of Kashmir through proxy warfare, initiated by President Zia Ul Haq in 1988 after the failure of "Operation Gibraltar."

According to a report compiled by the Joint Intelligence Committee (JIC) of India in 1995, ISI spent about Rs 2.4 crore per month to sponsor its activities in Jammu and Kashmir. Although all groups reportedly received arms and training from Pakistan, the pro-Pakistani groups were reputed to be favored by the ISI. As of May 1996, at least six major militant organizations, and several smaller ones, operated in Kashmir. Their forces were variously estimated at between 5,000 and 10,000 armed men.

The oldest and most widely known militant organization, the Jammu and Kashmir Liberation Front (JKLF), spearheaded the movement for an independent Kashmir. This group declared a cease-fire in 1994. The most powerful of the pro-Pakistani groups is the Hezb-ul-Mujahedin. The other major groups are Harakat-ul Ansar, a group which reportedly has a large number of non-Kashmiris in it, Al Umar, Al Barq, Jaish-e-Mohammad, and Lashkar-e Toiba, which is also made up largely of fighters from Afghanistan and Pakistan. Many of these militants were trained in Afghanistan, where several ISI agents were killed during U.S. air strikes in 1998 against terrorist training camps. Since the defeat of the Taliban, militant training camps have moved to Pakistani Kashmir.

ISI has been reported to operate training camps near the border of Bangladesh where members of separatist groups of the northeastern states, known as the "United Liberation Front Of Seven Sisters"

[ULFOSS] are trained with military equipment and terrorist activities. These groups include the National Security Council of Nagaland [NSCN], People's Liberation Army [PLA], United Liberation Front of Assam [ULFA], and North East Students Organization [NESO].

Pakistan's military leader, General Pervez Musharraf, has attempted to rein in the ISI. Since September 11th, Islamic fundamentalists have been purged from leadership positions. This includes then-ISI head Lieutenant General Mahmood Ahmed, who was replaced in October 2001 by Lieutenant General Ehsanul Haq.

Additional reforms of the ISI have been made. Most notable was the decision to disband the Kashmir and Afghanistan units. Both these groups have promoted Islamic fundamentalist militancy throughout South Asia. Some officials have been forced to retire and others have been transferred back to the military. Intelligence experts have estimated that these moves would slash the size of the ISI by close to 40%.

OFFICE OF INTER-SERVICES PUBLIC RELATIONS (ISPR)

Officially, the Office of Inter-Services Public Relations (ISPR) closely controls and coordinates release of military news and access to military sources. The press has traditionally avoided negative coverage of the armed forces, and the ISPR has served to hold press coverage of military matters under close restraint. Leaks, while not uncommon, are carefully managed: it is common knowledge that journalists, routinely underpaid, are on the unofficial payrolls of many competing interests, and the military (or elements within it) is presumed to be no exception. Rumors of intimidation, heavy-handed surveillance, and even legal action to quiet the unduly curious or nondeferential reporter are common.

The competitive nature of Pakistani politics helps to ensure press freedom, since the media often serve as a forum for political parties, commercial, religious, and various other interests, as well as influential individuals, to compete with and criticize each other publicly. Although the press does not criticize Islam as such, leaders of religious parties and movements are not exempt from the public scrutiny and criticism routinely experienced by their secular counterparts.

This pattern of control and restraint has loosened somewhat. Early in 1997 -- after an election in which corruption in high places was the principal issue -- the press published charges of corruption and misuse of office against senior navy and air force officers and the navy chief was forced to resign. In the summer, the deaths of several air force cadets while undergoing training prompted newspaper reports of brutal training officers and procedures, and those found responsible were held to public account.

Detailed public discussion of the military as an institution is severely hampered since any published discussion, let alone criticism, of the defense budget is proscribed by law. However, late in 1997 this code of silence was undermined when a National Assembly committee, by discussing defense appropriations and corruption in defense contracts in an open session, made possible (and legal) newspaper coverage of the same issues.

In a case followed closely by the press and human rights groups, journalist Humayun Fur, bureau chief of the Urdu daily Mashriq, was arrested by intelligence agency operatives on 28 June 1997 and imprisoned on charges of "anti-State activities." Fur was found guilty by a military court in September and sentenced to 5 years' imprisonment. A handout issued by the Defense Ministry stated that the court convicted Fur of espionage for passing sensitive state secrets to personnel from a "foreign diplomatic mission" in Islamabad (two Indian High Commission staff members were expelled in connection with the case in September). Human rights groups expressed concern that Fur was tried by a military court and urged that he be retried in an open court under civil law. The press reported that Fur was only the second journalist in the country's history to be tried by court martial. Fur was released in October after the chief of army staff remitted the unserved portion of his sentence on humanitarian grounds because of Fur's ill-health.

MILITARY INTELLIGENCE

The three main intelligence agencies in Pakistan are ISI, Military Intelligence [MI] and the Intelligence Bureau [IB]. Each agency has its own specific responsibilities, but all share the common goal of preserving Paksitan's national security. Since any significant domestic or foreign political activity impinges on national security, there has traditinally been considerable overlap in the activities of these three agencies.

Prior to the imposition of Martial Law in 1958, Military Intelligence reported to the Commander-in-Chief of the Army (C-in-C). When martial Law was promulgated in 1958 all the intelligence agencies fell under the direct control of the President and Chief Martial Law Administrator, and the three intelligence agencies began competing to demonstrate their loyalty to Ayub Khan and his government. The ISI and the MI became extremely active during the l964 presidential election keeping politicians, particularly the East Pakistanis, under surveillance.

Military Intelligence activities include operations in Sindh against Indian intelligence operatives. This organization, implicted in arrests of innocent people, monitors the activities of the leaders of political opposition groups.

SPECIAL SERVICES GROUP

The Soviet invasion of Afghanistan made Pakistan a country of paramount geostrategic importance. Pakistan's top national security agency, the Army's Directorate for Inter-Services Intelligence, monitored the activities of and provided advice and support to the mujahidin, and commandos from the Army's Special Services Group helped guide the operations inside Afghanistan.

SURVEYOR GENERAL OF PAKISTAN

Survey of Pakistan
The Surveyor General of Pakistan
Murree Road, P.O. Box No. 1068
Rawalpindi, Pakistan
Tel: +92-51-455229
Fax: +92-51-453960

The responsibility for topographic mapping and aerial photography lies with the Surveyor General of Pakistan [SGP]. Established in 1947, the Survey of Pakistan (SOP) is based in Rawalpindi with a number of regional offices distributed at urban centers throughout Pakistan. SGP is a civil organization which, for security reasons, is headed by a Surveyor General and works under the strict control of Army General Headquarters (GHQ). Colonel C.A.K. Innes-Wilson, a Royal Engineers officer who joined the Survey of India which mapped the subcontinent, was the first Surveyor General of Pakistan.

All departments which require topographic maps make their request to SGP and many are permanently registered with it for mapping and aerial photographs procurement. The SOP performs these functions under the auspices of the Ministry of Defence (MOD). Organisationally, the SOP is overseen by the Surveyor General (SG) who is a direct military appointee and a senior uniformed officer. The SG reports directly to the Secretary of Defence. Under the SG are two Deputy SG's (I and II) who manage the operational departments of the agency and a Senior Technical Advisor. These departments are divided into Regional Directorates for Topographic Mapping including the Northern region centred in Peshawar, Eastern region (Lahore), Western region (Quetta) and finally, the Southern region in Karachi. Responsibility for fields surveys and the maintenance/update of topographic maps are sub-divided according to these geographic areas.

Three other operational directorates exist within the SOP which include the Directorate of Photogrammetry (Rawalpindi), Directorate of Printing and Map Publications (Rawalpindi) and the Directorate of the Survey Training Institute (Islamabad). The Photogrammetry Directorate is responsible for the commissioning and flying of aerial photography, followed by map interpretation and production from these source data.

MINISTRY OF INTERIOR

FEDERAL INVESTIGATIVE AGENCY

Before independence, the security forces of British India were primarily concerned with the maintenance of law and order but were also called on to perform duties in support of the political interests of the government. The duties of the police officer in a formal sense were those of police the world over: executing orders and warrants; collecting and communicating upward intelligence concerning public order; preventing crime; and detecting, apprehending, and arresting criminals. These duties were specified in Article 23 of the Indian Police Act of 1861, which (together with revisions dating from 1888 and the Police Rules of 1934), is still the basic document for police activity in Pakistan.

The overall organization of the police forces remained much the same after partition. Except for centrally administered territories and tribal territories in the north and northwest, basic law and order responsibilities have been carried out by the four provincial governments. The central government has controlled a series of specialized police agencies, including the Federal Investigative Agency, railroad and airport police forces, an anticorruption task force, and various paramilitary organizations such as the Rangers, constabulary forces, and the Frontier Corps.

Benazir Bhutto appointed Rehman Malik as chief of the Federal Investigation Agency which then launched a secret war against the Islamists, which amounted to a direct attack on the ISI. The Pakistani military was equally dismayed by reports of FIA contacts with the Israeli secret service, the MOSSAD, to investigate Islamist terrorists. The FIA leadership under Bhutto also angered Islamist elements because they allowed the extradited Ramzi Yousaf to the US for trial on the New York Trade Centre Bombing. One of the first acts of President Leghari after dismissing Benazir Bhutto on 05 November 1996 was to imprison the Ghulam Asghar, head of FIA, suspended on non specified corruption charges, and Rehman Malik, Addl. Director General FIA, was also arrested.

The Federal Investigation Agency conducts the investigations on receiving reports of corruption, either through the P.M.'s Accountability and Coordination Cell or directly from the public. After the investigations, the cases are referred to the Chief Ehtesab Commissioner for trial by the Ehtesab courts. However, the Chief Ehtesab Commissioner, Mr Mujaddad Ali Mirza, has complained that the Federal Investigation Authority and the Anti-Corruption Police have failed to cooperate with the Commission.

Police tactics in British India were never gentle, but in contemporary Pakistan, according to the Herald, a magazine published in Karachi, "The police have institutionalized torture to a point where it is viewed as the primary method of crime detention. Police torture has become so commonplace that it has slowly lost the capacity to shock and disgust." These charges were echoed by Amnesty International's especially bleak appraisal of Pakistan's human rights situation in its June 1992 "International News Release" report. The report, reflecting the law and order breakdown in Sindh and the government's reaction to it, stated that government opponents often are harassed, placed under arrest, and detained for unspecified periods of time. Scores of prisoners of conscience have been held for their political activities or religious beliefs. The practice of repeatedly bringing false charges against members of the political opposition is a widely used tactic in Pakistani politics and has been used to arrest thousands of opposition party activists. According to the United States State Department's Country Reports on Human Rights Practices for 1993, there were no significant efforts in 1992 or 1993 to reform either the police or the judicial system, and authorities continued to be lax in their prosecution of abuses in these areas. Pakistani and international human rights organizations have demanded that steps be taken to reverse the trend by bringing torturers to justice and by taking such procedural steps as reducing the time prisoners spend in places of first arrest, where most torture takes place.

Torture is a particularly acute problem in cases in which the suspect is thought to have committed a political crime, but it is not uncommon in serious criminal cases. General police brutality in handling all suspects is routine. Police frequently act without warrants or other proper authorization, and individuals disappear into the criminal justice process for weeks before they can be found and, through writs of habeas corpus, be brought into regular judicial channels. Rape of prisoners, both male and female, is common. Prisoners often die in detention but are reported as killed in the course of armed encounters. Police also are alleged to extort money from families of prisoners under threat of ill treatment. The performance of the police and their failure to act against political groups that run their own torture machinery are especially bad in Sindh, but there is no Pakistani who looks on an encounter with the police with equanimity.

NARCOTICS CONTROL DIVISION

Prior to April 1989, narcotics matters were dealt in the Ministry of Interior, and the Pakistan Narcotics Control Board (PNCB), the field organization, was an attached department of the Ministry. As the complexity of narcotics problem had grown globally, and the drug abuse had proliferated in Pakistan. Narcotics Control Division was set up in April, 1989.
The Anti Narcotics Task Force (ANTF) and the PNCB are the law enforcement arms of the narcotics Control Division. The PNCB was set up in 1973. This Department essentially performs the coordinating, controlling and supervisory functions.

The ANTF is newly set up Force under the Narcotics Control Division. The functions of this Force are to inquire into and investigate all offences relating to, or connected with preparation, production, transportation, trafficking or smuggling of intoxicants, narcotics and chemical precursors or reagent used in the manufacture of narcotics or dangerous drugs or assets therefrom or any offence committed in the course of the same transaction under any law for the time being in force, including any attempt or conspiracy to commit, or any abutment of any such offence.

The presence of two law enforcement agencies with almost the same functions, under the Narcotics Control Division, necessitated their reorganization so that the resources and manpower of these two organizations could be jointly put to use for more effective narcotics law enforcement. The Government has since placed these two organizations under the command of the Directorate General of ANTF.

Institutional changes have also been made at the highest level. A Policy Review Board has been set up under the chairmanship of the Minister for Narcotics Control with Provincial Ministers of Home and Health Departments as its members to meet twice a year and review the implementation of Government's policy in all areas of narcotics control. Under this arrangement the narcotics issues will remain under continuous review and evaluation of the political leaders. In addition, a Narcotics Interdiction Committee comprising heads of Federal and Provincial Law Enforcement Agencies has been set up to meet periodically and review and evaluate the narcotics interdiction measures and performance of the agencies concerned in this regard.

U.S.-PAKISTAN JOINT WORKING GROUP ON COUNTERTERRORISM AND LAW ENFORCEMENT

On May 8, 2002, Assistant Secretary for International Narcotics and Law Enforcement Affairs Rand Beers, Coordinator for Counterterrorism Ambassador Francis Taylor, Assistant Secretary for South Asian Affairs Christina Rocca, and U.S. Department of Justice Deputy Assistant Attorney General

Bruce Swartz hosted the first meeting of the U.S.-Pakistan Joint Working Group on Counterterrorism and Law Enforcement. Pakistan's Minister of Interior, Mr. Moinuddin Haider, led the Pakistani delegation. Deputy Secretary of State Richard Armitage delivered opening remarks. Minister Haider is also meeting with National Security Advisor Condoleezza Rice, Attorney General John Ashcroft, Director of the FBI Robert Mueller, and other officials in the Department of State.

The two governments discussed a broad range of bilateral law enforcement issues, including counternarcotics, counterterrorism, extradition, money laundering, trafficking in persons, demand reduction and drug abuse control, alternative development and poppy eradication, police and legal system reform, and issues related to the repatriation of Pakistani nationals detained in the United States in connection with immigration proceedings.

The two governments agreed to strengthen their cooperation in these areas, and to hold another Joint Working Group meeting in approximately six months, with specific follow-up meetings in the interim.

The Joint Working Group was announced during Pakistani President Pervez Musharraf's official visit to Washington in February 2002. Among the United States agencies participating were the Department of State, the Department of Justice, the Federal Bureau of Investigation, the Drug Enforcement Agency, and the Immigration and Naturalization Service. In addition to Minister of Interior Haider, representatives of Pakistan's Federal Investigative Agency, National Crisis Management Center and Anti-Narcotics Force participated.

PAKISTAN'S INTER-SERVICES INTELLIGENCE (ISI)[2]

The intelligence community of Pakistan, which was once described by the "Frontier Post" of Peshawar (May 18,1994) as its "invisible government" and by the "Dawn" of Karachi (April 25,1994) as "our secret godfathers" consists of the Intelligence Bureau (IB) and the ISI. While the IB comes under the Interior Minister, the ISI is part of the Ministry of Defence (MOD). Each wing of the Armed Forces has also its own intelligence directorate for tactical MI.

The IB is the oldest dating from Pakistan's creation in 1947. It was formed by the division of the pre-partition IB of British India. Its unsatisfactory military intelligence (MI) performance in the first Indo-Pak war of 1947-48 over Jammu & Kashmir (J & K) led to the decision in 1948 to create the ISI, manned by officers from the three Services, to specialise in the collection, analysis and assessment of external intelligence, military and non-military, with the main focus on India.

Initially, the ISI had no role in the collection of internal political intelligence except in Pakistan-Occupied Kashmir (POK) and the Northern Areas (NA--Gilgit and Baltistan). Ayub Khan, suspecting the loyalty and objectivity of the Bengali police officers in the Subsidiary Intelligence Bureau (SIB) of the IB in Dacca, the capital of the then East Pakistan, entrusted the ISI with the responsibility for the collection of internal political intelligence in East Pakistan.

Similarly, Z.A.Bhutto, when faced with a revolt by Balochi nationalists in Balochistan after the liberation of Bangladesh in 1971, suspected the loyalty of the Balochi police officers of the SIB in Quetta and made the military officers of the ISI responsible for internal intelligence in Balochistan.

Zia-ul-Haq expanded the internal intelligence responsibilities of the ISI by making it responsible not only for the collection of intelligence about the activities of the Sindhi nationalist elements in Sindh

---

[2] by B. Raman

and for monitoring the activities of Shia organisations all over the country after the success of the Iranian Revolution in 1979, but also for keeping surveillance on the leaders of the Pakistan People's Party (PPP) of Mrs.Benazir Bhutto and its allies which had started the Movement for the Restoration of Democracy (MRD) in the early 1980s. The ISI's Internal Political Division had Shah Nawaz Bhutto, one of the two brothers of Mrs.Benazir Bhutto, assassinated through poisoning in the French Riviera in the middle of 1985, in an attempt to intimidate her into not returning to Pakistan for directing the movement against Zia, but she refused to be intimidated and returned to Pakistan.

Even in the 1950s, Ayub Khan had created in the ISI a Covert Action Division for assisting the insurgents in India's North-East and its role was expanded in the late 1960s to assist the Sikh Home Rule Movement of London-based Charan Singh Panchi, which was subsequently transformed into the so-called Khalistan Movement, headed by Jagjit Singh Chauhan. A myriad organisations operating amongst the members of the Sikh diaspora in Europe, the US and Canada joined the movement at the instigation and with the assistance of the ISI.

During the Nixon Administration in the US, when Dr.Henry Kissinger was the National Security Adviser, the intelligence community of the US and the ISI worked in tandem in guiding and assisting the so-called Khalistan movement in the Punjab. The visits of prominent Sikh Home Rule personalities to the US before the Bangladesh Liberation War in December, 1971, to counter Indian allegations of violations of the human rights of the Bengalis of East Pakistan through counter-allegations of violations of the human rights of the Sikhs in Punjab were jointly orchestrated by the ISI, the US intelligence and some officials of the US National Security Council (NSC) Secretariat, then headed by Dr.Kissinger.

This covert colloboration between the ISI and the US intelligence community was also directed at discrediting Mrs.Indira Gandhi's international stature by spreading disinformation about alleged naval base facilities granted by her to the USSR in Vizag and the Andaman & Nicobar, the alleged attachment of KGB advisers to the then Lt.Gen.Sunderji during Operation Bluestar in the Golden Temple in Amritsar in June, 1984, and so on. This collaboration petered out after her assassination in October,1984.

The Afghan war of the 1980s saw the enhancement of the covert action capabilities of the ISI by the CIA. A number of officers from the ISI's Covert Action Division received training in the US and many covert action experts of the CIA were attached to the ISI to guide it in its operations against the Soviet troops by using the Afghan Mujahideen, Islamic fundamentalists of Pakistan and Arab volunteers. Osama bin Laden, Mir Aimal Kansi, who assassinated two CIA officers outside their office in Langley, US, in 1993, Ramzi Yousef and his accomplices involved in the New York World Trade Centre explosion in February, 1993, the leaders of the Muslim separatist movement in the southern Philippines and even many of the narcotics smugglers of Pakistan were the products of the ISI-CIA collaboration in Afghanistan.

The encouragement of opium cultivation and heroin production and smuggling was also an offshoot of this co-operation. The CIA, through the ISI, promoted the smuggling of heroin into Afghanistan in order to make the Soviet troops heroin addicts. Once the Soviet troops were withdrawn in 1988, these heroin smugglers started smuggling the drugs to the West, with the complicity of the ISI. The heroin dollars have largely contributed to preventing the Pakistani economy from collapsing and enabling the ISI to divert the jehadi hordes from Afghanistan to J & K after 1989 and keeping them well motivated and well-equipped.

Even before India's Pokhran I nuclear test of 1974, the ISI had set up a division for the clandestine procurement of military nuclear technology from abroad and, subsequently, for the clandestine purchase and shipment of missiles and missile technology from China and North Korea. This division, which was funded partly by donations from Saudi Arabia and Libya, partly by concealed allocations in Pakistan's State budget and partly by heroin dollars, was instrumental in helping Pakistan achieve a military nuclear and delivery capability despite its lack of adequate human resources with the required expertise.

Thus, the ISI, which was originally started as essentially an agency for the collection of external intelligence, has developed into an agency adept in covert actions and clandestine procurement of denied technologies as well.

The IB, which was patterned after the IB of British India, used to be a largely police organisation, but the post of Director-General (DG), IB, is no longer tenable only by police officers as it was in the past. Serving and retired military officers are being appointed in increasing numbers to senior posts in the IB, including to the post of DG.

In recent years, there has been a controversy in Pakistan as to who really controls the ISI and when was its internal Political Division set up. Testifying before the Supreme Court on June 16,1997, in a petition filed by Air Marshal (retd) Asghar Khan, former chief of the Pakistan Air Force, challenging the legality of the ISI's Political Division accepting a donation of Rs.140 million from a bank for use against PPP candidates during elections, Gen. (retd) Mirza Aslam Beg, former Chief of the Army Staff (COAS), claimed that though the ISI was manned by serving army officers and was part of the MOD, it reported to the Prime Minister and not to the COAS and that its internal Political Division was actually set up by the late Z.A.Bhutto in 1975.

Many Pakistani analysts have challenged this and said that the ISI, though de jure under the Prime Minister, had always been controlled de facto by the COAS and that its internal Political Division had been in existence at least since the days of Ayub Khan, if not earlier.

The ISI is always headed by an Army officer of the rank of Lt.Gen., who is designated as the Director-General (DG). The present DG is Lt.Gen.Mahmood Ahmed. He is assisted by three Deputy Directors-General (DDGs), designated as DDG (Political), DDG-I (External) and DDG-II (Administration). It is divided into the following Divisions:

* The Joint Intelligence Bureau (JIB)---Responsible for all Open Sources Intelligence (OSINT) and Human Intelligence (HUMINT) collection, inside Pakistan as well as abroad.

* The Joint Counter-Intelligence (CI) Bureau: Responsible for CI inside Pakistan as well as abroad.

* The Joint Signals Intelligence Bureau (JSIB): Responsible for all communications intelligence inside Pakistan and abroad.

* Joint Intelligence North (JIN): Responsible for the proxy war in Jammu & Kashmir and the control of Afghanistan through the Taliban. Controls the Army of Islam, consisting of organisations such as Osama bin Laden's Al Qaeda, the Harkat-ul-Mujahideen (HUM), the Lashkar-e-Toiba, the Al Badr and Maulana Masood Azhar's Jaish-e-Mohammad (JEM). Lt.Gen.Mohammad Aziz, presently a Corps Commander at Lahore, is the clandestine Chief of Staff of the Army of Islam. It also controls all opium cultivation and heroin refining and smuggling from Pakistani and Afghan territory.

* Joint Intelligence Miscellaneous (JIM): Responsible for covert actions in other parts of the world and for the clandestine procurement of nuclear and missile

technologies. Maj Gen (retd) Sultan Habib, an operative of this Division, who had distinguished himself in the clandestine procurement and theft of nuclear material while posted as the Defence Attache in the Pakistani Embassy in Moscow from 1991 to 93, with concurrent accreditation to the Central Asian Republics (CARs), Poland and Czechoslovakia, has recently been posted as Ambassador to North Korea to oversee the clandestine nuclear and missile co-operation between North Korea and Pakistan. After completing his tenure in Moscow, he had co-ordinated the clandestine shipping of missiles from North Korea, the training of Pakistani experts in the missile production and testing facilities of North Korea and the training of North Korean scientists in the nuclear establishments of Pakistan through Capt. (retd) Shafquat Cheema, Third Secretary and acting head of mission, in the Pakistani Embassy in North Korea, from 1992 to 96. Before Maj.Gen. Sultan Habib's transfer to ISI headquarters from Moscow, the North Korean missile and nuclear co-operation project was handled by Maj.Gen.Shujjat from the Baluch Regiment, who worked in the clandestine procurement division of the ISI for five years. On Capt.Cheema's return to headquarters in 1996, the ISI discovered that in addition to acting as the liaison officer of the ISI with the nuclear and missile establishments in North Korea, he was also earning money from the Iranian and the Iraqi intelligence by helping them in their clandestine nuclear and missile technology and material procurement not only from North Korea, but also from Russia and the CARs. On coming to know of the ISI enquiry into his clandestine assistance to Iran and Iraq, he fled to Xinjiang and sought political asylum there, but the Chinese arrested him and handed him over to the ISI. What happened to him subsequently is not known. Capt.Cheema initially got into the ISI and got himself posted to the Pakistani Embassy in North Korea with the help of Col.(retd) Ghulam Sarwar Cheema of the PPP.

* Joint Intelligence X (JIX): Responsible for administration and accounts.

* Joint Intelligence Technical (JIT): Responsible for the collection of all Technical Intelligence (TECHINT) other than communications intelligence and for research and development in gadgetry.

* The Special Wing: Responsible for all intelligence training in the Armed Forces in the Defence Services Intelligence Academy and for liaison with foreign intelligence and security agencies.

Since 1948, there have been three instances when the DG,ISI, was at daggers drawn with the COAS. The first instance was during the first tenure of Mrs.Benazir Bhutto as Prime Minister (1988 to 1990). To reduce the powers of the ISI, to re-organise the intelligence community and to enhance the powers of the police officers in the IB, she discontinued the practice of appointing a serving Lt.Gen, recommended by the COAS, as the DG, ISI, and, instead appointed Maj.Gen. (retd) Shamsur Rahman Kallue, a retired officer close to her father, as the DG in replacement of Lt.Gen.Hamid Gul in 1989 and entrusted him with the task of winding up the internal intelligence collection role of the ISI and civilianising the IB and the ISI. Writing in the "Nation" of July 31,1997, Brig.A.R.Siddiqui, who had served as the Press Relations Officer in the army headquarters in the 1970s, said that this action of hers marked the beginning of her trouble with Gen.Beg, the then COAS, which ultimately led to her dismissal in August,1990. Gen.Beg made Maj.Gen.Kallue persona non grata (PNG), stopped inviting him to the Corps Commanders conferences and transferred the responsibility for the proxy war in J & K and for assisting the Sikh extremists in the Punjab from the ISI to the Army intelligence directorate working under the Chief of the General Staff (CGS).
The second instance was during the first tenure of Nawaz Sharif (1990-93), who appointed as the DG,ISI, Lt.Gen.Javed Nasir, a fundamentalist Kashmiri officer, though he was not recommended by the COAS for the post. Lt.Gen.Asif Nawaz Janjua, the then COAS, made Lt.Gen.Nasir PNG and

stopped inviting him to the Corps Commanders conferences. Despite this, Lt.Gen.Janjua returned to the ISI the responsibility for the proxy war in J & K and for assisting the Sikh extremists.
During her second tenure (1993-96), Mrs. Bhutto avoided any conflict with Gen.Abdul Waheed Kakkar and Gen. Jehangir Karamat, the Chiefs of the Army Staff in succession, on the appointment of the DG,ISI. Her action in transferring part of the responsibility for the operations in Afghanistan, including the creation and the handling of the Taliban, from the ISI to the Interior Ministry headed by Maj.Gen. (retd) Nasirullah Babar, who handled Afghan operations in the ISI during the tenure of her father, did not create any friction with the army since she had ordered that Lt.Gen. Pervez Musharraf, then Director-General of Military Operations, should be closely associated by Maj.Gen.Babar in the Afghan operations.
However, sections of the ISI, close to Farooq Leghari, the then President of Pakistan, had Murtaza Bhutto, the surviving brother of Mrs.Benazir, assassinated outside his house in Karachi in September,1996, with the complicity of some local police officers and started a disinformation campaign in the media blaming her and her husband, Asif Zirdari, for the murder. This campaign paved the way for her dismissal by Leghari in November,1996.
The third instance was during the second tenure of Nawaz Sharif (1997-99) when his action in appointing Lt.Gen. Ziauddin, an engineer, as the DG,ISI, over-riding the objection of Gen.Musharraf led to the first friction between the two. Gen.Musharraf transferred Lt.Gen.Mohammad Aziz, the then DDG,ISI, on his promotion as Lt.Gen. to the GHQ as the CGS and transferred the entire Joint Intelligence North (JIN), responsible for covert actions in India and Afghanistan to the Directorate-General of Military Intelligence (DGMI) to be supervised by Lt.Gen.Aziz. It is believed that the JIN continues to function under the DGMI even after the appointment of Lt.Gen.Mahmood Ahmed as the DG, ISI, after the overthrow of Sharif on October 12,1999. Gen.Musharraf, as the COAS, made Lt.Gen.Ziauddin PNG and stopped inviting him to the Corps Commanders' conferences. He kept Lt.Gen.Ziauddin totally out of the picture in the planning and implementation of the Kargil operations. After the Kargil war, Nawaz Sharif had sent Lt.Gen.Ziauddin to Washington on a secret visit to inform the Clinton Administration officials of his concerns over the continued loyalty of Gen.Musharraf. After his return from the US, Lt.Gen.Ziauddin went to Kandahar, as ordered by Sharif, to pressurise Mullah Mohammad Omar, the Amir of the Taliban, to stop assisting the anti-Shia Sipah Sahaba Pakistan and to co-operate with the US in the arrest and deportation of bin Laden. On coming to know of this, Gen. Musharraf sent Lt.Gen.Aziz to Kandahar to tell the Amir that he should not carry out the instructions of Lt.Gen.Ziauddin and that he should follow only his (Lt.Gen.Aziz's) instructions.
These instances would show that whenever an elected leadership was in power, the COAS saw to it that the elected Prime Minister did not have effective control over the ISI and that the ISI was marginalised if its head showed any loyalty to the elected Prime Minister.
In their efforts to maintain law and order in Pakistan and weaken nationalist and religious elements and political parties disliked by the army, the ISI and the army followed a policy of divide and rule. After the success of the Islamic Revolution in Iran in 1979, to keep the Shias of Pakistan under control, the ISI encouraged the formation of ant-Shia Sunni extremist organisations such as the Sipah Sahaba . When the Shias of Gilgit rose in revolt in 1988, Musharraf used bin Laden and his tribal hordes from the North-West Frontier Province (NWFP) and the Federally-Administered Tribal Areas (FATA) to suppress them brutally. When the Mohajir Qaumi Movement (MQM---now called the Muttahida Qaumi Movement) of Altaf Hussain rose in revolt in the late 1980s in Karachi, Hyderabad and Sukkur in Sindh, the ISI armed sections of the Sindhi nationalist elements to kill the Mohajirs. It then created a split between Mohajirs of Uttar Pradesh origin (in Altaf Hussain's MQM) and those of Bihar origin in the splinter anti-Altaf Hussain group called MQM (Haquiqi--meaning real). In Altaf Hussain's MQM itself, the ISI unsuccessfully tried to create a wedge between the Sunni and Shia migrants from Uttar Pradesh.
Having failed in his efforts to weaken the PPP by taking advantage of the exile of Mrs.Benazir and faced with growing unity of action between Altaf Hussain's MQM and sections of Sindhi nationalist elements, Musharraf has constituted a secret task force in the ISI headed by Lt.Gen.Mahmood Ahmed, the DG, and consisting of Lt.Gen.(retd) Moinuddin Haider, Interior Minister, and Lt.Gen.Muzaffar Usmani, Deputy Chief of the Army Staff, to break the PPP, the MQM and the Sindhi nationalists.

This task force has encouraged not only religious political organisations such as the Jamaat-e-Islami (JEI) of Qazi Hussain Ahmed, the Jamiat-ul-Ulema Islam (JUI) of Maulana Fazlur Rahman etc, but also sectarian organisations such as the Sipah Sahaba and the Lashkar-e-Jhangvi of Riaz Basra, living under the protection of the Taliban and bin Laden in Kandahar in Afghanistan, to extend their activities to Sindh.

These organisations have now practically got out of the control of the ISI. Instead of attacking the PPP, the MQM and the Sindhi nationalists and bringing them to heel as Musharraf had hoped they would, they have taken their anti-Shia jehad to Sindh and have been recruiting a large number of unemployed Sindhi rural youth for service with the Taliban. Sindh, which was known for its Sufi traditions of religious tolerance, has seen under Musharraf a resurgence of the street power of the JEI and the JUI, which had been practically driven out of the province in the 1980s, by the PPP, the MQM and the Sindhi nationalists, and has seen in recent months anti-Shia massacres of the kind used by Musharraf in Gilgit in 1988. Over 200 Shias have been gunned down, including 30 doctors of Karachi, and the latest victims of the sectarian Frankenstein let loose by Musharraf in Sindh have been Shaukat Mirza, the Managing Director of Pakistan State Oil, and Syed Zafar Hussain Zaidi, a Director in the Research Laboratories of the Ministry of Defence, located in Karachi, who were gunned down on July 28 and 30,2001, respectively. The Lashkar-e-Jhangvi has claimed responsibility for both these assassinations.

As a result of the policy of divide and rule followed in Sindh by the ISI under Musharraf, one is seeing in Pakistan for the first time sectarian violence inside the Sunni community between the Sunnis of the Deobandi faith belonging to the Sipah Sahaba and the Lashkar-e-Jhangvi and the Sunnis of the more tolerant Barelvi faith belonging to the Sunni Tehrik formed in the early 1990s to counter the growing Wahabi influence on Islam in Pakistan and the Almi Tanzeem Ahle Sunnat formed in 1998 by Pir Afzal Qadri of Mararian Sharif in Gujrat, Punjab, to counter the activities of the Deobandi Army of Islam headed by Lt.Gen.Mohammed Aziz, Corps Commander, Lahore.

The Tanzeem has been criticising not only the Army of Islam for injecting what it considers the Wahabi poison into the Pakistan society, but also the army of the State headed by Musharraf for misleading the Sunni youth into joining the jehad against the Indian army in J & K and getting killed there in order to avoid the Pakistani army officers getting killed in the jehad for achieving its strategic objective. The ISI, which is afraid of a direct confrontation with the Barelvi organisations, has been inciting the Sipah Sahaba and the Lashkar-e-Jhangvi to counter their activities .

This has led to frequent armed clashes between rival Sunni groups in Sindh, the most sensational of the incidents being the gunning down of Maulana Salim Qadri of the Sunni Tehrik and five of his followers in Karachi on May, 18,2001, by the Sipah Sahaba, which led to a major break-down of law and order in certain areas of Karachi for some days.

Musharraf, the commando, believes in achieving his objective by hook or by crook without worrying about the means used. In his anxiety to bring Sindh under control and to weaken the PPP, the MQM and the Sindhi nationalists, he has, through the ISI, created new Frankensteins which might one day lead to the Talibanisation of Sindh, a province always known for its sufi traditions of religious tolerance and for its empathy with India.

Musharraf is under pressure from sections of senior army officers concerned over these developments to suppress the Sipah Sahaba and the Lashkar-e-Jhangvi. He and Lt.Gen.Haider have been making the pretence of planning to do so. It is to be seen whether they really would and, even if they did, whether they would or could effectively enforce the ban on them.

In India, there is a point of view in some circles that the only way of effectively countering the ISI activities against India is to have an Indian version of the ISI, with extensive powers for clandestine intelligence collection, technology procurement and covert actions and that the proposed Defence Intelligence Agency (DIA) should be patterned after Pakistan's ISI rather than after the DIA of the US and the Defence Intelligence Staff (DIS) of the UK, which are essentially agencies for the analysis and assessment of military intelligence in a holistic manner, with powers for clandestine collection only during times of war or when deployed in areas of conflict and with no powers for covert action.

The principle of civilian primacy in the intelligence community is widely accepted in all successful democracies and the discarding of this principle in Pakistan sowed the seeds for the present state of affairs there. In our anxiety for quick results against the ISI, we should not sacrifice time-tested principles as to how intelligence agencies should function in a democratic society.

In the 1970s,Indian policy-makers wisely decided that the Indian intelligence should not get involved in clandestine procurement of denied technologies since the exposure of any such procurement could damage the credibility and trustworthiness of the Indian scientific and technological community in the eyes of other countries.
This is what has happened to Pakistan. Its intelligence community did some spectacular work in clandestine procurement and theft of technologies abroad. But, once the details of this network were exposed, post-graduate students of Pakistan in scientific subjects, its academics, research scholars and scientists are looked upon with suspicion in Western countries and find it difficult to enter universities and research laboratories for higher studies and research and get jobs in establishments dealing in sensitive technologies and are less frequently invited to seminars etc than in the past. In its anxiety to catch up with India in the short term, Pakistan has damaged its long-term potential in science and technology.
(The writer is Additional Secretary (retd), Cabinet Secretariat, Govt. of India, and, presently, Director, Institute For Topical Studies, Chennai. E-Mail: corde@vsnl.com)

PHILIPPINES

NATIONAL INTELLIGENCE COORDINATING AGENCY

http://www.gov.ph/
http://www.army.mil.ph/

The period following the overthrow of the Marcos regime brought important changes to the Philippines' intelligence and security structure. During the martial law era (1972-81), the volume and scope of government intelligence activity had greatly expanded. The preeminent intelligence agency was the National Intelligence and Security Authority, headed by General Fabian Ver, a close Marcos confidant and chief of staff of the Philippine armed forces. By the end of Marcos's tenure, the National Intelligence and Security Authority and the rest of the country's intelligence apparatus were heavily focused on tracking the president's political opponents. Security agents were suspected of numerous human rights abuses.

The revamp of the nation's intelligence system commenced with Aquino's rise to power. The new government significantly curtailed intelligence operations and purged many of General Ver's operatives. Drafters of the 1987 constitution installed legal safeguards against the kind of abuses committed by the Marcos intelligence and security apparatus. The National Intelligence and Security Authority, tainted by its close association with the deposed president, was renamed the National Intelligence Coordinating Agency and refocused its efforts away from political opposition leaders to internal security threats, especially the communist insurgency. Notable intelligence successes against the communist rebels during the late 1980s were an apparent result of this reorientation. Government operatives repeatedly captured top CPP and NPA cadres, prompting devastating purges within the insurgent ranks as guerrillas attempted to ferret out the sources of intelligence penetrations.

In 1990 Aquino issued an executive order authorizing her national security adviser to oversee the National Intelligence Coordinating Agency and other elements of the intelligence community. The adviser was empowered to audit the agencies and was charged with ensuring that they were responsive to the needs of the president and the National Security Council. The secretaries of national defense and justice, whose departments performed intelligence functions, were directed to work with the national security adviser to fulfill the president's mandate.

The Department of Justice's principal intelligence-gathering organ, the National Bureau of Investigation, was formed in 1936 as the Division of Investigation and patterned after the United States Federal Bureau of Investigation. The bureau's principal mission was to assist the Philippine Constabulary and police in crime detection and investigation, freeing them to concentrate on maintaining peace and order. Collection of intelligence on internal security threats was considered a related function.

The Department of National Defense, meanwhile, maintained an extensive intelligence apparatus. Although little was publicly revealed about its organization or operation, it was known that the military's principal intelligence organ was the Intelligence Service of the AFP. Headed by a brigadier general, Intelligence Service units operated throughout the country. Their mission in 1990 included not only pursuing insurgents, but also gathering information on military coup plotters and participants. The military services, too, maintained their own intelligence arms. The regimental-size Intelligence and Security Group supported the army while the Constabulary Security Group served Philippine Constabulary leaders. The division of responsibilities among these military intelligence agencies, as well as the institutional mechanisms, if any, that were set up to coordinate their activities, were unclear.

ARMED FORCES OF THE PHILIPPINES INTELLIGENCE SERVICE

POLAND

INTELLIGENCE AGENCIES

http://aw.gov.pl/eng/bip/index.html

Wspolnota Informacyjna Rzadu *Government Intelligence Community*
Agencja Wywiadu

Foreign Intelligence Agency
Agencja Bezpieczenstwa Wewnetrznego

Internal Security Agency
Wojskowe Sluzby Informacyjne
Military Intelligence Services

GOVERNMENT INTELLIGENCE COPMMUNITY

Particular competences of the Head of the Foreign Intelligence Agency include organizing the cooperation aimed at the exchange of any information material for the external security and international position of the Republic of Poland among government administration bodies in the frame of the Government Intelligence Community.

• The Government Intelligence Community is AN AUXILIARY BODY OF THE PRIME MINISTER constituting the team for the exchange of information material for the external security and international position of the Republic of Poland among the government administrations bodies as well as for the analysis of such information and forecasting threats in the above respect.

• The Government Intelligence Community was established in institutional terms (as the team) on 9 September 2002, while regulations referring to procedures of the exchange of information constituting the subject of its works entered into force on 1 October 2002.

• The foundation of the Government Intelligence Community fulfils the statutory disposition stating that such kind of cooperation is organized by the Head of the Foreign Intelligence Agency and satisfies the delegation for the Prime Minister to define an appropriate procedure for such exchange of information as well as requirements for bodies participating therein (Art. 41 sec. 1 and 2 of the Internal Security Agency and Foreign Intelligence Agency Act of 24 May 2002 - Ustawa z dnia 24 maja 2002 r. o Agencji Bezpieczeństwa Wewnętrznego oraz Agencji Wywiadu).

Tasks of the Government Intelligence Community include:

- exchange of any information material for the external security and international position of the Republic of Poland among government administration bodies;
- collecting, processing and analyzing information constituting the subject of exchange;
- expressing opinions on information constituting the subject of exchange;
- indication of bodies, institutions and organizations to which information constituting the subject of exchange are to be submitted - together with the Government Intelligence Community opinion;
- forecasting - based on information constituting the subject of exchange - any threats for the external security and international position of the Republic of Poland.

Information exchanged in the frame of the Government Intelligence Community and constituting the subject of its works refer in particular to:

- external threats aimed at the security, defense, independence, territorial integrity and inviolability of the territory of the Republic of Poland;
- threats to international alliances, political systems and military pacts the Republic of Poland is a party to;
- international terrorism, extremism and international groups of organized crime;
- international trading in weapons as well as goods, technologies and services of a strategic importance for the security of the Republic of Poland and for the international peace and security;
- performance of international agreements pertaining to disarmament and threats connected with a proliferation of mass destruction weapons and their carriers;
- threats existing in the areas of international conflicts and crises;
- threats for performance of goals of the Republic of Poland foreign policy;
- threats to economic interests of the Republic of Poland.

Composition of the Government Intelligence Community:

- Head of the Foreign Intelligence Agency - chairman of the Government Intelligence Community;
- undersecretary of state in the Ministry of Foreign Affairs - deputy chairman of the Government Intelligence Community;
- secretary of the Government Intelligence Community;
- members:
    - secretary of state in the Ministry of Internal Affairs and Administration;
    - secretary of state in the Chancellery of the Prime Minister performing duties associated with international contacts of the Prime Minister;
    - undersecretary of state in the Ministry of National Defense;
    - undersecretary of state in the Ministry of Economy;

- undersecretary of state in the Ministry of Finance;
- Deputy Head of the Internal Security Agency;
- Deputy Head of the Military Information Services.

Works of the Government Intelligence Community may be also attended - with regular voting rights - by:

- a representative of the National Security Bureau, indicated by the Head of such Bureau.

Deputy chairmen, secretary and members of the Government Intelligence Community are appointed and dismissed by the Prime Minister upon request of the Head of the Foreign Intelligence Agency.

In addition other persons - representing bodies, institutions or organizations competent in affairs constituting the subject of works, provided that they fulfill requirements enumerated in regulations on protection of classified information, may participate in the works of the Government Intelligence Community, based on the invitation from the chairman and only in the advisory capacity.

The government administration bodies transfer any information material for the external security and international position of the Republic of Poland to the Head of the Foreign Intelligence Agency immediately after obtaining the same, and if possible - in the contents and form in which they obtained the foregoing.

The Head of the Foreign Intelligence Agency presents such obtained information on the next meeting of the Government Intelligence Community. Other persons remaining in its composition may also present such information on the meeting of the Community also.

The Head of the Foreign Intelligence Agency, in accordance with determinations of the Government Intelligence Community, immediately provides appropriate addressees with the aforementioned information - together with the Community opinion.

The chairman convenes meetings of the Government Intelligence Community every two weeks, on dates indicated in the work schedule or upon the initiative of the chairman or upon request of the Community member.

Meetings of the Government Intelligence Community are of a secret nature and the disclosure of any information and documents constituting the subjects of exchange and effects of works of the Community takes place with due regard to regulations on protection of classified information.

The chairman of the Government Intelligence Community provides the Prime Minister, by the end of January each year, with report on the Government Intelligence Community operations in the previous year.

The Chancellery of the Prime Minister provides the service of the Government Intelligence Community.

The Government Intelligence Community performs periodically (at least quarterly) analyses of information constituting subjects of exchange through the preparation of the Joint Analysis of the Government Intelligence Community. Such analyses include also forecasts of threats to the external security and international position of the Republic of Poland.

The Head of the Foreign Intelligence Agency presents the Joint Analysis of the Government Intelligence Community to:

- the President of the Republic of Poland,
- the Marshall of the Sejm,
- the Marshall of the Senate,
- the Prime Minister.

The Government Intelligence Community may also determine other addressees of the Joint Analysis of the Government Intelligence Community.

FOREIGN INTELLIGENCE AGENCY

Director
of Cabinet of the Head
of the Foreign Intelligence Agency
Col. Andrzej Kolczyński
Address for correspondence
02-634 Warszawa
ul. Miłobędzka 55
telephone (48) (0-prefix-22) 640-50-19
fax (48) (0-prefix-22) 640-50-70
(48) (0-prefix-22) 640-50-33
e-mail poczta@aw.gov.pl

Please send any correspondence referring to the website of the Foreign Intelligence Agency to the following e-mail address:
e-mail serwis@aw.gov.pl

FOREIGN INTELLIGENCE AGENCY

http://www.abw.gov.pl/EN/Eng_glo.htm

AGENCJA BEZPIECZEŃSTWA WEWNĘTRZNEGO
00-993 Warszawa
ul. Rakowiecka 2A
email: poczta@abw.gov.pl
(ABW zastrzega sobie prawo do nieodpowiadania na wszystkie listy)

OFICER DYŻURNY ABW
Tel. (022) 58-57-910, (022) 56-59-110

SKARGI I WNIOSKI
Tel. (022) 58-59-192 (w godz. 8 - 16)

RZECZNIK PRASOWY SZEFA ABW
mjr Magdalena Stańczyk
Tel. (022) 84-53-015, 56-59-191, 56-59-292

The ABW is the Polish special service responsible for the matters of the protection of the state's internal security and its constitutional order. The Headquarters of the ABW, located in Warsaw, is composed of 16 units, among other things, of the following Departments: of Counterintelligence; of Counteracting Corruption, Terrorism and Organised Crime; for the Protection of Classified Information; of Telematics Security, as well as of 5 Bureaus, for example: Bureau of Record and Archives, Legal Bureau.

The country structure of the ABW is composed of 15 regional branches, placed in the capitals of provinces.

The tasks of the ABW, among other things, include: fighting threats to internal security of the state and its constitutional order as well as exposing the crimes of espionage, terrorism, breach of the state secret, corruption of persons holding public posts, and crimes aimed against the economic foundations of the state, crimes of proliferation of the ABC weapons and trade in drugs on an international scale.

The ABW provides appropriate bodies with information that may be vital for the protection of the state's internal security and its constitutional order and performs the functions of the national security authority. It also has the investigatory powers analogous to those of the Police.

LEADERSHIP

The Internal Security Agency (ABW) is led by the Head of the ABW,
Mr Andrzej Barcikowski.

Andrzej Barcikowski was born on 27 April 1955 in Warsaw. In 1977 he graduated from the University of Warsaw. He studied political science. In 1983 defended his doctoral thesis at Warsaw University.

In 1977 - 1983 he worked at the Faculty of Journalism and Political Science of the UW. In 1984 - 1990 he occupied main posts at the Central Committee of the Polish United Workers' Party (KC PZPR) in the units responsible for political programmes and analyses. In 1990 - 94 an employee of the Polish branch of a British IT concern, the ICL.

In 1995 - 96 - Director of the Office of the Supervisory Board of the Polish Development Bank.

In 1996 - 1997 Director General of the Office of the Council of Ministers and Chief of the Co-operative of Advisors to Prime Minister Włodzimierz Cimoszewicz. In 1997 Chief of the Political Cabinet of the Prime Minister.

In 1998 - 2000 held main positions at publishing houses MUZA S. A. (company ltd. by shares) and MUZA EDUKACYJNA Ltd. From January 2001 - Deputy Director of the Organisation Department of BRE Bank S. A. (company limited). Member of the Chapter of the Polish Promotion Trade Mark "Teraz Polska" (It's Time for Poland Now - conferred on the best Polish products).

From 1996 Member of the Committee of the Office of Public Orders. Member of the Democratic Left Alliance Ethics Commission. From October 2001 to April 2002 - undersecretary of state at the Ministry of Internal Affairs and Administration. From April to the end of June 2002 Chief of the Office of State Protection. Since 29 June 2002 - Head of the Internal Security Agency (ABW).

LEGAL BASES

1. The basic legal acts

The basic legal act regulating the Internal Security Agency's scope of action as well as the duties and powers of its officers is the Internal Security Agency and Foreign Intelligence Agency Act of 24 May 2002 (Journal of Laws No. 74, item 676).

2. The oversight of the Special Services

The organs of the civil oversight are both legislative bodies (the Sejm Commission for the Special Services), executive (the Prime Minister, appropriate ministers), as well as judicial bodies and the Supreme Chamber of Control.

In April 1995, by virtue of the amended Sejm resolution of 30 July 1992, the Sejm Commission for the Special Services was set up. The tasks of the Commission are concentrated on assessing legal and normative acts (bills and regulations) of general character concerning the special services, along with giving opinions on the directions of their work.

The Commission gives opinions on the directions of the activity of the special services, basing on the information presented by the heads of these services, examines the annual reports of the heads of the ABW, AW and WSI (Military Intelligence Services) and it gives opinions on the requests concerning the appointment of particular persons as heads and deputy heads of the special services. The realm of the Commission's activities includes also assessing draft budgets in the part concerning the special services as well as assessing the report on the execution of this budget. Among other aspects that are assessed are the cooperation between the special services subordinated to the Minister of Internal Affairs and Administration and to the Minister of National Defence, as well as their cooperation with other services and military units supervised by the Minister of Internal Affairs and Administration. The members of the Commission also assess the cooperation between the special services and organs of state administration, prosecuting organs, and they examine complaints concerning the activity of the special services.

In 2002, the Sejm of IV term appointed new members of the Sejm Commission for the Special Services. The Sejm decided that the Commission will be composed of 9 MPs: 3 from the Democratic Left Alliance (SLD), and one from each of the following parties: Citizens Platform (PO), Self-Defence (Samoobrona), Law and Justice (PiS), Polish Peasant Party (PSL), League of Polish Families (LPR), Union of Labour (UP). Thereby members of the Commission became: Marian Marczewski (SLD), Józef Gruszka (PSL), Andrzej Grzesik (Samoobrona), Marian Janicki (UP), Zdzisław Kałamaga (SLD), Bogdan Lewandowski (SLD), Antoni Macierewicz (KN), Konstanty Miodowicz (PO), and Zbigniew Wasserman (PiS). The current chairman of the Commission is Andrzej Grzesik.

The Committee for Special Services acts under the Council of Ministers as a consultative and advisory body in the matters of programming, overseeing and coordinating the activity of the ABW, AW, and Military Intelligence Services. The tasks of the Committee include formulating assessments or expressing opinions in, among other things, the matters of appointing and dismissing the Head of the ABW, setting up the directions and action plans for the special services, giving opinions on detailed draft budgets and projects of legal acts concerning the special services. The members of the

Committee also assess the execution of the statutory tasks of the special services, among other things, in the matters of organising the exchange of important information among the government administration organs and in the field of classified information protection.

The Committee is headed by the Prime Minister, run by the Secretary and composed of: the minister responsible for internal affairs, minister responsible for foreign affairs, Minister of National Defence, minister responsible for public finance, National Security Advisor to the President (head of the National Security Bureau). The sessions of the Committee are also attended by: the Head of the ABW, Head of the AW, Chief of the Military Intelligence Services, and Chairman of the Sejm Commission for the Special Services.

In the field of applying by the special services the measures of intelligence techniques and measures of correspondence control, the supervising bodies are the Prosecutor General and the District Court of Warsaw.

The Supreme Chamber of Control (NIK) checks the activity of the ABW in relation to its execution of the budget and to the execution of acts of law and other legal acts concerning the financial, economic, organisational, and administrative activity.

PORTUGAL

http://www.sis.pt

The Intelligence System of the Portuguese Republic (SIRP) is presently regulated by Law no. 30/84 dated of 5 September. This law has been amended, respectively, by Laws nos. 4/95, dated of 21 of February 15/96, dated of 30 of April, and 75-A/97, dated of 22 of July.

Statutory Law of SIRP entrusts the intelligence services with the duty of assuring, whilst respecting the Constitution and the Rule of Law, the production of intelligence required for the safeguarding of national independence and internal security.

SIRP is fed with information collected by two services, which in turn have clearly distinct functions:

- Security and Intelligence Service (SIS);
- Military and Defence Strategy Intelligence Service (SIEDM).

SIS SIS is the organism assigned with the production of intelligence that contributes for the safeguarding of internal security and prevention of sabotage, terrorism, espionage, and those acts, that by their very nature, may alter or destroy the constitutionally established State and the Rule of Law.
SIEDM SIEDM is the organism entrusted with the production of intelligence that contributes to the safeguarding of national independence, national interests, external security of the Portuguese State, the fulfilment of Armed Forces missions and military security.
SIS and SIEDM are dependent to the Prime Minister;

- SIS through the Interior Minister;
- SIEDM through the Defence Minister.

The activities developed, as within the ambit of SIRP, obey to several principles:

- principle of respect for the Constitution and the Rule of Law;

- principle of respect for rights, freedoms and guaranties;
- principle of legality of competencies; SIRP objectives are to be attained, exclusively, through the exercise of those competencies determined in SIRP Statutory Law;
- principle of specificity of competencies; each service is confined to the activities of research and treatment of information that is specifically within its competencies;
- principle of limited action: SIS and SIEDM agents and servants cannot exercise powers, practice acts or develop activities which are within the ambit of those judicial competencies, and others, attributed to entities with police functions, being expressly forbidden the detention of individuals or the initiation of criminal proceedings;
- principle of exclusivity: other services are expressly forbidden from the conduction of activities and pursuit of objectives identical to the ones determined by SIEDM Statutory Law;
- principle of confidentiality and State secret: servants and agents of the intelligence services are required to respect a rigorous duty of confidentiality as regards accessed information; information related with SIS and SIEDM activities are protected as secrets of State.

The organic structure of SIRP is systematised as follows:

- Parliament elects the members of the Oversight Board for the Intelligence Services and proceeds to the hearing, in parliamentary commission, of the nominated SIS and SIEDM Director-Generals;
- Prime-Minister co-ordinates the activities of the intelligence services, presides the Intelligence Oversight Board and informs the President of the Republic;
- the action of the Prime-Minister is assisted by the Intelligence Oversight Board;
- the Intelligence Oversight Board is permanently assisted by a Technical Commission;
- the Technical Commission is presided by the respective Secretary General;
- SIS is dependent to the Prime-Minister through the Interior Minister;
- SIEDM is dependent to the Prime-Minister through the Ministry of Defence;
- the Republic's General Prosecutor selects the members of the Data Centres Oversight and Accountability Commission.

SIRP Statutory Law describes in greater detail the competencies of the following entities: Prime Minister, Intelligence Oversight Board, Technical Commission, the Oversight and Accountability Council of Intelligence, and Data Centres Oversight and Accountability Commission.

To the Director General is entrusted the function of assuring the proper operation of SIS and that it maintains faithful, in its performance, to its legal aims and objectives.

In particular, the Director General has the competency to:

- direct, through the hierarchical structure, the activities of the service and inspect, supervise and co-ordinate in such manner that ensures the effective attainment of the service's institutional ends;
- preside the Administrative board;
- direct the activity of the Data Centre;
- execute the Prime Minister and the Minister of Interior's determinations, as well as the deliberations of the oversight and accountability organs defined in SIRP Statutory Law;
- nominate and discharge personnel, with the exception of those appointed by the Prime Minister and the Minister of Interior;
- exercise within the legal boundaries disciplinary measures;
- guide the elaboration of SIS budget;
- elaborate SIS annual report.

The nomination of SIS Director General is preceded by hearing of the appointee before a parliamentary commission.
The Director General is assisted by two Deputy Director Generals, and is replaced in case of absence and any impediments, by the one who has been appointed to that effect.

INTELLIGENCE AGENCIES

Sistema de Informações da República Portuguesa (SIRP) Intelligence System of the Republic of Portugal

Serviço de Informações de Segurança Security Intelligence Service
Serviço de Informações Militares
Military Intelligence Service
Serviço de Informações Estratégicas de Defesa e Militares (SIEDM)
Strategic Defense and Military Intelligence Service

In the 1940s the secret police, called the International Police for the Defense of the State (Policia Internacional e de Defesa do Estado - PIDE), although under jurisdiction of the Ministry of Justice, was in fact controlled directly by Salazar. Under revisions of the law after 1954, PIDE officers were entitled to act as inquiring magistrates empowered to detain for trial persons suspected of crimes against the state. Suspects were routinely arrested without warrants and often held for months without specific charges brought against them and without access to legal assistance. Disappearance and torture were commonplace. Agents of PIDE carried out covert operations within communist organizations, the government-run labor unions, the armed forces, the universities, and the Portuguese emigrate communities abroad. During the 1960s and 1970s, PIDE directed its efforts to suppressing opposition to the war effort in the African colonies, particularly on university campuses, and to tracking down anti-regime terrorists responsible for bombing military and strategic installations.

Although PIDE was renamed the General Security Directorate (Direccao Geral de Seguranca--DGS) by Marcello Caetano's government, it retained its old image. The abhorrence felt for it was so strong that it was abolished in Portugal the day after the Caetano regime was toppled. Abuses by the security apparatus were subsequently reported in detail in the Portuguese press, causing even more revulsion among the public.

The lingering specter of PIDE and DGS as pillars of the authoritarian regime in the memory of the Portuguese people delayed the establishment of a new civilian intelligence agency for more than a decade. Following an Armenian terrorist attack on the Embassy of Turkey in 1983, the assassination of a Palestine Liberation Organization representative at a Socialist International conference the same year, and a number of domestic terrorist attacks, the Portuguese government became convinced of the need for a new intelligence agency. In 1984, the Intelligence System of the Republic of Portugal (Sistema de Informacoes da Republica Portuguesa -SIRP) was established in 1986. SIRP was intended to be the parent body for three separate intelligence services: the Security Intelligence Service (Servico de Informacoes e Seguranca -SIS), the Military Intelligence Service (Servico de Informacoes Militares \SIM), and the Defense Strategic Intelligence Service (Servico de Informacoes Estrategicas de Defesa -SIED).

SISTEMA DE INFORMACOES DA REPUBLICA PORTUGUESA [SIRP] (INTELLIGENCE SYSTEM OF THE PORTUGESE REPUBLIC)

The intelligence system of the Portuguese Republic is regulated under Law 30/84 of 5 September 1984. The legal frame of the SIRP attributes the responsibility to the information services to ensure, respecting the law and the Constitution, the production of intelligence necessary to safeguard national independence and guarantee internal security.

The SIRP is fed by information collected by two services with differing functions:

- the Security Information Service (SIS)
- the Strategic Military and Defense Information Service (SIEDM)

The SIS is an organization charged with the production of intelligence that contributes to the safeguarding of internal security, prevention of sabotage terrorism, espionage and practices which, by their nature, could alter or destroy the constitutionally established state.
SIEDM is an organization charged with the production of intelligence that contributes to the safeguarding of national independence, national interests, the external security of the Portuguese State, and in the execution of the missions of the Armed Forces and for military security.
Both SIS and SIEDM fall under the Prime Minister:

- SIS, by way of the Minister of Internal Administration
- SIEDM, by way of the Minister of National Defense

The legal frame of the SIRP defines the organic structure of the Intelligence System of The Portuguese Republic.
This organic structure is articulated in the following manner:

- the Republic Assembly elects members of the Counsel of Legalization from the Intelligence Services through a parliamentary committee, or is directly appointed by the Director General of the two services.
- the Prime Minister has various authorities with regard to the SIRP: coordinate the activities of the Intelligence Services, preside over the superior council of Intelligence and to inform the President of the Republic.
- the action of the Prime Minister is overseen by the superior council of intelligence.
- the superior council of intelligence is supervised, in permanency, by a technical committee.
- the technical committee is comprised of the respective Secretary General, who presides, and the directors general of SIS and SIEDM.
- the SIS falls under the Prime Minister, under the Ministry of Administration.
- the SIEDM falls under the Prime Minister under the Ministry of National Defense.
- the Attorney General of the republic elects members of the committee of Legalization (seems like an Inspector General to me).

The undertaken activities of the SIRP obey various principles:

- the principle of respect of the Constitution and the law.
- the principle of respect of directives, freedoms and guarantees.
- the respect of the legality of attributes and authorities, the finalities of the SIRP will be exclusively realized by way of the attributes and authorities set forth in the legal frame of the SIRP.
- the principle of specificity of attributes: each service can perform its activities dealing with intelligence with respect to its specific attributes.
- the principle of limitation of the operating area: the functionaries and agents of the SIS and SIEDM are not able to exercise abilities, or perform activities in the legal establishment (court system) or in the police establishment, being expressly prohibited the detention of individuals or legal proceedings.
- the principle of exclusivity: it is prohibited that other services overtake identical activities or objectives to those foreseen in the legal frame of the SIRP.

- the principles of protection of secret(s) of the State: the functionaries or agents of the intelligence services are obligated to maintain a rigorous vigilance over the information to which they have access, and information related to the activities of the SIS and SIEDM are protected by State Secret.

ABBREVIATIONS

AR - Assembleia da Republica
(Republican Assembly)
MDN - Ministro da Defesa Nacional
(Minister of National Defence)
EMGFA - Estado-Maior-General das Forcas Armadas
(General Staff of the Armed Forces)
CFSI - Conselho de Fiscalizacao dos Servicos de Informacoes
(Council of Legalization of the Intelligence Services; Inspector General)
PGR - Procuradoria-Geral da Republica
(Attorney General of the Republic)
DIMIL - Divisao de Informacoes Militares
(Military Intelligence Divisions)
CFCD - Comissao de Fiscalizacoes
(Legal Oversight Committee)
SIEDM - Servico de Informacoes Estrategicas de Defesa e dos Centros de Dados
(Military Strategic Defence and Military Intelligence Service)
PM - Primeiro-Ministro
(Prime Minister)
MAI - Ministerio da Administracao Interna
(Ministry of Internal Administration)
CSI - Conselho Superior de Informacoes
(Superior Intelligence Council)
SIS - Servico de Informacoes de Seguranca
(Security Intelligence Services)
CT - Comissao Tecnica
(Technical Committee)
CA - Conselho Administrativo
(Administrative Council)
DG - Director-Geral
(Director General)
SAAG - Servico Administrativo e de Apoio Geral
(Administrative General Support Service)
CC - Conselho Consultivo
(Consultative Council)
SI - Servico de Informatica
(Information Service)
SO - Servicos Operacionais
(Operational Services)
DGA - Director-Geral Adjunto
(Adjunct Director General)
DR - Delegacoes Regionais
(Regional Delegations)

SERVIÇO DE INFORMACOES DE SEGURANCA [SIS] (SECURITY INFORMATION SERVICE)

The SIS was created in 1984 under the frame of SIRP. One year later, in 1985, the law decree 225/85 of 4 July approved the Organization of the SIS.

The SIS is a public service, dependent on the Prime Minister by way of the Ministry of Internal Administration, and integrated in the SIRP. The frame of the SIRP, or SIS, is the only organization charged with the production of information (intelligence).

The SIS enjoys administrative and financial autonomy and is located in Lisbon. There could be other created delegations of the SIS in other points of the country. In actuality, the SIS has delegations in Porto, Ponta Delgada, Funchal and Faro. In the environment of its specific attributes, the SIS has the authority to proceed in a systematic and precise manner, in the analysis, production and storage of intelligence.

From a territorial point of view, this authority coïncides with that of the sovereign powers of the Portuguese State.
All Public Administration Services, central, regional and local, and institutes and public businesses and concessions are obligated to give their cooperation to the SIS. A special obligation to collaborate is imposed upon the security forces and services as set forth in the law of Internal Security.
The SIS, in turn must:

- cooperate with SIEDM
- communicate with competent authorities in criminal investigation and in the execution of penal action or in illegal criminal facts, safe-guarding the law of State Secret(s)
- communicate with competent authorities, under the terms of the law news and information dealing with internal security matters and in the prevention and repression of criminality.

The SIS can cooperate with partner foreign organizations under the frame of international treaties assumed by the Portuguese State and within the limits of its specific attributes. This cooperation is subject to the Prime Minister's guidance, through the superior council of Intelligence. The activities of the SIS are considered, in all its effects, classified in the interest of the Internal Security of the State.

SERVIÇO DE INFORMAÇÕES DE SEGURANÇA SECURITY INTELLIGENCE SERVICE

Therefore, the Basic Law assumes that **freedom** and **security** are two rights closely intertwined: freedom is only authentic and full if it can be enjoyed where personal security exists; on the other hand, the right to security is nothing more than the guarantee of the free exercise of basic rights.

The basic right to security is twofold: it can be a **negative** concept, as a subjective right to security, a right to be defended from eventual aggressions on the part of the State apparatus; and a **positive** concept, as a right to protection, through the State apparatus, against aggressions or threats from another.

Therefore the positive conception of a basic right to security, requires an action by the State through the establishment of a **policy of security,**

Such policy of security perceives two different aspects: **internal security** and **external security.** External security is normally connected with national defence. Its purpose is defined in Article 273, s.2, of the Constitution: "National defence aims at affirming the respect for constitutional order, democratic institutions and international conventions, national independence, territorial integrity, and freedom and security of the population against any aggression or external threats".

If on the one hand it is not difficult to grasp the fundamental concept of external security, that is not the case of internal security.

In the definition laid down in Law no. 20/87, of 12 of July (Internal Security Law), internal security is "an activity developed by the State in order to maintain order, security, and public peace, protect juridical values and persons, prevent criminality and contribute in the assurance of the normal operation of democratic institutions, the regular enjoyment of rights and fundamental freedoms, and the respect for democracy and the Rule of Law.

Law no. 20/87 clearly enunciates the principles and aims of internal security:

- internal security is designed to protect juridical values and persons, and not to threaten them;
- internal security aims at ensuring the normal exercise of rights and fundamental freedoms of citizens;
- internal security is concomitant to the respect for democracy and the Rule of Law, and is exercised according to the law, namely penal and procedural law, and organic laws of the security services;
- measures undertaken in the ambit of a policy of security are destined mainly to the protection of life and the integrity of persons, public peace and democratic order, and directed at violent or highly organised criminality, in particular terrorism and espionage.

Amongst the principles of organic and functional nature, are:

- the principle of unity for each security force or service within national territory as a whole;
- the general principle of cooperation of all citizens in the attainment of internal security objectives;
- the principle of cooperation and coordination of security forces and services;
- the principle of exclusiveness of operation of each security force and service in the ambit of the functions they are entrusted with;
- the public and rigorously apolitical nature of security forces and services.

Further, the Law of Internal Security defines the attributions of the distinct entities in a security policy context:

- Parliament contributes in framing internal security policies and in the supervision of its execution. It is within its competencies, the election of members of the Oversight Board for Intelligence Services.
- Government, which is responsible for the conduction of an internal security policy and, through the Council of Ministries, the delineation of general directives of that same policy together with its execution; the drafting and assurance of resources; approves the co-ordination plan between security forces and services; determines the rules for classification and circulation of official documents; and accredits those persons that should have access to classified documents.
- Prime-Minister, who co-ordinates the action of cabinet members in matters regarding Internal Security, propounds to the Council of Ministers the plan for the coordination of security forces and services, supervises the inter-ministerial activity for the adoption of adequate measures in case of a serious threat to internal security, and finally, informs the President of the Republic on matters regarding the conduction of internal security policy. Some of these competencies may be delegated to the Interior Minister;
- the Superior Council for Internal Security, which is an inter-ministerial organ of consultation in matters of security;
- the Cabinet for the Co-ordination of Security, which is a specialised organ of consultation for technical and operational co-ordination of the security forces and services activities, operating under the direct supervision of the Prime-Minister, or by delegation, under the Interior Minister;

- Security forces and services:
- Republican National Guard;
- Criminal Police;
- Immigration Office;
- Organisms of Maritime Authority Systems and Correspondent Organisms of Aeronautical Authority Systems;
- Security and Intelligence Service.

The Intelligence System of the Portuguese Republic (SIRP) is presently regulated by Law no. 30/84 dated of 5 September. This law has been amended, respectively, by Laws nos. 4/95, dated of 21 of February 15/96, dated of 30 of April, and 75-A/97, dated of 22 of July.

Statutory Law of SIRP entrusts the intelligence services with the duty of assuring, whilst respecting the Constitution and the Rule of Law, the production of intelligence required for the safeguarding of national independence and internal security.

SIRP is fed with information collected by two services, which in turn have clearly distinct functions:

- Security and Intelligence Service (SIS);
- Military and Defence Strategy Intelligence Service (SIEDM).

SIS SIS is the organism assigned with the production of intelligence that contributes for the safeguarding of internal security and prevention of sabotage, terrorism, espionage, and those acts, that by their very nature, may alter or destroy the constitutionally established State and the Rule of Law.
SIEDM SIEDM is the organism entrusted with the production of intelligence that contributes to the safeguarding of national independence, national interests, external security of the Portuguese State, the fulfilment of Armed Forces missions and military security.
SIS and SIEDM are dependent to the Prime Minister;

- SIS through the Interior Minister;
- SIEDM through the Defence Minister.

The activities developed, as within the ambit of SIRP, obey to several principles:

- principle of respect for the Constitution and the Rule of Law;
- principle of respect for rights, freedoms and guaranties;
- principle of legality of competencies; SIRP objectives are to be attained, exclusively, through the exercise of those competencies determined in SIRP Statutory Law;
- principle of specificity of competencies; each service is confined to the activities of research and treatment of information that is specifically within its competencies;
- principle of limited action: SIS and SIEDM agents and servants cannot exercise powers, practice acts or develop activities which are within the ambit of those judicial competencies, and others, attributed to entities with police functions, being expressly forbidden the detention of individuals or the initiation of criminal proceedings;
- principle of exclusivity: other services are expressly forbidden from the conduction of activities and pursuit of objectives identical to the ones determined by SIEDM Statutory Law;
- principle of confidentiality and State secret: servants and agents of the intelligence services are required to respect a rigorous duty of confidentiality as regards accessed information; information related with SIS and SIEDM activities are protected as secrets of State.

The organic structure of SIRP is systematised as follows:

- Parliament elects the members of the Oversight Board for the Intelligence Services and proceeds to the hearing, in parliamentary commission, of the nominated SIS and SIEDM Director-Generals;
- Prime-Minister co-ordinates the activities of the intelligence services, presides the Intelligence Oversight Board and informs the President of the Republic;
- the action of the Prime-Minister is assisted by the Intelligence Oversight Board;
- the Intelligence Oversight Board is permanently assisted by a Technical Commission;
- the Technical Commission is presided by the respective Secretary General;
- SIS is dependent to the Prime-Minister through the Interior Minister;
- SIEDM is dependent to the Prime-Minister through the Ministry of Defence;
- the Republic's General Prosecutor selects the members of the Data Centres Oversight and Accountability Commission.

SIRP Statutory Law describes in greater detail the competencies of the following entities: Prime Minister, Intelligence Oversight Board, Technical Commission, the Oversight and Accountability Council of Intelligence, and Data Centres Oversight and Accountability Commission.

The Intelligence Oversight Board is the inter-ministerial organ of consultation and co-ordination in matters of intelligence.

Under the presidency of the Prime-Minister, the Intelligence Oversight Board is constituted by:

- Vice-Prime-Ministers, if any;
- Ministers of State and Presidency, if any;
- Minister of Interior;
- Minister of Defence;
- Minister of Justice;
- Minister for Foreign Affairs;
- Minister of Finance
- Minister for the Republic and Autonomous Region of the Azores;
- Minister for the Republic and Autonomous Region of Madeira;
- President of the Regional Government of Madeira
- President of the Regional Government of the Azores
- Head of General Staff of the Armed Forces;
- Director-General of SIS;
- Director-General of SIEDM;
- General-Secretary for the Technical Commission.

The Intelligence Oversight Board has the following competencies:

- advice and assist the Prime-Minister in the co-ordination of the Intelligence Services;
- opiniate upon all matters submitted by the Prime-Minister or, under his authorisation, by any of its members, in the subject of intelligence;
- propose the orientation of activities to be developed by the intelligence services.

The Intelligence Oversight Board is assisted, permanently, by the Technical Commission.

The **Consulting Board (CC)** was created through the operation of SIS Organic Law, and is a consulting organ that responds directly to the Interior Minister.

The Consulting Board is constituted by:

- the Commander in Chief of the National Republican Guard;
- the Commander in Chief of the Public Security Police;
- the Director General of the Criminal Police;
- the Director of the Immigration Office;
- the Commander in Chief of the Maritime Police;
- SIS Director General;
- SIS Deputy Directors.

On the other hand, at the request or determination by the Minister of Interior other entities may participate at Consulting Board meetings.
The Consulting Board has the following competencies:

- advise the Minister of Interior, upon matters regarding internal security Intelligence;
- propound to the Minister of Interior the adoption of adequate measures destined to the centralisation, handling, and employment of all information that is of interest to the furthering of SIS objectives;
- analyse the necessary mechanisms in order to effectuate the duty of cooperation as between SIS and other public institutions.

Oversight and Accountability Board of the Intelligence Services is an organ that oversees the operation of the intelligence services.

The Oversight and Accountability Board of the Intelligence Services controls and supervises the activities of the intelligence services, assuring the respect for the Constitution and the Law, particularly in the ambit of rights, freedoms and fundamental guaranties of citizens.

It is constituted by three citizens of recognised integrity and in their full enjoyment of civil and political rights, elected by Parliament under a secret ballot and qualified majority.

The mandate of its members is of four years, only interrupted by parliamentary determination, which is undertaken according to the terms of the elective procedure.

The operation of Statutory Law of SIRP is not restricted to the mere attribution -to the Oversight and Accountability Board of the Intelligence Services – of a generic competency enabling it to supervise the intelligence services. This competency of supervision is regulated in more detail, conferring to the Intelligence Oversight Board the power to:

- consider the report of SIS and MDSIS activities;
- obtain from SIS Director-General and MDSIS Director-General, on a bimonthly basis, an integral list of the processes in course, and it may require and obtain additional accounts, as it deems necessary;
- be informed, through the Interior Minister and Defence Minister, of governmental guidelines regarding investigative information;
- obtain from the Intelligence Oversight Board and from the Technical Commission any account over matters concerning the operation of the SIRP;
- inspect SIS and MDSIS headquarters or secondary installations;

- ask for any information contained in SIS Data Centres and MDSIS Data Centres;
- report to Parliament, at the very least on an annual basis, on matters regarding the operation of intelligence services;
- propound to government the conduction of investigative or sanctioning procedures and inquests;
- pronounce over any legislative initiatives concerning SIRP, or organisational methods, and administrative, financial or personal management of SIS and MDSIS.

In addition, the Oversight and Accountability Council of the Intelligence Services supervises the methods applied to exchange information as between the two services, and deliberates upon reports of the Armed Forces activities in relation to specific operational information.

SIRP Statutory Law foresees the existence of **data centres** in the Intelligence services.

Still, these data centres are autonomous from each other, they cannot be linked.

On the other hand, they are subjected to the control of the Oversight and Accountability Commission of Data Centres.

SIS has a Data Centre, encharged with the processing and conservation of data and information relative to SIS institutional attributions.

The Data Centre is directed by a servant of the service with the status of departmental director, and is nominated and discharged by the Minister of Interior, under the advice of the Director General.

The conduction of the Data Centre is assured by SIS Computer Services staff.

The Director General of SIS directs the activities of the Data Centre.

With the exception to the Oversight and Accountability Commission, no entity unrelated with SIS may have direct access to the Data Centre. Even the access by SIS servants or agents is regulated by a Ministerial Order of the Minister of Interior.

The **Administrative Board** is the competent organ for the administration of budgetary appropriations

The Administrative Board is constituted:

- by the Director General, who presides it;
- by the Assistant Directors;
- by the General Administration Director.

ROMANIAN

INTELLIGENCE AGENCIES

http://www.presidency.ro
http://www.sri.ro/

Office of the President
Romanian Intelligence Service [*Serviciul roman de informatii (SRI)*]
Guard and Protection Service (SPP)
Foreign Intelligence Service [*Serviciul de informatii externe (SIE)*]
Ministry of National Defence
General Directorate for Defense Intelligence
Ministry of Internal Affairs
General Directorate for Intelligence and Internal Protection
Directia generala de informatii si protectie interna
Ministry of Justice
Independent Service for Protection and Anticorruption
Serviciul independent pentru protectie si anticoruptie (SIPA)

FOREIGN INTELLIGENCE SERVICE

Office of the Foreign Intelligence Service (SIE) at :
Phone :(+40 21) 203.41.37 Fax : (+40 21) 203.41.63
(+40 21) 203.44.47

E-mail
relatii_presa@sie.ro
relatii_publice@sie.ro

Address : 280 - 282, Bucureşti - Ploieşti Road , District 1, Bucharest
and at the Post Office no. 41, P.O. Box no. 59, Bucharest.

The Foreign Intelligence Service is a fundamental institution of the system of national security, established on constitutional grounds and subject to parliamentary oversight, which makes a specific contribution to safeguarding, upholding and pursuing Romania's interests, within the unitary conception set out in the Strategy of National Security.

According to the Strategy, the goals of the Service for the coming period and within a foreseeable prospective are priority aimed at substantially enhancing the performance of its activity, its focusing on the main courses of action established through strategic planning (combating asymmetric threats, first of all terrorism and trans-border crime, foreign counterintelligence, promoting Romania's political and economic interests, foreign liaison etc.).

Another element of particular importance has been added, namely, supporting the process of Romania's European and Euro-Atlantic integration, by cementing and making adequate use of the relations of partnership forged with similar services in the West-European countries.

The new context created in the international environment has entailed a deep reassessment of concepts in the area of security and has imposed a rethinking of the role and the broadening of the responsibilities of the intelligence services in democratic countries. For its part, the Foreign Intelligence Service has established its own strategy, which aims to turn the service into a modern, efficient and flexible one, endowed with a high degree of compatibility and interoperability with opposite structures in democratic countries, capable of giving a timely and qualified response to social commands.

It is our belief that the pro-active civil support of the Romanian society, including through developing the model of security culture promoted by intellectual elites, the enhancement of the quality of communication with the civil society and the correct propaganda through the media will pose incentive elements for consecrating the Foreign Intelligence Service as a modern institution devoted to protecting and promoting Romania's vital interests.

RUSSIA

INTELLIGENCE AGENCIES

Security Council
Defense Council
Committee for State Security [KGB]
Komitet Gosudarstvennoi Bezopasnosti

Foreign Intelligence Service (SVR)
Sluzhba Vneshney Razvedki
Central Intelligence Service [CSR]
Centralnaya Sluzhba Razvedky
Federal Security Service (FSB)
Federal'naya Sluzhba Bezopasnosti
Federal Counterintelligence Service (FSK)
Federal'naya Sluzhba Kontr-razvedky
Federal Agency for Government Communications & Information (FAPSI)
Federal'naya Agenstvo Pravitel'stvennoy Svayazi i Informatsii
State Technical Commission [GosTekhKomissiya]
Gosudarstvennaya Tekhnicheskaya Komissiya
Federal Protective Service (FSO)
Federal'naya Sluzhba Okhrani
Main Administration for the Protection of the Russian Federation (GUO)
Glavnoye Upravlenie Okhrani Rossiiskoy Federatsii
Presidential Security Service [PSB]
Prezidentskaya Sluzhba Bezopasnosti
Federal Border Service [FPS]
Federal'naya Pogranichnaya Sluzhba
SECURITY MINISTRY OF RUSSIA (MBR)
Ministerstvo Bezopasnosti Rosii

MINISTRY OF DEFENSE (MOD)
Main Intelligence Directorate (GRU)
Glavnoye Razvedovatel'noye Upravlenie (GRU)
MINISTRY OF INTERNAL AFFAIRS (MVD)
Ministerstvo Vnutrennikh Del
Interlinked System for Recognizing Enemies [SOUD]
Sistema Objedinyonnogo Uchota Dannych o Protivnike
Intelligence Related Facilities
Intelligence Programs and Activities
Intelligence Related Documenation

INTELLIGECEN AND SECURITY SERVICES DEVELOPMENT

Gorbachev Era

After gaining the post of general secretary in March 1985, Gorbachev moved with unprecedented speed to implement personnel changes in the party and government. His success in getting rid of so many potential political opponents in such a short time surprised Western Soviet experts, particularly because Gorbachev did not have a substantial power base or patronage network of his own when he took office. Gorbachev apparently relied on the same bases of support that Andropov had used in his ascent to the top, which included the KGB. According to Western experts, Gorbachev appealed to the KGB for help in purging the Brezhnev old guard. The main vehicle used by Gorbachev in carrying out these purges was the anticorruption campaign. By the late summer of 1985, hardly a day passed without a report in the press on cases on bribery, embezzlement, or other forms of economic crime. In addition to high-level party and state officials, MVD and Procuracy employees came under fire for their failure to uncover crimes. Even MVD chief Vitalii Fedorchuk fell victim to Gorbachev, losing his post in early 1986. Fedorchuk's replacement, Aleksandr Vlasov, was a former party apparatchik (see Glossary) with no experience in law enforcement.

Although the regular law enforcement agencies were subjected to sharp attacks for their failure to combat crime, the KGB remained unscathed, despite the fact that it was empowered by law to investigate certain types of economic crime. There was some turnover in key KGB posts, but these changes were not nearly as widespread as were the changes in the CPSU apparatus and in other state agencies.

Numerous signs pointed to the fact that the Gorbachev leadership was cultivating good relations with the KGB by maintaining its high prestige and political status. KGB chairman Chebrikov was promoted to full membership in the Politburo just a month after Gorbachev came to power. He also figured prominently in the Soviet media. At the Twenty-Seventh Party Congress in February-March 1986, for example, he delivered a speech that was an unprecedented assertion of the power and authority of the KGB.

Although Gorbachev continued to rely on the KGB in his drive to purge the party and state apparatus of corrupt officials, toward the end of 1986 signs indicated that his relations with this organization were becoming strained. The KGB cannot have been pleased about the reformist polices promoted by Gorbachev, in particular openness in the media and liberalization of cultural norms. Calls for reform of the judicial and legal systems, voiced with increasing frequency in the autumn of 1986, signified that the Gorbachev leadership was attempting to curtail arbitrary KGB actions against citizens. This attempt became even more apparent in January 1987, when Chebrikov acknowledged, on the front page of *Pravda,* that employees of the KGB had committed illegalities. Such an acknowledgment of KGB abuses was unprecedented. Even during the Khrushchev era, when the crimes of Stalin's security police were exposed, the KGB was never criticized in the press. Observers speculated that, having depended initially on KGB support to purge the Brezhnevites, Gorbachev decided by early 1987 that he was strong enough to embark on reforms that might antagonize this institution.

It was not long, however, before signs of opposition to Gorbachev's policies arose, and a "conservative backlash" occurred. Although the opposition appears to have been led by disgruntled party leaders such as Egor K. Ligachev, the second-ranking member of the Politburo, the KGB probably joined forces with these conservatives. Chebrikov's comments, in particular his strident speech delivered in September 1987, made it clear that the KGB would not allow the democratic reforms to go too far: "There must be a clear awareness that the restructuring is taking place in our state and society under the leadership of the Communist Party, within the framework of socialism and in the interests of socialism. This revolutionary process will be reliably protected against any subversive intrigues." The subsequent ouster of a leading proponent of Gorbachev's reforms, Moscow party chief Boris El'tsin, was an indication of the strength of the opposition to Gorbachev.

Although he made some strategic retreats in early 1988, Gorbachev continued to pursue his policy of *perestroika*, and exposures of illegal KGB activities continued. Even more threatening for the KGB were unprecedented revelations about security police terror under Stalin. Although the role of the police in the purges had been discussed since the Khrushchev era, *glasnost'* resulted in a much more devastating critique of the role of the police during this period. Ethnic unrest of various nationalities, together with increasingly bold political demands by the Soviet intelligentsia, also presented the KGB with significant challenges. In a speech delivered in mid-April, Chebrikov expressed concern that things were going too far and that some individuals were "unleashing a wide-ranging arsenal of methods of social demagoguery and substituting bourgeois liberalism for the essence of the concept of socialist democracy." Subsequently, in October 1988 Chebrikov lost his position as chief of the KGB and was replaced by Vladimir Kriuchkov.

POST-SOVIET DEVELOPMENTS

KGB spetsnaz forces were assigned to storm the Russian Parliament building early on 21 August 1991 and seize key leadership personnel, including Boris Yeltsin. Units assigned this mission included the Al'fa (Alpha) counterterrorist group subordinate to the KGB's Seventh Main Directorate (Surveillance), and commanded by Hero of the Soviet Union, General Major Viktor Karpukhin. Another KGB unit was under the KGB's First Chief Directorate (Foreign Operations) and intended principally for operations abroad. It was commanded by an officer identified only as Col. Boris B. However, the commanders on the scene decided not to execute thes plan, and some Alpha subgroup commanders and personnel refused to take part in the action, which contributed to the failure of the coup against Gorbachev, and ultimately the collapse of the Soviet Union.

On 21 August 1991 Vladimir Kryuchkov, KGB head and one of the leaders of the coup, was arrested. The next day, a reformer, Vadim Bakatin, was appointed in Kryuchkov's place. On 24 October 1991 Mikhail Gorbachev signed a decree abolishing the KGB.
The Soviet Union's Committee for State Security dissolved along with the USSR in late 1991. However, most of its assets and activities have continued through several separate organizations.

- The Foreign Intelligence Service [SVR] was the first element of the KGB to establish a separate identity [in October 1991] incorporating most of the foreign operations, intelligence-gathering and intelligence analysis activities of the KGB First Chief Directorate.
- The Federal Agency for Government Communications and Information [FAPSI], the Russian counterpart to the US National Security Agency. Formed in February 1994, FAPSI replaced the Administration of Information Resources (AIR) at the Presidential Office, which was formed from the KGB Eighth Chief Directorate and the Sixteenth Directorate, and like the NSA is responsible for communications security and signals intelligence.
- Some 8,000-10,000 troops that formerly constituted the KGB Ninth Directorate, which guarded the Kremlin and key offices of the CPSU, joined the Federal Protective Service [FSO - Federal'naya Sluzhba Okhrani - formerly known as the Main Administration for the Protection of the Russian Federation (GUO - Glavnoye Upravlenie Okhrani)] and the 1,000 man Presidential Security Service [PSB] with responsibilities similar to the American Secret Service.
- Internal security functions previously performed by the Second, Third and Fifth Chief Directorates and the Seventh Directorate were initially assigned to a new Ministry of Security. But agency was disbanded December 1993 and replaced by the Federal Counterintelligence Service. This 75,000-person agency was subsequently redisgnated the Federal Security Service (FSB).

On 30 October 1997 the State Duma today voted down a draft federal law "On State Security Agencies in the Russian Federation" submitted by Sergey Skurikhin, a deputy of the Liberal Democratic Party of Russia [LDPR]. It was backed only by LDPR leader Vladimir Zhirinovskiy, and opposed by the factions of the CPRF [Communist Party of the Russian Federation], Our Home is Russia, Yabloko, and the Agrarian deputies group. A total of 148 deputies voted in favor of the draft law, 129 voted against; and with 11 abstentions. The Russian president and the Russian government did not support the adoption of the draft law. The law proposed the creation in Russia of a new state agency, the Russian Ministry of State Security, recombining Federal Security Service, the Foreign Intelligence Service, and the Federal Agency for Government Liaison and Information.

In recent years the government appears to have dramatically augmenting the MVD forces. While some [disputed] reportss claim that these forces now number 800,000 men, officially the MVD forces are acknowledged to include a force of 264,000. Equiped with with heavy weapons and structured and organized to carry out purely military operations against external enemies, recent changes in the number, training, and mission of MVD forces suggest concern about domestic unrest. In February 1997 Interior Minister Anatoly Kulikov, a general with a well-deserved reputation as a hard-liner, was elevated to the rank of deputy prime minister.

On 04 July 1994, FBI Director Louis Freeh and then-Russian Interior Minister Viktor Yerin signed a protocol providing for joint law enforcement efforts, which included opening an FBI attache office in Moscow.

The Ministry of Internal Affairs is responsible for 743 correctional labor institutions, 168 pretrial detention facilities, and 13 prisons. In addition, the MVD maintains 60 educational labor colonies for juveniles. In 1994 the MVD received only 87 percent of its funds allocated by the federal budget. As a result, it is estimated that prisons were able in fact to provide only 60 to 70 percent of the daily food rations they envisioned providing and only 15 to 20 percent of needed medications and medical care. Prisoners and detainees must rely on families to provide them with extra food and routine medicines.

A range of decrees, orders and instructions, often marked "secret", regulate the actions of the Ministry of Internal Affairs (MVD). Most of these documents have not been published and are not made available upon request. MVD orders and instructions are issued for service purposes and are not supposed to be copied in any way or presented to organizations, societies, agencies, which are not involved in the monitoring of the functioning of the corrective labour institutions. The internal MVD instruction *"Internal Regulation Rules of the Correctional Labour Institutions"* of 1992 details the rules and limitations concerning day-to- day life in places of confinement. Special Order No. 13 of the MVD (15 January 1993) reintroduced the reduced norm of nutrition, previously abolished in 1988, for prisoners at penitentiaries serving disciplinary punishments in the so-called punishment-isolator (known by its Russian acronym SIZO), punishment cell (kartser) and in solitary confinement cells.

Another secret MVD instruction facilitates the practical training of the special purpose detachments of MVD and OMON at SIZOs and correctional labour colonies. The instruction reportedly allows these units practice their skills on prisoners.

During 1996 the Moscow Center for Prison Reform reported that according to official MVD statistics over 3,000 detainees died in IVSs (temporary holding isolators) and SIZOs and over 9,000 convicts died in prisons and penal colonies.

MVD forces are carrying out various kinds of peacekeeping operations inside Russia, notably in Chechnya. Yeltsin began the invasion of Chechnya on 11 December 1994, intending to to seal off Grozny, eliminate illegal armed formations, and end the participation of the Russian army, transferring authority to the MVD and establishing a temporary government. MVD tasks included reestablishing law and order in the republic, ensureing that public utilies began functioning again, and, together with the FSK, setting up operational investigation groups.

Human Rights Watch and the OSCE have documented several instances in which Ministry of Internal Affairs forces in Chechnya abducted civilian noncombatants as well as Chechen separatist soldiers. According to government statistics, government forces detained 1,308 Chechen noncombatants without arrest warrants in the period up to June 30, 1995. Of that number, the Government admits to still holding 141. The Government claims that the others have been released, but documenting these statements has been difficult.

A wave of contract killings started in 1990, and by 1993 the number of contract murders had increased, with no arrests and little investigation. In most of these cases the killers were never identified, or where the killers were known they were not caught. In a few cases where the killers were identified, they turned out to be former or active officers of the MVD Special Purpose Detachment, OMON, hired by criminalized businessmen to carry out the crime.

SECURITY AND DEFENSE COUNCILS

The President of the Russian Federation directly controls the activities of the intelligence, law enforcement, and defense activities of the Russian government. Intelligence activities are overseen by the Russian National Security Council and coordinated through the Permanent Interbranch Commissions of the National Security Council and their Chairmen. In addition to the three foreign intelligence agencies, the intelligence community also controls the Federal Customs Service and the newly organized Federal Security Service. The Federal Customs Service can provide the intelligence services with detailed information on the movement of goods and equipment in and out of Russia. Proprietary information such as customer lists could be derived from declarations made to the Customs Service. The Federal Security Service incorporates the functions of the Main Administration for the Protection of the Russian Federation and the Federal Counterintelligence Service. The combination of these functions has returned much of the internal security and counterintelligence functions formerly held by the KGB to a single agency.

While the centralized Soviet decisionmaking system dominated by the Politburo and the Central Committee has been abolished, new national security decisionmaking structures have been marked by improvisation and ad hoc responses.

Security Council

The Russian Security Council was established to provide a high-level forum within which Russia's president can interact directly and concurrently with his key ministers and agency heads. However like the US National Security Council (NSC) the Russian Security Council is not a deliberative body that arrives at decisions on its own. Decisions are made by the President, , who chairs the Security Council, and issues executive orders or decrees. Although the Security Council was intended to be the primary forum for the integration and coordination of security policy, it has has proven to be relatively ineffective in coordinating policy. Gen. Alexander Lebed, who was appointed secretary of the Security Council in June 1996, sought to make the Security Council an operational instrument for coordinating and integrating foreign and security policy. But he was replaced before his plans could be implemented. Lebed's successor, Ivan Rybkin, has little experience in security affairs, and the Council has primarily been preoccupied with Chechnya and internal security issues.

Defense Council

The Defense Council, established in July 1996 as part of the Presidential Apparatus, is charged with advising the president on important decisions on military policy. In addition to the Defense Ministry, membership includes other ministries and bodies such as the Interior Ministry and Border Guards. Initially set up to counterbalance Lebed's Security Council, under its secretary Yuri Baturin the Defense Council has become a key forum for the formulation and coordination of defense policy.

INTELLIGENCE COORDINATION

In early 1997 it was reported that a draft presidential edict contemplated the creation of a center to coordinate the activities of the FSB [Federal Security Service], the SVR [Foreign Intelligence Service], the FAPSI [Federal Government Communications and Information Agency] (and, according to some reports, the FPS [Federal Border Service]). Candidates to head the coordination center included Yevgeniy Savostyanov, a former geophysicist and counterintelligence officer currently serving as deputy presidential chief of staff, Yuriy Baturin or Sergey Stepashin.

FEDERAL SECURITY SERVICE[3]

fsb@fsb.ru
Phone: (095) 914-22-22

[3] Successor KGB USSR

Information Services: тел.: (095) 914-43-69 (круглосуточно)

Central Office:

Moscow, Kuznetskiy Most 22
тел.: (095) 924-31-58

Press Office

Moscow, 101000, Lubyabnja 2
Phone (095) 914-39-08
Fax (095) 975-24-70
press@fsb.ru

Logistics and Supply Department" umto@fsb.ru
Military Conterintelligence Department: Электронная почта uvkr@fsb.ru
Military Medical Department: Электронная почта vmu@fsb.ru
Inspection Department: Электронная почта insp@fsb.ru
Information Department: Электронная почта uioord@fsb.ru
Special Operation Center: Электронная почта csnsput@fsb.ru
Investigation Department: Электронная почта invest@fsb.ru

Research Department: Электронная почта unto@fsb.ru
Special Communication Department: Электронная почта sps@fsb.ru
International Cooperation Department: Электронная почта ums@fsb.ru
Radio Counterintelligence Department: Электронная почта drad@fsb.ru
Special Technical Programs Department: Электронная почта uotm@fsb.ru
Public Security Department: Электронная почта usb@fsb.ru
Public Information Department: Электронная почта ooi@fsb.ru

ORGANIZATION

The basic organizational structure of the FSB was created in 1954, when the reorganization of the police apparatus was carried out. In the late 1980s, the KGB remained a highly centralized institution, with controls implemented by the Politburo through the KGB headquarters in Moscow.

STRUCTURE

The KGB was originally designated as a "state committee attached to the Council of Ministers." On July 5, 1978, a new law on the Council of Ministers changed the status of the KGB, along with that of several other state committees, so that its chairman was a member of the Council of Ministers by law. According to the 1977 Soviet Constitution, the Council of Ministers "coordinates and directs" the work of the ministries and state committees, including the KGB. In practice, however, the KGB had more autonomy than most other government bodies and operated with a large degree of independence from the Council of Ministers. The situation was similar with the Supreme Soviet, which had formal authority over the Council of Ministers and its agencies. In 1989 the actual powers of the Supreme Soviet, however, gave it little if any power over KGB operations.

The KGB was a union-republic state committee, controlling corresponding state committees of the same name in the fourteen non-Russian republics. (All-union ministries and state committees, by contrast, did not have corresponding branches in the republics but executed their functions directly through Moscow.) Below the republic level, there existed KGB administrations (*upravleniia*) in the *kraia* (see Glossary) and oblasts (see Glossary). In the Russian Republic, however, there was no separate KGB. Oblast KGB administrations in the Russian Republic were subordinated directly to the central KGB offices in Moscow. At the lower levels, autonomous *okruga* (see Glossary), cities, and *raiony* (see Glossary) had KGB departments or sections.

The KGB also had a broad network of special departments in all major government institutions, enterprises, and factories. They generally consisted of one or more KGB representatives, whose purpose was to ensure the observance of security regulations and to monitor political sentiments among employees. The special departments recruited informers to help them in their tasks. A separate and very extensive network of special departments existed within the armed forces and defense-related institutions.

Although a union-republic agency, the KGB was highly centralized and was controlled rigidly from the top. The KGB central staff kept a close watch over the operations of its branches, leaving the latter minimal autonomous authority over policy or cadre selection. Moreover, local government organs had little involvement in local KGB activities. Indeed, the high degree of centralization in the KGB was reflected in the fact that regional KGB branches were not subordinated to the local soviets (see Glossary), but only to the KGB hierarchy. Thus, they differed from local branches of most union-republic ministerial agencies, such as the MVD, which were subject to dual subordination.

The KGB was directed by a chairman--who was formally appointed by the Supreme Soviet but actually was selected by the Politburo-- one or two first deputy chairmen, and several (usually four to six) deputy chairmen. Key decisions were made by the KGB Collegium, which was a collective leadership body composed of the chairman, deputy chairmen, chiefs of certain KGB directorates, and one or two chairmen of republic KGB organizations.

Functions and Internal Organization

As a state committee with ministerial status, the KGB operated on the basis of a statute (*polozhenie*), confirmed by the Council of Ministers, that set forth in legal terms the KGB's powers and duties. Unlike the majority of statutes governing ministerial agencies, the KGB's statute was not published. Nevertheless, Soviet textbooks on administrative law offered useful statements about the KGB's role and functions. The KGB's tasks were generally defined in official Soviet publications as encompassing four areas: the struggle against foreign spies and agents, the exposure and investigation of political and economic crimes by citizens, the protection of state borders, and the protection of state secrets. In addition, the KGB was charged with a wide range of preventive tasks, which were designed to eliminate the causes of both political and ordinary crimes. In other words, the KGB was tasked with ferreting out potential threats to the state and preventing the development of unorthodox political and social attitudes among the population.

Western estimates of KGB manpower have ranged from 490,000 in 1973 to 700,000 in 1986. There are no published estimates of the KGB budget. Many KGB personnel were institutions to which they were assigned, and the KGB received support and services from the military and other institutions, rendering a meaningful budgetary accounting particularly problematic.

Official Soviet sources did not discuss the internal structure of the KGB in detail. Nevertheless, some information on KGB organization and functions has been revealed by Soviet defectors and other sources. In 1988 the KGB had five chief directorates and three known (possible another) directorates that were smaller in size and scope than the chief directorates, as well as various other administrative and technical support departments.

> The **First Chief Directorate (Foreign Operations)** was responsible for all foreign operations and intelligence-gathering activities. It was divided into both functional services--training and management of covert agents, intelligence analysis, and collection of political, scientific, and technological intelligence--and geographic departments for different areas of the world. The Directorage included a spetsnaz group formed in August 1981 to conduct external reconnaissance, sabotage, training

and security missions, though in practice the unit was particularly active in internal-security actions.

The **Second Chief Directorate** was responsible for internal political control of Soviet citizens and foreigners residing within the Soviet Union, including both diplomats and tourists.

The **Third Chief Directorate [Armed Forces]**dealt with military counterintelligence and political surveillance of the Soviet armed forces. The Armed Forces Directorate was divided into twelve major departments that oversaw all the various military and paramilitary formations of the Soviet government. Officers from the Directorate were stationed at every echelon of Soviet armed forces down to the company level, in each military district, with every naval group, at each military front. These KGB officers reported through their own chain of command to KGB headquarters.

The **Fifth Chief Directorate** also dealt with internal security. Created in 1969 late 1960s to combat political dissent, it took up some of the tasks previously handled by the Second Chief Directorate. The Fifth Chief Directorate had special operational departments for religious dissent, national minorities, the intelligentsia and the artistic community, and censorship of literature.

The **Seventh Directorate (Surveillance)** handled surveillance, providing personnel and technical equipment to follow and monitor the activities of both foreigners and suspect Soviet citizens. Much of this work was centered in the Moscow and Leningrad areas, where tourists, diplomats, foreign students, and members of the Soviet intelligentsia were concentrated. The *Al'fa* (Alpha) counterterrorist group was subordinated to Seventh Main Directorate. Alpha was involved in many counterterrorist and internal-security missions since its formation in 1974 and was heavily active in special-operations tasks in Afghanistan.

The **Eighth Chief Directorate** was responsible for the highly sensitive area of communications. The Communications Directorate was tasked with monitoring foreign communications. The Directorate was also responsible for the cryptological systems used by KGB divisions, the transmission of communications to KGB stations overseas, and the development of secure communication equipment.

The **Ninth Directorate** [Guards Directorate] provided bodyguards for principal Party leaders and their families, and the Kremlin and other major government facilities around the Soviet Union.

The **Sixteenth Directorate** [former State Communications Department] maintained the telephone and radio systems used by all Soviet government agencies.

The **Border Troops Directorate** protected Soviet land and sea borders.

In addition to the various directorates and a special network of training and education establishments, the KGB included a variety of other organizations: a personnel department, a secretariat, a technical support staff, a finance department, an archives, an administration department, and a party committee. Most of these bodies had counterparts within the different directorates. Party committees, which existed in every Soviet organization, handled political indoctrination of personnel. Heads of party committees arranged regular meetings to discuss party matters and served as liaisons between the party and the KGB at various levels, although party membership was probably universal among

KGB employees. At the republic level, KGB organization was probably similar to that of the central KGB, although republic KGBs did not supervise units of the Border Troops, which were administered centrally. Nor did they include functions of the Third Chief Directorate, which was organized primarily along military service lines or by military district. In addition, functions such as communications and foreign espionage may have been administered only in Moscow.

DOMESTIC SECURITY AND THE COMMITTEE FOR STATE SECURITY

The KGB had a variety of domestic security functions. It was empowered by law to arrest and investigate individuals for certain types of political and economic crimes. It was also responsible for censorship, propaganda, and the protection of state and military secrets.

Legal Prerogatives

In carrying out its task of ensuring state security, the KGB was empowered by law to uncover and investigate certain political crimes set forth in the Russian Republic's Code of Criminal Procedure and the criminal codes of other republics. According to the Russian Republic's Code of Criminal Procedure, which came into force in 1960 and has been revised several times since then, the KGB had the authority, together with the Procuracy, to investigate the political crimes of treason, espionage, terrorism, sabotage, anti-Soviet agitation and propaganda, divulgence of state secrets, smuggling, illegal exit abroad, and illegal entry into the Soviet Union. In addition, the KGB was empowered, along with the Procuracy and the MVD, to investigate the following economic crimes: stealing of state property by appropriation or embezzlement or by abuse of official position and stealing of state property or socialist property (see Glossary) on an especially large scale.

In carrying out arrests and investigations for these crimes, the KGB was subject to specific rules that were set forth in the Code of Criminal Procedure. The Procuracy was charged with ensuring that these rules were observed. In practice, the Procuracy had little authority over the KGB, and the latter was permitted to circumvent the regulations whenever politically expedient. In 1988 closing some of these loopholes was discussed, and legal experts called for a greater role for the Procuracy in protecting Soviet citizens from abuse by the investigatory organs. As of May 1989, however, few concrete changes had been publicized.

It is important to note that the KGB frequently enlisted the MVD and the Procuracy to instigate proceedings against political nonconformists on charges that did not fall under the KGB's purview. Dissidents were often charged for defaming the Soviet state and violating public order. Sometimes the KGB arranged to have them charged for ordinary crimes, such as hooliganism or drug abuse.

THE FOREIGN INTELLIGENCE ROLE OF THE COMMITTEE FOR STATE SECURITY

The KGB played an important role in furthering Soviet foreign policy objectives abroad. In addition to straightforward intelligence collection and counterintelligence, the KGB participated in the Kremlin's program of active measures. KGB officials also contributed to foreign policy decision making.

Organization

The First Chief Directorate of the KGB was responsible for KGB operations abroad. The longtime head of the First Chief Directorate, Vladimir Kriuchkov, who had served under Andropov and his successors, was named head of the KGB in 1988.

The Second Chief Directorate also played a role in foreign intelligence in 1989. It recruited agents for intelligence purposes from among foreigners stationed in the Soviet Union, and it engaged in counterintelligence by uncovering attempts of foreign intelligence services to recruit Soviet citizens.

FIRST CHIEF DIRECTORATE

The First Chief Directorate was responsible for all international Soviet clandestine activities, apart from military intelligence collection by the GRU and political initiatives of the Communist Party itself.

ILLEGALS DIRECTORATE (DIRECTORATE S)

Directorate S recruited, trained, and managed KGB officers assigned to foreign countries under false identities. Most of the staff of the Directorate have either served as illegals, or have served abroad under diplomatic cover.

SCIENTIFIC AND TECHNICAL DIRECTORATE (DIRECTORATE T)

Directorate T was created from the former Department 10 in 1963 to intensify the acquisition of Western strategic, military and industrial technology. By 1972 Directorate T had a headquarters staff of several hundred officers subdivided into four Departments in addition to specialists stationed at major Soviet embassies around the world. The Directorate's operations were coordinated with the scientific and technical collection activities of other KGB elements, and with the the State Scientific and Technical Committee (GNTK).

PLANNING AND ANALYSIS DIRECTORATE (DIRECTORATE I)

Directorate I was established in 1969 to review past operations as a guide to improving future initiatives, although in practice it was said to function more as a dumping-ground for aging or inept officers.

INFORMATION SERVICE (SPECIAL SERVICE I)

Special Service I was responsible for the correlation and dissemination of routine intelligence collected by the First Chief Directorate, apart from technical intelligence collected and processed by Directorate T. Other related responsibilities included publication of a weekly intelligence summary for Party leaders, briefing officers prior to foreign assignment, conducting special studies at Central Committee direction. The products of the Information Service did not consist of finished estimative intelligence, but rather of raw reports that were provided to senior leaders who drew their own conclusions.

COUNTERINTELLIGENCE SERVICE (SPECIAL SERVICE II)

Special Service II was tasked countering foreign intelligence agencies, including penetrating foreign security, intelligence and counter-intelligence services to undermine their effectiveness in countering the activities of the KGB. Special Service II was also responsible for the security officers tasked with monitoring Soviet civilians stationed abroad, including Soviet nationals working as correspondents, trade representatives, Aeroflot clerks, or any other capacity.

DISINFORMATION DEPARTMENT (DEPARTMENT A)

Department A was responsible for clandestine initiatives and campaigns to influence foreign governments and publics, as well to shape perceptions of individuals and groups hostile to Soviet interests. The majority of the Departments activities were implemented by other KGB elements, or other Soviet organizations.

EXECUTIVE ACTION DEPARTMENT (DEPARTMENT V)

Department V was responsible for "wet affairs" (*mokrie dela*) -- murders, kidnappings, and sabotage -- which involve bloodshed. Previously known as the Thirteenth Department or Line F, the Department was enlarged and redesignated in 1969, and tasked with sabotaging critical infrastructure so as to immobilize Western countries during future crises. The Department employed officers stationed in Soviet embassies, illegals stationed abroad, and the services of professional.

GEOGRAPHIC DEPARTMENTS

The operational core of the First Chief Directorate lay in its geographical departments [numbering ten in the early 1970s and growing to eleven by the late 1980s]. The geographic Departments were responsible for the majority of the KGB enterprises abroad. The duties of this department included the staff of KGB "legal" Residencies [*rezidenty*] in Soviet embassies, operating under legal cover while engaged in intelligence collection, espionage, and active measures, as well as KGB illegals [apart from those operating under assignment from the Executive Action and Disinformation Departments]. They also managed operations initiated through international communist-front organizations, as well as other agent of influence operations.

1ST DEPARTMENT

United States and Canada

2ND DEPARTMENT

Latin America

3RD DEPARTMENT

United Kingdom, Australia, New Zealand, and Scandinavia

4TH DEPARTMENT

Federal Republic of Germany, Austria

5TH DEPARTMENT

France, Italy, Spain, the Netherlands, Belgium, Luxembourg, and Ireland

6TH DEPARTMENT

China, North Vietnam, North Korea

7TH DEPARTMENT

Japan, India, Indonesia, the Philippines, and the rest of Asia

8TH DEPARTMENT

Arab nations, Yugoslavia, Turkey, Greece, Iran, Afghanistan, and Albania

9TH DEPARTMENT

English-speaking nations of Africa

10TH DEPARTMENT

French-speaking nations of Africa

OTHER DEPARTMENTS

11TH DEPARTMENT

The 11th Department, formerly known as the Advisers Department, conducted liaison with counterpart services in Cuba and Eastern European countries.

12TH DEPARTMENT

The 12th [Cover Organs] Department provided KGB personnel with cover jobs in other Soviet institutions, as diplomats, journalists, tourists, or delegates to conferences.

13TH DEPARTMENT

The 13th Department provided secure communications with Residencies, officers, and agents in the field.

14TH DEPARTMENT

The 14th Department supplied forged passports and other documents, invisible writing materials, incapacitating chemicals, and other technical devices required in Foreign Directorate operations. Specialists in Soviet embassies monitored local communications and provided technical assistance to the Residency.

15TH DEPARTMENT

15th Department maintained the operational files and archives of the First Chief Directorate.

16TH DEPARTMENT

The 16th Department performed routine personnel functions and recruits prospective staff officers for the First Chief Directorate. Many officer candidates were recruited from the Institutes of International Affairs and Eastern Languages in Moscow.

INTELLIGENCE AND COUNTERINTELLIGENCE

KGB intelligence gathering in the West increased markedly after the era of détente began in 1972. Détente permitted a vast influx of Soviet and East European diplomatic, cultural, and commercial officials into the United States and other Western countries. KGB officers and their East European counterparts operated under various guises, posing as diplomats, trade officials, journalists, scientists, and students. The proportion of Soviet citizens abroad who were engaged in intelligence gathering was estimated to range from 30 to 40 percent in the United States to over 50 percent in some Third World countries. In addition, many Soviet representatives who were not intelligence officers were nevertheless given some sort of assignment by the KGB.

Apparently, the First Chief Directorate had little trouble recruiting personnel for its foreign operations. The high salaries, military rank, access to foreign currency, and opportunity to live abroad offered attractive enticements to young people choosing a career. First Chief Directorate recruits were usually graduates of prestigious higher education institutions and had knowledge of one or more foreign languages. The KGB had a two-year postgraduate training course for these recruits at its Higher Intelligence School located near Moscow.

The KGB was the primary agency responsible for supplying the Kremlin with foreign intelligence. According to former Soviet diplomat Arkady Shevchenko, Moscow cabled out questions on a daily basis to KGB *rezidenty* abroad to guide them in their tasks. In addition to political intelligence, KGB officers concentrated increasingly on efforts to acquire advanced Western technology.

The KGB reportedly acted as a collector of militarily significant Western technology (in the form of documents and hardware) on behalf of the Military Industrial Commission of the Presidium of the Council of Ministers. This commission coordinated the development of all Soviet weapons systems, along with the program to acquire Western technology, and it levied requirements among the KGB, the Main Intelligence Directorate (see Glossary), and several other agencies, including those of East European intelligence services. The KGB and the GRU increased their technical collection efforts considerably in the early 1980s, when the number of requirements levied on them by the Military Industrial Commission rose by about 50 percent.

The Andropov era saw a greater orientation in the KGB toward electronic espionage--communications intercepts and satellites--to supplement intelligence gathered by agents. According to Robert Campbell, the Soviet Union deployed at least three satellites for intelligence collection. Some of the intelligence may have been strictly military and therefore collected by the GRU, but the KGB reportedly also made use of these satellites.

Active Measures

Active measures were clandestine operations designed to further Soviet foreign policy goals and to extend Soviet influence throughout the world. This type of activity had long been employed by the Soviet Union abroad, but it became more widespread and more effective in the late 1960s. Among these covert techniques was disinformation: leaking of false information and rumors to foreign media or planting forgeries in an attempt to deceive the public or the political elite in a given country or countries. The United States was the prime target of disinformation, in particular forgery operations, which were designed to damage foreign and defense policies of the United States in a variety of ways.

Defectors reported that the Soviet Union and its allies circulated forged documents--often purporting to be speeches, letters, or policy statements by United States officials--containing false information. The use of international front (see Glossary) organizations and foreign communist parties to expand the Soviet Union's political influence and further its propaganda campaigns was another form of active measures. The World Peace Council was the largest and most important of Soviet front groups. Together with the International Department of the Central Committee, the KGB funneled money to these organizations and recruited Soviet agents to serve on their administrative bodies.

Other active measures involved support for terrorists and insurgents. As of 1989, there was no direct, public evidence that Soviet citizens had planned or orchestrated terrorist acts by groups from Western Europe or the Middle East, but there was much indirect evidence to show that the Soviet Union did support international terrorism. The Soviet Union maintained close relationships with a number of governments and organizations that were direct supporters of terrorist groups. The Soviet Union sold large quantities of arms to Libya and Syria, for example, and also maintained a close alliance with the Palestine Liberation Organization (PLO), providing it with arms, monetary assistance, and paramilitary training. Moscow's surrogate, Cuba, played a central role in Latin American terrorism by providing groups with training, arms, and sanctuary, and the Soviet Union's East European satellite states often served as middlemen or subcontractors for channeling aid to terrorist groups. Although the KGB, with some exceptions, avoided direct involvement with terrorist operations, it played an important role in diverting aid to these groups and providing the Soviet leadership with intelligence reports on their activities.

The KGB also was heavily involved in the support of "wars of national liberation" in the Third World. Together with satellite intelligence services, the KGB helped to organize military training and political indoctrination of leftist guerrillas, as well as providing arms and advisers. The manipulation of wars of national liberation enabled the Soviet Union to influence the political future of the countries in question and to make their new governments more responsive to Soviet objectives. The Soviet regime concentrated mainly on African countries until the late 1970s but then extended its support for "national liberation movements" to Central America, where it has regularly employed the services of Cuba.

The KGB relied heavily on the intelligence services of satellite countries in carrying out both active measures and espionage operations. The intelligence services of the German Democratic Republic (East Germany), Czechoslovakia, Poland, Hungary, Bulgaria, and Cuba formed important adjuncts to the KGB. Although formally subordinated to their own governments, these satellite intelligence services were, according to many Western experts, heavily influenced by the KGB. A former official in the Czechoslovak intelligence service stated that Soviet intelligence was informed about every major aspect of Czechoslovak intelligence activities, and Soviet advisers (called liaison officers) participated in planning major operations and assessing the results. As far back as the 1960s, the KGB introduced a new element of coordination with the satellite intelligence services through the creation of departments for disinformation in East German, Czechoslovak, and Hungarian intelligence services and the establishment of direct lines of communication from these departments to the KGB.

Soviet active measures involved not only KGB and satellite intelligence services but also several other Soviet agencies, which all participated in a coordinated effort to further Soviet policy objectives. In addition to the KGB, the Central Committee's International Department took a leading role in directing and implementing active measures.

INFLUENCE ON FOREIGN POLICY

The KGB participated in the foreign policy decision-making process at the highest level because its chief was a member of the Politburo. At the same time, it influenced the formulation of foreign policy at a lower level as an executor of that policy, a provider of information, and a generator of ideas, solutions, and alternatives. Thus, for example, when the Kremlin decided to invade Czechoslovakia in 1968, KGB chief Andropov, who was an expert on Eastern Europe and had a direct line of intelligence from Czechoslovakia, presumably influenced the decision-making process significantly. Furthermore, the KGB, as the main provider of intelligence to the leadership, was in a position to influence decision making by screening and interpreting the information. The KGB probably favored the invasion because of the threat posed by a possible spillover of unrest into the Soviet Union. Also, efforts by Czechoslovak reformers to reorganize their security police jeopardized KGB operations in Czechoslovakia. Considerable evidence showed that the KGB, in order to bolster the prointerventionist position, used intelligence and covert action to produce proof of counterrevolution in Czechoslovakia.

Andropov did not always favor military intervention as a solution to international problems, however. Other considerations, such as the Soviet Union's international image, no doubt affected his views on the 1979 invasion of Afghanistan (which he reportedly did not favor) and the 1980-81 Polish crisis (where he probably was among those who opposed an invasion). Both these crises occurred at a time when the KGB was trying to mobilize West European public opinion against plans by the North Atlantic Treaty Organization (NATO) to introduce intermediate-range missiles in Europe.

Chebrikov did not have Andropov's foreign policy expertise when he took over as head of the KGB in 1982, but his admission to the Politburo gave him a voice in foreign policy at the highest level. In addition, many Western experts believe that the KGB chairman served on the Defense Council, an important collegial decisionmaking body that provided top-level coordination for defenserelated activities of the Soviet government. Chebrikov's numerous trips to Eastern Europe after he became head of the KGB indicated that he was personally involved in KGB operations beyond Soviet borders, and his forceful advocacy of Soviet "counterpropaganda" efforts abroad implied a commitment to a strong foreign policy role for the KGB. Kriuchkov, who became head of the KGB in 1988, had been extensively involved in foreign operations as the chief of the First Chief Directorate of the KGB.

INTERNAL SECURITY TROOPS

The government of the Soviet Union had several bodies of troops under its control for the purpose of ensuring internal security. These troops included the Border Troops and Security Troops of the KGB and the Internal Troops of the MVD.

BORDER TROOPS OF THE COMMITTEE FOR STATE SECURITY

The Border Troops, distinguishable by green piping on their uniforms, were organized under the KGB's unnumbered Border Troops Directorate, which was headed in 1989 by Army General Viktor Matrosov. He was assisted by one or more first deputy chiefs, several deputy chiefs, and a chief of staff. Within the directorate, a political administration provided political indoctrination and surveillance on behalf of the party. Western specialists reported that there was an intelligence administration within the Border Troops Directorate, but this had not been confirmed by Soviet sources.

The Border Troops strength was estimated in 1989 to be in the range of 230,000 men, down from the estimated 300,000 personnel in the early 1970s. Although under the operational authority of the KGB, the Border Troops were conscripted as part of the biannual call-up of the Ministry of Defense, and their induction and discharge were regulated by the 1967 Law on Universal Military Service, which covered all armed forces of the Soviet Union.

The legal status, duties, and rights of the Border Troops were set forth in the Law on the State Border, confirmed by the Supreme Soviet on November 24, 1982. Article 28 defined the basic duties of the Border Troops. Their duties included repulsing armed incursions into Soviet territory; preventing illegal crossings of the border or the transport of weapons, explosives, contraband, or subversive literature across the border; monitoring the observance of established procedures at border crossing points; monitoring the observance by Soviet and foreign ships of navigation procedures in Soviet territorial waters; and assisting state agencies in the preservation of natural resources and the protection of the environment from pollution. Border guards were authorized to examine documents and possessions of persons crossing the borders and to confiscate articles; to conduct inquiries in cases of violations of the state border; and to take such actions as arrest, search, and interrogation of individuals suspected of border violations.

The Border Troops Directorate administered approximately nine border districts (*pogranichnye okruga*), which covered the nearly 63,000 kilometers of the state border. Border district boundaries were distinct from civil or military district boundaries. The nine border districts were subdivided into detachments (*otriady*), covering specific sections of the border, border command posts (*pogranichnye komendatury*), passport control points (*kontrol'no-propusknye punkty*), and border outposts (*zastavy*). The border area was divided into a border zone, which included the territory of the district and settlements adjacent to the state border, and the border strip, which was approximately two kilometers in depth, running directly along the border. Only permanent residents or those who had obtained special permission from the MVD could enter the border zone. Entry into the border strip was forbidden without special permission from the Border Troops.

Soviet sources repeatedly stressed that a border guard was not only a soldier but also a defender of Soviet ideology. His mission entailed sensitive political tasks, such as detecting subversive literature, and shooting citizens attempting to escape across the border. Enlisted men were trained with their operational units, whereas officers were trained in special Border Troops schools, such as the **Dzerzhinskii Higher Border Command School** and the **Higher Border School** in Moscow. Military-political officers received training at the **Voroshilov Higher Border Military Political Academy**, founded in the 1930s and located outside Leningrad. In 1972 a higher border military-political school was created in Golytsin, near Moscow. More recently, higher border command faculties were set up at the **Frunze Military Academy** and the **Lenin Military-Political Academy**. The period of instruction at the Dzerzhinskii Higher Border Command School was four years. Officer candidates, who were screened carefully by their local KGB offices before admittance, took general higher education courses along with specialized military and political studies.

To ensure a high level of discipline among personnel of the Border Troops, much attention was devoted to political training and indoctrination. For this purpose, a network of political organs, the **Political Directorate** of the Border Troops, was established within the Border Troops. It had political departments within all the border districts, detachments, and education institutions, and a network of full-time party political officers worked among all troop units. They conducted political study groups, gave propaganda lectures, and worked to increase the level of combat effectiveness among the troops.

SECURITY TROOPS OF THE COMMITTEE FOR STATE SECURITY

The KGB's Security Troops, which numbered about 40,000 in 1989, provided the KGB with a coercive potential. Although Soviet sources did not specify the functions of these special troops, Western analysts thought that one of their main tasks was to guard the top leadership in the Kremlin, as well as key government and party buildings and officials at the republic and regional levels. Such troops were presumably under the Ninth Directorate of the KGB.

The Security Troops also included several units of signal troops, which were reportedly responsible for installation, maintenance, and operation of secret communications facilities for leading party and government bodies, including the Ministry of Defense. These troops were probably under the command of the Eighth Chief Directorate. Other special KGB troops were intended for counterterrorist and counterinsurgency operations. Such troops were reportedly employed, along with the MVD's Internal Troops, to suppress public protests and disperse demonstrations, such as that of the Crimean Tatars in July 1987 and those in the republics of Armenia and Azerbaydzhan in March 1988. Special KGB troops also were trained for sabotage and diversionary missions abroad.

LUBYANKA KGB HEADQUARTERS

Lubyanka Square in downtown Moscow is the site of the site of the *Lubyanka* head-quarters of the KGB. KGB directors from Lavrentiya Beriya to Yuriy Andropov had their office on the third floor of the building. The center of the square was dominated centre by a statue of Felix Dzerzhinsky, founder of the first communist secret police, the Cheka. Like many others, the statue was removed in August 1991.
The Lubyanka actually consists of three buildings. The main yellow building, which is often shown on television, predates the Revolution and was taken over by the Bolsheviks in 1918. Containing the Lubyanka prison, this building is now the headquarters of the Border Troops, and it also contains a single Federal Security Service (FSB) Directorate. The Federal Security Service headquarters building is the gray one to left side, No. 1/3. whose construction began under Andropov and was finished under Chebrikov.
Since 1984 (when KGB chief Yuri Andropov became chairman of the Communist Party and decided to improve the KGB's public image) tourists have been able to visit a KGB museum in a gray stone building behind the Lubyanka. The upper floors are KGB offices, but the ground floors are used for conferences and a clubroom for retired KGB offices, featuring a disco, among other things. And since the Soviet collapse in 1991, Russia's intelligence agencies have tried to create an impression of openness, giving guided tours through the yellow Lubyanka. The new KGB Museum, which is open to the public, is housed in the Lubyanka building. Across the square from the Lubyanka is *Dyetsky Mir* (Children's World), the largest children's shop in the country.

\EMBASSY WASHINGTON, DC

2650 Wisconsin Avenue, NW
Washington, DC
In 1973 the US agreed to allow the Soviet Union construct new embassy facilities on a tract of land on Mt. Alto in the District of Columbia. Mount Alto, at an altitude of 350 feet, is is the third highest point in the District, enjoying a direct visual line to the Capitol, the White House, the Pentagon, and the State Department. The Soviets originally wanted to locate a new embassy in Chevy Chase, MD, but the US Government objected. They then chose a site in midtown Washington, and again the US objected. The US subsequently identified the the Mt. Alto site and persuaded the Soviets to accept it. The location of the new Soviet embassy was offered to the Soviets at a time when electronic surveillance techniques and the potential for their further development were not fully understood in

the West. The Soviet acquisition of Mt. Alto embassy site was not the result of a Soviet conspiracy, but rather it was the consequence of a bad judgment on the part of the United States.
Soon after construction started, concerns were expressed that if the Soviets occupied the new Embassy site, their electronic equipment would be capable of intercepting all communications dealing with national security flowing in and out of Washington, unless encrypted, as well as ordinary business and personal conversations. Soviet The embassy could have been used as a platform to conduct highly sophisticated electronic surveillance of the US government, to facilitate Soviet espionage, and the purchase and theft of US high technology.
Subsequently it was decided to prevent the Soviet Union from occupying new embassy buildings on Mount Alto until the US had acquired a new embassy location in Moscow of substantially equal character. The issue of embassy locations is very complicated, and became even more convoluted after the US discovered Soviet bugging devices in the structure of the new American embassy. The National Security Agency (NSA) and the Central Intelligence Agency (CIA) both objected to allowing the Soviet Union [and Russia] to use the embassy at Mt. Alto.

SERBIA

In summer 2002, the Serbian Assembly passed a law separating the State Security Service (Resor Drzavne Bezbednosti -- RDB) from the Serbian Ministry of Internal Affairs (MUP) and transforming it into a new civilian controlled agency, the Security Intelligence Agency (Bezbednosno-Informativna Agencija -- BIA).

SECURITY INTELLIGENCE AGENCY *BEZBEDNOSNO-INFORMATIVNA AGENCIJA -- BIA*

http://www.bia.sr.gov.yu/
bia@bia.sr.gov.yu

Sphere of Agency's activity includes the following:

a) Counterintelligence
Gathering, analyzing, processing and evaluating information on the engagement of foreign intelligence services and certain individuals, groups and organizations on the territory of the Republic of Serbia that are directed against the security of the Republic of Serbia.

b) Intelligence
Through the activities carried out both abroad and at home on gathering, analyzing, processing, and evaluating information of political, economic, security and military nature that indicate intentions and possibilities of covert activities directed against the security of the Republic of Serbia.

c) Other security activities
Prevention of activities directed against organized crime, criminal acts with elements of foreign, internal and international terrorism as well as most sever criminal acts against humanity and international law and constitutional order.

FREQUENTLY ASKED QUESTIONS

1. What are the basic activities of BIA?

- BIA gathers and processes information that concern the protection of security of the Republic of Serbia, detects, and prevents activities directed against undermining and disturbing the constitutional order of the Republic of Serbia **(see Article 2 of the Law on BIA)**.

2. Who controls activities of the Agency?

- BIA activities are controlled by the National Assembly and Government of the Republic of Serbia. **(see Chapter IV of the Law of BIA)**.

3. How can citizens recognize members of BIA?

- Members of BIA have official identity cards with the "Security Information Agency's" sign, identification number and photo **(photos of official identity cards)**.

4. Do the members of BIA carry weapons?

- Yes, but only those members having status of person with full or limited authorization with written permition for carrying weapons on the back of their identity cards **(photos of official identity cards)**.

5. Does BIA have agents?

- BIA is authorized to use services of individuals for the activities and benefit of the Agency **(see Article 10 of the Law on BIA)**. Agent can be a person older than 18 years, with foreign, domestic citizenship or without citizenship, who is prepared to cooperate consciously, continuously and in secrecy, with the aim to protect the security of the Republic of Serbia an it's citizens.

6. How can one get authorization for the interception of communications?

- According to the Law, BIA can intercept communications only with previously obtained written decision of the Supreme Court of Serbia and the authorization of the Agency Director **(see Articles 9, 14 and 15 of the Law on BIA)**.

7. Who can become a member of BIA?

- Formally, every citizen of Serbia and Montenegro older than 18 years, physically and mentally healthy, against whom no charges have been brought and who meets the requirements for the job he/she applies for **(see Human Resources)**.

8. Do armed forces exist under the structure of BIA?

- BIA does not have special armed formation in its structure, and in accordance with lawfully defined areas of activity, the priority of the Agency is the information activity in the function to protect the security of the R Serbia. Many people connect the former Unit for Special Operations (JSO) with BIA, thinking that it is its integral part. Dating November 2001, JSO was formally separated from State Security Service (RDB) and continued to function as part of the structure of the Ministry of Interior of Serbia. In July 2002, RDB was transformed into BIA, when any kind of legal framework for the existence of armed forces in the structure of BIA seized.

"The Agency carries out tasks relating to the security of the Republic of Serbia; the discovery and prevention of activities which threaten to undermine or disturb the constitutional order of the Republic of Serbia; the acquisition, processing and analysis of security-intelligence information relevant to the security of Republic of Serbia; informing the competent state authorities about security issues; and other responsibilities determined by the Law " - Article 2 of the Law on BIA.

If you have the information about the following:

- organized crime

- internal and international terrorism
- criminal acts against humanity and International Law
- undermining and disturbing constitutional order

endangering the security in the country

SLOVAKIA

INTELLIGENCE PROFILE

CZECH REPUBLIC

Once part of the Holy Roman Empire and, later, the Austro-Hungarian monarchy, Czechoslovakia became an independent nation at the end of World War I. Independence ended with the German takeover in 1939. After World War II, Czechoslovakia fell within the Soviet sphere of influence. In 1968, an invasion by Warsaw Pact troops ended the efforts of the country's leaders to liberalize party rule and create "socialism with a human face." Anti-Soviet demonstrations the following year ushered in a period of harsh repression. With the collapse of Soviet authority in 1989, Czechoslovakia regained its freedom through a peaceful "Velvet Revolution." On 1 January 1993, the country underwent a "velvet divorce" into its two national components, the Czech Republic and Slovakia.

INTELLIGENCE IN CZECHOSLOVAKIA

The following intelligence organizations were active in Czechoslovakia until 1993.

- Sbor Narodni Bezpecnosti -SNB- (National Security Corps)
- Verejna Bezpecnost -VB- (Public Security)
- Statni Bezpecnost -StB- (State Security)
- Pohranicni Straz (Border Guard)
- Protivzdusna Obrana (Anti Aircraft Defense)
- Federal Directorate of Intelligence Services -FSZS-
- Hlavni Sprava Rozvedky -HSR- (controlled by the Main Directorate of the General Staff)
- Zpravodajska Sprava Generalniko Stab -ZSGS- (Intelligence Directorate of the General Staff)

The Ministry of Interior controlled the armed security organizations in the country except for the regular armed forces and some prison guards.

The police in Czechoslovakia was not called police, but rather security. The National Security Corps comprises Public Security and State Security. Public Security was a uniformed force that performs routine police duties throughout the country. State Security, the former Secret Police, was at the same time an investigative agency, an intelligence agency, and a counter intelligence agency. Any activity that could possibly be considered anti-state fell under the purview of State Security. St a.k.a. Secret Police, was notorious for their cruelty and brutal methods of interrogation.

The SNB was an armed force, organized and trained as such but equipped to perform police rather than military functions. Its members are subject to military discipline and are under the jurisdiction of military courts. The Ministry of Interior operated its own higher level educational institute, which trained security personnel at different stages of their careers. The Advanced School of the National Security Corps in Prague, granted academic degrees to the SNB and the Border Guard, also under the Ministry of Interior.

Public Security performed routine police functions at all levels from federal to local. In 1987 it was reported to be a relatively small force for the extent of its responsibility, but it was augmented by volunteer auxiliary units. The federal minister of interior controlled other forces that could be ordered to assist Public Security if needed, and he could also request further help from the military.

Public Security and State Security units were deployed throughout the country and had headquarters at regional and district levels; there were 10 kraje and 114 districts in 1987. Public Security forces also established sections in rural areas. Both forces were under the ostensible supervision of the ministries of interior of the Czech and Slovak socialists republics. However, there seemed to be no question that operational direction of the security forces emanated from the Ministry of Interior at the federal level and that the two ministries of the component republics had administrative rather than supervisory functions.

Another militarized security force subordinated to the Ministry of Interior was the Border Guard, which was established in 1951 as a separate agency under the then-existing Ministry of National Security. The Border Guard was an armed force subject to the same military regulations that govern the CSLA. In mid-1987, in addition to the individual small arms carried by its personnel, the Border Guard also had some armored vehicles, antitank guns, and machine guns.

The main strength of the Border Guard has been deployed along the West German border since 1950. Smaller units patrolled the Austrian frontier as well as the borders with East Germany and Poland. Only a few units were stationed on the Hungarian and Soviet borders. The basic operational unit was the battalion, which was divided into companies and platoons and could be grouped into brigades for administrative purposes. The federal minister of interior could call the Border Guard to supplement security forces if necessary, and in wartime it could be assigned to the army either to serve specialized guard functions or to fight as infantry. Members of the Anti Aircraft Defense helped the Border Guard by instituting air patrols. The portion of the border with Hungary formed by the Danube River was patrolled by the Border Guard, which used launches and patrol boats equipped with radar and infrared sighting devices.

Clandestine Radio in Czechoslovakia

In his article "Twenty Five Years Ago in Prague", Don Moore describes the role of the Czechoslovakian clandestine stations in 1968, when the USSR invaded the country. Parts of the article are reprinted hereafter with kind permission of Don.

> « With the fall of Communism in Europe several years behind us, it's hard to remember what Cold War tensions were like. Yet, twenty- five years ago this month, the Cold War became extremely cold when the Soviets invaded Czechoslovakia. As so often in modern warfare, radio was there to play an important role.
>
> At 2200 UTC on August 20, at least 250,000 Warsaw Pact troops -mostly Soviets, but also East Germans, Poles, Bulgarians, and Hungarians - crossed into Czechoslovakia. News of the invasion traveled slowly to the capital, and not until 01:00 did Czechoslovak Radio broadcast the first news of it to a startled world. Shortwave listeners reported that Radio Prague's external services carried on with their normal prerecorded broadcast, without any mention of the invasion. The Prague Radio Building on Vinohrodska Street, just behind the National Museum in the Central City, would be the center of resistance. Within minutes of the radio's invasion announcement, Czechoslovak youths began gathering on Vinohrodska Street. Using wood, stones, buses and trolley cars, they began constructing massive barricades across the street.
>
> At 8:00 a.m. Soviet troops surrounded the station building. A woman announcer reported this to the listeners, noting that, "*They are going to silence our voices, but*

they cannot silence our hearts." The microphone was passed from hand to hand as the announcers asked the audience to remain calm and have courage. One man held the microphone to the window so the listeners could hear machine gun fire outside. As her companions sobbed in the background, the first woman announcer came back on and reported, "*They have entered the building, but we are still here and will be with you as long as we can hold out ... we are behind Dubcek and we will never give up, NEVER.*" Then the national anthem was played.

Surprisingly, only 7 Czechoslovaks were killed in the two battles for the radio station, out of a total of 23 killed in Prague and other cities. Later in the afternoon, thousands of citizens carrying a blood splattered flag made a funeral procession along Vinohradska Street in honor of the fallen in the battle for Radio Prague.

Within half an hour of Radio Prague's fall, a clandestine anti-Soviet broadcaster came on the air in Prague. Gradually others were added elsewhere in the city, and in cities such as Brno, Pilsen, and Ceske Budejovice. Around the country, local radio staffs left their studios and took to the airwaves from secret locations.

At first, the clandestines provided news and moral support for the resistance. As they became more organized, the stations actually began to orchestrate the resistance. Then, as the resistance centered on the clandestine network, the stations became a sort of quasi-government for a nation without a real one. Their slogan was "*Jsme s v mi; bud'te s n mi!*", or "*We are with you; be with us!*" Although the underground stations denounced the Soviet invasion, they always stressed their loyalty to the Socialist system as represented by Dubcek and his "Prague Spring". Rather than being anti-Communist, they supported a liberal form of Communism. And they always pointed out that they were "free, legitimate" radio stations of the Czechoslovak people.

Surprisingly, in concentrating on closing down official Czechoslovak radio studios, the Soviets didn't bother to occupy several key medium and long wave transmitter sites. Radio technicians then set up make-shift studios and connected them to the usual high-powered transmitters on their normal frequencies! Soon, however, the Soviets wised up and occupied the transmitter sites, too.

By this time, the free radios had set up a number of a hodgepodge of true clandestine transmitters. Some came from the Czechoslovak army and others from factories, especially the Tesla Electronics Equipment plant. In other cases amateur transmitters were pressed into service. Still others were put together at the moment with whatever parts were at hand.

The stations worked together, and soon a true clandestine network came together. Up to nineteen stations took turns broadcasting for fifteen minutes at a time on the same frequency. Each station had local and national news, plus coded messages for members of the resistance. Numbered codes signaled the end of a transmission so the next station in the link could come on. At first the breaks between stations were choppy with as much as five minutes of dead air. Later the engineers became so proficient that the switches were often not even noticeable. During their time off the air, some stations moved their transmitter to a new site before their next turn, as a further guard against discovery.

The clandestine operators didn't limit themselves to radio. They put on at least four underground TV stations also. The broadcasts were highly professional, and in addition to news carried a lot of comedy programs making fun of the invasion. Humorous Russian lessons were especially popular, as was a satirical tour for visitors of the sites of occupied Prague.

Although the Czechoslovak clandestine broadcasts caught the Soviets by surprise, the Soviets had their own clandestine stations, too. Just a few hours after the invasion began, Radio Vltava came on 210 meters, claiming to be a Czechoslovak station and justifying the invasion as the will of the Czechoslovak people. The broadcasts, however, were in Russian-accented Czech and broken Slovak. The free radios announced Radio Vltava's frequency to their listeners and invited them to listen to it for amusement. Radio Vltava was actually located in East Germany, and eventually its frequency was taken over by Radio Berlin International. Later at least three other Soviet-operated clandestine stations broadcast briefly to Czechoslovakia. One, Vysilac Zare (Dawn Transmitter), pretended to be pro-Dubcek, but careful monitoring proved it to be a subtle attempt at spreading disinformation among the underground.

Finally, the invaders located a list of government-registered hams and the troops systematically began shutting them down one by one. Others stations realized the fight was over and shut down on their own. On Thursday, August 29, the last free radio station, on 950 kHz at a location near the Austrian border, closed down. The radio battle for Czechoslovakia was over. »

SLOVAKIA

COUNTRY NAME:

Slovenska Republika (Slovak Republic or Slovakia) with capital Bratislava

ADMINISTRATIVE DIVISIONS:

8 regions; Banskobystricky, Bratislavsky, Kosicky, Nitriansky, Presovsky, Trenciansky, Trnavsky, and Zilinsky.

MILITARY BRANCHES:

Ground Forces, Air and Air Defense Forces, Territorial Defense Forces, and Civil Defense Force.

GENERAL:

After centuries under foreign rule, mainly by Hungary, the Slovaks joined with their neighbors to form the new nation of Czechoslovakia in 1918. Following the chaos of World War II, Czechoslovakia became a communist nation within Soviet-ruled Eastern Europe. Soviet influence collapsed in 1989, and Czechoslovakia once more was an independent country turning toward the West. The Slovaks and the Czechs agreed to separate peacefully on 1 January 1993. Slovakia has experienced more difficulty than the Czech Republic in developing a modern market economy.

INTELLIGENCE/SECURITY:

The following security agencies are reportedly active in Slovakia;

- SIS -Slovenska Informacni Sluzba (Slovak Information Service)
- Border and Aliens Police
- Defense Ministry Intelligence-Security Service
- Internal Security

- Office of Civil Protection
- Office of Nuclear Surveillance

Little is known about the Slovak intelligence services (SIS). Recently some embarrassing facts were revealed by the head of the SIS, Vladimir Mitro. Mitro says that during the time that Meciar ruled in Slovakia, the SIS has been involved in abduction and murder, including kidnapping of President Michal Kovac's son, Michal junior, in 1995. SIS is also accused of inciting neo-Nazism and racism in the Czech Republic, in an attempt to destabilize the neighboring country.
In contrast with the Czech Republic, the StB's structure has never been fully dismantled in Slovakia. Many of its surveillance devices were left basically intact, and are apparently still being used. Today, the Slovak intelligence agency SIS operates much as the Czechoslovak StB did before 1989.
An RFE report says: « *Cameras hidden under jackets draped over one shoulder, walkie-talkies in the shape of fountain pens, small microphones hidden under cuffs and lapels -- all standard tools in the days of the StB -- are back in Bratislava and other big cities. Indeed, intelligence experts say that those instruments are now accompanied by even more up-to-date technology, including disposable one-time-use microphone-transmitters the size of a lead pellet that can be shot at a target's back and clings to him until he brushes it off.* »

CZECH REPUBLIC

COUNTRY NAME:

Ceska Republika (Czech Republic) with capital: Praha (Prague)

ADMINISTRATIVE DIVISIONS;

73 districts: Benesov, Beroun, Blansko, Breclav, Brno-Venkov, Bruntal, Ceske Budejovice, Ceska Lipa, Cesky Krumlov, Cheb, Chomutov, Chrudim, Decin, Domazlice, Frydek-Mistek, Havlickuv Brod, Hodonin, Hradec Kralove, Jablonec nad Nisou, Jesenik, Jicin, Jihlava, Jindrichuv Hradec, Karlovy Vary, Karvina, Kladno, Klatovy, Kolin, Kromeriz, Kutna Hora, Liberec, Litomerice, Louny, Melnik, Mlada Boleslav, Most, Nachod, Novy Jicin, Nymburk, Olomouc, Opava, Pardubice, Pelhrimov, Pisek, Plzen-Jih, Plzen-Sever, Prachatice, Praha-Vychod, Praha Zapad, Prerov, Pribram, Prostejov, Rakovnik, Rokycany, Rychnov nad Kneznou, Semily, Sokolov, Strakonice, Sumperk, Svitavy, Tabor, Tachov, Teplice, Trebic, Trutnov, Uherske Hradiste, Usti nad Labem, Usti nad Orlici, Vsetin, Vyskov, Zdar nad Sazavou, Zlin, Znojmo, and 4 municipalities: Brno, Ostrava, Plzen, and Praha.

MILITARY BRANCHES:

Army, Air and Air Defense Forces, Civil Defense, Railroad Units.

INTELLIGENCE/SECURITY:

In the short period after the collapse of the Soviet authority in 1989 till 1994, when the BIS was formed, a number of Czechoslovak and -later- Czech organizations have been active. Here is a rundown:

- UOUD -Urad Pro Ochranu Ustavy a Demokracie (Office for the Protection of the Constitution and Democracy)
  16.2.1990 - 19.12.1990
- FIS -Federální Informaèní Sluzba (Federal Information Service)
  20.12.1990 - 30.6.1991
- FBIS -Federální Bezpeènostní Informaèní Sluzba (Federal Security Information Service)
  1.7.1991 - 31.12.1992

- BIS ER -Bezpeènostní Informaèní Sluzba Èeské Republiky (Security Information Service of the Czech Republic)
  1.1.1993 - 29.7.1994
- BIS -Bezpeènostní Informaèní Sluzba (Security Information Service)
  constituted on 30.7.1994 under Act No. 154/1994

  The following intelligence/security agencies are currently active:

- BIS - Bezpecnostni Informacni Sluzba (Security Information Service)
- UDV - Bureau of Documentation and Investigation of Communist Crimes
- Military Intelligence Service / Military Defence Intelligence
- UZSI - Urad Pro Zahranicni Styky a Informace (Office for Foreign Relations and Information)

« Act No. 153 of July 7, 1994 on the Intelligence Services of the Czech Republic » gives a description of the tasks of the various agencies.
The Security Information Service (BIS) secures information on

a. schemes and activities directed against the democratic foundations, the sovereignty and territorial integrity of the Czech Republic,
b. the intelligence services of foreign powers,
c. activities endangering state and official secrets,
d. activities the consequences of which may jeopardize the security or major economic interests of the Czech Republic,
e. information regarding organized crime and terrorism.

The Office for Foreign Relations and Information (UZSI) secures information of foreign provenance which is important for the security and protection of the foreign political and economic interests of the Czech Republic.
The Military Intelligence secures information on

a. schemes and activities which pose a military threat to the Czech Republic,
b. the intelligence services of foreign powers in the area of defence,
c. schemes and activities directed against the interests of safe-guarding the defence of the Czech Republic,
d. activities endangering state and official secrets concerning the defence of the Czech Republic.

The intelligence services fulfill further tasks as defined by specific legislation or international treaties by which the Czech Republic is bound.

RELATED NUMBERS STATIONS

The related numbers stations can be grouped in five 'families'. For clarity's sake I will use the ENIGMA designators here. Station profiles can be found in previous N&O's. Most of the stations are gone for a while now. S31 went down the drain late last year. The survivors are S10, S10E, M07, M10, M10E, and S17C.

- Family IX :
  G18

- Family IXA:
  S10, S10A. S10B, S10C, S10D, S10E, M07, M10, M10A M10B, M10C, M10D, M10E
- Family IXB: S05, S05A, S05B, S15, S16, M06, M06A.
  This was station OLX, operated by the Ministry of Interior. They even sent our QSL cards! (pictures attached)
- Family IXC:
  S17, S17A, S17B, S17C, S18, S19, S19A, M39
- Military :
  S31 (1122 and 2136 kHz. Around for over 30 years, now defunct.

SPAIN

STRUCTURE OF THE SPANISH INTELLIGENCE COMMUNITY:

Presidencia del Gobierno
Presidency of the Government
Comisión Delegada del Gobierno Para Asuntos de Inteligencia
Delegate commission of the Government for Matters of Intelligence
Ministerio de Defensa
Ministry of Defence

CENTRO NACIONAL DE INTELIGENCIA CNI NATIONAL INTELLIGENCE CENTER

http://www.cni.es

Armed Forces
Centro de Inteligencia de las Fuerzas Armadas CIFAS
Center of Intelligence of the Armed Forces
Army
Centro de Inteligencia y Seguridad
Intelligence and Security Center
Navy
Sección de Informacion
Section of Information
Air force
División de Información
Division of Information
Ministerio del Interior
Ministry of Interior
Secretaria de Estado de Seguridad
State Security Secretariat
Guardia Civil
Civil Guard
Servicio de Información de la Guardia Civil
Information Service of Civil Guard
Cuerpo Nacional de Policia
National Police Corps
Comisaría General de Información
General Commissariat of Information

SOUTH AFRICA

INTELLIGENCE AGENCIES

National Intelligence Co-ordinating Committee [NICOC]
South African Secret Service [SASS]
National Defence Force Intelligence Division
National Intelligence Agency [NIA]
South African Police Service [SAPS]

INTELLIGENCE COMMUNITY

THE MINISTRY

Minister for Intelligence
Ronald Kasrils

MINISTRY FOR INTELLIGENCE SERVICES

The Ministry for Intelligence Services was established on 1 September 1996 and assists the Minister for Intelligence in the supervision and general superintendence of the intelligence services; policy formulation; guidance and direction of the transformation process, and the general conduct of intelligence. The National Strategic Intelligence Amendment Act, 1998 (Act 37 of 1998), was approved by the National Council of Provinces in August 1998. The Act will ensure that the Minister and the intelligence services focus sufficiently on flashpoints when necessary. In terms of the Act, the Minister would have to ensure effective co-operation between the civilian intelligence services (ie National Intelligence Agency (NIA) and South African Secret Service (SASS)), the South African National Defence Force (SANDF) and the South African Police Services (SAPS), in consultation with the relevant Ministers.

NATIONAL INTELLIGENCE COORDINATING COMMITTEE (NICOC)

Mr MJ Maqetuka
Intelligence Coordinator

The National Intelligence Co-ordinating Committee (NICOC) was established on 1 January 1995 in accordance with the National Strategic Intelligence Act, 1994 (Act 39 of 1994).

NICOC consist of the Intelligence Co-ordinator as well as directors-general of the civilian intelligence bodies - the National Intelligence Agency (NIA) and the South African Secret Service (SASS); the Chief of the Intelligence Division of the South African National Defence Force (SANDF), and the Head of the Division: Crime Intelligence of the South African Police Services (SAPS).

NICOC is also supported by a staff complement which is responsible for day-to-day co-ordination.

In terms of the Act, NICOC is required to co-ordinate intelligence supplied by the members of the national intelligence structures and to produce and disseminate intelligence with regard to matters of national strategic importance. In order to facilitate co-ordination, NICOC has established Provincial Intelligence Co-ordination Committees (PICOC's) in the nine provinces and several functional committees.

NICOC's direct clients are the President, the Cabinet and the Cabinet Committee for Security and Intelligence Affairs. Other clients include government departments, Premiers, provincial governments and parliamentary committees.

CIVILIAN INTELLIGENCE

There are two civilian intelligence structures, namely the National Intelligence Service (NIA) and the South African Secret Service (SASS). NIA is responsible for domestic and counter-intelligence in order to enhance national security and the defend the Constitution, the interests of the State and the well-being of the people of South Africa. The Secret Service serves as the foreign intelligence department of the Government and its mission is to conduct intelligence in relation to external threats, opportunities and other issues that could affect the interests and well-being of South Africa, with the aim of promoting the national and security interests of the country and its citizens.

The objective of the intelligence community is to provide evaluated information with the following responsibilities in mind:

- safeguarding the Constitution
- promoting the interrelated elements of security, stability, co-operation and development, both within South Africa and in relation to Southern Africa
- upholding the individual rights enunciated in the chapter on Fundamental Rights (the Bill of Rights) contained in the Constitution
- intensifying collection efforts in crime in support of the SAPS crime intelligence task promoting South Africa's ability to face foreign threats and to enhance its competitiveness in a dynamic world achieving national prosperity while making an active contribution to global peace and other globally-defined priorities for the well-being of humankind.

OVERSIGHT AND CONTROL

Executive control is exercised by way of a civilian Ministry and a Cabinet committee. The civilian intelligence services are accountable to the Minister of Intelligence, who reports to the Cabinet through the Cabinet Committee for Security and Intelligence Affairs.

Parliament has also appointed a mechanism, the Joint Standing Committee on Intelligence (JSCI), legislated in the Intelligence Services Control Act, 1994 (Act 40 of 1994), which is able to order investigations into the intelligence community's activities.

Dr Siyabonya Cwele
Chairperson of the Joint Standing Committee on Intelligence (JSCI)

The Intelligence Services Control Act, 1994 (Act 40 of 1994) also makes provision for the appointment of an Inspector-General for Intelligence. In November 1999, the Intelligence Services Control Amendment Bill was passed by the National Assembly and the National Council of Provinces. It brought Act 40 of 1994 into line with the Constitution, which sets a two-thirds majority in the National Assembly for the appointee's approval.

The Inspector-General will investigate complaints about alleged maladministration, abuse of power, transgressions of laws and policies, corruption and improper enrichment within the intelligence services. The Bill gives the Inspector-General wide powers of access to information and the right to get access to any intelligence, information or premises within or outside the control of the intelligence service in order to perform these functions. The Inspector-General will be responsible for:

- monitoring compliance by the intelligence services with their policies
- submitting certificates to the Minister of reports given to heads of service
- submitting reports to the Joint Standing Committee about investigation of complaints by members of the public against the intelligence services.

In addition to the above, the Auditor-General and Standing Committee on Public Accounts (SCOPA) monitor the relevant intelligence budgets, while the Constitution provides for protection against State abuse through the Public Protector and the Human Rights Commission.

NATIONAL INTELLIGENCE AGENCY

Private Bag X87
Pretoria
0001

MINISTRY: Head of Communication (Media Liaison)
Ms L Daniels
Cell: 082 418 3389

NIA: Head of Communication
Ms P Ndlovu
Tel: (012) 427 4510
Fax: (012) 427 5150

Switchboard: (012) 427 4000

Fax: (012) 427 4651

You are welcome to email us for more information or provide us with information through the following email addresses:

Careers opportunities: careers@nia.gov.za
To submit operational information: noc@nia.gov.za
General information and enquiries: info@nia.gov.za

Mission

- To provide critical and unique intelligence that alerts government and its partners of threats and opportunities.
- To ensure a secure environment that will promote and foster government initiatives geared to attain and sustain a society free from fear and want.
- To develop and nurture a professional and dedicated workforce that is beyond reproach.

FUNCTIONS AND MANDATE

The National Strategic Intelligence Act of 1994 defines the primary functions of NIA as being to gather, correlate, evaluate and analyse domestic intelligence to:

- identify any threat or potential threat to the security of the Republic or its people;
- supply intelligence regarding any such threat to the National Intelligence Co-ordinating Committee (NICOC);
- gather departmental intelligence at the request of any interested department of state and without delay to transmit such intelligence that constitutes departmental intelligence to the relevant department;
- fulfil the national counter-intelligence responsibility and for this purpose to conduct and co-ordinate counter-intelligence to gather, correlate, evaluate, analyse and interpret information regarding counter-intelligence to identify any threat or potential threat to the security of the Republic or its people;
- inform the President of any such threat;
- supply (where necessary) intelligence relating to any such threat to the South African Police Services (SAPS) for the purposes of investigating any offence or alleged offence.

DIRECTOR GENERAL & DEPUTY DIRECTORS GENERAL

Director General	Deputy Director General Corporate Services	Deputy Director General Operations
Mr BL Masetlha	**Ms NST Majola-Pikoli**	**Mr LG Njenje**

In view of these functions, NIA is responsible for the following:
To fulfil a proactive, anticipatory or early warning role of scanning and assessing the total (economic, social, political and environmental) domestic security situation to identify and report to the policy maker or executive departments any signs or warning signals of threats or potential threats to the constitutional order and the safety of the people.
To perform a reactive monitoring role of tracking events when a threat/crime has been identified or a crisis has already arisen, without duplication of the role of other executive departments. The purpose of this monitoring role is mainly to enhance investigation and prosecution by providing tactical information and intelligence to enforcement and prosecution institutions and to decide the extent and implications of threats or potential threats to the national security of the Republic and the safety of the people.
To provide an integrated multi-analytical strategic projective assessment of patterns, trends and of security relevant issues, to provide strategic early warning and to enhance NIA's support/involvement in policy formulation.

SUDAN

INTELLIGENCE AGENCIES

`Al Amn al-Dakhili' (Internal Security) `
Al Amn al-Khariji' (External Security)

SWEDEN

INTELLIGENCE AGENCIES

Militära underrättelse- och säkerhetstjänsten (MUST)
Military Intelligence and Security Service
Säkerhetspolisen (SAPO)
Swedish Security Police
FRA
Swedish SIGINT Organization
Totalförsvarets forskningsinstitut (FOI)
Swedish Defence Research Establishment
Försvarets materielverk
Swedish Defence Materiel Administration

SWITZERLAND

INTELLIGENCE PROFILE

Switzerland's independence and neutrality have long been honoured by the major European powers, and Switzerland was not involved in either of the two World Wars. The political and economic integration of Europe over the past half century, as well as Switzerland's role in many UN and international organizations, has strengthened Switzerland's ties with its neighbours. However, the country did not officially become a UN member until 2002. Switzerland remains active in many UN and international organizations, but retains a strong commitment to neutrality.

	: Swiss Confederation / Switzerland
Country name	
Local name	: Schweizerische Eidgenossenschaft / Schweiz (German), Confédération Suisse / Suisse (French), Confederazione Svizzera / Svizzera (Italian)
Capital	: Bern
Administrative divisions	: 26 cantons; Aargau, Appenzell Ausser-Rhoden, Appenzell Inner-Rhoden, Basel-Landschaft, Basel-Stadt, Bern, Fribourg, Geneve, Glarus, Graubunden, Jura, Luzern, Neuchatel, Nidwalden, Obwalden, Sankt Gallen, Schaffhausen, Schwyz, Solothurn, Thurgau, Ticino, Uri, Valais, Vaud, Zug, Zurich

MILITARY BRANCHES

Army, Air Force, Frontier Guards, Fortification Guards

INTELLIGENCE

- Swiss Intelligence Services (SIS)
- Directorate for Strategic Intelligence (SND)
- Military Intelligence Service (MND)
- Air Force Intelligence Service (LWND)
- Federal Office of Police (BAP)
- Service for Prevention and Analysis (DAP)

This is a compilation of facts open to the public and personal experiences. The VBS (DDPS) and SND have homepages, but don't try the link for a detailed description of the SND - it does not (and presumably never will) open. The best sources are the archives of the parliament.

SWISS INTELLIGENCE SERVICES (SIS)

For a long time after WW II Switzerland kept its behaviour of a hedgehog and the Secret Services didn't make an exception; they were in charge at will. Before their reorganisation the services were rather a threat than a protection for the country. This remark excludes the exceptionally good job performed during WW II.

The so-called "Fichenaffäre" (surveillance scandal) 1989 however turned the country upside down. Without any political control many thousand of citizens had been filed - up to a quantity of 700.000(!) individual files. The Swiss were shocked. Finally, examination for everybody was granted - the author included. For years he had been frisked at the airport, photos were taken. They obviously did not digest my STRATCOMINT task in a time when I had negotiations for my employer in the GDR about the sale of scientific equipment for research on toxics in Rügen. A tiny ballpoint mark in my passport made customs watchful. Later on, when I could not enter a certain Islamic country with my passport stamped in Israel, I got a new one - and never again have been frisked. This is just one example, how amateurish Swiss Home Intelligence acted. As a result of the political earthquake following the "Fichenaffäre", all relevant services became re-organised, the parliamentary control functions became enhanced and nowadays are rather effective.

- CONNECTIONS OF SIS WITH OTHER ORGANISATIONS

As it is usual SIS too is looking for informations to trade in. Since 1971 SIS is member of the Berne Club. Intelligence office heads of 17 European countries meet annually. According to the Dutch Security Service BVD the 2000 agenda for example covered the subject of European integration. Another organisation, which exchanges data on international political violence, is the Kilowatt Group, founded in 1977. Members are EU countries, Canada, Norway, Switzerland, CIA and FBI, South Africa and Israel with Mossad and Shin Beth. The group is dominated by Israel because of its strong position in the information exchange on Arab based terror group in Europe and the Middle East.
SIS is not mentioned as a member of the Trevi Group.
In 1990 it became clear Italy has had a secret stay-behind army named "Gladio". Founded in 1959 by the Italian Secret Service SIFAR and supported by NATO and CIA it had to be dissolved by the Italian Senate amid public protests.
However, others of those secret armies existed elsewhere:

- "Absalon" in Denmark
- "ROC" in Norway
- "SDRA8" in Belgium and - of course -
- "P-26" in Switzerland.

Support to these organisation was given by ACC (Allied Clandestine Committee), linked to SHAPE (NATO Supreme HQ Europe). The Belgian Secret Service SGR organised the last meeting in October 1990.
Swiss P-26 was completed with P-27 for Secret Communications. The crew consisted of 400 people - a number of 1000 was the target. Weapons, explosives and up-to-date equipment for nearly every possible "case" were stored in several places. No doubt the Swiss Intelligence Service was aware - or part - of the story. The question remains, how the relationship was between NATO and P-26 in a neutral country. P-26 and P-27 have been smashed 1991 by a parliamentary commission.

- SIS' STRUCTURE

The Federal Department for Defence, Civil Protection and Sports (DDPS) operates the

- Directorate for Strategic Intelligence (SND)
- Military Intelligence Service (MND)
- Air Force Intelligence Service (LWND)

The Federal Department of the Interior operates the

- Federal Office of Police (BAP)
- Service for Prevention and Analysis (DAP).

SND

The Directorate for Strategic Intelligence (SND) is responsible for the procurement of information from foreign countries for all Federal Departments. This includes OSINT, HUMINT and COMINT. 9 out of 10 information are of economic nature. Main target areas are the Balkans, Central Asia, India, Pakistan, Middle East and Northern Africa. The SND also collects data on the proliferation on mass destruction weapons supporting the agreement of Helsinki and others.

MND

The Military Intelligence Service (MND) provides COMINT and SIGINT in the interior and exterior. Some of its bases are used in parallel by the DAP. The MND will scan, locate and analyse sources of electromagnetic waves. If necessary it is prepared to use ECM (Electromagnetic Counter Measures). Training post for the "Funkaufklärer" (COMINT) soldiers is PE-19, the barracks in Jassbach. After basic schooling the specialists are transferred to the EKF Bat 51 to 53 (Electronic Warfare Batalions). Candidates for STRATCOMINT must have attended trainig before recruitment. A privatly operated school (ILT) is in charge for the Morse training. Training post is PE-20, the barracks of Heimenschwand. Once trained soldiers are transferred to EKF Bat 46. The third, important, base is located in Zimmerwald (PE-Z). The MND here works together with civil specialists from SWISSCOM and - I assume - DAP and SND.
Zimmerwald is packed with all kind of stuff:

- the usual antennas for HF/VHF/UHF reception
- dishes of ONYX system
- permanent GPS tracking station
- astronomical observatory and SLR (Satellite Laser Ranging) station
- Earth Tides Observatory
- permanent Ozon (O3) measuring station

There is a series of other, temporarily used, sites, the MND may use. Especially for COMINT on VHF there are those funny "field days" for recruits somewhere in the mountains for exercises in DF and UHF links. Locations of the stations for strategic DF are confidential and are therefore not disclosed here.

LWND

The Air Force Intelligence Service (LWND) seems to be a small unit, its task being the tactical reconnaissance for the Air Force itself. I didn't find any sources dealing with LWND.

BAP

The Federal Office of Police (BAP) will prosecute criminals as far as it is not a task for the cantonal polices (for example if explosives have been used or the trail leads to a foreign country). Informations for the BAP are procured by the DAP and - on demand and permission - by the SND. The service works closely together with SWISSCOM and the BAKOM (Swiss Authorities on Telecommunications) in all cases where criminals use cellular networks or unlicensed communication equipment. Although the DAP must apply for informations gained for example from SATCOMS, its role of course is delicate, as usual for services of MOI. The privatizing of companies like SWISSCOM adds some problems. SWISSCOM Broadcast runs all transmitters for the SRG (Swiss Radio and TV Company) - and does it also in wartimes for the emergency transmitters. SWISSCOM Broadcast staff doing their "normal" job is annually on duty on these stations.

Obviously there are many links between the services and some facilities are "double manned" giving rise for rumours. As an example one should mention the "*Hoher Kasten*", a mountain at the border in the Rhine valley, facing Austria. A huge antenna tower is visible. Declared as "*SWISSCOM multi purpose facility*", it houses VHF broadcast transmitters to serve the most western parts of Austria with their own programs, transmitters for REGA, the Swiss Rescue Airline and tracking receivers for Constant Volume Balloons (CVB) from Switzerland and Italy. Believing some sources, it was the intention of SIS to erect an impressive center for COMINT/ SIGINT on that place. To my knowledge it never has been realised, but my enquiry at the BAKOM only produced the answer that they "*unfortunately do not file technical details of the stations*".

ONYX

In 1997 the Federal Council decided to complete the classical COMINT by interception of SATCOM within the borders. Switzerland has not participated in NSA's ECHELON project, although this was an option for a certain time. It has been decided to develop a tailormade system which was called SATOS 3. The system is now in operation for a testing period and is called ONYX. In 2006 ONYX will be in full use for the SND.

ONYX has entirely been developed for COMINT/SIGINT, not for ELINT (RADAR, weapon guiding systems, etc). Switzerland is one of the believed 30 countries (in 2002) using such systems. The USA (NSA), with ECHELON (stations in US, UKUSA countries and affiliated), Great Britain GCHQ (stations in Gibraltar, Cyprus, Belize, Oman, Turkey and Australia) and France (DGSE) (stations in Dome, Kouru, Mayotte, Emirates and others) do possess global systems. Russias and Chinas possibilities are unknown.

ONYX is located in Leuk, Heimenschwand and Zimmerwald. It is operated by the SND. There are no antennas outside Switzerland. The size of the antennas is between 18 m and 4 m. How many there will be is not known, but "the number has to be doubled" (Parliamentary Commissions paper).

The SATCOM station Leuk was erected by SWISSCOM, could be accessed for guided tours and never was "secret". Since 2001 SWISSCOM abandoned the SATCOM business and sold the facilities to a US company (!).

Given the fact, that globally acting criminal organisations more and more use shortwaves (HF e-mail, etc), systems like ONYX mainly are used for the protection of economic interests.
The information for this profile was compiled by one of our Central European monitors. THANX!

ARMED FORCES INTELLIGENCE SERVICE (AIS)

The AIS is tasked with reconnaissance and intelligence at the operational and tactical levels if the armed forces are called up for civil affairs support or active duty. The AIS is also charged with the training of intelligence officers for the armed forces.

THE AIR FORCE INTELLIGENCE SECTION

The AFIS is responsible for intelligence, particularly on technical matters, that is directly necessary for air force operations. In addition it gathers information within the armed forces' area of interest, analyzes this information and forwards it to the AIS. The Air Force Intelligence Section is under operational control by the Deputy Chief of Staff for Intelligence.

FEDERAL OFFICE OF POLICE *BUNDESAMT FÜR POLIZEI (BAP)*

The BAP is Switzerland's domestic security and counterintelligence agency.

SYRIA

INTELLIGENCE PROFILE

BACKGROUND

Following the breakup of the Ottoman Empire during World War I, Syria was administered by the French until independence in 1946. In the 1967 Arab-Israeli War, Syria lost the Golan Heights to Israel. Since 1976, Syrian troops have been stationed in Lebanon, ostensibly in a peacekeeping capacity. In recent years, Syria and Israel have held occasional peace talks over the return of the Golan Heights.

Country name	: Al Jumhuriyah al Arabiyah as Suriyah (Syrian Arab Republic)
Short name	: Suriyah / Syria
Capital	: Damascus
Administration	: Syria has 14 provinces: Al Hasakah, Al Ladhiqiyah, Al Qunaytirah, Ar Raqqah, As Suwayda', Dar'a, Dayr az Zawr, Dimashq, Halab, Hamah, Hims, Idlib, Rif Dimashq, Tartus

MILITARY BRANCHES:

Syrian Arab Army, Syrian Arab Navy, Syrian Arab Air Force (includes Air Defense Forces), Police and Security Force

INTELLIGENCE AGENCIES:

- Idarat al-Amn al-'Amm
- Idarat al-Amn al-Siyasi
- Shu'bat al-Mukhabarat al-'Askariyya
- Idarat al-Mukhabarat al-Jawiyya

All Syrian intelligence services are under direct control of the president. The agencies have overlapping functions so that Syria is not dependent on any one of them.

IDARAT AL-AMN AL-SIYASI
POLITICAL SECURITY DIRECTORATE

This organisation is responsible for detecting signs of organized political activity against the regime. This involves surveillance of suspected political dissidents, as well as the activities of foreigners in Syria. The agency also monitors all print and audiovisual media.

IDARAT AL-AMN AL-'AMM
GENERAL INTELLIGENCE DIRECTORATE

This Directorate is the main civilian intelligence service in Syria. It is divided into three branches;

- The internal security division is responsible for internal surveillance of the population in general;
- The external security division;
- The Palestine division, which monitors the activities of Palestinian groups in Syria and Lebanon.

SHU'BAT AL-MUKHABARAT AL-'ASKARIYYA
MILITARY INTELLIGENCE SERVICE

Syria's military intelligence service, headquartered at the Defense Ministry complex in Damascus, is formally responsible for the usual range of military surveillance operations, planning, etc. that one would expect. In addition, it is responsible for providing military and logistical support to Palestinian, Lebanese, and Turkish extremist groups, monitoring (and often assassinating) political dissidents abroad, and coordinating the activities of Syrian and Lebanese military forces stationed in Lebanon.

IDARAT AL-MUKHABARAT AL-JAWIYYA
AIR FORCE INTELLIGENCE DIRECTORATE

Despite its name, this intelligence service is not primarily concerned with providing information to the air force. It's evolution into Syria's most secretive and fearsome intelligence service has a great deal to do with the fact that Hafez Assad was once commander of Syria's air force. After he assumed power in 1970, Assad turned to this intelligence service, dominated by men that he knew well (and in most cases had appointed himself), to undertake sensitive domestic and international operations.

On the domestic level, Syrian air force intelligence has frequently spearheaded operations against Islamist opposition elements in the country. It played a leading role in the regime's suppression of Muslim Brotherhood revolt during the 1970's and early 1980's. More recently, air force intelligence agents reportedly led the nationwide manhunt for members of the Islamic Liberation Party (Hizb al-Tahrir) in Dec. 1999.

The Directorate has also been central to the regime's sponsorship of international terrorism. It's agents, frequently stationed abroad in Syrian embassies and in branch offices of Syria's national airline, have directly coordinated dozens of terrorist operations.

CONTACTS

Syrian Cabinet
Cabinet of Ministers (Includes Ministries of state and of State for Cabinet and Services Affairs)
Shahbandar Street
Tel 222600 /2221000/ 2110212

Ministry of Foreign Affairs
Muhajereen, Shora Avenue
Tel. 3331200/4/ 3337200
Fax. 3320686**Ministry of Justic**
Eal-Nasre Street
Tel. 2214105/ 220302
Fax. 2246250

SYRIA'S INTELLIGENCE SERVICES: A PRIMER

Syria's four main intelligence services are (or were) directly under the control of the Syrian president and have overlapping functions so that the regime is not overly dependent on any one of them. Each operates in near total secrecy (most of the information below was compiled by MEIB from scattered reports in the Arab press and interviews with knowledgable Syrian sources). None of the services are permitted full access to information about all of its counterparts or the identities of agents working in the other services. Even within each service, commanders of different divisions often reported directly to Assad, rather than to their nominal superiors. Whether the intelligence chiefs will show Bashar the same kind of unquestioned loyalty is anyone's guess.

The Political Security Directorate [Idarat al-Amn al-Siyasi]

The Political Security Directorate (PSD) is responsible for detecting signs of organized political activity that run counter to the interests of the regime. This involves surveillance of suspected political dissidents, as well as the activities of foreigners residing in the country and their interaction with locals. The PSD also monitors all print and audiovisual media.

The commander of the PSI is Maj. Gen. Adnan Badr Hassan, an Alawite from Homs. He has held this position since 1987.

General Security Directorate [Idarat al-Amn al-'Amm]

The General Security Directorate (GSD) is the main civilian intelligence service in Syria. It is divided into three branches. The internal security division is responsible for internal surveillance of the population in general--a duty which clearly overlaps with that of the PSI. The purpose of this redundancy, notes one prominent scholar of the Ba'athist regime, is to ensure that Assad "has always in the security field two strings to his bow . . . acting in a manner not unlike that of Napoleon, who pressed into service a secret police under Fouché and simultaneously organized a counterpolice to check on Fouché."[1] The other two divisions of the GSD are external security (equivalent to the CIA) and the Palestine division, which monitors the activities of Palestinian groups in Syria and Lebanon.

The director of the GSD is Maj. Gen Ali Houri, a member of the Ismaili sect of Shi'ite Islam.[2] It is noteworthy that until Houri's appointment last year, this position had *always* been held by a member of the Sunni Muslim community. The dismissal of Houri's predecessor, Lt. Gen. Bashir al-Najjar, in July 1998 (and his subsequent imprisonment on corruption charges) was part of a larger trend over the past two years of removing the relatively few Sunnis who held top posts in the security apparatus.[3] The deputy chief of the GSD, Muhammad Nassif, is a retired military officer who heads the powerful Alawite Khayr Bek clan. Nassif had been a central figure in relations with Iran and Lebanese Shi'ite militias in south Lebanon for quite some time and formerly headed the internal security division of the GSD.

The current head of internal security for the GSD is Bahjat Suleiman, a key political advisor to Bashar Assad who was appointed to this position last year. It is unclear who heads the external security division. One source contacted by MEIB said that Gen. Ghazi Kanaan, the head of Syrian military intelligence in Lebanon, currently occupies this position. While this is plausible in light of Kanaan's presence at Syrian-Turkish security talks last year, we've been unable to confirm this claim. The head of the Palestine division was last reported to be Hisham Bakhtiar, but this information is two years old. It is difficult to establish with certainty the current occupants of these two positions because these divisions are rarely mentioned in the Syrian press.

Military Intelligence [Shu'bat al-Mukhabarat al-'Askariyya]

Syria's military intelligence service, headquartered at the Defense Ministry complex in Damascus, is formally responsible for the usual range of military surveillance operations, planning, etc. that one would expect. In addition, it is responsible for providing military and logistical support to Palestinian, Lebanese, and Turkish extremist groups, monitoring (and often assassinating) political dissidents abroad, and coordinating the activities of Syrian and Lebanese military forces stationed in Lebanon.

Gen. Assef Shawkat

The current head of military intelligence is Gen. Hassan Khalil, 63, who was appointed to this position five months ago to replace Gen. Ali Douba. Khalil, an Alawite from Latakia, had served as Douba's deputy since 1993. MEIB has learned from informed sources, however, that the main decision-maker in this service is *not* Khalil, but the recently-appointed deputy chief of military intelligence, Gen. Assef Shawkat. Shawkat, also an Alawite, is the husband of Bashar Assad's older sister Bushra.

Air Force Intelligence [Idarat al-Mukhabarat al-Jawiyya]

Despite its name, this intelligence service is *not* primarily concerned with providing information to the air force. It's evolution into Syria's most secretive and fearsome intelligence service has a great deal to do with the fact that Hafez Assad was once commander of Syria's air force. After he assumed power in 1970, Assad turned to this intelligence service, dominated by men that he knew well (and in most cases had appointed himself), to undertake sensitive domestic and international operations. For nearly thirty years, the service was commanded by Maj. Gen. Muhammad al-Khouli, a trusted advisor whose office was adjacent to Assad's in the presidential palace.

On the domestic level, Syrian air force intelligence has frequently spearheaded operations against Islamist opposition elements in the country. It played a leading role in the regime's suppression of Muslim Brotherhood revolt during the 1970's and early 1980's. More recently, air force intelligence agents reportedly led the nationwide manhunt for members of the Islamic Liberation Party (Hizb al-Tahrir) in December 1999.

Air force intelligence has also been central to the regime's sponsorship of international terrorism. It's agents, frequently stationed abroad in Syrian embassies and in branch offices of Syria's national airline, have directly coordinated dozens of terrorist operations. The most well-documented example was the attempted bombing of an Israeli airliner at London's Heathrow airport in April 1986. The subsequent investigation revealed that the primary culprit, Nizar Hindawi, who had duped an unsuspecting woman into carrying explosives onto the aircraft, was operating in coordination with Haitham Sayid, the deputy chief of Syrian air force intelligence at that time. As a result of this fiasco, an international warrant for Sayid's arrest was issued and Britain broke diplomatic ties with Syria (they were restored four years later when Syria joined the allied coalition against Iraq).[4]

Gen. Ibrahim Hueiji, the current head of air force intelligence, is an Alawite from the Haddadin tribe. He was elected to the Ba'ath party's central committee on June 17.

[1] Hanna Batatu, *Syria's Peasantry, the Descendants of Its Rural Notables, and Their Politics* (Princeton University Press, 1999), p. 240.
[2] The Ismailis (sometimes called the "Seveners" because they recognize only seven imams rather than twelve), split from orthodox Shi'ite Islam in the eighth century, They constitute about 1% of the population of Syria. Much like the Alawite minority in Syria, who constitute 11% of the population, the Ismailis have historically feared Sunni Muslim dominance and have thus tended to be very supportive of the Assad regime.
[3] In 1998, it was widely reported in the Arab press that Lt. Gen. Mahmoud Shaqa was appointed to this position (see, for example, *Al-Quds Al-Arabi,* 6 July 1998), but these reports were erroneous.
[4] Declassified files of the East German Stasi intelligence agency have recently shed light on the involvement of Syrian intelligence in other terrorist attacks overseas, most notably the 1983 bombing of a Frech Cultural Center in West Berlin. See Daniel Pipes, *Syria Beyond the Peace Process* (Washington, DC: Washington Institute for Near East Policy, 1996), p. 115.

TAIWAN

INTELLIGENCE & SECURITY AGENCIES

National Security Council (NSC)

Ministry of National Defense

Military Intelligence Bureau
Army
Navy
Air Force
Coast Guard
Military Police Command
National Security Bureau

Interior Ministry
National Police Administration

Justice Ministry
Investigation Bureau

The primary objective of the ROC's defense policy is to defend Taiwan, the Pes- cadores, Kinmen, and Matsu. This entails establishing a fighting force of sufficient readiness to guard the nation and protect its people. The direct and most serious threat to the ROC's national security remains the unwillingness of Peking to renounce the use of military force against Taiwan. Thus, while ROC national defense strategy calls for balanced development of the three Armed Forces, naval and air supremacy receive first priority. In addition to current defensive preparations, a long-term policy of developing an elite fighting force and self-sufficiency in defense technology is also being strictly followed. This calls for restructuring the Armed Forces, streamlining command levels, renovating logistical systems, merging or reassigning military schools and upper-ranking staff units, as well as reducing the total number of men in uniform.

The defense budget for the ROC military has been reduced annually during the past decade and has become more and more open to public scrutiny. The downward trend in ROC military expenditures was especially evident in fiscal 1994, when the budget shrank 4.65 percent. The defense budget is becoming increasingly public. In fiscal 1996, only 36 percent of the budget was considered confidential, in comparison to 51 percent in fiscal 1993 and 46 percent in 1994, respectively. The defense budget for fiscal 1996 will occupy just under 23 percent of the total government budget, down from 24.5 percent of the previous year.
The thinking behind changes to the ROC's Armed Forces over the past few years reflects a shift from equal stress on offense and defense to assuring defense. This strategic principle, as implemented under the Ten-Year Troop Reduction Plan , has led to a targeted force of less than 400,000 troops by the year 2003 and an increase in the ratio of combat troops to overall military manpower.

The allocation of resources among the three services will give priority to air superiority and control of the seas in defensive operations, as well as to coastal defense. Accordingly, a ten-year program is to be implemented in three phases, including the development of a practicable table of organization for the three services to facilitate training and carry out peacetime missions, elimination of overlapping staff units in the three major services, and consolidation of the General Staff Headquarters of the Ministry of National Defense (MND) and the general headquarters of the three services, transferring non-military tasks to organizations outside the MND.

Second-generation weapon systems used by the three armed services are also being actively updated. These include the inception of four E-2T air defense warning systems, the formation of the first Ching-kuo indigenous defense fighter (IDF) squadron, the commissioning of the Cheng-kung and Knox-class missile frigates, and taking delivery of a second batch of AH-1W attack helicopters and OH-58D reconnaissance helicopters.

MINISTRY OF NATIONAL DEFENSE

Article 36 of the ROC Constitution stipulates that the president of the republic "shall have supreme command of the land, sea and air forces of the whole country," and Article 3 of the Organic Law of the Executive Yuan states that "the Executive Yuan shall establish (among others) a Ministry of National Defense." According to the Organization Law of the MND , the ministry shall be in charge of the defense affairs of the whole country, and the minister shall be a civilian. The current defense minister is Chiang Chung-ling .

Within the Ministry of National Defense is the General Staff Headquarters (GSH), under which are the various services, including the Army, Navy, Air Force, Combined Services Forces, Armed Forces Reserve Command/Coast Guard Command, and Military Police Command. In charge of military affairs, the GSH is headed by a chief of the general staff, who acts, in the military command system, as chief of staff to the president for operational matters; while in the administrative system, he serves as chief of staff to the minister of national defense. The current chief of the general staff is General Lo Pen-li .

The Ministry of National Defense is responsible for formulating military strategy, setting military personnel policies, devising draft and mobilization plans, delineating supply distribution policies, arranging for the research and development of military technology, compiling data for the national defense budget, setting military regulations, conducting court martial proceedings and administering military law. The ministry itself has a Minister's Office ; Departments of Manpower , Materials , and Law ; a Bureau of the Comptroller , and the Judge Advocates Bureau .

GENERAL STAFF HEADQUARTERS, MND

In charge of the planning and supervision of joint war activities, political warfare, personnel, military intelligence, operations, education and training, logistics, organization and equipment calibration, communications, military archives management, and medical services, the General Staff Headquarters, MND contains the Office of the Chief of the General Staff ; the Department of Supervision and Inspection ; the General Political Warfare Department ; Offices of the Deputy Chiefs of the General Staff for Personnel , Intelligence , Operations , Logistics , and Planning ; the Bureau of Communications and Electronics ; the Military History and Translation Bureau ; the Military Medical Bureau ; and the General Affairs Bureau .

COMBINED SERVICES FORCE GENERAL HEADQUARTERS

The Combined Services Force General Headquarters is in charge of ordinance, military maps, and communication equipment for the ROC Armed Forces. It also provides support and services commonly needed by all Armed Forces services, such as finance, surveying, engineering, rear echelon administration, purchase and procurement, and armament appraisal and testing.

ARMED FORCES RESERVE COMMAND

Shortly after the ROC government announced the lifting of the Emergency Decree and the termination of the Period of National Mobilization for Suppression of the Communist Rebellion , the Taiwan Garrison General Headquarters (TGGH) was deactivated, and two new commands were created to assume partial responsibility for tasks formerly performed by the TGGH: the Armed Forces Reserve Command (AFRC), which is mainly in charge of reservist management and mobilization affairs; and the Coast Guard Command (CGC), responsible for matters of coastal security.

Units	Address	Tel.	E-mail
Foreign Affairs Department, National Police Administration	7, Sec. 1, Chungshiao E. Road, Taipei City	(02)23213175	npafad01@npa.gov.tw
Foreign Affairs Police Corps, National Police Administration	7, Sec. 1, Chungshiao E. Road, Taipei City	(02)23940238	service@npa.gov.tw

Alien Detention Center, National Police Administration	105, Tapu Road, Sanshia, Taipei County	(02)26730091-3	service@npa.gov.tw
Section Four, Bureau of Immigration	15, Guangjou Street, Taipei City	(02)23899983	foudi@ms1.immigration.gov.tw
Immigration Corps, Aviation Police Bureau	27, Hanching N. Road, Dayuan Shiang, Taoyuan County	(03)3982243	eyes@dns.apb.gov.tw
Foreign Affairs Section, Aviation Police Bureau	27 Hanching N. Road, Dayuan Shiang, Taoyuan County	(03)3982242	eyes@dns.apb.gov.tw
Foreign Affairs Section, Keelung Harbor Police Bureau	5-1, Chungcheng Road, Keelung City	(02)24258461	adm2818@mail.klhph.gov.tw
Foreign Affairs Section, Taichung Harbor Police Bureau	2, Chungheng 4th Road, Wuchi Jen,Taichung County	(04)26565849	thpb0301@mail.thpb.gov.tw
Foreign Affairs Section, Kaohsiung Harbor Police Bureau	24, Penglai Road, Kushan District, Kaohsiung City	(07)5515183	p2715@mail.khb.gov.tw
Foreign Affairs Section, Hualien Harbor Police Bureau	13 Gangkou Road, Hualien City, Hualien County	(03)8222701	mod@mail.hlhb.gov.tw
Foreign Affairs Division, Taipei Municipal Police Department	96, Yanping S. Road, Taipei City	(02)23817494	fad@webmail.tmpd.gov.tw
Foreign Affairs Division, Kaohsiung Municipal Police Department	260 Chungcheng 4th Road, Kaohsiung City	(07)2215796	evb00@kmph.gov.tw
Foreign Affairs Section, Taipei County Police Bureau	57 Mingchu Road, Panchiao City, Taipei County	(02)29614809	tcp2122@tcpsung.gov.tw
Foreign Affairs Division, Ilan County Police Bureau	23, Weishui Road, Ilan City, Ilan County	(039)353921	t004@imail.ilcpb.gov.tw
Foreign Affairs Division, Keelung City Police Bureau	205 Shin-Er Road, Keelung City	(02)24252787	klcg2080@mail.tpg.gov.tw
Foreign Affairs Division, Taoyuan County Police Bureau	3, Shienfu Road, Taoyuan City, Taoyuan County	(03)3335107	tyhp14-3@mail.tyhp.gov.tw
Foreign Affairs Division, Hsinchu County Police Bureau	12, Kuanming Sixth Road, Tsubei City, Hsinchu County	(035)557953	dragon0270@sinamail.com
Foreign Affairs Division, Hsinchu City Police Bureau	1, Chungshan Road, Hsinchu City	(035)242103	1051@ems.hccg.gov.tw
Foreign Affairs Division, Miaoli County Police Bureau	2 Miaoli Fuchien Road, Miaoli City, Miaoli County	(037)356950	m19905@ems.miaoli.gov.tw
Foreign Affairs Division, Taichung County Police Bureau	225, Chungshan Road, Fongyuan City, Taichung County	(04)25285475	tcpa2122@dns.tcpa.gov.tw
Foreign Affairs Division, Taichung City Police Bureau	588, Sec. 2,Wenshin Road, Taichung City	(04)23273875	tcpbbb01@mail.tpg.gov.tw
Foreign Affairs Division, Nantou County Police Bureau	669, Chungshin Road, Nantou City, Nantou County	(049)2234302	fad@mail.ncpb.gov.tw
Foreign Affairs Division, Changhua County Police Bureau	778, Sec. 2, Chungcheng Road, Changhua City, Changhua County	(04)27619872	jb01@ms1.chpb.gov.tw
Foreign Affairs Division, Yunlin County Police Bureau	100, Sec. 3, Dashiue Road, Yunlin City, Yunlin County	(05)5329033	fap@mail.ylhpb.gov.tw

Foreign Affairs Division, Chiayi County Police Bureau	3, East Sec., Shianher 1st Road, Taipao City, Chiayi County	(05)3620220	2074@m2.cypd.gov.tw
Foreign Affairs Division, Chiayi City Police Bureau	195, Chungshan Road, Chiayi City	(05)2236695	mb01@mail.ccpb.gov.tw
Foreign Affairs Division, Tainan County Police Bureau	3, Chungcheng Road, Shinying City, Tainan County	(06)6354531	foreignaffairs@mail.tncp.gov.tw
Foreign Affairs Division, Tainan City Police Bureau	37, Nanmen Road, Tainan City	(06)2229704	tnc762@yahoo.com.tw
Foreign Affairs Division, Kaohsiung County Police Bureau	388, Guangyuan Road, Fengshan City, Kaohsiung County	(07)7452830	ki@mail.kcpb.gov.tw
Foreign Affairs Division, Pingtung County Police Bureau	119, Chungcheng Road, Pingtung City, Pingtung County	(08)7336283	ptb001@ptpolice.gov.tw
Foreign Affairs Division, Hualien County Police Bureau	21, Fuchien Road, Huanlien City, Hualien County	(038)224023	fad@mail2.hlpb.gov.tw
Foreign Affairs Division, Taitung County Police Bureau	268, Chungshan Road, Taitung City, Taitung County	(089)334756	V2122@mail.ttcpb.gov.tw
Foreign Affairs Division, Penghu County Police Bureau	26, Chiping Road, Magung City, Penghu County	(06)9270870	yenju651115@kimo.com.tw
Administration Division, Kinmen County Police Bureau	15, Chingshan Road, Chingcheng Jen, Kinmen County	(0823)25653	inhwab@mail.kpb.gov.tw
Administration Division, Lienchiang County Police Bureau	260, Chiehshou Tsun, Nangan Hsian, Lienchiang County	(0836)22421-2192	ogoven@pchome.com.tw

MANPOWER STRUCTURE

A person in the ROC military may be an officer , a noncommissioned officer (NCO) , or an enlisted man . He may be serving on either a volunteer or a conscript basis, and may be on active duty or reserve status.

OFFICERS

Officers in the ROC military generally come from three backgrounds. They might be graduates of military academies who become career officers , graduates of different specialized military schools who serve shorter terms of duty , or college graduates who have passed a written test to become reserve officers.

Approximately 15 percent of the officers commissioned each year are graduates from different military academies; another 45 percent are graduates of specialized military schools; and the remaining 40 percent are reserve officers.

The ratio of officers to NCOs is currently 1:2.4, while that to enlisted men is 1:2.6. Thus, the ratio of officers to soldiers as a whole in the ROC Armed Forces is around 1:5, which is close to the 1:6 ratio of the US Armed Forces, and almost equals that of the Japanese Self-Defense Force (1:4.98).

NONCOMMISSIONED OFFICERS

NCOs constitute the backbone of basic units of the Armed Forces, and are increasingly depended upon to train troops and develop their combat performance. In recent years, however, most senior NCOs have retired, leaving the current proportion of career NCOs too low and the percentage of

NCO reservists in service too high. Reservists are on active duty for a very limited period of time, making it difficult for them to keep up with changes in the operation and maintenance of ever-more sophisticated weapons and equipment. Solutions to this problem lie in reconfiguring the NCO organizational structure and recruiting new NCOs.

Conscripts

The Military Service Law of the ROC stipulates that all males in the Republic of China shall fulfill military service. Article 3 of the law states: "Male persons shall be liable for military service on January 1 of the year immediately following the year during which they reach the age of 18, and shall no longer be drafted for service beginning on December 31 of the year during which they reach the age of 45." Citizens who have been sentenced to imprisonment for longer than seven years are prohibited from entering the military.

Under the Military Service Law, military conscription is administered jointly by the Ministry of National Defense and the Ministry of the Interior . The former is responsible for securing an adequate number of conscripts and training them, while the latter determines the sources of the conscripts and ensures their rights and benefits. Generally, conscripts undergo a minimum of two months of basic training before receiving their 22-month unit assignments.
Male senior high, vocational high, and college students whose studies would be interrupted by military conscription can defer their induction until after graduation. Students who are admitted to a university or college undergo two months of basic training in the summer before their freshman year. Upon graduation, they re-enter the military to fulfill the remainder of their two-year commitment.

Young men in poor health are exempt from military conscription. Those in average health may serve in the National Guard . Draftees from impoverished families may apply for service in this unit, giving them reserve status and allowing them to stay with their families. In addition, the only son of parents who are over seventy may also apply for National Guard service to fulfill his military obligation.

Military Mobilization

The ROC defense strategy calls for maintaining a minimum force in peacetime and mobilizing a large number of troops in the event of war. The reservist system plays a key role in such a policy by facilitating instantaneous mobilization and instant combat readiness. At present, registered reservists in the ROC amount to about 3.8 million persons, or more than 18 percent of the general population. After a man is discharged from active duty, he must report to his local military reserve unit, a subunit under the Armed Forces Reserve Command. Reservists are organized into different units according to their military occupational specialty (MOS). Since a prolonged mobilization recall might adversely affect both the livelihood of a reservist and the overall economic development of the country, annual reservist training is usually conducted through recalls. An MOS refresher training course is conducted, and each reservist is notified of his unit combat mission and relative location.

DEFENSE R&D

Research and development of national defense technology is often in direct proportion to the degree of a nation's industrialization. While the ROC industrial sector has made considerable progress over the past decade, most of it has in fact been confined to machining components and light manufacturing. The MND has long made use of the National Defense Industrial Development Fund to assist public and private enterprises in cultivating qualified technical personnel and purchasing facilities, transferring advanced technology, and developing a more sophisticated production base that one day promises a fully self-reliant defense industry. The MND has issued the Defense Science and Technology Development Plan to strengthen cooperation between the academic and industrial sectors, and has, along with several cabinet-level institutions such as the National Science Council , the Ministry of Education , and the Ministry of Economic Affairs , set up the Executive Committee for the Development of Defense Science and Technology (ECDDST). With its two subdivisions, the Academic Cooperation Group and the Industrial Cooperation Group , the ECDDST taps academic resources for researching defense technology and makes use of the industrial sector to develop and manufacture weaponry and armaments.

CHUNGSHAN INSTITUTE OF SCIENCE AND TECHNOLOGY

As the leading institution for the research, development, and design of defense technology in the ROC, the Chungshan Institute of Science and Technology (CIST) contains some 6,000 scientists and more than 8,000 technicians.

With its headquarters in Lungt'an , Taoyuan County, the CIST has facilities stretching over nearly 6,000 acres scattered throughout Taiwan, and is divided into four major research divisions: aeronautics, missiles and rockets, electronics, and chemistry. The CIST has six centers for systems development, systems maintenance, quality assurance, materials R&D, aeronautic development, and missile manufacturing. Each research division or research center has a director in charge of the research and development of its specialty, while planning units have project chairmen responsible for R&D program management and system integration. The CIST jointly conducts independent research and development of weapon systems with the Aero Industry Development Center , which is now under CIST supervision; some manufacturing units of the Combined Services Force; academic institutions; and public and civilian industries.
To date, a number of weapon systems have been domestically designed, tested, and produced on a mass scale by the CIST. These include the Kung-feng 6A rocket, the Hsiung-feng I and Hsiung-feng II SAMs, artillery fire control systems, naval sonar systems, naval electronic warfare systems, and the Tzu-chiang trainer aircraft . The CIST has produced or plans to produce Tien-kung I and Tien-kung II SAMs, and Tien-chien AAMs. The institute is also developing the Tien-chien II AAM system. To date, the first squadron of 20 prototype IDF fighters has been completed and turned over to the ROC Air Force.

A proposal to privatize the Aero Industry Development Center was approved by the Legislature on May 16, 1995. This conversion from military to private status, under the supervision of the Ministry of Economic Affairs, is intended to facilitate the transfer of ROC military aeronautic know-how to the private sector while enabling the center to form joint ventures with high-tech foreign manufacturers. This in turn is expected to bring advanced aviation technology into Taiwan to accelerate the growth of the nation's aerospace industry. A period of three-and-a-half years has been granted to the center to carry out full privatization.

NATIONAL SECURITY BUREAU

The National Security Bureau was established on March 1, 1955, falling directly under the National Defense Council (NDC). In 1967 the National Security Council (NSC) was set up to replace the NDC, and the NSB became a subsidiary organ under the NSC. The National Security Bureau put police and the re-organized secret peace-keeping intelligence agencies under its control. Under the National Security Bureau's command, there were: (1) administrative organizations such as Police Administration Office, Bureau of Exit and Entry Control, Investigation Bureau of Justice Department; (2) military agencies such as Taiwan Garrison Command Headquarters, General Political Combat Unit, Military Intelligence Bureau and Military Police Headquarters; (3) KMT organizations such as Social Work Committee, (Chinese) Mainland Maneuvers Committee and Overseas Maneuvers Committee, among which directly affecting the daily life of the Taiwanese were Police Administration Office, Bureau of Investigation, Garrison Command, Military Police and Social Works Committee.

The National Security Bureau was feared by the people, like the police force in the Japanese occupation era. Its headquarters, located at 110 Yangteh Boulevard of Yang Ming Mountain, a suburb of Taipei, was referred to as the "Mystical 110", where no visitor or reporter were admitted except taking pictures from outside the gate. The successive bureau chiefs were exclusively military officer in the rank of a general, and the bureau was nicknamed "Taiwan's KGB" or "TKGB".

On January 1, 1994, shortly after the respective organic laws of the NSC and NSB were promulgated by the order of the ROC President on December 30, 1993, the National Security Bureau became a legal institution.

Since its establishment, the NSB has striven to perform its duties on the one hand, and on the other hand, to be responsive to the changing demands of the society by adapting its line of duties and setting up relevant regulations and systems. In 1994, the organic law of the NSB was passed by the legislature, establishing the NSB as a fully legalized organ of the government in charge of the coordination of national security intelligence and special service missions. Based on the guidelines of operating with strict adherence to the law, remaining neutral in the execution of duties, and separating intelligence collection from law enforcement, the NSB has mapped out a blueprint for the future.

The NSB Organic Law is based on the principle of "separating intelligence functions from law enforcement." It authorizes the NSB to integrate and coordinate matters concerning national security intelligence work, set up a viable framework for national intelligence operations, as well as compile and evaluate strategic information that has a direct bearing on national security. The intelligence is forwarded to national policy-makers and other relevant authorities. Legally authorized law enforcement organs are charged with the maintenance of social order. The setting up and functioning of this mechanism fall in line with intelligence units in democratically advanced countries.
In view of the unique features and actual requirements of intelligence work, several articles are stipulated in the NSB's Organic Law:

- The NSB is empowered to coordinate with competent authorities about providing needed cover to assist certain intelligence operations.
- Intelligence information and its sources shall be kept confidential, unless otherwise authorized by the NSB.
- The NSB's annual budget estimates shall be treated confidentially. In the wake of closed-door screening by legislators, the budget in question shall be concealed in those of other government agencies.

It is the National Security Bureau's duty to keep abreast with the latest developments in the international community, mainland China, and Taiwan, so as to safeguard the stability and prosperity of Taiwan and fulfill its responsibilities of collecting and assessing intelligence of strategic importance to national security. As stipulated by the NSB's Organic Law, the Bureau is authorized to integrate, coordinate and support national security-related intelligence operations conducted by various functional organizations within the intelligence and law enforcement community.

In addition to managing intelligence relevant to national security, it also takes charge of planning special tasks and is responsible for guiding, coordinating, and supporting the intelligence affairs of the Military Intelligence Bureau of the National Defense Ministry, the Telecommunications Development Division, the Coastal Defense Headquarters, the Military Police Headquarters, the National Police Administration of the Interior Ministry, and the Investigation Bureau of the Justice Ministry. This is also a special feature of the NSB since martial law was lifted.

As result of institutionalizing operations, the NSB now has six divisions -- divisions in charge of international intelligence, intelligence about mainland China, intelligence relevant to Taiwan's security, analysis of the nation's strategic intelligence, scientific and technological intelligence and telecommunications security, and control and development of secret codes and facilities.

COORDINATION MEETING FOR NATIONAL SECURITY INTELLIGENCE (CMNSI)

The NSB also runs the Coordination Meeting for National Security Intelligence (CMNSI) through concerted efforts with other related branches of the government so as to integrate intelligence resources and assets. According to Article 2 and 17 of the Organic Law of the NSB, the NSB is authorized to convene CMNSI to integrate, counsel, coordinate and support the overall security intelligence efforts for national security and development. The Meeting is presided over by the Director General of the NSB and attended by heads of the concerned intelligence and law enforcement agencies, while individuals from other related organizations will attend the Meeting upon invitation if deemed necessary. The CMNSI is in charge of planning, coordinating, and providing support for the nation's overall intelligence efforts targeting national security.
Structurally, the CMNSI is divided into four functional coordination meetings:

- Coordination Meeting for International Operations (SMIO)
- Coordination Meeting for Operations in Mainland China (CMOMC)
- Coordination Meeting for Operations in the Taiwan Region (CMOTR)
- Coordination Meeting for the Collection of Technological Intelligence (CMCTI)

SPECIAL SERVICE COMMAND

As stipulated in the NSB Organic Law, the NSB is charged with the duty of working in conjunction with relevant agencies to ensure the safety of the President, Vice President, their family, former Presidents and other specified persons, including candidates of presidential and vice presidential elections from the deadline of the registration date to the day after voting. Staff members at the NSB Special Service Command Center need to keep in mind the importance of maintaining safety while adopting a citizen-friendly attitude at all times. Special agents need to exercise wisdom and courage when striking a balance between the two. Wisdom refers to the integration of memory, comprehension, adaptability, judgement and creativity. Courage calls for perseverance and sacrifice. Both qualities need to be cultivated through education, training and management of everyday life.

INVESTIGATION BUREAU

The Ministry of Justice Investigation Bureau [MJIB] is a governmental, judicial, investigation agency that takes the responsibilities of "Safeguarding National Security; Maintaining Social Stability and Protecting the People's Well-being". In accordance with the Article No. 2 of "The MJIB's Organizational Ordinance, ROC", this bureau is responsible for the investigation on violations against national security and interests, and matters concerning internal security.

In 1947, the Constitution of ROC was promulgated and put into effect. Then in 1949, the "Investigation Bureau of the Ministry of Interior" was established in Kuanchew to complete and strengthen what is an integral part of law enforcement in a constitutional government. That was the beginning of MJIB. It was the first government investigation agency ever legalized in this country. Mr. Ji Yuan-Fo was assigned to be the first Director General, and in Dec. of the same year the Bureau was relocated along with ROC government to Taipei, Taiwan. Another reorganization took place on June 1st, 1956. At that time the Bureau was renamed the "Investigation Bureau of Ministry of Judicial Administration". Afterwards the Bureau started to take up major investigation & internal security issues concerning national safety and violation against national interests. In the wake of the 1955 transformation, Mr. Ji was retained at the head office. On August 1st, 1980, owing to the renewal the R.O.C.'s judicial systems, the Bureau was given its present, permanent title, "MJIB".

Since October 30, 1998, the MJIB function has been redefined, by an Executive Yuan decree, in the following nine items that cover crime-prevention and investigation.

- Sedition
- Treason
- Unauthorized disclosure of national secrets
- Corruption and bribery during election
- Drug trafficking
- Organized crime
- Major economic crime and money laundering
- National affairs
- Other matters relating to national security and interests, specifically assigned by superior government authorities

MJIB conducts investigations on information indicating potential espionage & its activities and how it may affect political stability, financial order and social peace. It gather intelligence on the transforming and developing of local partisans and factions that adversely affect administration and provincialism, as well as the state of "peace & order" during elections, in which vote-buying and violence are singled out.

It monitors high-profile movements, including unlawful gathering or parades, major petitions, complaints illegal, demonstrations or contingencies that affect peace and order. Investigations conducted on racketeers, concealed weapons among triads, smuggling & drug-trafficking and triad supporters.

Maintaining internal security is one of the major functions of MJIB. Maintaining national secrets is the equivalent of safeguarding national security. In pursuance to the "Organization Provision of MJIB", the Bureau is responsible for investigation and internal security involving the offenses of treason, sedition and other violations endangering national security interests. In other words, to safeguard national security is of primary importance and this is followed by maintaining national interests, and protecting the people's well-being are among the rest of the functions of the Bureau. Counter-espionage and infiltration are the cornerstone for security and stability. Indications and evidence obtained from intelligence and past cases of this Bureau verify that enemy espionage agents on certain occasions have sneaked into Taiwan island under legal, as well as other illegal covers. They are suspected of various methods of information collection, prowling, stealing technology, disrupting economic and social order. In this regard, the Bureau makes an effort, besides a full grasp of general situations, in planning and placing tactile preparations to dig out clues for effective countermeasures.

In dealing with enemy espionage, all-out support and participation are called for from various sectors of society.

The ROC government passed rudimentary legislation of opium-related offenses of the "Criminal Code." Later on, in the reinforced legislations enacted to strengthen control, and to impose additional penalties upon drug-use and its spread the following laws were enacted: the "Ordinance of Eliminating Illicit Drugs"; the "Narcotics Control Statute." MJIB, pursuant to its duties mandated by law, has taken charge of the task of wiping out illicit drugs & narcotics.

TURKEY

MILLI ISTIHBARAT TESKILATI (MIT) (NATIONAL INTELLIGENCE ORGANIZATION)

DUTIES, POWERS AND RESPONSIBILITIES OF THE MIT

The Turkish National Intelligence Organization was founded as a body subordinate to the "Prime Ministry", under Law 644 on the Turkish National Intelligence Organization , dated July 6, 1965. This Law, after being in force for 18 years, has been replaced by Law 2937 titled as the Law on the State Intelligence Services and the Turkish National Intelligence Organization as of January 1, 1984 as a result of the efforts paid to eliminate any deficiencies, troubles, and gaps that were come across during the practice of the previous law, and to adapt it to the rapidly changing and improving world conditions.

In Law 2937, the organization and the main tasks of the MIT have been described in general terms, and both secrecy and rapid action/adaptation to changing circumstances have been obtained through arranging the other issues regarding the number, names, detailed tasks and the inner structures of the units by confidential regulations which would be approved by the Prime Minister.

Another aspect of Law 2937 which makes it different from Law 644 is that under Law 2937, the MIT has been subordinated directly to the "Prime Minister". The MIT has been subordinated directly to the "Prime Minister", taking into consideration the fact that in accordance with the Constitution, the Cabinet and the Prime Minister are jointly responsible for carrying out the general policy of the Government.

Duties

Powers

Responsibilities

Duties and Responsibilities of the Other State Institutions and Organizations With Regard to National Intelligence

Secrecy of The Information and Documents

Permission for Criminal Prosecution

Permission for Testimony

HISTORY OF THE MIT

Increasing need of nations to get information in advance about each other's political, social, economic, military activities and expectations have obliged them to establish some formations exclusively charged with collecting information.

In our country, the efforts to establish an intelligence organization that would function in a systematic and organized manner were started during the last years of the Ottoman Empire. In that period, in order to preserve the political unity, to prevent the separatist activities, and particularly to follow the activities of the foreign nations mostly focused on the Middle East, the need had emerged to give a centralized and organized nature to the intelligence activities, then being carried out on an individual and limited basis. The first intelligence organization was established on August 05, 1914 by Enver Pasha under the name of TESKILAT-I MAHSUSA (Special Organization). That organization, which had undertaken important missions and had carried out military and paramilitary activities during the First World War, was dissolved at the end of the war, following the Mondros Truce of October 30, 1918.

In the period that followed the Mondros Truce, a new intelligence unit was formed in late 1918 under the name of KARAKOL CEMIYETI (Police Guild). This new organization carried out many important missions during the National Liberation War through providing arms to people and to small armed groups for fighting against the occupation forces in Anatolia, and also through providing supplies and equipment to the national forces. When Istanbul was occupied on March 16, 1920, the activities of that organization had come to an end with the arrest of its members.

After the dissolution of the KARAKOL CEMIYETI, various intelligence groups were formed. One of these groups, namely the HAMZA GRUBU (Hamza Group), which was established on September 23,

1920, changed its name to FELAH GRUBU (Felah Group) on August 21, 1921, and continued its activities until the end of the National Liberation War.

ASKERI POLIS TESKILATI (Military Police Organization- shortly called as A.P. or P) was founded by the Turkish General Staff on July 18, 1920 with the aim of putting an end to the chaos prevailing among the different intelligence organizations and countering the enemy's espionage activities and propaganda infiltrating the army ranks. Later, as a result of the need felt for a unit to collect information, "The Intelligence Branch" was formed. This organization, which had carried out successful missions during the war, was dissolved on March 19, 1921.

The vacuum that arose in the intelligence activities with the dissolution of the Askeri Polis Teskilaty, was filled in a short time with the establishment of TEDKIK HEYETI AMIRLIKLERI (Inspection Board Directorates) again by the Turkish General Staff in various Anatolian provinces during the period between April 01, 1921- June 22, 1922. Later, in the light of the previous experiences and with the aim of reaching the newly established objectives, another intelligence group named MUDAFAA-I MILLIYE (National Defense) was founded, this time under the instructions of Mustafa Kemal. On May 03, 1921, the Turkish Grand National Assembly officially approved the establishment of that organization, which was called shortly as "MIM MIM"

While the TEDKIK HEYETI AMIRLIKLERI were carrying out their activities in Anatolia, the "MIM MIM" achieved to establish in Istanbul an extensive network of spies and intelligence consisting of a large cadre of military and civilian officers. The MIM MIM conducted very important duties during the National Liberation War, like organizing the activities to secretly transfer weapons and ammunitions to Anatolia, and infiltrating the enemy headquarters, foreign missions, and groups collaborating with the enemy to get important information and documents. This organization, which also maintained cooperation during the war with other groups established to collect information about the enemy, was dissolved on October 05, 1923, following the liberation of Istanbul.

During the period which followed the dissolution of intelligence organizations and foundation of the Republic of Turkey, the intelligence activities had been carried out until the year 1926 by the intelligence unit within the Turkish General Staff.

At the beginning of 1926, Ataturk had given the order for the establishment of a modern intelligence organization having the same standards with those in the developed countries. Colonel Oberst Walter Nikolai, a Polish originated officer who had guided Germany's intelligence activities during the World War I, was called on to undertake that duty. With the participation of the cadre that had been trained in European countries, and under the official order (January 06, 1927) of Field Marshal Fevzi CAKMAK, Chief of General Staff, the first intelligence organization of the Republic of Turkey was established under the name of MILLI EMNIYET HIZMETI- MAH (National Security Service).

REPUBLIC OF TURKEY
GENERAL STAFF HEADQUARTERS
DEPARTMENT OF INTELLIGENCE
Nr : 10152
Ankara
January 06, 1927

THE DIRECTORATE OF THE NATIONAL SECURITY SERVICE

The Organization of National Security has been established with its headquarters based in ANKARA, and its branches for the time being in the provinces of ISTANBUL, IZMIR, ADANA, DIYARBAKIR, and KARS. These provincial branches are directly subordinate to the General Headquarters.

The intelligence services previously being carried out by the Military Inspection bodies, will henceforth be run under the control of the Organization of National Security.

Chief of General Staff
Field Marshal FEVZI CAKMAK

Sukru Ali Ogel had been appointed as the first Director of MAH, which still keeps its importance as a symbol in the eyes of the MIT members, since it firmly connects the historical roots of the MIT to the future.

MAH, which had undergone during its history some small-scale structural changes in consistent with the emerging needs, had successfully conducted Turkey's intelligence activities until the year 1965.

With a view to have the intelligence to be collected on every subject relevant to the formulation of the State's national security policy gathered at one center, the Turkish Grand National Assembly passed on July 22, 1965 the law 644, under which the name of the organization was changed as the MILLI ISTIHBARAT TESKILATI- MIT (National Intelligence Organization). The same law also provided for the control of the organization by an Undersecretary that would be subordinate only to the Prime Minister in the fulfillment of duties defined under the law.

The MIT had carried out its duties for about 19 years under the provisions of Law 644. However, the rapidly changing conditions and new developments had brought the need for new legal arrangements. To that end, on November 01, 1983 Law 2937 on the State Intelligence Services and the National Intelligence Organization was passed. This law was put into effect as of January 01, 1984.

The MIT, which has a modern structural organization and closely follows every kind of technological developments that would help the achievement of national objectives, and its experienced professional and technical staff is successfully fulfilling its duties defined under the law in a manner firmly devoted to the principles of pluralist democracy, supremacy of law, impartiality and human rights.

The historical information presented above was prepared through a study of various books written about the war of national liberation, and some open sources. However, studies have already been started to prepare a much more detailed historical survey of our Organization, to be based on the documents kept in our own archives as well as the State archives. This historical study will be completed and released to the public opinion on the 75th Anniversary of the establishment of the MIT.

UKRAINE

Security Service of Ukraine
33 Volodymyrska St.
Kyiv-34, Ukraine, 01034
Tel.: (+380 44) 226-2564.
Fax.: (380 044) 229 3040

The SBU Public Reception Office is responsible for:

- receiving visitors arriving at the SBU Headquarters;
- considering citizens` appeals;
- receiving reports of SBU officers and petitions of its employees.

The SBU Headquarters and its regional offices provide for receiving visitors twenty-four hours a day. During working hours visitors are received in the SBU Public Reception Office by operatives and senior officials of the Security Service of Ukraine. There is a schedule of reception in the SBU Public Reception Office for visitors to meet with the SBU senior officials. The schedule is placed on the wall inside the SBU Public Reception Office. During non-working hours visitors are received by executive and operative officers on duty and, if necessary, by senior officials and operatives of the departments concerned.
The access to the SBU Public Reception Office is free for any visitor.
The telephone of the SBU Public Reception Office is

ORGANIZATION

The SBU's system consists of the Headquarters of the Security Service of Ukraine, regional SBU offices, the Main Office of the SBU in the Autonomous Republic of Crimea, military counterintelligence elements, and educational, research, and other establishments.

The organizational structure of the SBU is determined by the President of Ukraine. By coordinating and monitoring activities of the other elements of the SBU, the Headquarters of the Security Service of Ukraine is responsible for national security.

SENIOR SECURITY SERVICE OFFICIALS

The chief of the Security Service of Ukraine is in charge of the SBU Headquarters, directing the operations and the work of the SBU as a whole. He is personally responsible for fulfillment of the tasks incumbent on the SBU.

The chief of the Security Service of Ukraine is appointed by the Verkhovna Rada of Ukraine upon recommendation by the President of Ukraine. The chief of the Security Service of Ukraine is assisted in carrying out his by the deputies, appointed by the President of Ukraine upon his recommendation.

Head of the Security Service of Ukraine	Igor Petrovych SMESHKO Colonel General
Deputy Head of the SBU	Anatoliy Pavlovych GERASYMOV Lieutenant General
Deputy Head of the SBU	Ihor Vasylovych DRIZHCHANY Lieutenant General of Justice
Deputy Head of the SBU	Mykola Serhiyovych OBYKHOD Lieutenant General of Justice
Deputy Head of the SBU - head of Main Directorate for Combating Corruption and Organized Crime	Yevhen Volodymyrovych SERHIYENKO Major General
Deputy Head of the SBU	Serhiy Ivanovych TUZ Lieutenant General
Deputy Head of the SBU	Volodymyr Volodymyrovych SHEREMETA Colonel General

HISTORY

The Security Service of Ukraine (SSU) (*Sluzhba Bespeky Ukrayiny (SBU)*), which encompasses law enforcement and intelligence functions, is the authority responsible for ensuring the state security of Ukraine.

he need to reform the former Union and republican systems of state security authorities arose right after Ukraine declared its independence. On September 20, 1991, by adopting the Regulation "On Establishment of the National Security Service of Ukraine," the Verkhovna Rada of Ukraine (Ukraine's Parliament) liquidated the State Security Committee of the Soviet Socialist Republic of Ukraine (Ukrainian KGB).

In the shortest possible time, it was necessary to resolve issues relating to the formation of new departments while staffing them with professionally trained officers committed to building up independent Ukraine, and creating a regulatory and legislative framework. On March 25, 1992, the Verkhovna Rada of Ukraine approved the Law "On the Security Service of Ukraine," which became yet another proof of Ukraine's firm course toward building a democratic state ruled by law. Unlike their predecessors, officers of the new Ukrainian Security Service got an opportunity to operate based on an explicit legal base - the Laws of Ukraine "On the Security Service of Ukraine," "On Operational and Investigative Activities," "On Organizational and Legal Principles in the Fight against Organized Crime, " "On State Secrets", "On the Fight against Corruption," etc.

Being conscious of new internal and external political realities that took shape after Ukraine declared its independence and guided by Ukraine's intention to become a member of the world community of civilized democratic states that would play an important role in the world, the SBU has unconditionally gave up the idea of applying an embracing global approach and using the image of the main enemy or hostile side, as well as uncivil and inhumane methods of operation in its activities. From the very outset, the SBU provided active assistance to the country's top echelon in resolving extremely important issues by priority directions of the statehood development, year by year building up its potentials and responding with flexibility to changes in operating conditions. The SBU, as a special-purpose law enforcement authority established in conformity with new principles, has its own role in the system of state authorities.

Nowadays, the SBU is capable of carrying out fully any of the tasks that are specified by the Law of Ukraine "On the Security Service of Ukraine" or set by senior state officials. To this purpose, a special emphasis is laid on top priority and most important tasks, which are appropriate only to a secret service and which can not be resolved by anyone except the security services.

These tasks include protection of state sovereignty, the constitutional system, the state's territorial integrity, the economic, scientific and technical, and defense potentials of Ukraine, the vested interests of the state and the rights of its citizens from spying and subversive activities of foreign intelligence services, as well as from encroachment of separate organizations, groups, or individuals. Dedicated efforts are being made with respect to prevention, identification, preclusion, and detection of crimes against the peace and security of the world, as well as against terrorism, corruption and organized crime in the domains of administration and economy, and other illegal acts directly endangering vital interests of Ukraine.

Intelligence and counterintelligence activities have been the most important functions of the SBU*. But the point is that new policies in this domain are introduced and relevant adjustments to the way they are carried out are made depending on the changes taking place in the world, in particular in the area of international relations. Abandoning the "totalitarian" concept in carrying out counterintelligence search, the Ukrainian Security Service implements differentiated policies for organizing countermeasures against foreign intelligence services. In the new historical period, the

SBU's position on implementation of counterintelligence measures is grounded on a principle subordinated to provisions of the legislation in force to protect on this basis civil rights and freedoms, society and public interests both within and outside the territory of Ukraine by specific means and methods appropriate for a state security service.

n compliance with the prescribed requirements, counterintelligence officers have terminated illegal activities of several foreign intelligence agents and frustrated efforts of some Ukrainian citizens to pass abroad information of a political, scientific, technical, or economic nature.

In 1992, the SBU uncovered and stopped the espionage activities of G. Sarkisian, a stateless person, and A. Tkachenko, a Ukrainian citizen, who collected information on modern anti-aircraft missiles, fulfilling the tasks of a foreign intelligence service in this country. In 1994, Ukrainian counterintelligence conducted an operation aimed at quashing acts of provocation against Ukraine by a 32-year old Swede Eric Olaf Estenson, which resulted in his expulsion from this country and extradition to Swedish authorities. While in Ukraine, Estenson planned to obtain parts of nuclear warheads, from which he intended to assemble a 20-30 megaton nuclear bomb in Stockholm to blackmail the Swedish government into providing $2 billion as financial assistance to Ukraine.

There are many examples of other successful counterintelligence operations. In particular, the Ukrainian counterintelligence prevented a number of efforts to smuggle large shipments of armaments from and into the territory of Ukraine. The SBU also thwarted attempts to steal technologies and dual-use materials from Ukraine and to carry out illegal operations with nuclear materials and radioactive substances. Due to these preventive measures, Ukraine succeeded in meeting its obligations with respect to non-proliferation of mass destruction weapons and delivery vehicles.

In compliance with the legislation in effect, the SBU carries out information processing and analysis to support Ukrainian state officials in the implementation of Ukraine's foreign and domestic policies aimed at state development, strengthening of defense and economic capabilities, and fostering of international cooperation. Information and analytical support of central and local Ukrainian authorities is one of the priority activities of the Security Service of Ukraine. Assessments, proposals, and prognoses made by SBU analysts play a significant role in the information and analysis support system of state decision making. They also constitute the basis of an internal system for detecting and counteracting internal and external threats to national security. The highest appraisal for the work of SBU analysts, and the SBU as a whole, is when their information products are utilized at the governmental level to make relevant decisions.

SBU's officers strive to focus their efforts on the protection of the most vital spheres of society. At present, the economy is one of such spheres. Just for that reason, it has been quite natural for the SBU to establish the Department for National Economy Counterintelligence Protection within its structure. This department is designated to be the leading element within the SBU's system charged with the development of strategies and tactics for the protection of national economic interests, and detection and preclusion of economic crimes.

In accordance with its authority, the Security Service of Ukraine carries out counterintelligence activities to counteract large scale embezzlement of public or collective property, stealing, or illicit use of budget resources in financial, banking, and credit sectors, as well as funds drawn from privatization or foreign trade. In this connection, the Security Service is involved in monitoring the receipt and use of ear-marked state and foreign loans.It also participates in the returning of currency assets from abroad and in expert assessment of large contracts with foreign companies. One of the SBU's tasks is to counteract money laundering. Thus, the Security Service operates not only in order to protect but also to improve the economy.

From the very beginning of its establishment it has been one of the top priorities for the Security Service to combat terrorism. In many countries this problem has superseded other threats and has come to the forefront. Just because of the preventive and protective measures that were taken, there has been no large scale and grave acts of terrorism in Ukraine. Recently, some terrorist actions have been uncovered in cooperation with other law enforcement bodies.

In particular, the SBU has averted illegal extremist acts against several diplomatic missions that some foreign individuals intended to commit in the territory of Ukraine. Any attempts to unfold preparation of terrorist acts or find shelter from criminal prosecution for such activities while staying in Ukraine are and will be decisively stopped by the Security Service.

There has been no manifestations of terrorism in Ukraine in its classical notion. However, sometimes the SBU has to deal with various threats to commit violence against Ukraine's politicians, representatives of public authorities at all levels, and leaders of political parties and civic organizations, as well as with kidnapping and hostage taking.

Taking into account the seriousness of the problem, a number of laws was adopted in Ukraine with an objective to foster the effectiveness of combating terrorism. In addition, a new area of responsibility of Ukrainian law enforcement officers has been legislatively established -- to ensure security of individuals participating in criminal justice. Within the SBU, the Directorate for Combating Terrorism and Protection of Criminal Justice Participants deals with such issues. Its officers conducted over 300 operations to apprehend particularly dangerous criminals and to free hostages. There have been no cases associated with harm coming to persons who are under protection of the Directorate's officers. Law enforcement measures, in particular those taken by the Security Service of Ukraine, that were coordinated with the leadership of the country made it possible in some areas to stem or localize unlawful activities of criminal organizations. Special units responsible for combating corruption and organized crime are faced with tasks to be more effective against existing criminal organizations that commit interregional and transnational crimes.

In order to fulfill this task, the Security Service of Ukraine has activated and continues its operations to combat drug trafficking, which are particularly targeted at exposing and eliminating interregional and transnational drug trafficking organizations, transportation routes of narcotics and drug raw materials into Ukraine and via its territory. In 1997 and 1998, officers of the Security Service of Ukraine prevented in cooperation with customs officers and border controllers a number of attempts of transnational narcocartels, in particular Colombian and African ones, to organize a peculiar "transit bridge" for moving large shipments of "heavy" drugs (cocaine, hashish, and heroin) to Western Europe through the territory of Ukraine. As a result of three operations alone, law enforcement officers seized 624 kilograms of cocaine, 250 kilograms of cocaine paste, and over six tons of hashish worth of hundreds of million dollars at black market prices.

For the successful conduct of such operations, the SBU has established close contacts with Interpol and foreign law enforcement agencies. Considering the global character of these problems, various questions are currently resolved in close cooperation with foreign intelligence and security services. In the meantime, the SBU has reached agreements on liaison and cooperation with foreign intelligence services and law enforcement agencies of over 50 countries. These partnership contacts provide for effective work and bring good results.

On the basis of agreements that have been concluded, meetings and joint consultations are held to discuss issues on combating organized crime, terrorism, narcotrafficking, etc., and to exchange opinions and information. Meetings of the Council of Heads of CIS Security Services (SORB) are held regularly. This results in successful conduct of operations on seizure of large shipments of drugs, arms, and smuggled goods, and leads to arrests of criminal organizations' members. The arrest of A. Mnjoyan, an inhabitant of Yerevan, was one of the first such notable cases, when agents of SBU's special units mounted an operation in the southern Ukrainian city of Odessa in response to a request by senior officials of the National Security State Administration of the Republic of Armenia. He was sought for committing five made-to-order and two attempted murders. In particular, among his victims were the former head of the National Security State Administration of the Republic of Armenia and the mayor of Yerevan.

At present, one cannot but take into the account the cardinal changes that have recently taken place in the understanding of security. This notion embraces a fairly broad circle of questions that are of concern to each country. In addition to protection of territorial integrity, inviolability of national borders, and military, economic, and political factors, the question relates to the security of the entire region or, in other words, the ability of states to jointly meet new challenges and threats, in particular proliferation of weapons of mass destruction, drug trafficking, international terrorism, organized crime, illegal migration, and environmental disasters. So, while in the present operating conditions in the world, which continuously vary and are characterized by a greater openness of society, increased cooperation at all levels, and Ukraine's active entering into the world community, the Security Service of Ukraine makes all possible efforts for the state to be on firm ground in Europe and in the world.

Thus, the concept of the new Ukrainian security service is based on the SBU's commitment to protect the interests of the Ukrainian people and national and human values.

The SBU constantly informs the public on various aspects of its activities by reporting results of its operations in the mass media. Publicity has become an essential condition in the functioning of the Security Service. Many people write letters or visit the SBU to show their worries and concerns about the development of some events. Visitors are received at the SBU's Public Reception Office, located on: 35, Volodymyrska St., Kyiv, Ukraine. A repousse on the facade of its two-storied building indicates that the prominent Ukrainian scholar, historian, and statesman Mykhailo Hrushevskyi worked in it between 1927 and 1930.

In fulfillment of the prescribed tasks, the Security Service of Ukraine makes all possible efforts to ensure peace and order in Ukraine and that the results of its efforts coincide with the hopes of its compatriots.

UKRAINE: MAIN INTELLIGENCE DIRECTORATE

The Main Intelligence Directorate of the Security Service of Ukraine (GUR SBU), which was established as a functional element within the Headquarters of the Security Service of Ukraine on December 28, 1991, carries out intelligence activities to ensure the national security in the spheres which are vital for Ukraine.
The main task of the GUR SBU is to safeguard the person, the state, and the society against possible external threats by assisting with the following:

- formation and implementation of both domestic and international policies of Ukraine;
- solving problems relating to defense potentials, social and economic development, and science and technology progress; and
- finding ways of dealing with other questions associated with the national security of Ukraine and safeguarding its interests abroad.

It has been also determined that one of the key tasks of GUR SBU is to support the functioning of Ukrainian establishments abroad and to provide for the secure stay of their employees and members of their families, as well as other Ukrainian citizens sent abroad on a tour of duty in cases when they are aware of state secrets.

Combating international organized crime, in particular terrorism and drugs trafficking, is yet another priority in GUR's activities.

UNITED KINGDOM

INTELLIGENCE AGENCIES

Central Intelligence Machinery Joint Intelligence Committee (JIC)

Minister of Defense
Defence Procurement Executive
Directorate General Command Information Systems
Defence Intelligence Staff [DIS]
Defence Intelligence and Security Centre
Defence Geographic and Imagery Intelligence Agency
Military Survey Defence Agency
Royal Air Force
Joint Air Reconnaissance Intelligence Centre (JARIC)
Strike Command
No 7010 (VR) Photographic Interpretation Squadron

Foreign and Commonwealth Secretary
MI6 Secret Intelligence Service (SIS)
Government Communications Headquarters (GCHQ)

Home Secretary
MI5 Security Service
National Criminal Intelligence Service (NCIS)
Metropolitan Police [Scotland Yard]
"DA" Notices (formerly "D" Notices)

GCHQ - Government Communications Headquarters

GCHQ plays a vital role in protecting the security of the nation's official and military communications and advising government and industry on communications and computer security. In addition GCHQ studies a wide range of telecommunications and other electronic signals to provide Britain with crucial defence and foreign intelligence.

M15 Security Service

M15 was set up to counter espionage against British organisations by foreign powers. In recent years its remit has widened to include counter-terrorism, subversion and organised crime. [unofficial]

M16 Security Service

The role of M16 is to obtain and provide information relating to the actions or intentions of persons outside the British Islands, and to perform other tasks relating to the actions or intentions of such persons. [unofficial]

NCIS - The National Criminal Intelligence Service

Britain's National Criminal Intelligence Service (NCIS) was launched in April 1992 to provide leadership and excellence in criminal intelligence.

CENTRAL INTELLIGENCE MACHINERY

The Central Intelligence Machinery is the central mechanism, based in the Cabinet Office, for the tasking, co-ordination and resourcing of the United Kingdom's intelligence and security Agencies, for scrutinising their performance and for reporting on the intelligence they produce. The 1994 Intelligence Services Act placed the functions of the Secret Intelligence Service (SIS) and Government Communications Headquarters (GCHQ) on a statutory footing for the first time. There is greater openness on the expenditure of the Agencies; a combined Single Intelligence Vote is now published annually. And a new Official Committee has been set up to examine the plans of the Security Service and to review its work.

MINISTERIAL COMMITTEE ON THE INTELLIGENCE SERVICES (IS)

In their day-to-day operations the Intelligence and Security Agencies operate under the immediate control of their respective Heads who are personally responsible to Ministers. The Prime Minister is responsible for intelligence and security matters overall and is supported in that capacity by the Secretary of the Cabinet. The Home Secretary is responsible for the Security Service; the Foreign & Commonwealth Secretary for SIS and GCHQ. The Secretary of State for Defence is responsible for the Defence Intelligence Staff (DIS) which forms an integral part of the Ministry of Defence.

There is also a Ministerial Committee on the Intelligence Services (IS), whose Terms of Reference are "To keep under review policy on the security and intelligence services" For example, the Committee considered the policy issues connected with the Intelligence Services Act. The Prime Minister is its chairman and the other members are the Deputy Prime Minister, Home, Defence and Foreign & Commonwealth Secretaries and the Chancellor of the Exchequer.

PERMANENT SECRETARIES' COMMITTEE ON THE INTELLIGENCE SERVICES (PSIS)

Ministers are assisted in the oversight of the Agencies by the Permanent Secretaries' Committee on the Intelligence Services (PSIS) which scrutinises the Agencies' annual expenditure forecasts, management plans and intelligence requirements, as part of the Public Expenditure Survey arrangements. These plans, together with the recommendations of the PSIS, are then submitted to Ministers, who agree the appropriate level of funding for the Agencies through the Single Intelligence Vote (SIV). For 1996-97 this is £751 million. PSIS is chaired by the Secretary of the Cabinet and its members are the Permanent Under Secretaries of the Foreign & Commonwealth Office, Ministry of Defence, Home Office and Treasury. The Intelligence Co-ordinator acts as adviser to PSIS, and chairs an advisory committee, known as the Preliminary Committee, which conducts the first scrutiny of the Agencies' Expenditure Forecasts.

CABINET OFFICIAL COMMITTEE ON SECURITY (SO)

The Committee has the responsibility to review the performance of the Security Service against plans and objectives, examine future Service priorities and to advise the Cabinet Secretary and PSIS as appropriate. Its membership comprises senior officials from the Treasury, Foreign & Commonwealth Office, Home Office, Department of Trade & Industry, Ministry of Defence, Department of Social Security, Scottish Office, Northern Ireland Office, GCHQ, Security Service, SIS, Office of Public Service and the Cabinet Office. The Home Office provides the Chairman and the secretariat functions are provided from the central intelligence machinery within the Cabinet Office.

SECURITY AND INTELLIGENCE CO-ORDINATOR

Sir David Omand KCB has been appointed to the post of Security and Intelligence Co-ordinator and Permanent Secretary, Cabinet Office. This new Permanent Secretary post is being created to enhance the capacity at the centre of Government to co-ordinate security, intelligence and consequence management matters and to deal with risks and major emergencies should they arise.

Sir David has been Permanent Secretary at the Home Office, Director of the Government Communications Headquarters (GCHQ), and Deputy Under Secretary of State for Policy at the Ministry of Defence. He was also a member of the Joint Intelligence Committee (JIC) for five years, and will rejoin the JIC in this appointment. He is currently Chairman of the Centre for Management and Policy Studies.

DEFENCE INTELLIGENCE STAFF [DIS]

The Defence Intelligence Staff, part of the Ministry of Defence and funded within the defence vote, is an essential element of the central intelligence machinery. The Defence Intelligence Staff is the main provider of strategic Defence Intelligence to the Ministry of Defence, and the Armed Forces and is also a key element of the United Kingdom's central intelligence machinery. Located in the Old War Office Building, Whitehall, the DIS supports other Government Departments with advice and intelligence assessments; these assessments also play a special role in support of analysis and operations undertaken by NATO and the WEU.

The Defence Intelligence Staff can trace its ancestry back to 1946, when the Joint Intelligence Bureau (JIB) was established under the direction of General Keith Strong, General Eisenhower's British wartime Chief of Intelligence. It was created in 1964 by the amalgamation of all three service intelligence staffs and the civilian Joint Intelligence Bureau to form an integrated body able to serve the Ministry of Defence and the Armed Forces and other Government Departments.

The task of the DIS is to analyse information from a wide variety of sources, both overt and covert. In order to make decisions, Ministry of Defense [MOD] policy-makers, military planners and force commanders need an accurate view of world developments, timely warning of impending crises, and informed reporting on areas where British forces are or may be deployed. These are the tasks of the Defence Intelligence Staff, which produces assessments drawing on material from a variety of sources, including both open literature and classified reports. These assessments range from studies of the characteristics of weapon systems held by potential opponents, to the analysis of the influences at work in any part of the world where the United Kingdom has important interests.

The DIS is a mixed organisation of serving officers and civilian research staff, scientific staff and linguists. The head of the DIS is the Chief of Defence Intelligence (CDI), a serving 3 star officer who may be drawn from any of the three services, who reports to the Chief of the Defence Staff and the Permanent Secretary of the MOD. CDI is responsible for the overall co-ordination of defence intelligence throughout the Armed Forces and single-Service commands. The Chief of Defence Intelligence is responsible for the work of the DIS and is charged also with the overall direction of intelligence within the defence community. CDI is deputy chairman of the Joint Intelligence Committee, which produces authoritative intelligence assessments on behalf of the UK intelligence community and which is the main national instrument for advising on intelligence collection priorities and the assessment of the results.

The provision of intelligence support to the Peace Implementation Force (IFOR) in the former Yugoslavia has been allocated a significant proportion of the resources available to the Defence Intelligence Staff (DIS). The DIS runs a full-time Yugoslav Crisis Cell, which can call upon the in-depth expertise of all directorates within the DIS, including military, infrastructure, technical and industries analysts and the embargo monitoring cell. All assessments are rapidly and securely disseminated to British forces operating as part of the IFOR deployment via the Joint Headquarters at the same time as they are passed to the Department. Wherever possible and appropriate, they are sent to Allies operating alongside our own forces in the former Yugoslavia, both through the NATO communications system and via the intelligence liaison staffs resident within the DIS itself.

The DIS are also involved in the setting up of the WEU Situation Centre and Intelligence Section. The DIS submits Weekly Intelligence Summaries to the Intelligence Section, supplemented by weekly briefing on the situation in the former Yugoslavia. It has also responded to ad hoc requests from the Section for more detailed briefing on particular areas. The DIS will continue to work with WEU partners to refine current arrangements and to improve the WEU's ability to receive and circulate intelligence.

The DIS has a total staff of 4,600 both military and civilian, about 700 of whom are located in the DIS Headquarters in the Old War Office Building. The remaining staff work in the DIS Defence Agencies or at other units in the UK and overseas. Serving members of the Armed Forces make up approximately 60% of the manpower of the DIS. The DIS is divided into two main parts - the Defence Intelligence Analysis Staff (DIAS) and the Intelligence and Geographic Resources Staff (IGRS). In addition, other staffs dealing with finance, personnel, Departmental management, and information systems and communications report directly to CDI.

The civilian Deputy Chief of Defence Intelligence (DCDI) heads the Defence Intelligence Analysis Staff (DIAS), which is responsible for providing global defence intelligence assessments and strategic warning. The DIAS is able to draw upon classified information provided by the Government Communications Headquarters, the Secret Intelligence Service, the Security Service, Allied intelligence services and military intelligence collection assets, in addition to diplomatic reporting and a wide range of open-source information.

The Intelligence & Geographic Resources Staff (IGRS) is headed by the Director General Intelligence and Geographic Resources (DGIGR), a serving 2-star military officer who may be drawn from any of the three services. DGIGR manages six discrete policy branches in the Old War Office Building with responsibility for oversight of the collection and provision of specialist intelligence and geographic information to Defence. DGIGR is also the "Owner" of the three DIS Defence Agencies: the Defence Intelligence and Security Centre (DISC), the Joint Air Reconnaissance Intelligence Centre (JARIC), and Military Survey. On 10 May 1999, the then Parliamentary Under-Secretary of State announced that two of these agencies -- JARIC and Military Survey -- would merge on 1 April 2000 into a new agency, the Defence Geographic and Imagery Intelligence Agency.

DEFENCE INTELLIGENCE AND SECURITY CENTRE

Chicksands, Shefford
Beds SG17 5PR

The Defence Intelligence and Security Centre (DISC) is located at Chicksands in Bedfordshire. The Agency was created on 1 October 1996 to integrate all intelligence and most security training into a single tri-Service organisation. Core functions are to provide: training in intelligence and security disciplines, training in conduct after capture, and advice on intelligence and security policy. The Defence Intelligence and Security Centre trains the Armed Forces and other intelligence agencies in intelligence and security disciplines, and conduct after capture. It also contributes advice on appropriate intelligence and security policy matters, and maintains an operational capability. In 1998/99, it employed an average of 484 staff and its net operating cost was £27 million.

MILITARY SURVEY DEFENCE AGENCY

Elmwood Avenue
Feltham
Middlesex TW13 7AH

Military Survey was established as a Defence Agency on 2 April 1991. Its role is to ensure the provision of geographic and geospatial support to defence planning, training and operations - providing the Armed Forces with the mapping they require throughout the world. Its net operating costs in 1998/99 were £91.4 million and it employed an average of 1,078 staff. The Chief Executive Military Survey is the ultimate Defence authority on geographic matters and has overall responsibility worldwide for geographic personnel in the UK and overseas. Military Survey supports a small central staff in MOD Main Building and occupies a number of sites at Feltham, Hermitage near Newbury, Tolworth, Guildford and Münchengladbach in Germany.

On 10 May 1999, the then Parliamentary Under-Secretary of State announced that two of these agencies -- JARIC and Military Survey -- would merge on 1 April 2000 into a new agency, the Defence Geographic and Imagery Intelligence Agency. Sources and Resources

JOINT AIR RECONNAISSANCE INTELLIGENCE CENTRE (JARIC)

RAF Brampton
Huntingdon
Cambs PE18 8QL

The Joint Air Reconnaissance Intelligence Centre (JARIC) is based at RAF Brampton, near Huntingdon. It has a total staff of about 500, comprising service personnel from all three services and approximately 144 civil servants. During 1998/99, it employed an average of 465 staff and had net operating costs of £20.7 million. It acts as the Department's centre of excellence for the production of imagery intelligence. Its role is to exploit and analyse imagery from all available sources and produce intelligence products and services to meet the requirements of MOD and the operational Commands. It provides this intelligence to military commanders and the Government, in support of current military operations, defence planning and wider intelligence matters. JARIC is also tasked with provision of trained and experienced personnel in support of specific military operations.
The Secretary of State for Defence announced on 19 July 1995 that the joint air reconnaissance intelligence centre was a candidate for defence agency status. The Joint Air Reconnaissance Intelligence Centre launched as a Defence Agency on 19 April 1996.

JARIC's role as an operational enabler was significantly enhanced by the Strategic Defence Review [SDR]. The Agency was extensively reorganised early in 1999 to bring a closer alignment with post-SDR customer requirements and to take full advantage of new technology. The reorganisation was undertaken on the basis of an internal Business Process Re-engineering (BPR) study, commissioned by the CE, and aimed at improving the Agency's effectiveness.

The performance of JARIC is monitored by the Agency Owner's Advisory Board, which is chaired by JARIC's "Owner", the Director General Intelligence and Geographic Resources, DGIGR, and is made up of the Agency's major customers and its Non-Executive Director. The Chief Executive of JARIC formally reports his progress against Key Targets to the Owner's Board twice a year and also through the Owner's Quarterly Performance Reviews. The first Owner's Board to review the 1998-99 Key Targets met on 7 October 1998 and the second met on 24 February 1999.

Although photographic processing remains the mainstay of much of the agencies' current business, digital technology is opening up new techniques for imagery analysis that are likely to be increasingly in demand, including for example computer-generated 3-D visualisations and the merging of multi-source images. The agencies envisage that they will have an increasingly overlapping requirement for new technologies to provide these capabilities.

Phase 1 of the program to enhance JARIC's ability to exploit digital imagery was implemented in late 1998. This gave JARIC an improved ability to respond to customers' requirements. The final Phase 2 of the program is being managed by the Defence Procurement Agency (DPA), which, subject to scrutiny, will be taken forward as part of a joint submission with the Military Survey's MDS project (Mil Svy Digital Geographic Information and Production Management System), and is planned to be implemented in 2001. It will replace all JARIC's legacy systems with state-of-the-art technology. To enable JARIC to respond to these new demands, there is a continuing need for connection to modern defence communications systems.

For Resource Accounting and Budgeting (RAB) purposes JARIC is in the process of developing Customer Supplier Agreements (CSAs) with its main customers. It also works closely with those customers through the JARIC Customer Tasking Group (JCTG) where improved procedures are now being introduced to manage and prioritise requirements placed on JARIC. Customer surveys were conducted in 1996 and 1997, the latter by the Defence Analytical Services Agency (DASA). A further survey is currently under way, under the sponsorship of the JARIC Customer Tasking Group (JCTG). Additionally, each product dispatched from JARIC is accompanied by a mini-questionnaire inviting comments from the recipients. The results from successive surveys have shown a high level of customer satisfaction with the Agency's products and services.

JARIC Defence Agency occupies a building belonging to Royal Air Force Brampton. The Agency is therefore dependent on its landlord to work with the providers of public utilities and services such as air conditioning. JARIC has been involved in three major estate relocation/rationalisation studies since 1996. The first, in January-July 1996, the Collocation of Defence Intelligence Units (CDIU) Phase 2 study, employed outside consultants to determine the viability of moving JARIC to the DIS site at Chicksands. The decision was taken to leave JARIC in situ. The subject was revisited in connection with the SDR programme in early 1998. The two main options in this study were the relocation of JARIC to either Feltham or a green field site. Once again, the substantial costs of relocation, re-calculated to a 1998 cost base militated against a move and the decision, once again, was taken to leave JARIC at Brampton. More recently, JARIC has been involved in discussions on the future use of the Brampton estate post the demise of RAF Logistics Command in November 1999.

The case for merging the Military Survey and JARIC Defence Agencies into a single agency was considered under the Strategic Defence Review. The study, which was completed in September 1998, concluded that there were a number of drivers, mainly in the medium to long term, recommending the merger of Military Survey and JARIC. These would secure improved operational effectiveness and better service to defence. Early implementation of a merger was recommended. On 10 May 1999, the then Parliamentary Under-Secretary of State announced that two of these agencies -- JARIC and Military Survey -- would merge on 1 April 2000 into a new agency, the Defence Geographic and Imagery Intelligence Agency.

DEFENCE GEOGRAPHIC AND IMAGERY INTELLIGENCE AGENCY [DGIA]

On 10 May 1999, the then Parliamentary Under-Secretary of State announced that two of these agencies -- JARIC and Military Survey -- would merge on 1 April 2000 into a new agency, the Defence Geographic and Imagery Intelligence Agency. The case for merging the Military Survey and JARIC Defence Agencies into a single agency was considered under the Strategic Defence Review. The study, which was completed in September 1998, concluded that there were a number of drivers, mainly in the medium to long term, recommending the merger of Military Survey and JARIC. These would secure improved operational effectiveness and better service to defence. Early implementation of a merger was recommended.

DGIA is based at four main UK sites: Feltham in West London, Brampton near Huntingdon, Tolworth in Surrey and Hermitage near Newbury. The Headquarters is at Feltham, alongside its largest business unit, the Defence Geographic Centre. DGIA has some 1,700 staff; over half are civilians and all three Services are represented. The Agency acts as the Department's centre of excellence for the production of imagery intelligence and geographic information in support of current military operations, defence planning, general intelligence requirements and wider Government interests.

No 7010 (VR) Photographic Interpretation Squadron RAuxAF

The Sqn's role is to provide operational Photographic Interpretational (PI) to support the RAF
No 7010 Flt was formed in Apr 1953. The Flight's role was to exploit strategic imagery at the joint Air Reconnaissance Intelligence Centre (JARIC), then at RAF Nuneham Park in Oxfordshire.
In 1965, it became the first reserve unit to augment RAF Germany during Exercise ROYAL FLUSH.
In Aug 1982, Her Majesty The Queen approved the issue of a crest to the flight. In allusion to the flight's role, the emblem of a human eye is portrayed with a wing embellishment and set in front of a roundel. The motto VOCATI VENIEMUS may be freely translated as 'when summoned we shall be there'. No 7010 Flt became No 7010 (VR) Sqn on 5 April 1997, when the RAFVR was amalgamated with the RAuxAF.

Over the years, the balance of emphasis has shifted from provision of Strategic Intelligence towards support to tactical reconnaissance squadrons. That said, No 7010 Sqn continues to provide Strategic Intelligence support to JARIC (now at RAF Brampton), while supporting the tactical operations of Tornado GR1 A and Jaguar GRI aircraft. In addition, the Sqn supports both HQ Allied Rapid Reactions Corps (ARRC) and HQ AIRCENT in Germany.

SECRET INTELLIGENCE SERVICE MI6

CONTACTS

The MI5 Phoneline for providing information to the Service

Since March 1998 a public telephone number – the MI5 Phoneline: 020 7 930 9000 – has been available for those wishing to provide information to the Service to assist it in its work. Members of the public may for instance become aware of activities which they think may be relevant to the Service's functions: others may be personally involved with groups investigated by the Service, or closely associated with them, and may have information to offer via the Phoneline. As an alternative to the Phoneline, information may be sent in writing to the Service's Enquiries Desk (details below). Any information provided, and the identities of callers, will be treated with the greatest care.

The MI5 Phoneline should not be used for enquiries about the Service, including employment opportunities, which should be sent instead to the Enquiries Desk. In addition, it should not be used for reporting information about imminent threats to life or property, which should be passed to the police using the 999 system, or via the Anti-Terrorist Hotline – 0800 789321 – which is for giving the police information about a terrorist incident which has happened or is about to occur.

Enquiries about the Service

Members of the public who wish to write to the Security Service, including those with enquiries about joining the Service, should contact:

The Enquiries Desk
PO Box 3255
London SW1P 1AE

All correspondence will be treated in the strictest confidence.

How to Complain

Members of the public who believe that the Security Service has acted improperly in relation to them or to their property and who wish to complain should write to:

The Security Service Tribunal
PO Box 18,
London SE1 0TZ

Members of the public who believe that their post or telephone calls have been intercepted in breach of the Act and who wish to complain should write to:

The Interception of Communications
Act Tribunal
PO Box 12376,
London SW1P 1XU

The Secret Intelligence Service, sometimes known as MI6, originated in 1909 as the Foreign Section of the Secret Service Bureau, under RNR Commander, later Captain, Sir Mansfield Cumming, which was responsible for gathering intelligence overseas. By 1922 Cumming's section had become a separate Service with the title SIS. Cumming signed himself 'C'; his successors have done so ever since.

The Special Operations Executive (SOE) was established in 1940, partly from the then Section D of SIS. After the War it was disbanded and some of its members were reabsorbed into SIS.

With the passing of the Intelligence Services Act, SIS was placed on a statutory footing under the Foreign & Commonwealth Secretary to whom it is responsible for all aspects of its work. The Act defines the functions of the Service and the responsibilities of its Chief, as well as establishing control and oversight arrangements. The Service's principal role is the production of secret intelligence in support of Her Majesty's Government's security, defence, foreign and economic policies within the framework of requirements laid upon it by the JIC and approved by Ministers. It meets these JIC requirements for intelligence gathering and other tasks through a variety of sources, human and technical, and by liaison with a wide range of foreign intelligence and security services. Specific operations are subject to longstanding procedures for official and ministerial clearance.

As the CIA is known as "The Company," SIS is known internally as "The Firm" and to other agencies as "The Friends." SIS is based at 85 Albert Embankment, Vauxhall Cross in London (known to those who work there as "Legoland"). MI6 also paid for a number of telephones located in a busy street in south London (Borough High Street in Southwark, opposite the Police Station) which has been identified as the spy training centre. The main training centre is Fort Monckton, a Napoleonic fort on the south coast at Gosport in Hampshire. What is thought to have been MI6's former City of London office is located in an office block in the Square Mile.

OPERATIONS

Each year the Security Service submits its analysis of the various threats and, thus, its priorities and plans for the future, for scrutiny and validation by an inter-departmental Whitehall committee. This committee, known as SO(SSPP), also reviews the Service's performance against the previous year's plans. It is a sub-committee of the Official Committee on Security (SO), 'SSPP' standing for 'Security Service Priorities and Performance'. Its terms of reference include the review of the Service's performance against plans and objectives, and examination of future Security Service priorities. The committee is chaired by the Home Office and its membership comprises senior officials drawn from a range of departments with particular knowledge of the Service's work in countering threats.
The Security Service is not the only organisation with responsibilities bearing on national security, or involved in collecting intelligence about security threats.

Others play important roles within their own specific functions, notably the Secret Intelligence Service (SIS), Government Communications Headquarters (GCHQ), Departments of State and the law

enforcement agencies. The Security Service works as an integral part of the UK's overall intelligence effort, alongside SIS and GCHQ. The three agencies assist one another in the pursuit of their functions. The Service is in close contact with relevant departments in its work, particularly the Home Office, Foreign and Commonwealth Office, Ministry of Defence and Northern Ireland Office. There is a close operational relationship between the Service and UK police forces, who are responsible for taking many of the actions arising from the Service's work. The Service also cooperates closely with other UK law enforcement bodies, such as HM Customs and Excise, and with the armed services. Overseas, the Service receives assistance from a wide range of foreign security and intelligence services (nearly 100 in all). These productive relationships are key to the Service's ability to tackle threats to UK interests internationally.
The particular role of the Security Service is to:

- investigate – to obtain and then to collate, analyse and assess secret intelligence about threats;
- counter – to act, and enable others to act, to counter specific threats;
- advise – to keep Government, and others as appropriate, informed of the threats, and to advise on the response, including protective security measures;
- assist – to provide relevant assistance to other agencies, organisations and departments.

In its approach to its work the Service aims to achieve a strategic advantage over the 'targets' of its investigations. Over time, the Service seeks to build up a detailed body of knowledge about target organisations, their key personalities, infrastructure, plans and capabilities. This enables the Service to assess the level and nature of the threat they pose which, in turn, informs the further deployment of intelligence resources to counter their activities. This is a cyclical process involving adjustments being made continually on the basis of new intelligence or events.

The assessment of threats is thus a central and distinctive component of the Service's work and provides the basis of decisions about resource allocation, counter-action and protective measures. The Service's judgments about the magnitude of the various threats to national security, and hence the distribution of the Service's efforts, are subject to scrutiny and validation by a senior inter-departmental committee (SO(SSPP)) and then by Ministers. Similarly the Service's judgments on its priorities are adjusted in the light of the national requirements for intelligence drawn up by the Joint Intelligence Committee (JIC) which are also approved by Ministers. Sources of Intelligence

In carrying out its statutory functions the Service draws on the following principal sources of secret intelligence:

- the interception of communications;
- eavesdropping, which involves covertly monitoring the speech of targets under investigation;
- surveillance (following and observing); and
- agents within target organisations.

In Security Service terminology an 'agent' is a human source working within or close to a target organisation, who provides intelligence in secret to the Service. Agents are not members of the Service.

At any one time the Service may be conducting many investigations, but only a few will draw on the full range of techniques. In planning deployments, the Service aims to operate with the minimum of intrusion and expense, and in proportion to the threat. In complex investigations, several different techniques will be used in combination, and much of the skill lies in deciding the most effective blend.

Organisations which pose a threat to national security often go to considerable lengths to prevent and detect efforts to investigate their activities. The Security Service aims to gather intelligence while ensuring that the targets under investigation remain unaware of the Service's interest in them. Clearly there is a need to prevent the compromise of a potentially successful investigation while it is running, but the Service also needs to look to the future. Keeping secret the details of intelligence methods is important if the Service is to retain them for use in future intelligence operations. Secrecy is also vital to ensure the safety of individuals, including agents.

The Security Service Act makes the Director General responsible for ensuring that there are effective arrangements within the Service to control the acquisition and disclosure of information. A major aspect of this control is a structure of internal mechanisms designed to ensure that the Service responds only to genuine threats, and does so with proper regard for the law, proportionately to the threat, and with appropriately senior authorisation for intrusive measures. These essential safeguards are also designed to allow fast-moving investigations to proceed swiftly, with proper authorisation, but without being hampered by unnecessary bureaucracy.

OPERATIONS UNDER INTERCEPTION AND 'PROPERTY' WARRANTS

Operations to intercept mail and communications on the public telecommunications network must be specifically authorised by a warrant signed by the Secretary of State under the Interception of Communications Act 1985 (IOCA). Interception warrants may only be issued if the Secretary of State considers that the warrant is necessary in the interests of national security, or for the purpose of safeguarding the economic well-being of the UK against threats from overseas, or in order to prevent or detect serious crime.

The Intelligence Services Act 1994 provides for the issue of 'property' warrants by the Secretary of State. The effect of a property warrant is to authorise otherwise unlawful entry into, or interference with, someone's property – for example, for the purpose of eavesdropping or conducting a clandestine search. Property warrants may only be issued if the Secretary of State is satisfied that the proposed action is necessary on the grounds that it is likely to be of substantial value in assisting the Service to fulfil its functions, and that what the action seeks to achieve cannot reasonably be achieved in another way. It is usually the Home Secretary who issues interception and property warrants for the Security Service.
All intended operations of this sort are subject to extensive scrutiny both within the Service and outside, for example at the Home Office. Final authorisation is a matter for the Secretary of State and is only given on the basis of a formal submission which contains a detailed account of why the warrant is required. The submission also sets out the nature of the threat, the intelligence background, and confirms that the scope of the operation falls within the statutory functions of the Service. Applications for warrants must be approved by senior managers within the Service, and are then scrutinised by senior officials before submission to the Secretary of State. Arrangements are in place for the most urgent cases to be processed quickly.

AGENTS

Agents represent one of the most important sources of secret intelligence. Agent operations are run by specially trained officers and can last for long periods, sometimes for many years. The Service attaches particular importance to ensuring that its agents – many of whom are inevitably at risk through their work for the Service – are managed securely. Management arrangements for agent operations are also designed to make sure that the case is kept under proper control, drawing on advice from the Service's legal advisers as necessary. For instance, a key objective is to avoid placing the agent in the role of agent provocateur, by enticing those on whom he or she is reporting to commit criminal acts which they would not otherwise have committed.

The Service pays close attention to the personal welfare of its agents, both during their agent career and after their active work for the Service has ended.

Surveillance

Surveillance operations involve the covert observation of targets under investigation in order to obtain intelligence about their movements and the identities of those with whom they are in contact. Surveillance is carried out by highly skilled, specialist officers who may work in vehicles, on foot or from fixed observation posts. The Service's surveillance section is practised at operating in concert with others, particularly the police.

Information Management and Record-keeping

Intelligence operations rely on high quality record-keeping and information management systems. Some intelligence leads are too fragmentary or imprecise to be of immediate value. Nevertheless, small details – for example, of the membership and modus operandi of target organisations – are important because they provide the raw material on which the assessment of individual threats is based, against which new intelligence is judged, and from which further investigations can be developed. The Service's record-keeping is central to supporting the capacity for sustained, integrated research and analysis which underpins all of the Service's work.

The Service's records include both paper files and computer records. Paper files remain for the present the main working documents of the Service, but computer-based documents are becoming increasingly important. The Service also makes extensive use of computer systems for the indexing and retrieval of its records. No government department or other agency has access to the Service's databases, although the relevant authorities will be given access as necessary to specific information for the purpose of court cases. Within the Service there are additional controls which limit access to particularly sensitive data relating to the Service's operations and investigations. Detailed criteria govern the opening of files on individuals and organisations. These criteria specify the circumstances in which opening a file and initiating enquiries are justified within the terms of the Service's statutory functions. They are kept under continual review and are formally checked for currency, relevance and propriety on an annual basis. In his report to Parliament for 1991, the Commissioner under the Security Service Act described in detail the Service's controls on its files.

The Service currently holds in total about 440,000 files which have been opened at some time since its establishment in 1909. Of these, approximately 35,000 files relate to Service administration, policy and staff, and 40,000 concern subjects and organisations studied by the Service. About 75,000 files relate to people or groups of people who have never been investigated by the Service such as those who have received protective security advice. This leaves about 290,000 files which relate to individuals who, at some time during the last 90 years, may have been the subject of Security Service enquiry or investigation. Of this 290,000 some 40,000 have been reduced to microfilm and placed in a restricted category to which Security Service staff have access only for specific research purposes. A further 230,000 files are closed so that staff may use them where necessary in the course of their current work, but may not make enquiries about the subjects of the files.

Therefore the great majority of the Service's file holdings do not relate to individuals who may be under current investigation by the Service. The number of files which fall within that category is around 20,000. Of that number, about one third relate to foreign nationals – typically members or associates of foreign intelligence services or terrorist groups, leaving approximately 13,000 active files on UK citizens.

Retention and Destruction of Files

The Service must take account of a number of potentially conflicting factors when considering the long-term retention of files which are no longer of current interest. There are some specific legal requirements. First, the Service has a responsibility to provide the Security Service Tribunal with any details it requires of enquiries made about a complainant, or of any disclosure made for vetting purposes, since the Security Service Act came into force in December 1989; relevant records must therefore be retrievable. The Service must also comply with the requirements of the Public Records

Act 1958 in identifying records of historical interest for permanent retention and eventual transfer to the Public Record Office. In practice, this means retaining files for future release that would otherwise have been destroyed as obsolete. The Service receives advice from the Public Record Office in judging which files to retain on historical grounds.

In November 1997 the Service transferred to the Public Record Office the first tranche of its own historical archives: its surviving records from the First World War. In considering the release of historical papers, the Service must take account of the need to protect former staff and agents. It remains a fundamental principle that the identities of agents must be protected. Privacy issues are also important. The Service must consider carefully whether it is proper to release into the public domain intelligence records which may reflect adversely on an individual who was suspected of criminality (for example, as a possible spy) but was never tried in court. Aside from these specific requirements, the general principle underlying the Service's file retention policy is that it seeks to retain only those records which will assist it in fulfilling its functions under the Security Service Act. The Service therefore keeps under review whether it might need its older records to fulfil its functions at a later time, such as for future investigations prompted by new intelligence. There is a balance to be struck between the possible intelligence value of retaining files and the need to ensure that files are not kept unnecessarily.

In the period between the Service's formation in 1909 and the early 1970s, large numbers of files (well over 175,000) were destroyed as they became obsolete or following a major contraction in the Service, most notably after the two World Wars. This sometimes caused problems, for example in the late 1960s when the Service faced difficulties investigating some spy cases because relevant records had been destroyed. It therefore became the Service's policy to retain records indefinitely. However, in the early 1990s, following the collapse of Soviet communism and the associated decline in the threat from subversion, the review and destruction process was reinstated. Since then more than 110,000 files have been destroyed or earmarked for destruction. The files under review for possible destruction have included those opened for counter-subversion reasons, and retained because Soviet and Warsaw Pact intelligence services had in the past sought to recruit spies from within certain subversive groups.

INTELLIGENCE AS EVIDENCE AND THE LAW OF DISCLOSURE

Since 1992 the Service's work has led to its becoming increasingly engaged in the criminal justice process. Intelligence material has been either adduced in evidence, or disclosed to the defence as 'unused material'. This has happened principally in the context of the Service's counter-terrorist work. Security Service officers gave evidence at nine trials between 1992 and April 1998, all of which led to convictions. The duty of prosecutors to make material available to the defence in criminal cases is set out in the Criminal Procedure and Investigations Act 1996. The Act recognises that the duty of disclosure must accommodate the need to protect sensitive information, the disclosure of which could damage important aspects of the public interest, such as national security. However, it is the courts – not the Service or the Government – that ultimately decide what must be disclosed in particular cases.

When planning and carrying out intelligence investigations that may lead to a prosecution, the Service has constantly in mind the requirements of both the law of evidence and the duty of disclosure. Security Service officers, working closely with members of law enforcement agencies, seek to ensure that operations are properly coordinated with a view to the possible use of the intelligence as evidence in court. For these reasons, as well as to ensure proper internal controls, the Service keeps detailed records of its operations, including all meetings with agents, eavesdropping, search and surveillance operations.

Where an investigation leads to a prosecution, the defence must be provided with material as required by the 1996 Act. Prosecuting counsel considers the Service's records and advises which of them are disclosable. If disclosure would cause real damage to the public interest by, for example, compromising the identity of an agent or a sensitive investigative technique, the prosecutor may apply to the judge for authority to withhold the material. Such applications take the form of a claim for public interest immunity (PII).

Claims for PII in relation to Security Service material are made by a certificate signed by the Home Secretary. In deciding whether a claim is appropriate, the Home Secretary carries out a careful balancing exercise between the competing public interests in the due administration of justice and the protection of national security. This exercise takes account of detailed advice from prosecuting counsel as to the relevance of the material to the issues in the case. If the Home Secretary considers that the balance comes down in favour of non-disclosure, a claim for PII will be made. But the decision on a PII claim is one for the judge alone. If a claim is successful, the judge will keep the decision under review throughout the proceedings.

Relationships

The Service's direct access to a network of national and international links is fundamental to its work. The Service liaises closely with a range of organisations and government departments both in the UK and overseas.

The Director General is appointed by the Home Secretary, in consultation with the Prime Minister, and the Service therefore has regular dealings with officials at the Home Office. The Service also has close links with the Foreign and Commonwealth Office, the Cabinet Office, the Northern Ireland Office, the Department of Trade and Industry and the Ministry of Defence, and advises all government departments and agencies on protective security matters. The central mechanisms for the coordination and resourcing of the UK's intelligence agencies are based in the Cabinet Office.

For GCHQ and SIS, the Joint Intelligence Committee (JIC) agrees the intelligence requirements and tasking to be laid upon them and these are submitted to Ministers for approval. These requirements are then reviewed annually in a process managed by the Intelligence Coordinator, and performance against them is reviewed at the end of each year by the JIC and by Ministers. The Director General is a member of the JIC. The Security Service contributes intelligence on some of the JIC's requirements, such as those relating to terrorism, but its overall priorities are determined not by the JIC but by its statutory remit to counter threats. In recognition of this, the Service's plans and priorities are validated and its performance reviewed annually by a separate Cabinet Office inter-departmental committee established for the purpose, called 'SO(SSPP)'.

Intelligence Agencies

The Security Service works closely with both SIS and GCHQ, whose statutory basis derives from the Intelligence Services Act 1994. The three agencies have different but related functions. The range of mutual assistance is wide, and is based on a closeness of relationship that promotes cooperation when a particular result can be achieved more effectively or more efficiently with another's help. For example, Security Service and SIS resources are shared in some support areas to avoid duplication. More formally, the Security Service is one of the many departments that place tasking on SIS and GCHQ through the JIC machinery to collect certain categories of intelligence. In the Service's case, this is intelligence relevant to the Service's functions to add to its own collection efforts. The Service is a major customer for intelligence produced by SIS and GCHQ in areas such as terrorism.

Police and other Law Enforcement Agencies, and the Armed Services

The Service also works closely with the UK's 55 police forces, particularly their Special Branches, and with other law enforcement agencies, such as HM Customs and Excise, and the National Criminal Intelligence Service. The Service receives assistance from the police in many areas of its work, provides information and assessments to them on the current threats, and collaborates closely with them in investigations which may result in criminal proceedings.

The Service provides support to the police in two main areas: in the field of serious crime, the Service works exclusively in support of the police and other law enforcement agencies; and in Northern Ireland the Service provides support to the Royal Ulster Constabulary, which has the lead role for intelligence work on terrorism related to Northern Ireland. (The Service has the equivalent role for all aspects of terrorism outside Northern Ireland.) The Service also works with the armed services on a range of security matters.

With Foreign Security and Intelligence Services Although the Service is charged with protecting national security as it relates to UK interests both in the UK and overseas, its primary focus is domestic and most of its staff are based in London. In many areas of its work it in consequence relies heavily on the support of SIS and seeks assistance from foreign security and intelligence services. To this end, the Service has links with nearly 100 services worldwide.

Executive Powers

The Security Service is a civilian organisation and its officers have no executive powers, such as the authority to detain or arrest people. It is not a 'secret police force'. Security Service investigations are shared with the police or other law enforcement agencies when there is a prospect of the arrest of people who are committing or planning criminal offences. In recent years, the Service has developed and applied procedures which enable its intelligence to be admitted as evidence in criminal proceedings. In addition, the Service may recommend to the Home Office or to the Foreign Office that known terrorists or foreign intelligence officers, for example, be refused entry to the UK, or be deported or expelled. However, the decision whether to do so lies outside the Service.

The Geographical Remit of the Security Service

Media reporting sometimes reveals confusion about the geographical scope of the Service's work. Threats to national security often come from abroad – for example, from foreign intelligence services or from foreign terrorist groups. Moreover, the scope of national security extends beyond the British Isles: British interests worldwide include diplomatic premises and staff, British companies and investments, and British citizens living or travelling abroad. Security threats to British interests anywhere in the world fall within the scope of the Service's functions as set out in the Security Service Act. In dealing with security threats overseas the Service cooperates closely intelligence agencies.

Assassination

The Service does not kill people or arrange their assassination. It is subject to the rule of law in just the same way as other public bodies.

The Service's Role in Employment Vetting

The Service's role in the vetting of candidates for employment in sensitive posts is based solely on checks against its records. Decisions on employing staff are the responsibility of the department concerned and the Service does not investigate or interview candidates on their behalf. The Security Service Act stipulates that the Service may only disclose information for use in deciding whether someone should be employed in sensitive work if it does so in accordance with arrangements approved by the Home Secretary. If, on checking, the Service finds that it has a substantial and relevant security record on an applicant, it may provide a summary assessment of the security information. However, the mere existence of a Security Service record does not necessarily mean that an assessment will be made. There is no 'blacklist'.

Whitehall 'Leak' Inquiries

The Service does not carry out inquiries into leaks of information from Government, except where national security may be affected. As part of its protective security role, it does give advice to

Government on security policy and practice and its protective security section 39 carries out audits of security arrangements within other departments on request. But it has no 'policing' role.

TRADE UNIONS AND PRESSURE GROUPS

It has often been alleged that in the past the Service systematically investigated trade unions and various pressure groups, such as the National Union of Mineworkers and the Campaign for Nuclear Disarmament.

The Service has never investigated people simply because they were members or office-holders of trade unions or campaigning organisations. But subversive groups have in the past sought to infiltrate and manipulate such organisations as a way of exerting political influence. To fulfil its function of protecting national security, the Service therefore investigated individual members of bona fide organisations when there were grounds to believe that their actions were "intended to overthrow or undermine parliamentary democracy by political, industrial or violent means". The Service investigated the activities of the subversive groups, but not the organisations they sought to penetrate.
When the Security Service Bill was debated in Parliament in 1988, the then Home Secretary, Douglas Hurd, spelt out the basis for the Service's work in this area:

> "It does not matter if . . . people have views on the structure or organisation of Parliament or if they are involved in seeking to change industrial practices in this country or to negotiate a better deal if they are members of trade unions, or if they seek to challenge or change the Government's policies relating to defence, employment, foreign policy or anything else . . . Its [the Service's] sole criterion in relation to a subversive threat is whether there is a deliberate intention to undermine parliamentary democracy and whether that presents a real threat to the security of the nation."

The subversive threat to parliamentary democracy in the UK is now negligible and the Service accordingly has no current investigations in this area.

THE ROYAL FAMILY, MINISTERS AND OTHER PUBLIC FIGURES

The Service is sometimes alleged to be responsible for routinely monitoring the private lives of people because they have a high public profile, including members of the Royal Family, Government Ministers, and Members of Parliament. This is not the case. For example in 1993, the Prime Minister, John Major, confirmed that the Service had had no involvement in any interception of the communications of members of the Royal Family.
The Service only investigates individuals whose activities fall within its statutory remit under the Security Service Act.

THE 'WILSON PLOT'

In his book Spycatcher, the former Security Service officer Peter Wright claimed that up to 30 members of the Service had plotted to undermine the former Prime Minister Harold Wilson. This allegation was exhaustively investigated and it was concluded, as stated publicly by Ministers, that no such plot had ever existed. Wright himself finally admitted in an interview with BBC1's Panorama programme in 1988 that his account had been unreliable.

SIR ROGER HOLLIS

It was claimed that former Director General of the Security Service, Sir Roger Hollis, was a Russian spy. The Trend inquiry of 1974 cleared Hollis of that accusation. Subsequently, the evidence of the former KGB officer Oleg Gordievsky confirmed this judgment.

ILLEGAL TELEPHONE TAPPING

The Service does not tap telephones illegally. In carrying out interception it fully complies with the provisions of the Interception of Communications Act 1985.

ACCESS TO SECURITY SERVICE FILES

No member of the public is permitted to see any Security Service files, except for historical records which have been declassified and released by the Public Record Office. Confidentiality is essential to protect details of investigational and operational techniques and to maintain the effectiveness of the Service. The dangers that would be posed by, for example, members of terrorist groups or foreign intelligence services embarking on 'fishing expeditions' in the Service's records are obvious. However, under the Security Service Act, anyone who is "aggrieved by anything which he believes that the Service has done in relation to him" may complain to the Security Service Tribunal. The Tribunal has access to any information it requires to adjudicate on a complaint.

ORGANIZATION - SECURITY SERVICE MI5

Structure of MI5 @Agentura.com, December 2003

The Security Service operates under the statutory authority of the Secretary of State (the Home Secretary), but it is not part of the Home Office. In a democracy there is an inherent tension between the existence of a Security Service with intrusive investigative capabilities and the preservation of individuals' privacy. As long as covert threats to the nation persist, the Service may need to invade the privacy of a very small minority in order to protect the security of the great majority. But there must also be safeguards. In addition to its own tightly drawn internal controls, the Service is subject to the following external oversight and accountability measures:

- The Director General is accountable under the Security Service Act 1989 to the Home Secretary. The Director General is appointed by the Home Secretary in consultation with the Prime Minister and is required to submit a report to them annually. The Director General is statutorily responsible for all aspects of the operations and efficiency of the Service, and for ensuring that it obtains and discloses information only in accordance with its functions under the Act.
- The Security Service Act provides for an independent Tribunal, supported by a Commissioner (a senior judge), to investigate complaints about the Service from members of the public. The Commissioner is also responsible for reviewing the issue by the Secretary of State of Property Warrants under the Intelligence Services Act 1994.
- The Interception of Communications Act 1985 also provides for a Tribunal, supported by a Commissioner (also a senior judge), to investigate complaints about interception of telephone or postal communications. The Commissioner is also responsible for reviewing the issue of interception warrants by the Secretary of State.
- Under the Intelligence Services Act 1994, the Service, together with SIS and GCHQ, is overseen by the Intelligence and Security Committee, a committee of Parliamentarians, on matters of expenditure, administration and policy.
- The Service's performance, plans and priorities are subject to external scrutiny and validation by a senior Whitehall committee, known as SO(SSPP), reporting to Ministers.

The Director General has one Deputy who is responsible for overseeing intelligence operations. There are five branches, each headed by a Director: three branches are engaged in intelligence investigations and in advising on protective measures to counter the various threats; the other two are responsible for intelligence collection, production and information management, and for personnel, security, finance and facilities management. There is also a Legal Advisers' department. In addition, the Service fills the post of Director and Coordinator of Intelligence (Northern Ireland), who reports separately both to the Director General and to the Secretary of State for Northern Ireland.

The Director General, Deputy Director General, the Directors and the Legal Adviser meet regularly as the Management Board of the Service to consider policy and strategic issues. In particular, the Management Board decides how the priorities and organisation of the Service should change to reflect shifts in the pattern and intensity of threats.

The Service currently employs around 1,900 people (a full-time equivalent strength of 1,860), who are mostly based at its headquarters at Millbank in central London. The Director General has a Deputy who oversees intelligence operations, and there are six Directors. The Service is divided into branches, each headed by a Director.

OVERSIGHT AND ACCOUNTABILITY

The Security Service Act 1989 sets out a number of statutory mechanisms for the accountability and control of the Service and its work. It:

- places the Service under the authority of the Secretary of State (the Home Secretary);
- sets out the responsibilities of the Director General; and
- provides for an independent Tribunal and Commissioner to deal with complaints about the Service from the public.

The Act also contained provisions, subsequently incorporated into the Intelligence Services Act 1994, for the issue of warrants by the Secretary of State authorising interference with property, and for the review by the Commissioner of the Secretary of State's exercise of this function. These statutory mechanisms have been considered and endorsed by the European Commission on Human Rights in a number of applications under the European Convention on Human Rights arising out of complaints to the Security Service Tribunal. The Service is also subject to various other forms of oversight and accountability, notably:

- the provisions of the Interception of Communications Act 1985, including a Tribunal to handle complaints about interception, and a Commissioner who is responsible for reviewing the Secretary of State's exercise of his functions in issuing warrants;
- oversight by the Intelligence and Security Committee (ISC), a committee of Parliamentarians which was established under the Intelligence Services Act 1994;
- external review and validation of the Service's priorities and performance by a senior Whitehall committee (SO(SSPP))
- Ministerial oversight of the Service's funding arrangements;
- scrutiny of the Service's spending plans by the Permanent Secretaries' committee on the Intelligence Services (PSIS), as part of the budgetary process; and
- scrutiny by the National Audit Office, which has access to any of the Service's financial records it requires.

The mechanisms for oversight of the Service have undergone many changes throughout its history, as different Governments have addressed the particular requirements of the day. Originally established under the Prime Minister's authority, and later under the Home Secretary with the Maxwell-Fyfe Directive to the Service of 1952, the Service is now accountable for its work via the range of oversight arrangements described above.

THE ROLES OF THE HOME SECRETARY AND THE DIRECTOR GENERAL

The Director General is appointed by the Home Secretary, in consultation with the Prime Minister. The Director General is personally responsible for:

- the operations and efficiency of the Service;

- making an annual report on the work of the Service to the Home Secretary and the Prime Minister;
- ensuring that the Service is politically impartial; and
- ensuring that the Service obtains and discloses information only in accordance with its statutory functions, or (in the case of disclosure) for the purpose of preventing or detecting serious crime, or for the purpose of any criminal proceedings.

The Director General's responsibilities in this last area are met by means of arrangements through which the day-to-day work of the Service is controlled. These internal mechanisms are designed to ensure that the work of the Service adheres to the principles that:

- the rule of law must be paramount; and
- that methods of investigation must be proportionate to the threat and authorised at an appropriate level.

The relationship between the Home Secretary and the Director General is of great importance. The Home Secretary receives briefing from the Director General on threats to national security and economic well-being and discusses with him or her matters of policy affecting the Service – for example, regarding resources or legislation. The Home Secretary is briefed by the Director General on major current investigations and has a close knowledge of the most sensitive aspects of the Service's work through the procedure by which the Home Secretary personally authorises warrants allowing the Service to intercept letters or telephone calls, or to interfere with property. The Home Secretary also receives independent advice and information from officials in the Home Office, who maintain close working links with the Service.

THE INTELLIGENCE AND SECURITY COMMITTEE (ISC)

The Intelligence Services Act 1994 established the Intelligence and Security Committee. Its remit is "to examine the expenditure, administration and policy" of the Security Service, SIS and GCHQ. The Committee comprises nine Parliamentarians, drawn from both the House of Commons and the House of Lords. The Committee is appointed by the Prime Minister in consultation with the Leader of the Opposition. No member may be a current Minister of the Crown. The Committee makes an annual report to the Prime Minister, who lays it before Parliament, subject to any exclusions on security grounds.

The Director General of the Security Service (as well as the Chief of SIS and the Director of GCHQ) has a statutory duty to provide the ISC with the information it requires. The agency heads may only withhold information from the Committee if it falls within certain categories of 'sensitive' information, as defined in the Intelligence Services Act. This includes details of sources, operations and methods, as well as information provided in confidence by allied foreign services. However, even such sensitive material may be made available to the Committee if the agency concerned considers that it would be safe to do so.
A decision by the head of one of the agencies to withhold sensitive information from the Committee is subject to review by the Secretary of State, who can order that it should be made available if he or she considers it desirable in the public interest.

THE SECURITY SERVICE TRIBUNAL

The Security Service Act 1989 provides for a Tribunal to investigate complaints about the Service from members of the public. The Tribunal consists of three senior members of the legal profession, appointed by Royal Warrant. Both the Tribunal and the Commissioner are independent of the Government. They visit the Service to examine its records as necessary. The Act states that anyone may complain to the Tribunal "if he is aggrieved by anything which he believes the Service has done in relation to him or to any property of his". The Tribunal must first establish whether the complainant has been the subject of enquiries by the Service. The Tribunal obtains this information directly from the Service, whose staff are under a legal duty to produce whatever information is required. They may also be interviewed by the Tribunal.

If the Tribunal finds that the Service has made enquiries about a complainant, it must establish whether the Service had reasonable grounds for so doing. Similarly, it may be alleged that the Service has disclosed information about the complainant for use in vetting for employment.

If this proves to be the case, the Tribunal must determine whether the Service had reasonable grounds for believing the information to be true. If a complaint is upheld the Tribunal must notify the complainant and report its findings to the Secretary of State and to the Commissioner. The Tribunal also has the power to order that enquiries be ended and records destroyed, and that compensation be paid to the complainant. Between the introduction of the Security Service Act in 1989 and the end of 1997 the Tribunal investigated 275 complaints. No complaint was upheld. In the great majority of cases, the complainants were unknown to the Service.

THE SECURITY SERVICE COMMISSIONER

The Security Service Act also established the office of the Security Service Commissioner. One of the Commissioner's responsibilities is to review the issue by the Secretary of State of property warrants under the Intelligence Services Act. It is also the Commissioner's function, if a complainant to the Tribunal alleges that the Service has interfered with his or her property, to investigate whether a property warrant was issued. If one was, he or she must also establish whether the Secretary of State acted properly in issuing it.

The Commissioner – a senior judge – has an important additional function. If, on investigating a complaint, the Tribunal concludes that it should not be upheld, but nonetheless decides that there should be an investigation into whether the Service has in any other respect acted unreasonably in relation to the complainant, it may refer the matter to the Commissioner. The Commissioner will then investigate and may report the findings to the Secretary of State, who has the power to take any appropriate remedial action. The Commissioner makes an annual report to the Prime Minister, who lays it before Parliament, subject to any deletions judged necessary on security grounds after consultation with the Commissioner.

A number of Security Service procedures, particularly concerning record-keeping, have been adjusted in response to issues identified by the Tribunal and subsequently investigated by the Commissioner. In his annual report for 1991, the Commissioner commented that:

> "There can be no doubt that the very existence of the Tribunal as a body empowered to investigate complaints provides the Security Service with a strong additional incentive to ensure that its procedures are designed to eliminate the chance of a complaint being found justified."

THE IOCA TRIBUNAL AND COMMISSIONER

Similar arrangements exist under the Interception of Communications Act 1985 (IOCA), to which other agencies such as the police and HM Customs and Excise are also subject. IOCA established a Tribunal, supported by a Commissioner, to deal with complaints from anyone who believes their communications may have been intercepted in breach of the Act. The Tribunal, which consists of five senior members of the legal profession, investigates whether a warrant has been issued and, if so, whether the requirements of the Act have been met. If it is found that the Act has been breached, the Tribunal must notify the applicant and report its findings to the Prime Minister. The Tribunal may also quash the warrant, order the destruction of copies of intercepted communications and direct the Secretary of State to pay compensation. In none of the cases it has investigated has the Tribunal found against the Service.

The Interception Commissioner, also a senior judge, reviews the issue by the Secretary of State of warrants under the Act, and also assists the Interception Tribunal as required. He or she regularly visits the Service to examine the intelligence requirement for interception warrants and to discuss individual cases. The Commissioner reports annually to the Prime Minister and may report at any time if it appears that the requirements of the Act have not been met. As for the Security Service Act Commissioner, the IOCA Commissioner's annual report is laid by the Prime Minister before Parliament, subject to any exclusions judged necessary on security grounds.

FACILITIES

MI5 has moved to new headquarters at Thames House, situated at Millbank near the Houses of Parliament. The building is a modern refurbishment of a listed building and retains many attractive and original features. It is air-conditioned with up to date workstations and office automation systems. It contains good facilities for staff including a restaurant, shop, multi-gym and squash courts.

MI5's old headquarters was at 140 Gower Street in Bloomsbury - within walking distance of Euston Tower. The MI5 telephone network has its center on the 17th floor of Euston Tower in central London, the base of MI5's "communications manager". MI5 ran a free 0800 number from Euston Tower for the convenience of operatives engaged in "watching" targets around the UK and forced to make calls from payphones.

GCHQ GOVERNMENT COMMUNICATIONS HEADQUARTERS

Bletchley Park
Cheltenham
GCHQ CSO Morwenstowe
GCHQ CSO Ascension Island
Menwith Hill
Columbia Annex [CANX]

GCHQ is a Civil Service Department under the Ministerial responsibility of the Secretary of State for Foreign and Commonwealth Affairs. GCHQ provides Government Departments and Military Commands with signals intelligence (Sigint) in accordance with requirements laid upon it by the JIC (as for SIS) in support of HMG's security, defence, foreign and economic policies.

GCHQ was established in 1946 as the post-War successor of the Government Code and Cipher School which had been the central Sigint organisation since 1919 and had made an outstanding contribution to the War effort at Bletchley Park, for example by decrypting German messages enciphered by the ENIGMA machine. In 1953 GCHQ moved to two sites on the outskirts of Cheltenham. In 2003, it is in the process of moving to a new, consolidated building known as the Doughnut. The Director of GCHQ is responsible to the Foreign & Commonwealth Secretary for all aspects of its work.

GCHQ derives signal intelligence by monitoring a variety of communications and other signals, such as radars. For this purpose it controls and administers the **Composite Signals Organisation** which operates from a number of locations in the UK and overseas. The Composite Signals Organisation Station, Morwenstowe [Bude, Cornwall] is directly subordinate to GCHQ. Like SIS and the Security Service, it also works in liaison with a range of foreign intelligence and security services.

CESG

In addition to providing signals intelligence, GCHQ also provides advice and assistance to Government Departments and the Armed Forces on the security of their communications and information technology systems. This task is undertaken by the **Communications Electronics Security Group** of GCHQ, which works closely with their customers and industry, as well as with the Security Service, to ensure that official information in such systems is properly protected. CESG is the UK's National Authority for the official use of cryptography, and the National Technical Authority for information security more generally. CESG's primary customers are people handling and processing official information - usually within government departments large and small and the three services, but also in agencies and firms carrying out work on government's behalf. CESG is in principle open to requests for advice from other sectors, but are not currently resourced to service these on any large scale. CESG now operates on a cost-recovery basis, charging for customer-specific services while providing general national authority services (policy, standards, etc) to the official community at large at no direct cost. Generally, CESG does not manufacture security equipment, but rather works closely with industry to ensure the availability of a range of suitable products and services to meet official needs, and of the infrastructures to support those services.

The Director of GCHQ is Mr. David Pepper. At the end of the Cold War some 6,000 people worked for GCHQ, with the total staff having declined to perhaps 4,500 by 1997. GCHQ's annual budget is estimated to exceed £400M.

UNITED STATES

U.S. GOVERNMENT INTELLIGENCE AGENCIES

FBI Web Site http://www.fbi.gov/ Home Page for the Federal Bureau of Investigation
U.S. Intelligence Community http://www.odci.gov/ic
Central Intelligence Agency http://www.odci.gov/cia Home Page of the Central Intelligence Agency
CIABASE http://webcom.com/%7Epinknoiz/covert/ciabasesearch.html A small portion of the larger CIA database- basically a search engine
U.S. State Department Foreign Travel Advisories http://travel.state.gov/travel_warnings.html Up-to-date travel advisories available from the State Department
FedWorld Search Site http://www.fedworld.gov/categor.htm
National Security Institute http://nsi.org/
U.S. Department of Defense Security Institute http://www.dtic.mil/dodsi/
Freedom of Information Act http://www.foia.ucia.gov
U.S. Defense Intelligence Agency http://140.47.5.4/
Bureau of Diplomatic Security- U.S. State Department http://www.heroes.net/indexorigin.html
U.S. Security Policy Board http://www.spb.gov/html/spb.html
Office of the Director of Central Intelligence World Wide Web Site http://www.odci.gov/ Link page to several sites related to the Central Intelligence Agency
U.S. Army Intelligence Center at Fort Huachuca http://huachuca-usaic.army.mil/
U.S. State Department Individual Country Reports gopher://gopher.umsl.edu/11/library/govdocs//bnotes Background notes on countries
U.S. CIA Individual Country Reports gopher://gopher.umsl.edu/11/library/govdocs//wf93/wflatest CIA World Factbook for each country
United States and International Government Military and Intelligence Agency Access http://www.sagal.com/ajax/

List of links to U.S. and International government sites
MILNET- U.S. Intelligence Agencies http://www.milnet.com/milnet/intell.htm
Foreign Intelligence Advisory Board (PFIAB) http://www.whitehouse.gov/WH/EOP/pfiab/index.html PFIAB provides advice to the President concerning the quality and adequacy of intelligence collection, of analysis and estimates, or counterintelligence, and of other intelligence activities.
United States Secret Service http://www.treas.gov/usss/
U.S. National Counter-Intelligence Center http://www.nacic.gov NACIC coordinates the U.S. government's effort to identify and counter foreign intelligence threats to U.S. national and economic security.
Central Intelligence Agency WorldFact Book 1997 http://www.odci.gov/cia/publications/factbook/index.html
CIA Kids Home Page http://www.odci.gov/cia/ciakids/index.html Games for children, historical highlights about famous Americans, a world geography quic, and links to other Federal internet sites with pages for children.
CIA Publications and Handbooks http://www.odci.gov/cia/publications/pubs.html A lengthy list of publications published by the CIA including the CIA World Factbook
CIA Directorate of Science and Techonology http://www.odci.gov/cia/dst
Usenet Group for the Central Intelligence Agency alt.politics.org.cia
National Reconnaissance Office http://www.nro.odci.gov/ The NRO designs, builds, and operates the nation's reconnaissance satellites.
Defense Intelligence Agency http://140.47.5.4/index.html As a Combat Support Agency of the Department of Defense, the DIA's mission is to provide timely, objective and cogent military intelligence to the warfighters--soldiers, sailors, airmen, marines--and to the decisionmakers and policymakers of the U.S. Department of Defense and the U.S. Government
Department of State Bureau of Intelligence and Research http://www.odci.gov/ic/dsbir.html The Bureau of Intelligence and Research (INR) is the State Department's primary source for interpretive analysis of global developments
Central Intelligence Museum http://laf.cioe.com/~dna A virtual museum of the CIA, spy gadgets and all! Not an official government site of the CIA.

US INTELLIGENCE AND SECURITY AGENCIES

NATIONAL

United States Intelligence Community
National Intelligence Council [NIC]
Counterintelligence Center [CIC]
DCI Center for Security Evaluation [CSE]
DCI Crime and Narcotics Center [CNC]
DCI Counterterrorist Center (CTC)
DCI National Virtual Translation Center [NVTC]
DCI Weapons Intelligence, Nonproliferation, and Arms Control Center [WINPAC]
DCI Special Security Center
National Counterintelligence Executive [NCIX]
Terrorist Threat Integration Center [TTIC]

Central Intelligence Agency

National Security Agency

National Reconnaissance Office

National Geospatial-Intelligence Agency (formerly NIMA)

Defense Intelligence Agency

Federal Bureau of Investigation

OTHER DEFENSE DEPARTMENT

Assistant to the Secretary for Intelligence Oversight

Under Secretary of Defense for Intelligence
Under Secretary of Defense for Policy

Assistant Secretary of Defense for Networks and Information Integration

Defense Information Systems Agency

Defense Advanced Research Projects Agency

Defense Protective Service

Defense Security Service

US Special Operations Command

Army
Army Deputy Chief of Staff for Intelligence
Intelligence and Security Command

Navy
Office of Naval Intelligence
Naval Security Group Command
Naval Criminal Investigative Service

Marine Corps

Air Force
Air Force Technical Applications Center
Air Intelligence Agency

OTHER FEDERAL AGENCIES

National Security Council
President's Foreign Intelligence Advisory Board
Office of National Drug Control Policy

Department of Homeland Security
Information Analysis and Infrastructure Protection

Energy Department
Office of Intelligence

Justice Department
Justice Intelligence Coordinating Council
OIG - Office of the Inspector General
OIPR - Office of Intelligence Policy and Review
DEA - Drug Enforcement Administration
NDIC - National Drug Intelligence Center
USNCB - U.S. National Central Bureau

ATF - Bureau of Alcohol, Tobacco, Firearms and Explosives

State Department
INR - Bureau of Intelligence & Research
INL - Bureau for International Narcotics and Law Enforcement Affairs
CT - Counterterrorism Office
DS - Bureau of Diplomatic Security

Treasury Department
Office of Intelligence Support
Office of the Under Secretary (Enforcement)
FINCEN - Financial Crimes Enforcement
FLETC - Federal Law Enforcement Training Center

National Archives and Records Administration
Information Security Oversight Office

GLOBAL INTELLIGENCE AGENCIES

- International Criminal Police Organization - INTERPOL and INTERPOL PR
- OECD Financial Action Task Force on Money Laundering (FATF)

EUROPOL

http://www.europol.eu.int

Europol, Raamweg47,
The Hague, The Netherlands
Postal address: PO Box 90850
NL-2509 LW
The Hague Tel.: +31 70 302 5000
Fax +31 70 345 5896
info@europol.eu.int

SUPPLEMENTS

INTELLIGENCE COLLECTION

"Sizing up opponents to assess dangers and distances is the proper course of action" (Sun Tzu)

Modern intelligence gathering has both an electronic and human face. The gathering, or collection, of intelligence is nothing more than stealing someone's secrets. It is done strategically, which means according to some direction, plan, or mission, and it is done competitively, which means that your opponents and allies are also most likely doing it, and it is done non-transparently, or in secret. The policymaking process which is informed by intelligence may be transparent, but the intelligence gathering process rarely is disclosed. The first requirement is that your target must have something worth stealing. If they don't have anything worth stealing, then all you're doing is snooping or doing research. In the world of business, this is known as the difference between competitive intelligence and market research. The military takes intelligence gathering seriously, as it is almost always collected for the purpose of assessing risks and hazards in preparation for the order of battle (IPB, or Intelligence Preparation of Battlespace). The most important thing to remember is that *there is no such thing as intelligence for intelligence's sake.* The whole purpose of gathering information about other's secrets and processing it into intelligence is to provide your leaders or policymakers with options to make policy more effective and efficient. There is no point in tasking, collecting, analyzing, and distributing intelligence products if there's no policy, issue, or anticipated issue on the table.

Intelligence gathering is also called collection, and collection takes place using open or closed sources. It may be helpful to review some definitions of intelligence, which would include the following. Intelligence is "the product resulting from the collecting and processing of information concerning actual and potential situations and conditions relating to domestic and foreign activities and to domestic and foreign or US and enemy-held areas" (Carl 1990). Intelligence is "secret knowledge of the enemy, a kind of knowledge which stands independently of the means by which it is obtained and the process by which it is distilled" (Troy 1991). The most basic intelligence process, or cycle, involves 3 steps: (1) collection; (2) analysis; and (3) synthesis. Collection will be outlined below. Analysis involves a variety of techniques to make conclusions or inferences. Synthesis normally produces a product, such as a chart, graph, table, summary, or other visual aid. The synthesis step is sometimes called fusion. There are additional steps which are worth mentioning because those are the ends to which intelligence is put: (4) policy; (5) arrest; and (6) war.

Some of the historical reasons for having steps or names for the separate processes of intelligence go back to the 6th century BC writings of Sun Tzu, who said it consisted of four basic elements (and possibly a fifth): collection, analysis, covert action, counterintelligence, and maybe opportunity analysis. Over the years, there have been many additions to this literature on the intelligence process, and some examples would include: Kahn's Law (O'Toole 1990): "*Emphasizing the offensive tends toward a neglect of intelligence.*" The First Corollary = Emphasizing the defensive tends toward an emphasis of intelligence ... The Second Corollary = Emphasizing the offensive tends toward an emphasis of counterintelligence ... The Third Corollary = In situations of stalemate, both sides tend to emphasize intelligence equally ... The Fourth Corollary = An offensive operation that acquires defensive aspects tends to increase the emphasis on intelligence. Let's look at the contemporary way the intelligence process is organized.

There are five different categories of intelligence:

- "Current" intelligence looks at day-to-day events
- "Estimative" intelligence looks at what might happen
- "Warning" intelligence gives urgent notice that something might happen

- "Research" intelligence is an in-depth study of an issue
- "Scientific and technical" intelligence is information on foreign technologies

There are five different collection "disciplines" of intelligence:

- HUMINT: Human Intelligence; the collection and processing of raw intelligence from a clandestine agent working in the field.
- IMINT: Imagery Intelligence; the collection, mapping, and interpretation of photographs from aerial units or satellites. Sometimes this speciality is also called PHOTINT.
- MASINT: Measurement and Signature Intelligence; a collective term bringing together disparate elements that do not fit within the definitions of Signals Intelligence, Imagery Intelligence, or Human Intelligence. This category usually consists of acoustic intelligence; radar intelligence; nuclear radiation detection; infrared intelligence; electro-optical intelligence; radio frequency, unintentional radiation; materials, effluent, and debris sampling; and electro optical and spectro-radiometric sources. MASINT also refers to Signals or Imagery Intelligence data streams which require specialized processing. As a finished product, MASINT is used primarily to support military commanders and other users on a national or tactical scale.
- OSINT: Open Source Intelligence; more than just newspaper clippings and the Internet, OSINT involves inventories of the full range of accessible, acknowledgeable, and unclassified private sector information sources. Some 80% of OSINT is not online, not available in English, and not available in the U.S. The purpose is to produce Just in Time: Just Enough intelligence, and the process involves discovery, discrimination, distillation, and delivery.
- SIGINT: Signals Intelligence; consisting of 4 subfields: (1) communications intelligence (COMINT); (2) electronics signals analysis, primarily ELINT and RADINT; (3) foreign instrumentation signals intelligence (technical and intelligence information derived from the collection and processing of foreign telemetry, beaconry, and associated signals), usually abbreviated TELINT; and (4) information derived from the collection and processing of nonimagery infrared and coherent or noncoherent light signals hidden by such techniques as spectrum-spreading or frequency-hopping, usually referred to as signals conversion analysis. Sometimes, a whole lot of sophisticated technology is unnecessary because, believe it or not, 5% of the enemies of the U.S. still use Morse code. COMINT, which is a subset of SIGINT for Communications Intelligence involves the interception and processing of foreign communications passed by radio, wire, or other electromagnetic means, and by the processing of foreign encrypted communications, however transmitted. Interception comprises search, intercept, operator identification, signal analysis, traffic analysis, cryptonalysis, decryption, study of plaintext the fusion of these processes and the reporting of results. Excluded from this definition are the interception and processing of unencrypted written communications, press and propaganda broadcasts. COMSEC, or Communications Security, is any measure taken to deny persons information derived from the national security, or any measure taken to ensure the authenticity of a telecommunications. ELINT, which is a subset of SIGINT for Electronics Intelligence involves the collection (observation and recording) and processing for subsequent intelligence purposes of the information derived from foreign noncommunications, electromagnetic radiations, emanating from other than atomic detonation or radioactive sources.

Basic intelligence gathering consists of collecting facts (data) and observations from open sources or clandestine sources. Then, it is patiently and rigorously analyzed, evaluated, compared, and integrated with other information and existing intelligence to arrive at conclusions relevant to the needs of policymakers. Trends and anomalies from the collected intelligence are processed carefully, and if the incoming intelligence seems to follow a pattern that pre-existing intelligence has indicated, this is often called "connecting the dots." If there is an anomalous, sharp spike in the quantity or quality of incoming intelligence, this is often called "increased chatter." The key to success is that once your collection elements are deployed, the intelligence coming in from them is rapidly compared in a pre-production process often called "cross-cueing" which ensures the possibility for timely dissemination of intelligence products. When basic intelligence collection products are compared to the kind of collected intelligence coming in from advanced methods (such as orbital or airborne sensors), this pre-production process is often called "fusion," although the terms cross-cueing and fusion are sometimes used interchangeably. The United States operates with a multi-level intelligence community where interoperability and collaboration are important and intelligence from different collection sources can move rapidly from one collection discipline to another.

All gathered intelligence is rated for its quality and reliability, and then it is exploited. It is customary to apply a simple alpha (A-F) and numeric (1-6) system on raw data, where the alphabetical characters represent the reliability of the source (A= completely reliable, F= unknown reliability) and the numerical characters represent the accuracy of the information (1= confirmed by other sources, 6= truth cannot be judged). There are very few intelligence gathering sources with an A-1 rating. In the pre-production analysis phase, cross-cued intelligence is evaluated by what is called "analysis of competing hypotheses." Using this approach, an analyst (or group of analysts) tries to identify all plausible explanations or conclusions about an issue in an effort to select the correct (or most correct) one. There is then a simultaneous comparison of how well the available information supports each potential hypothesis. The finished product is a NIE (National Intelligence Estimate) presented to the National Security Advisor for the President that lays out the probabilities or possibilities. There are always caveats or provisos to intelligence products, and in many ways they are affected by the mindsets of the analysts who have processed them. The field of intelligence work has its own folklore which provides many cautions for those who produce intelligence products, as follows:

- Whatever you think you know is incomplete
- At least some of it is wrong
- You can't know which parts of what you think you know are wrong;
- You can't know what you don't know
- You can't know how much you don't know.

INFILTRATION AND EXFILTRATION

Much of intelligence gathering at the clandestine level is a lot like undercover police work. Like the policeman's attitude toward the "stool pidgeon" or "snitch," it's important to note that to intelligence professionals (case officers or case handlers), an "agent" is a foreign national, an informant, someone committed to treason and "spying" on his or her own country. The theory behind working undercover is that it removes any impediments to acquiring information, and allows a number of activities such as surveillance, eavesdropping, use of informants, and espionage. It typically involves an assumed identity for a defined and considerable amount of time. Undercover work allows someone to circulate in areas where they are not ordinarily welcome. The job of anyone working undercover is to "make cases", in other words, to gather enough information to enable a successful outcome, remembering that the goal is to be a hunter, not a gatherer. The first rule of clandestine intelligence gathering is to go after the big game. You want the payoff to be big. You want the largest impact possible because you've maximized your gathering operation as much as possible.

A distinction is usually made between agents who are under cover and those who are under deep under cover. This is sometimes referred to as "legals vs. illegals" although more common terminology distinguishes between "official" and "unofficial" cover. Official cover refers to disguishing an intelligence officer as an attache or liaison officer at an embassy or overseas post. Nonofficial cover refers to someone in deeper disguise who is acting like a businessman, journalist, tourist, or college professor on an exchange program. Those people on nonofficial cover make up what is called the "NOC list" (for NonOfficial Cover), and the NOC list is a closely guarded secret because NOCs are either high level principal agents or staff employees under a variety of covers. There is usually no cover working officially out of an embassy because everyone knows embassies are a hub of espionage. If a case officer under official cover works out of an embassy, they can expect extensive surveillance of their every move, so usually such officers restrict their recruitment activities to third countries outside the country where their embassy is. On the other hand, NOCs usually have dual nationality, often require handling by an inside case officer, and employ covers that Rustmann (2002) distinguishes as "cover for status" (the legitimacy to live and work in a particular country) and "cover for action" (the aliases or identities which allow operations to be carried out).

Let's examine the stages of undercover work: THE EARLY STAGES -- The usual pattern is to bring someone in as the girlfriend or boyfriend of an infiltrator, and then distance themselves from that infiltrator. Once it's clear to all the parties involved that the undercover agent is single again, another undercover agent is brought in as the boyfriend or girlfriend of the first undercover agent. This allows the gathering unit to work as a team, which is better for safety. The initial targets are usually the "big" leaders of a group that has been infiltrated, but often the undercover operatives have to settle for going after the "small" fries, accumulating information and case material as they go. A supervisor or case officer usually makes the decision about whether enough important information has been accumulated to decide if and when the operation should be terminated, and a system will have usually been put in place for the operative to turn over evidence on a systematic basis or en masse at one time. THE MIDDLE STAGES -- some agents are allowed to create their own cover stories or legend, and this will depend upon the type of behavior involved (drugs, contraband, gambling, "subversive" groups, terrorism). The need may arise for false documents or computer records for such agents. This is not ordinarily done with minor cases. The need may also arise for creating various kind of setup situations in which the agent "proves" their criminality or loyalty by engaging in a staged showdown with police or a brush with the law. The staged encounter may also be an opportunity to supervise the agent. Since supervision and continued surveillance becomes more difficult as the operation progresses over time, agents are sometimes "busted" to give a progress report and let management know if they need more or less supervision. THE LATE STAGES -- some "deep cover" agents lose perspective, and go "native" so agencies have policies in place to help avoid this. Most agencies will call someone in who has been doing this kind of work too long so that they can salvage their usefulness as a regular employee, and in fact, this is a job benefit guaranteed by civil service rights. SIS and SES officers, of course, enjoy no such rights, and are allowed to be hired and fired at will. Danger, temptation, and paranoia play roles in the late stages, and it is always possible the person becomes a "rogue" agent who arranges their own private surveillance and protection.

RECRUITING INFILTRATORS

The safest way to steal anything is to recruit someone who can steal it for you and who never knows your true identity. This works for just about anything you want to do that's illegal and you don't want to get caught for. Once someone is recruited properly, you can use them for just about anything. They can be used for sabotage, deception, covert operations, assassination, sex, just about anything. The apparatus of most intelligence operations is built on lies, deception, and using people, generally foolish people. Using people generally follows a pattern:

- the recruit doesn't realize what they are going to be doing
- the recruiter fools them into thinking they aren't doing anything so terrible
- the recruiter traps them in situations where they have no choice but to whatever they're told to do

Employees of intelligence services don't consider themselves spies; they consider themselves recruiters of spies. Sometimes, they sneak into foreign countries and do spy work themselves, but they still primarily think of themselves as case officers, supervisors, or handlers. In actual practice, there is a vast bureaucracy of people backing up the spy and their handler, or case officer. In any clandestine operation, the upper eschelon of a spy bureaucracy consists of: (a) a regional desk officer, who oversees all HUMINT operations in that region of the world; (b) watch officers, who staff a 24-hour crisis center; (c) a counterintelligence officer, who oversees clandestine meetings between officers and agents; and (d) a reports officer, who acts as a liaison between officers in the field and analysts at headquarters. The spies themselves are considered a traitor, or a fool, and fools come in an amazing variety of forms:

1. People with loose lips, careless security attitudes (inadvertent spies)
2. People fleeing the rule of their own country (defectors)
3. People looking for a source of extra income (walk-ins)
4. People who have made a plea bargain with law enforcement (undercovers)
5. People tricked, bribed, or blackmailed (recruits)
6. People caught spying against you (double agents)

Spies are usually classified as PRIMARY or ACCESS agents. A primary agent is someone with actual access to the information you need. An access agent knows somebody who is more important, and serves as a gateway or portal to others. Recruiting spies is all about deception. Case officers regularly deceive spies as much as spies deceive the people they spy on. Those who recruit and manage spies, however, must always come off as honest and sincere friends, and tell believable lies. Much of tradecraft is the pursuit of skill at lying. Here's one of the most standard deceptions:

> The False Flag -- the case officer pretends to hold a nationality or be a person whom the target expects to be friendly to the target's own interests. *Some examples*: A Chinese businessman thinks he's working for the Republic of China when he is really spying for Taiwan; a student in Lima thinks he's passing documents to Cuban intelligence when it's actually the CIA.

Three resources that a recruiter will need, and plenty of it, are: money, drugs, and sex. Money is generally used to attract a recruit's attention, and sooner or later, it's all going to come down to money. Normally, the money will come from the budgets of the intelligence service; and at other times, activities will be self-financed. Drugs are generally used to service or create an addiction which is then used for blackmail purposes, if appropriate. Alcohol is the drug of choice, but anything that will build rapport and encourage talking is suitable. Sex almost never involves the case officer engaging in it with the recruit. Instead, the case officer uses prostitutes paid to pretend being innocent lovers, capitalizes on an ongoing affair, uses another recruit, or an innocent amateur.

THE STEPS OF RECRUITMENT

There are two phases to recruitment. PHASE ONE consists of Spotting, Evaluating, and actual Recruiting. PHASE TWO consists of Testing, Training, Handling, and Terminating the recruit. SPOTTING means looking for people who have access to the things you want. Handlers generally look for angry or desperate people in mid-level management positions. The best prospects are those who are ambitious and have been passed over for promotion. Secondarily, handlers look for clerks, secretaries, and "invisible" people in the organization. Often, they have personal problems or vices that can be worked as well as anger and desperation. In many cases, the case officer will have to settle for an access agent who can plant electronic surveillance devices.

EVALUATION means personality profiling. The prospect should be thoroughly evaluated in order to determine their possible motives. A sufficient cover story is also usually created at this step. A adequate cover story involves layers of deception. RECRUITING takes the form of meeting and getting to know the target. A close, personal relationship is cultivated, and trust is built. It starts with small, personal favors, an increase in rewards, and then the final step of asking someone to clearly betray their employer, government, coworkers, or lover. Blackmail is used as a last resort if the psychological ploys fail.

In the advanced second phase,

TESTING means checking your informant's information against known facts. Regardless of the reasons for error, if a spy doesn't produce credible information, they should be threatened with termination at this point, or dropped as a source. Spies are also often "fluttered" at this point, which means that they are given a polygraph examination, or interrogated.

TRAINING involves teaching the spy how to use specialized equipment and codes. One of the other important things the spy will want training in is escape and evasion tactics. Training should also involve coaching the person in how to spend money. HANDLING is a term short for "psychological handling" which usually involves the passing of control from yourself to another, usually superior, case officer. The handing off of spies is done for several reasons: so they don't get too close to their original recruiter; to make them feel they are getting better protection; and to make them feel they are getting promoted. Often, it has been your agency which has generated some fear, convincing the spy that their mother or other relative needs protection. Spies can be promoted all the way up to Admiral or General since it's only honorary rank.

TERMINATION is always done by the agency. The most common reason given for termination is budget problems. Usually, the person is allowed to immigrate and is given a new identity, a desk job, and sometimes a pension. Other times, they are allowed to get caught or killed. It's important to break off all contacts with a terminated agent. They cannot be allowed to quit or resign.

Case officers and their spies should work up a special communications code between them. It may involve the type of clothing worn, or a series of hand signals. At a minimum, the following should be able to be communicated without words:

- We need to meet so that we can talk
- I have material to pass on to you
- I think I am being followed
- You have a tail
- Everything in OK

Spies have copied, photographed, or memorized things, which they then pass on to their contacts. Most intelligence services use what are called COURIERS to handle all such exchanges and contacts. Sometimes, couriers are involved in the initial recruitment and training of a spy; and at other times, they're unrelated to the case. Professional messenger and postal services are also sometimes used. A traditional exchange is:

> The Dead Drop -- The spy and their courier have arranged a place, usually a dumpster or public garbage can where material is discarded and later picked up.

Telephone conversations are always avoided, as are computerized forms of communicating over the Internet. A few Internet exceptions exist, however, as the most popular form of exchange takes place not with encryption, but with postings in public bulletin boards or Usenet discussion groups. In other words, no direct computer-to-computer connections are allowed. SAFE HOUSES exist in almost every city. Most commonly, they are hotel or motel rooms; other times, a rental house or apartment. Safe houses are always constantly being rented, the purpose being that their newness prevents the planting of surveillance devices. Spies should always be blindfolded when taken to a safe house.

SEX AS A WEAPON

Sex is only one (1) of several methods for "turning" someone into an agent, traitor, or spy. Almost all the motives for becoming such a person are expressed in the acronym MICE (Money, Ideology,

Compromise, Ego). Sex falls under the Compromise category. The letter "C" (for Compromise) can itself be subdivided into three (3) distinct subparts:

- Heterosexual Compromise
- Homosexual Compromise
- Nonsexual Compromise

The theory behind the use of sex in espionage is based on Freudian theory, the idea that the sex drive is basic, so basic, in fact, that it is the basis of all other drives, a "generalized" drive, if you will. Additionally, the sex drive is compulsive or addictive. It cuts across intelligence. There are several known incidents in which the most powerful and intelligent people in politics or government have jeopardized their careers to satisfy a sexual urge or craving. The use of beautiful women in baited situations is known as planting a "honey trap", or more formally "entrapment." The Arab countries are said to know everything about NATO activities and plans because it has been so efficiently penetrated by Arab romeos. A rather interesting part of spy history involves the use of HOMOSEXUAL agents. Some of the most notorious spies in history have been homosexuals (the Cambridge Spy Ring) or sexual deviants (the KGB agent Geoffrey Prime). Most sexual deviants don't succeed in the spy business, but homosexuals apparently do. Instead of being called "honey-traps", a homosexual compromise situation is called "drone-traps".

NONSEXUAL COMPROMISES

Recruits are also often enticed into various "deals" which expose them to blackmail by the host country's intelligence services. Here's a list of various techniques:

- Black-marketing -- targets are threatened with exposure for buying contraband goods and services on the black market.
- Currency violations -- targets are threatened with exposure for violating currency laws of the host nation
- Security violations -- targets are threatened with exposure for violating "no trespassing" zones or being on government property of the host nation
- Criminal Law violations -- targets are threatened with prosecution for various criminal offenses that they have been setup in.

Any refugee or war criminal makes excellent material for recruitment. The immigration quota system is often used to threaten people. An applicant is converted into a spy by promises of moving quickly on their visa application (permission to leave the country) in return for agreeing to spy in their newly adopted countries. Some nations offer to pay all tuition expenses if the student, studying in the host country, agrees to engage in espionage.

TORTURE AND BRAINWASHING

Another technique is to capture and "turn" an enemy into one of your spies. This isn't as relied upon as it once was, as torture and interrogation techniques have found a more respectable place in intelligence gathering. All sorts of things can irritate a person like flashing lights at 85 cycles per minute which put you in a receptive state to believe anything. The study of slightly irritating things that rob you of your sense of control or self-confidence is the study of torture and brainwashing. Tough, physical methods are not necessary. In fact, you don't want to use pain because the subject will lie and tell you anything to make the pain stop, and their subconscious will commingle fact and fiction. Instead, a regime of psychological pressure or coercion is better. In the end, you want to completely destroy the subject's psyche, turn their mind upside-down, and win their cooperation freely and voluntary. This has been the standard way of interrogating captured terrorists for years. There's also no need for a good cop, bad cop routine. It's important all the interrogators be perceived as good.

Torture is, of course, prohibited by international law, but psychological coercion is not. Where the two cross over is anyone's guess, but I would imagine marathon interrogations, lasting two, three, or four days in length, are good examples of a crossover situation. However, a lot can be accomplished in less than a 48 hour period, if done right. To begin with, a captured subject is blindfolded, and driven or flown around at length (even if the interrogation site is nearby). The use of truth serum is not strictly prohibited by international law, but much more effective is giving somebody a placebo, and letting them believe it's a truth serum. Subjects are usually placed in a small cell (5' by 7'), surrounded by bright lights (sometimes flashing), and music (or more often) static is played over speakers. The conditions of the cell are usually cold and wet. These conditions take away the ability to reason properly. They are awakened and fed at irregular intervals to throw off their biological clock. Then, they are constantly told lies that their family and friends need them to cooperate. It should become clear to the subject that any talking, along lines that the interrogators want to hear, helps to alleviate some of these conditions. In return for talking, the lights or static may be dimmed, for example. Dry clothes and uninterrupted sleep may follow as further rewards.

Once the subject has started cooperating, you build them back up by restoring their sense of self. This sense of self-reference must always include at least one of the interrogators as a central figure, perhaps based on promises you'll watch out for them, take care of them, and look after them from now on. The goal is to create a Stockholm syndrome where the subject identifies and becomes loyal to the interrogators. Brainwashing is the political indoctrination and ideological conditioning of people held captive with the purpose of changing their loyalties. It has been used on captured civilians and servicemen in the hope of making them traitors. There are believed to be three (3) stages:

- Stage 1 -- produce chaos, distrust, & turmoil in the individual
- Stage 2 -- eradicate individualism, self-will & creativeness
- Stage 3 -- inculcate the foreign ideology & dogma to realign loyalty

Brainwashing is based on the theory that every person has its breaking point. Brainwashing is not the correct term to use, as the current politically correct (and more sociological) term is "coercive persuasion" or "social persuasion." People who have been brainwashed apparently do not realize it, and will usually passionately deny it. At best, they will admit to having "seen the light" in some miraculous way. The "miracle" analogy is appropriate because the concept of "conversion" in some religions is kind of like a brainwashing process. Similar techniques are used by human-potential trainers and in company retreats or training functions. High school pep rallies share some characteristics of brainwashing. The boot camp experience in military and law enforcement training is, to some degree, a type of brainwashing. Many diet programs use brainwashing techniques. Training in terrorist and criminal groups often involves brainwashing.

Repetitive music is the fastest way to produce an alpha state (an eyes-open altered state of consciousness in which people are 25 times more suggestible). There's no need for subliminal messages, just a rhythm close to the beat of the human heart, from 45 to 72 beats per minute. Words delivered at a rate of 45 to 60 beats per minute best accompany the suggestibility effect. People are more susceptible to brainwashing when they are cut off from the outside world, have to use bathroom facilities but are not allowed to, and have been deprived of food, sleep, drugs, tobacco, and caffeine. During brainwashing, the tone of human interaction must be deadly serious. Humor is only allowed, if at all, in Phase 3. Marching, chanting, and singing can produce suggestibility states, and it helps to demonize an enemy. The theory of how to demonize an enemy is to produce visual, creative images that access the RIGHT BRAIN. The left brain is too rational, so it's important to be creative and imaginative when demonizing. Brainwashing works best if the new enemy is an old friend, even somebody they once loved. This is easily seen with parental alienation syndrome, or the hate training that goes on when an ex-wife or ex-girlfriend brainwashes the children. Brainwashing is also engaged in by husbands against their wives in domestic violence situations.

The CIA has conducted secret experiments on brainwashing. One declassified paper written by L.E. Hinkle and H.E. Wolff supports the notion that the effects of brainwashing are only temporary. No one has ever perfected the art of brainwashing to produce lifelong, consistent behavior change. Some critics would say that brainwashing doesn't work, that what actually occurs is that the followers eventually form a new collective world-view. Legally, a brainwashing, or more accurately, "duress" defense exists at law. The famous lawyer, F. Lee Bailey tried it in the Patty Hearst case, but the jury wouldn't buy it. President Carter, however, commuted her sentence, and President Clinton granted her a pardon. The vast majority of brainwashing cases are civil, and consist of former cult members suing their former groups for torts of false imprisonment, emotional distress, or fraud. Professional "deprogrammers" exist and have helped win multimillion-dollar verdicts in the 1980's. The watershed case is *U.S. v. Fishman* (1990), which presumably eliminated brainwashing testimony from law. Probably the most serious work on the subject is the 1960's research on POWs by Shein and Lifton. According to Lifton (1961), the requirements for a really clean brainwash are:

- isolation of subjects
- control over their information
- debilitation
- degradation
- discipline and fear
- peer pressure
- performance of repetitive tasks
- renunciation of formerly held values

MIND CONTROL EXPERIMENTS

Experiments have also been conducted on mind control using drugs. The highly secretive project (code name MKULTRA where MK stands for Mind Killer) ran from 1953 to 1963. The Soviets had been putting spies on the stand and getting them to confess openly, so the U.S. wanted to develop a similar "truth serum" as well as come up with a way for captured agents to induce amnesia. American spies carried a deadly fish toxin to take in case of capture, but the CIA wanted something better. They experimented with LSD. Sidney Gottlieb, who managed the CIA's Technical Services Division, supervised the experiments in mind control (code name Operation Midnight Climax in San Francisco). Gottlieb played a crucial role in the death of Dr. Frank Olson, who worked for the US Army's biological weapons center at Fort Detrick. In 1953, Gottlieb gave the unwitting Olson some LSD, and Olson soon developed psychotic symptoms and jumped to his death from a hotel window. Gottlieb was also implicated with Harry Anslinger's Bureau of Narcotics and Dangerous Drugs, and the infamous Dr Ewen Cameron, a Canadien who experimented with electroshock and lobotomies. Cameron invented a particularly ghastly process called "psychic driving" whereby drugged and shocked patients would have tapes played sixteen hours a day, dictating their new personalities. Gottlieb also funded experiments by Dr. Harris Isbell at the Center for Addiction Research in Lexington, Kentucky. This center experimented on black heroin addicts, the most infamous experiment being when Isbell gave LSD to seven black men for seventy-seven straight days.

Besides psychotropic drugs like LSD and psilocybin, certain biotoxins intended to disable or kill have been used in national security work. The CIA has been implicated in little black bag jobs in the Congo, Iraq, and of course, with the endless poisons directed at Fidel Castro. There were also some less-than-honorable things done under the Operation Phoenix Program in Vietnam, such as prisoner experimentation. The Canadians, however, have been extensively involved in prisoner experimentation. In Canada, the most infamous prison doctor was George Scott, who served as director of the Canadian Army's psychological rehabilitation department during World War II. After the war, Scott teamed up with shrinks from Allan Memorial Institute, including the notorious Ewen Cameron, to launch a variety of drug, electroshock, sensory deprivation and pain tolerance experiments, using prisoners and patients at mental hospitals as guinea pigs. One of those patient was John Stanley Faulder, who in 1977 went on a killing spree after being "rehabilitated." Other famous victims of these Canadian experiments were Robert Renaud and Dorothy Proctor, each of whom has sued the Canadian government. By far, however, the most famous name in the history of mind control experiments is Timothy Leary, who's colorful career began as a research psychologist at the Kaiser Foundation, where he developed a personality test to help the authorities classify prisoners, and from there, Leary went on to become a lecturer at Harvard.

The "Leary Personality Test," as it was known, had attracted the attention of the chairman of the Dept. of Social Relations, Dr. Henry Murray, whose also experimented on Ted Kaczynski, the Unabomber. Murray's "Thematic Aptitude Test" was being used by the CIA, which then took up the "Leary Test." Ted Kaczynski was a student volunteer in the contracts that Harvard had with the Pentagon and CIA. Leary then went on to the Massachusetts Correctional Institute in Concord, and embarked on LSD and psilocybin experiments with prisoners as possible means for behavior modification. From there, Leary somehow managed to wind up in the country of Algeria, where Eldridge Cleaver, exiled information minister of the Black Panthers, had him put in jail, but the CIA helped spring Leary from jail.

USE OF PSYCHICS

Psychics have also been used by intelligence agencies. This means information obtained by paranormal means through extrasensory perception (ESP) or the use of psychic powers. The U.S. Intelligence Community (primarily the DIA) in the 1980s, spent millions of dollars investigating the feasibility of using psychics. Code-named Star Gate, the 10-year project was inspired by reports that the Soviets were using similar techniques. Police departments have also used psychics since the Jack the Ripper case, and in more modern times, with renowned psychic Jeanne Dixon and her prediction of the assassination of President Kennedy in 1963. Psychics have played a somewhat extensive role with crime fighting and national security. Psychics often use crystals in their investigations because they are believed to possess energies that are attuned with the paranormal world.

Another technique is dowsing, which is usually done with a pendulum over a map to locate missing people or objects. Different objects are used in dowsing, with some psychics preferring metal rods and others using wooden sticks much like someone searching for water or oil. Most psychics believe the accuracy of their information depends upon how understandable their spirit guide is, and often, this spirit guide is one of the victims of a murderer or someone who died with knowledge of the crime. A few psychics claim that a giant record of all the deceased exists in the netherworld, and it's all a matter of looking someone up. Visionary dreams are another source of psychic information, and these appear to be somewhat useful for geographic locations, like the site of a plane crash or what a catastrophe scene looks like. The term psychometrics is used by psychics for when something the victim owned, such as an article of clothing, is contacted (usually held to the forehead), and information about the owner is "sensed" from contact with that object. The famous psychic Uri Geller, who operated in the 1970s and 1980s became rich and famous for his ability to sense where undiscovered oil, coal, and diamond fields were located. Dorothy Allison assisted police with the Patty Hearst kidnapping in 1974 and the arrest of the Son of Sam in 1977. Renie Wiley established a police training school in Florida during the 1980s to train local police on how to work with psychics. Since the early 1990s, a group in California, calling themselves the Mobius group, consists of a team of 25 psychics who are ready to work on cases when called by the police. Psychic Michael Bromley, who has based his methods on Native American shamanism, has also been helping many police departments since the 1990s, especially with security at Olympic games.

Several American psychics were recruited and assigned to NSA headquarters in Ft. Meade in a joint NSA-CIA operation. The U.S. Navy also experimented with ship-to-shore telepathy using psychics stationed on submarines and ashore. There were some successes reported, such as the ability of psychics to predict the exact date of launchings of new enemy submarines and their missile complements. The DEA also reportedly took an interest in the program because it provided valuable information about drug trafficking routes. Despite these modest successes, the CIA shut down the program in 1995 after it was evaluated by outside consultants.

The report by consultants was entirely negative. In recent years, several psychics who allegedly were involved in these programs have come forward to tell their stories. Gerald O'Donnell (who maintains one of the websites listed below) claims to have worked for a European intelligence service. The most well-known former-CIA psychic is David Morehouse, author of the book *Psychic Warrior: Inside the CIA's Secret Program.* According to Morehouse, Operation Star Gate was part of much larger remote viewing experiments. The most secretive activity was Operation Grill Flame, which was at Ft. Meade and involved recruiting military volunteers to have their psychic powers tested. The tests of Operation Grill Flame involved hooking soldiers up to biofeedback devices and monitors to determine if they could "see" the contents of what's inside an envelope.

Apparently, seven soldiers out of thousands tested qualified for continued service in the project. These soldiers were called "viewers" and each of them was assigned a "monitor", or person that handled them. At first, the CIA used them for fairly passive things like getting inside the minds of engineers or military leaders overseas. In the initial stages, the CIA also took an interest in the ability of viewers to transcend time as well as space (apparently, remote viewing involves seeing the past as well as the future). Soon, however, the CIA required viewers to see things from the eyes of hostages being tortured or airline bombing victims on their way to a fiery crash. As can be expected, these horrific scenes had a mental deteriorative effect on the psychics. Many of the CIA's psychics needed counseling or therapy to keep up with the stress of their workload. Toward the end, the CIA tried getting the psychics to use their powers as weapons, to assassinate people from abroad and so forth. That was when almost all the psychics quit. Some of them tried to blow the whistle to Congress, but the whole matter was kept out of the news and the program was quickly shut down.

CONCLUSION: One can see the range of efforts that have been undertaken to make human, clandestine intelligence gathering more effective and efficient. Much of it has been unsavory, so to speak, but that is the history of it. HUMINT, or human intelligence, basically involves espionage activities, and it is a fact that enemy spies and enemy secrets have to be dealt with in human ways. Given the sorry history of trying to make HUMINT more sophisticated, it is likely that most agencies will seek to reduce their dependence on such sources, and turn to technical intelligence collection or open source exploitation. The dilemma will remain that there is no good substitute for an aggressive human intelligence collection system, but the problem is creating one in a manner consistent with constitutional principles and also in a manner which doesn't degrade women.

COUNTERINTELLIGENCE AND DATA COLLECTION

Counterintelligence (CI) is any effort to protect secrets, prevent an intelligence mechanism from being manipulated, and also to exploit the intelligence activities of another entity. It can be passive or active. Passive or defensive counterintelligence is called "security", and involves locating, screening, and identifying people, limiting their access to classified material, and instituting accounting systems to trace losses. Active counterintelligence is called "countermeasures", and involves specific protections using specific tactics such as neutralizing an enemy or putting them under surveillance. Covert action, or a covert operation, can be defined as anything falling between the extremes of diplomacy and war. *All covert action requires counterintelligence for protection.*

Counterintelligence also involves protection against assassination, kidnapping, espionage, and sabotage. Espionage, also called spying or running agents, involves access, infiltration, and penetration, and is probably best seen as a type of reconnaissance. Counterespionage is sometimes treated as synonymous with counterintelligence, but it is somewhat different in that the former is more aggressive. Counterespionage is primarily concerned with deception (sometimes called deception and denial) and counterintelligence is primarily concerned with monitoring. For example, counterespionage would try to stage fake accidents in which fake classified documents would fall into the hands of the enemy (in order to deceive them). It relies upon the skills of camouflage and forgery. Counterintelligence would normally try to keep the enemy's regular communication unaltered (for monitoring) to stay one step ahead of them, and to expose potential vulnerabilities that may be exploited later on.

Counterintelligence produces some of the most confusing disinformation in the world, and several nations play that game well, regularly producing a steady stream of deception that is allowed to be intercepted. The U.S., of course, is the leader at this (mainly thru leaks to the press), but it's interesting how other nations (who don't have a free press) operate. They often use their police agencies.

MAJOR NATIONS COUNTERINTELLIGENCE SERVICES

You'd be surprised how many so-called "allies" run counterintelligence operations against one another. Well, maybe not, since allies are likely to have slightly different vital interests, and are only "allies" as long as cooperation is to their advantage. In the meantime, they may be pursuing their own advantage in their own way.

ARGENTINA – A centralized National Intelligence Center (CNI) operates out of the Secretariat of State Intelligence (SIDE) with its own School of National Intelligence (ENI). Each branch of the military operates its own intelligence units. The police have two intelligence agencies in both the Policia Federal and the Gendarmeria Nacional.
AUSTRALIA – The Parliament, through its Joint Committee on Intelligence and National Crime Authority (NCA) oversee an Australian Secret Intelligence Service (ASIS), a Strategic Intelligence Branch (SPI), and a Counterterrorism Section (ICT). The military has a Defense Intelligence Organization (DIO) with a school of military intelligence (SMI). The Army has four intelligence agencies, including a Languages School (LANGS). The Navy has three agencies, including electronic intelligence units. The Royal Air Force has intelligence units. There are eleven different police agencies with intelligence functions.

CANADA – Two Oversight agencies (a Privy Council & a Review Committee) monitor the work of the two branches of military intelligence: communications (electronic surveillance) and national defense (human intelligence). There are three police intelligence agencies: the Royal Canadian Mounted Police (RCMP), the Criminal Intelligence Service Canada (CSIC), and the Canadian Security Intelligence Service (CSIS).

CHILE – A civilian centralized agency, the National Intelligence Directorate (DINA), operates as part of the National Information Center (CNI). The Military has a centralized Directorate of National Defense Intelligence (DIDN). The Ministry of Interior has a Directorate of Public Security and Information, and the police have the Investigations Police and the Carabineros.

CHINA – The Communist Party Central Committee controls the main Ministry of State Security (MSS), a Ministry of Public Security, the People's Liberation Army's Central Security Regiment (8341 Unit), a Second Military Department (military intelligence), and a Third Military Department (counterintelligence). The Chinese News Agency (Xinhua) is an intelligence agency, and so is the China Association for International Friendly Contacts.
ENGLAND – The two main agencies are the MI5 and MI6 (also called SIS for Secret Intelligence Service), each located in the Home Office and Foreign Office, respectively. The Home Office also contains Scotland Yard and the National Criminal Intelligence Service (NCIS). The Foreign Office also contains an electronic intelligence agency (the GCHQ). The military has a senior Defense Intelligence Staff (DIS), a Royal Air Force Joint Air Reconnaissance Intelligence Centre (JARIC), and a counterterrorism Strike Command. All are overseen by a Joint Intelligence Committee (JIC).

FRANCE – The Secretary of Defense oversees a Directorate for External Security (DGSE), a Directorate for Military Intelligence (DRM), and a Directorate for Protection & Security (DPSD). In addition, there's an Electronic Warfare and Intelligence Brigade (BRGE), an Information Systems

Security agency (SCSSI), and an Interministerial Office for Information (DISSI). The Air Force has an intelligence unit, as well as the Army an Air Reconnaissance Wing (54th Intelligence Wing). The French Foreign Ministry operates an Analysis and Forecasting Center as well as an agency for electronic interceptions (CNCIS). The French Interior Ministry contains four intelligence agencies; one Central, one Territorial, one for Republican Security, and one for the Judicial Police.

GERMANY – Pre-reunification agencies that are still active include the main organization located in the old West German Chancellor's office, the Federal Intelligence Service, or BND (Bundesnachrichtendienst). The former East German organization, the Stasi, began dismantling in 1990. The reunification government has two intelligence agencies: the Federal Office for Protection of the Constitution; and the Federal Office for Information Technology Security (economic intelligence and computer espionage). The military has three intelligence agencies: the ANBw, the AFMBw, and MAD (Militaerischer Abschirmdienst).

INDIA – A centralized Joint Intelligence Committee with its own Research and Analysis Wing (RAW) and Intelligence Bureau (IB) oversees intelligence agencies in the Ministry of External Affairs: the Joint Cipher Bureau, numerous Army intelligence units, an Air Force intelligence unit, and two Navy Intelligence units; in the Ministry of Home Affairs: a Central Bureau of Investigation (CBI), five specialized police agencies, including a counterterrorism Rapid Action Force (RAF) and an Industrial Security Force; in the Ministry of Finance, a centralized Economic Intelligence Council with at least five specialized agencies, including Revenue Intelligence (DGRI), a Narcotics Control Bureau (NCB), and Tax Evasion Units.
INDONESIA – There are three civilian intelligence agencies within the DPKN Council for the Enforcement of Security and Law: the KOPKAMTIB (Operational Command); the BAKORSTANAS (Coordinating Agency for National Stability); and BAKIN (Intelligence Coordinating Agency). There are numerous military intelligence agencies, the centralized ones being KASSPSPOL (Sociopolitical Affairs), BAIS (Strategic Intelligence), and OPSUS (Special Operations). The Army, Navy, and Air Force each have their own intelligence units. Both the People's Police and Civilian Militia have their own intelligence units, and the Attorney General's Office also has one.

IRAN – The most well-known central agency is in the Ministry of Security and is called SAVAK although there are at least three other fairly centralized intelligence agencies: the Ministry of Intelligence and Security (MOIS), a Joint Committee for Special Operations, and an organization called VEVAK. There's one military intelligence agency, and one civilian-run agency: Jerusalem Force, Guardians of the Islamic Revolution.
IRAQ (prewar) – A National Security Council oversees a Special Security Service (SSS), an Iraqi Intelligence Service (IIS), something called Project 858, Airforce Intelligence, Military Intelligence, and a General Security Service. There are also intelligence units in the Special Republican Guard (SRG) and Republican Guard (RG) as well as the group called Saddam's Martyrs.

ISRAEL – Three known intelligence agencies: the Mossad (foreign affairs), Shin Bet (internal affairs), and Aman (military intelligence). Of these three, Shin Bet works the most closely with police intelligence. There are also at least two intelligence agencies posing as educational institutions: the Bureau of Scientific Relations and the Center for Political Research.

MEXICO – There are about four intelligence agencies under the President's Office; one is the Center for Research on National Security (CISEN); and three of them have to do with crime – Special Prosecutor's Office for Crimes Against Health (FEADS), National Institute for Combating Drugs (INCD), and the Center for Drug Control Planning (CENDRO). The Attorney General's Office also operates about three intelligence agencies: the National Institute for Drug Trafficking, and units in the Federal Judicial Police (PJF) and Federal District Judicial Police (PJDF). The military has a centralized Second Section (S-2) and electronics intelligence unit (DGT), but the Navy has its own strong intelligence unit.

NEW ZEALAND – Parliament subsumes three agencies: the Intelligence and Security Committee (I&SC); the Security Intelligence Service (SIS); and the Government Communications Security Bureau (GCSB). The police have two agencies: a Criminal Intelligence Bureau (CIB) and a Financial Intelligence Unit (FIU). There's also a market (economic) intelligence unit located in the Department of Trade. New Zealand plays a significant role in IntelSat.

NIGERIA – A Provisional Ruling Council oversees the operations of three main intelligence agencies: the Nigerian Security Organization (NSO), the National Intelligence Agency (NIA), and the State Security Service (SSS). There are also intelligence units in the National Guard, the Ministry of Internal Affairs, and a Special Bodyguard Unit. The military has one, centralized intelligence agency called the Defense Intelligence Agency (DIA), and the police have two: a Federal Investigation and Intelligence Bureau (FIIB) and a National Drug Law Enforcement Agency.

NORTH KOREA – The President is the top man. The Korean Worker's Party Central Committee, the Central People's Committee, and the Political Security Dept. are the second-tier. The Korean Workers Party Central Committee (KWP) runs cadre (leaders) training schools which are responsible for producing and placing foreign espionage agents, including training for some world terrorist groups. The People's Committee oversees the Armed Forces, and most intelligence activities are located in a large special branch of the armed forces called the Special Purpose Forces (SPF). There's a large Naval Intelligence branch, with ships and subs used for electronic espionage. The Air Force is also involved in electronic intelligence. The Army handles weapons development in a series of underground tunnels.

PAKISTAN – A joint military-civilian Intelligence Bureau serves as a central agency while four military intelligence agencies operate independently along with two police intelligence agencies: the Federal Investigation Authority (FIA) and the Narcotics Control Division.

RUSSIA – The Security Council and Defense Council jointly oversee the civilian agencies, consisting of the Committee for State Security (KGB), the Foreign Intelligence Service (SVR), the Central Intelligence Service (CSR), the Federal Security Service (FSB), and the Federal Counterintelligence Service (FSK). In addition, there's a Federal Agency for Electronic Information (FAPSI) and a Presidential Security Service. Military agencies include the Main Intelligence Directorate (GRU), the Interlinked System for Recognizing Enemies (SOUD), and others. There are a number of police, civilian, and academic intelligence agencies in Russia.

SERBIA – Civilian agencies are located in the Ministry for Foreign Affairs (SMIP) and the Information and Documentation Service (SID). Military agencies include a centralized Counterintelligence Service (KOS), an Army Special Forces Intelligence Corps (Red Berets), and Navy and Air Force intelligence units. Police forces include a State Security Service (SDB), a Special Force Police (Red Berets), a Special Antiterrorist Force (SAJ), and a Special Police Unit (PJM). There are three civilian agencies: the Volunteer Guard ("Tigers"), the "Gray Wolves", and the "White Eagles".

SPAIN – The Ministry of Interior contains four intelligence agencies including the police organizations: a civilian Civil Guard, a national Police Corps, a Commissariat of Intelligence, and a Foreign Intelligence Brigade. The Ministry of Defense has a centralized intelligence center, and all three branches (Army, Air Force, Navy) have special intelligence sections.
TAIWAN – A National Security Council presides over Army, Navy, Air Force, and Coast Guard intelligence agencies, and there's also a National Security Bureau, all mostly military in nature. There are separate police intelligence agencies in the Ministries of Interior and Justice.

EXAMPLES OF COVERT OPERATIONS

Covert action is any activity carried out in a concealed or clandestine manner, primarily to make it difficult, if not impossible, to trace the activity back to the sponsoring intelligence agency. There is quite a bit of literature available on the topic, much of it critical and questioning whether covert action is a standard part of foreign policy or just an essential part of intelligence operations. Defenders of the need for covert action argue that it provides an intermediate step between failed diplomacy and outright war. Current law (the Hughes-Ryan Amendment to the Foreign Assistance Act of 1961) requires that the President deem any proposed covert action as important to national security.

Godson (1994) probably has the most popular book on the subject, although he combines covert action and counterintelligence, two very different intelligence disciplines. Covert action has been practiced by all Presidents, from Washington to Lincoln (Knott 1996). According to a 1948 National Security Council document, covert operations are defined as: "propaganda; economic warfare; preventive direct action, including sabotage, anti-sabotage, demolition and evacuation; and subversion against hostile states, including assistance to underground resistance movements, guerrillas and refugee liberation groups, and support of indigenous anti-communist elements in threatened countries of the free world." Here are some examples:

OPERATION AJAX (SHAH OF IRAN)

One of the first U.S. covert operations was to preserve the regime of the Shah of Iran, and keep the country from falling into Russian hands. Propping up the Shah proved to be quite difficult, for he was not well liked by his people. Through persuasion and payoffs, the CIA was able for many years to prevent the Iranian military from staging a coup. The CIA would even go so far as to stir things up a bit in the Middle East so Iran could rally around a common enemy. Whenever the Shah appeared in public (as he often did on trips), the CIA saw to it that for every anti-Shah protester, there was at least another pro-Shah protester. The Shah developed his own security service, called SAVAK, and although the CIA tried to develop a relationship with it, SAVAK had its own agenda, and frequently resorted to proactive assassination. The CIA was dissuaded by SAVAK from becoming involved with the rising tide of Islamic Revolutionary Forces in Iran until it was too late.

PANAMA

This pattern of the CIA being used, exploited, outfoxed, and downright manipulated by local security services would continue for some time, and indeed happened again in Panama with General Manuel Noriega. Throughout the 1970s and 1980s, the U.S. used Panama as a staging area for covert operations in Latin America and the Caribbean. The U.S. became so dependent on Noriega and the flow of communication going in and out of Panama that there was little the U.S. could do when Noriega became involved with drug dealers. Eventually, the U.S. had to take him down, but there were many antecedent attempts by the CIA to deal with the Noriega problem. Noriega had risen to power as an intelligence chief himself, and he proved to be a formidable adversary in cloak and dagger games.

BAY OF PIGS

Near the end of his term (1960), President Eisenhower told the CIA to prepare a plan to invade Cuba and overthrow Castro. The Kennedy administration, who inherited the plan, decided not to provide sufficient air cover when the 1,400 CIA guerillas trained in Guatemala landed on the beaches at the Bay of Pigs in Cuba. The invasion force never made it past the beach. They were supposed to take three beachheads, hold them for three days, hook up with 500 internally placed guerrillas who would join them, the rebellion would begin, and the whole country would rise up against Castro.

The Bay of Pigs disaster reverberated for many years. Stories had to be concocted about what happened, and the "mercenaries did it" story kind of stuck, although a few of the survivors who weren't cut down on the beach make it back to tell the real story. Some of these survivors remained on the CIA payroll, and were put to use by G. Gordon Liddy during the Watergate break-in. Others who were taken prisoner by Castro were released a couple of years later when the U.S. agreed to pay a $62 million ransom in medicine and food raised by U.S. corporations. It turned out that Castro's intelligence knew all along about the invasion. He had rounded up as many as 200,000 of his own people to prevent a revolution, and he had all sorts of military hardware on the beach -- tanks, artillery, and mines. One of the CIA's agents, a Cuban major, Florentino Azpillage, turned out to be a double agent, and was feeding the CIA disinformation as well as informing Castro of CIA plans. After the Bay of Pigs, Kennedy became more determined than ever to get Castro. He launched Operation Mongoose, a sabotage and insurgency subversion plan. They contaminated sugar being exported by Cuba and made numerous raids along the Cuban coast for many years, occasionally strafing any Cuban officials and Soviet advisors on shore. Interestingly, the American Mafia was also interested in assassinating Castro. The reason being that Castro had shut down the lucrative gambling casinos in Cuba. On about the same day that the Mafia hit squad was to sneak into Cuba (with CIA assistance), President Kennedy was assassinated in Dallas. The coincidence would trigger suspicion that a vengeful Castro played a part in Kennedy's murder, or some other deal was cut between the Mafia and Castro.

CHILE

In 1964, the CIA spent millions of dollars to support the election of Chile's Christian Democratic Party. It would have to spend more than that in subsequent years because the popular candidate was Socialist Party leader Salvador Allende Gossens who was committed to land reform and nationalization of industry (particularly U.S. owned copper mining companies). In 1970, the CIA went all-out to stop the Allende regime from coming to power. They engaged in propaganda campaigns, electioneering, vote fraud, control of the press, radio, films, pamphlets, posters, graffiti, and direct mailings. They tried bribing every important leader in the nation with $250,000 each. Nixon authorized the CIA to coordinate a military coup and explore the possibilities of economic warfare, creating a financial and economic panic. The CIA recruited a couple of generals who agreed to stage a coup, and provided them with weapons and ammunition for an assassination squad. Despite several blunders in which the plotters assassinated themselves, general Pinochet's coup was eventually successful in 1973. Allende was shot dead while in bed with his mistress in the Presidential Palace. The cover story was that he shot himself, but Allende was not the only one to die -- over 25,000 Chileans died in the bloody coup. A series of CIA-supported assassinations of remaining supporters of the old regime took place until 1976. The U.S. would support the Pinochet government for many years to come.

MUNICH WORLD GAMES

In 1972, terrorist members of the Black September organization (a spin off of the PLO) seized 11 Israeli athletes in the Olympic Village. They demanded the release of over 200 Arabs from Israeli prisons. German authorities cooperated with the hostage takers by making an escape plane available. Israeli Prime Minister Golda Meir and Defense Minister Moshe Dyan called in a secret hit squad of the MOSSAD. The Mossad not only quickly took out the terrorist hostage takers, but every other member, friend, or relative of this particular spin off group, no matter where they were in the world, all simultaneously at the same time. It was a spectacular, worldwide, planned execution.

AFGHANISTAN

In 1979, the Russians grew tired of their old puppet government in Afghanistan, and decided to stage a coup in order to put somebody else in power besides Amin, whom they didn't like. The KGB-led operation was a blatant example of "wet affairs" carried out by Directorate S of Department 8 of the KGB. They infiltrated the Presidential palace cooking staff, and poisoned the food and drink for several days. All that did was kill off the President's extensive staff of taste testers. On Christmas Day, 1979, the Russians had had enough, and sent two armored columns right up to the door of the Presidential Palace. The KGB Alpha Squad commandos, dressed in Afghan uniforms, made it look like a coup, killing Amin and his mistress in the palace.

PRIVATE MILITARY FORCES

It's not well-known, but there are number of corporations who can be hired to perform mercenary-type actions. These groups are most frequently used as an alternative to U.N. peacekeeper troops.

Globalpolicy.org maintains a list of links to them, and articles about them. Private military firms (PMFs) have been a tool for covert and clandestine action for years, although some of these firms, like MPRI, are anything but covert and consist of former Pentagon officers. PMFs are operating on a global scale every day, and some governments of some countries (most commonly in Africa) regularly hire mercenary forces as the only protection they need or want. An increasing number of Western governments are turning to mercenary troops because they are reluctant to send in their own troops. The problem, however, is that sex rings, deals with dictators, misused military training and tragic accidents sometimes result from use of this secretive industry, and it's a $2 trillion a year industry. Sometimes, they do some good, but morality isn't something a PMF is known for. Singer (2003) does an excellent job of fairly reviewing PMFs, and not just focusing on the role they played in Sierra Leone, but as many areas of the world where they are known to operate.

ESPIONAGE AND TRADECRAFT

The Intelligence Community operates on the basis of CODE WORDS for just about everything. There is a technical distinction between a code word and a nickname. A code word is usually a single, five-letter word selected from a list contained in a document known as JANAP 299 (Joint Army, Navy, Air Force Publication). A code word always is assigned a classified meaning. A nickname usually consists of two words and is assigned an unclassified meaning.

TOP SECRET UMBRA, for example, indicates that information about the operation with the code word "umbra" is top secret. Employees may have a nickname for this operation like "spoke wheel" which implies that it's got something to do with transportation, and may or may not remind the employee of the cover story; in this case, the possible use of bicycle tires for something. Often, the nickname implies something the exact opposite of the real operation: SKYBORNE for an underseas operation, e.g., or WATERLOG for an space operation. Sometimes, four-letter code words are used, like GYRO, for instance. Whenever you see a four letter code word, this usually means that the information it refers to was obtained from intercepted communications by top officials from foreign countries. Other four-letter code words refer to mail openings and information obtained from foreign books. Classified documents are often labeled with all the associated code words; like TOP SECRET UMBRA GAMMA GYRO SKYBORNE WATERLOG. Each word may have a different security classification requirement. In this case, the employee would have to have the security clearance for each level. A clearance for GAMMA might not suffice for WATERLOG, e.g. This has resulted in the commonly-seen whiteout or blackout through certain sentences in reports, because the most classified material has been made unreadable.

TRADECRAFT GLOSSARY OF TERMS

BLIND DATE -- A meeting between an unknown intelligence officer and an agent, usually of separate governments, at a place of one or the other's choosing.
BLOWBACK -- A deception planted abroad to mislead people in other countries, but then coming back to the originating country through public media channels, intended to deceive one's own government as well.

CLOAK AND DAGGER -- The traditional game played by spies and spy agencies, compared to the game of "cops and robbers" played by law enforcement. The word "cloak" means to hide and the term "dagger" means to kill. It technically refers to the art of making somebody disappear without a trace, but has become slang for any kind of traditional spy operation.

COUNTERxxxxxx -- 3 basic types: COUNTERespionage, which protects classified materials or agents from being "collected" by feeding the enemy false information;

COUNTERintelligence, which protects people, organizations, or installations from assassination, infiltration, or sabotage as well as disrupting foreign intelligence gathering by acting on enemy plans

before they can be carried out; and COUNTERmeasure, a means of countering a specific enemy threat, such as in electronic countermeasures.
COVER -- A protective guise used by a person, organization, or installation to conceal true affiliation or sponsorship. If great care is used to construct a totally false identity, this is called a LEGEND. If it's just a light cover which consists of just a business card, address, and phone number to withstand a less than thorough inquiry, this is called being BACKSTOPPED.

DEAD DROP -- An exchange of information without the two operatives meeting face to face. Notes and materials, for example, are left in an airport locker or a tree stump.
DEFECTOR -- The most common way in which spies are recruited and/or prosecuted for espionage. A defector repudiates his or her country and comes forward to the enemy (walk-in) in possession of information of value. A defector-in-place is one who denounces their country but does not leave. In such cases, the person becomes a "mole", remaining in place where they can funnel information of value.
DISINFORMATION -- The creation and dissemination of false information to injure a target. A typical practice would involve forging false documents and leaking copies to the press, for example. Another technique would involve using scientifically produced propaganda to influence citizens under the spell of another power. In times of war, disinformation consists of leaking false war plans and the like.

DOUBLE AGENT -- Anyone working for more than one intelligence service, providing information or disinformation about each agency to the other.

HONEY TRAP -- A term used to describe the use of sex to blackmail or pressure someone into participating in an intelligence operation, or create a situation in which the target can be blackmailed at a later time. *see Raven and Swallow.*

ILLEGAL -- An agent performing intelligence work in a foreign country who passes him or herself off as not really a citizen of the country they are from; a standard recruitment ploy. Also, a term for anyone under deep cover of a legend.

INFORMER -- A person who knowingly or unknowingly provides information or intelligence.
MOLE -- A high-level agent who is hidden within an enemy organization who normally only provides information or intelligence in cases where it would be extremely valuable.
PRODUCT -- The final result of an intelligence analysis produced for the consumer or user; may be oral, written, or graphic.

RATFUCKER -- A term used to describe an infiltrator who has been planted in an organization.

RAVEN -- Name for a male agent used to seduce females or other males.
SLEEPER -- A technique used (extensively by the Germans and Russians) by intelligence services to plant an immigrant into a foreign country, and then activate him or her at a later time when needed.

SUCKING DRY -- A term (originally Russian in origin) to describe the process of debriefing an agent after he or she comes home from a mission.

SWALLOW -- Name for a female agent used to seduce men or other females.
TURN -- Turning somebody is to transform an agent into a double agent. The most common methods are: threat of execution; and blackmail, often involving sex. Sometimes, patriotism and money are used.

WET WORK -- A term used to describe intelligence operations involving murder or assassination.

ESPIONAGE AS SPYING

Espionage is spying. To historians, it's the world's second oldest profession. To criminologists, it's a crime against government. To practitioners, it's the exercise of tradecraft in the Great Game of governments. Tradecraft is any technique or trick that substantiates a view of the work as a skilled occupation or craft. The most common operational skills for espionage work involve surveillance and running agents. At the barest minimum, there are only three basic requirements of an espionage operation: (1) a way for the agent to get a hold of someone in case of emergency; (2) a way for the intelligence officer to get information from the agent; and (3) a way to pay the agent. Those who do the actual spying are called agents. Their supervisors are called officers.

Spying is not considered a crime against government by the government that employs them, only by the government upon which they're spying. If the spy is a double agent or spies against their own country, then they're guilty of treason or being a traitor. Treason is a rather loose word that involves aiding or abetting your country's enemies, and is often tossed around with cases of ideological dissent or protest. Spies are always at risk of becoming traitors. In the U.S., the crime of espionage is covered by Title 18, Chapter 37, Sections 792-799 of the U.S. Code, and includes the following offenses:

- Harboring or concealing an enemy of the United States
- Gathering, transmitting, or losing defense information
- Gathering or delivering defense information to aid a foreign government
- Photographing or sketching defense installations
- Using aircraft to photograph defense installations
- Publication or sale of photographs of defense installations
- Disclosure of classified information
- Violation of Intelligence Community regulations

One of the most frequently cited definitions of espionage is "the act of obtaining, delivering, transmitting, communicating, or receiving information about the national defense with an intent, or reason to believe, that the information may be used to the injury of the United States or to the advantage of any foreign nation" (Office of the National Counterintelligence Executive).

THE HISTORY OF ESPIONAGE

Although some trace the origins of spying to the time of Moses in the Bible, many experts point out the contributions of the ancient spy master, Sun Tzu (500 BC) who said there were five classes of spies:

(1) Local spies - recruited agents who are inhabitants of an enemy territory
(2) Moles - recruited agents who are officials in an enemy government
(3) Double agents - recruited enemy spies who are used for your own purposes
(4) Doomed spies - spies used for deception purposes and expendable
(5) Surviving spies - spies who produce intelligence on your enemies

Sun Tzu said - "When all five kinds of spy are hard at work, none can discover the secret system, or "divine manipulation of the threads." It is the commander's most precious resource. More intimate relations ought to be maintained with your spies than with your own army. None should be more liberally rewarded. In no other field should greater secrecy be preserved. Sun Tzu went on to say:

(1) Spies must possess a certain intuitive sagacity
(2) They should be managed with benevolence and straight forwardness
(3) Spies are ingenious, so make certain of the truth of their reports
(4) Be subtle, but use your spies for every kind of warfare
(5) All spies are expendable

Whether the object be to crush an enemy, storm a territory, or kill an official, it is always necessary to begin by finding out the names of the attendants, the aides-de-camp, and door-keepers and sentries of the official in question. Such assistants make up the playing field for spying because it's where your recruits and replacements come from.

When the enemy's spies come to spy on you, they must be sought out, tempted with bribes, led away and comfortably housed. Thus they will become double agents and available for our service. It is through the information brought by the double agent that we are able to acquire and employ local and inward spies. It is owing to his information, again, that we can cause the doomed spy to carry false tidings to the enemy.

Lastly, it is by his information that the surviving spy can be used on appointed occasions. The end and aim of spying in all its five varieties is knowledge of the enemy; and this knowledge can only be derived, in the first instance, from the double agent . Hence it is essential that the double agent be treated with the utmost liberality.

Sun Tzu also stressed the necessity of counterintelligence. An intelligence service is a two-edged sword. It is of no use unless it can be trusted beyond any shadow of doubt, but the fact that it is trusted leaves it dangerously vulnerable to its compromise by enemy agents. An intelligence service reduces the mass of data, often contradictory, straining for a leader's attention: instead of ten versions of the nature of a problem, the leader has just one. This minimizes confusion, but it allows your enemies an easy and single target for penetration and deception.

It is in the nature of counter-intelligence that you never quite know what you're doing. This can make it appear silly or childish. Outsiders sometimes suggest that the melodramatic intrigue of the intelligence business be junked entirely; but even if all the spies were let go, and all the field stations closed down, counterintelligence would necessarily remain, for reason that a vulnerable intelligence service is worse than none at all. Once that point has been conceded, all the rest of the clandestine enterprise comes tumbling after, because *the best way to protect one's service is to penetrate the enemy's.* The game of espionage will always go on because even allies will spy upon another, not just enemies.

American history traces spying to the American Revolution. Espionage, counterintelligence, and covert action have been important tools of U.S. political leaders since the founding of the Republic. During the Revolutionary War, General George Washington and patriots such as Benjamin Franklin and John Jay directed a broad range of clandestine operations that helped the colonies win independence. They ran networks of agents and double agents, employed deceptions against the British army, launched sabotage operations and paramilitary raids, used codes and ciphers, and disseminated propaganda and disinformation to influence foreign governments. America's founders all agreed with General Washington that "the necessity of procuring good intelligence is apparent and need not be further argued." Nathan Hale, of course, was America's most famous spy, and everyone knows his famous quote in 1776 when he was about to be hanged: "I only regret that I have but one life to lose for my country."

Presidents in the early republic were actively involved in intelligence activities--especially covert actions. In his first State of the Union message, Washington requested that Congress establish a "secret service fund" for clandestine activities. Within two years, the fund represented over ten percent of the federal budget. Thomas Jefferson drew on it to finance the United State's first covert attempt to topple a foreign government, one of the Barbary Pirate states, in 1804-05 (it failed). James Madison employed agents of influence and clandestine paramilitary forces to acquire territory in the Florida region from Spain during 1810-12. Several presidents dispatched undercover agents on espionage missions overseas. One spy, disguised as a Turk, obtained a copy of a treaty between the Ottoman Empire and France. Also during this period, Congress tried to exercise oversight of the secret fund, but President James K. Polk rebuffed the lawmakers, saying "The experience of every nation on earth has demonstrated that emergencies may arise in which it becomes absolutely necessary ... to make expenditures, the very object of which would be defeated by publicity." (The Polk Doctrine)

In the Civil War both Union and Confederacy extensively engaged in clandestine activities. They acquired intelligence from clandestine agents, military scouts, captured documents, intercepted mail, decoded telegrams, newspapers, and interrogations of prisoners and deserters. Neither side had a formal, high-level military intelligence service. The North's principal spymasters were Allen Pinkerton and Lafayette Baker--who both proved most effective at counterespionage--and military officers George Sharpe and Grenville Dodge. The Confederacy had a loose array of secret services that collected intelligence and conducted sabotage and other covert actions. Three of the South's most celebrated agents were women--Rose Greenhow, Belle Boyd, and Antonia Ford. In 1864, Confederate operatives tried to organize antiwar elements in Indiana, Illinois, and Ohio into a secession movement, and set a rash of fires in New York City in an attempt to burn it down. Northern and Southern agents in Europe engaged in propaganda and secret commercial activities. Overall, the North was more effective at espionage and counterintelligence, while the South had more success at covert action. The hard won expertise and organization built up during the Civil War was demobilized and dispersed after the war.

The United States' first formal, permanent intelligence organizations were formed in the 1880s: the Office of Naval Intelligence (the oldest, established in 1882) and the Army Military Intelligence Division. They posted attachés in several major European cities principally for open-source collection. When the Spanish-American War broke out in 1898, the attachés switched to espionage. They created informant rings and ran reconnaissance operations to learn about Spanish military intentions and capabilities--most importantly, the location of the Spanish Navy. One US military officer used well-placed sources he had recruited in the Western Union telegraph office in Havana to intercept communications between Madrid and Spanish commanders in Cuba. The U.S. Secret Service--in charge of domestic counterintelligence during the war--broke up a Spanish spy ring based in Montreal that planned to infiltrate the U.S. Army.

When World War I started in 1914, the United States' ability to collect foreign intelligence had shrunk drastically because of budget cuts and bureaucratic reorganizations. The State Department began small scale operations against the Central Powers in 1916, but not until the United States declared war on Germany in 1917 did Army and Navy intelligence receive infusions of personnel and money. The most significant advance for U.S. intelligence during the war was the establishment of a permanent communications security (COMSEC) agency in the Army-the forerunner of the National Security Agency. Meanwhile, the Secret Service and military counterintelligence aggressively interdicted numerous German covert actions inside the United States that included psychological warfare, political and economic operations, and dozens of acts of sabotage against firms and factories supplying munitions for the war effort. The Justice Department's Bureau of Investigation (forerunner of the FBI) took on a counterintelligence role as early as 1916, and Congress passed the first federal espionage law in 1917.

Between the wars, American intelligence officers concentrated on codebreaking and counterintelligence operations against Germany and Japan. Notwithstanding Secretary of State Henry Stimson's dictum that "gentlemen do not read each other's mail," by 1941, the United States had built a world class military intelligence capability, consisting of the "Black Chamber", or Section 8 (Cryptography) of Military Intelligence, under Herbert Yardley (Black Chamber being an old French phrase for any government agency that opens and reads mail), the Army's Signal Intelligence Service (SIS which later became the 2nd Signal Service Battalion responsible for SIGINT) under William Friedman, and several Navy Intelligence Agencies (a cryptography unit and a photography interpretation unit were the most prominent additions to ONI). Working backward from intercepts, Friedman's team cracked the Japanese Purple cipher. During the 1930s, the FBI launched an extremely effective counterintelligence attack on German and Japanese espionage and sabotage operations in the Western Hemisphere, infiltrating many networks and arresting dozens of agents.

The Bureau had less success against Soviet efforts to penetrate U.S. governmental and economic institutions.

As American entered World War II in 1941, President Franklin Roosevelt created the country's first peacetime, civilian intelligence agency--the Office of the Coordinator of Information--to organize the activities of several agencies. Soon after, however, the United States suffered its most costly intelligence disaster when the Japanese bombed Pearl Harbor. That failure -- a result of analytical misconceptions, collection gaps, bureaucratic confusion, and careful Japanese denial and deception measures -- led to the establishment of a larger and more diversified intelligence agency in 1942, the Office of Strategic Services (OSS), forerunner to the CIA.

The OSS (sometimes referred to as Oh So Secret) contained a number of people who went on to become great Americans, like Allen Dulles, Arthur Schlesinger, Arthur Goldberg, Gene Fodor (originator of the Fudor guides to foreign countries), filmmaker John Ford, and cookbook author Julia Childs. The OSS essentially set up offices around the world and recruited informants from the other side until they had a network of agents. Later, the OSS would begin participating in joint military operations, specializing in parachuting behind enemy lines to hook up with the underground. They were as likely to be involved in traditional espionage as they were in unconventional sabotage, subversion, and guerrilla activities. In the Pacific, before the start of the Vietnam War, it was the OSS who first set foot in that country to try and help out the French and the HoChi Minh government. The OSS officially became the CIA in 1947.

From the beginning, the CIA (as an independent organization as proposed by Truman) was resented by military intelligence, the FBI, and the press. It was dubbed a "Super Gestapo" agency with vaguely worded authorization to do anything "relating to national security." Their principal function, however, was to coordinate and correlate the intelligence collected by other agencies, and they gained power essentially by forcing the military and FBI to cooperate.

Fairly quickly, the CIA got many of its agents into "attache" positions at embassies around the world. They then, along with assistance from the military, took an interest in photo reconnaissance as well as ground stations to intercept communications. They were able to put all this in place in two years, by 1949. Soon, the CIA was controlling secret flights. By 1951, the CIA was a model for the world. Everyone, especially Israel, was convinced they needed to consolidate intelligence into one agency like the U.S. did.

By 1991, when it was evident the Cold War was coming to an end, there was much debate about the continued need for espionage and agencies like the CIA. People argued that the world was still a dangerous place, filled with risks for "low intensity warfare". Many of America's spy agencies restructured their operations to work with military agencies, to monitor terrorism and drug trafficking more closely, and to focus on protecting U.S. economic rather than political interests. In light of Scowcroft Commission Reports since 2001, intelligence agencies are still restructuring.

FAMOUS INTELLIGENCE FAILURES

One of the most well-known failures was OPERATION BARBAROSSA, a deep penetration mission that took Russian intelligence by surprise. In 1941, Hitler staged an operation invading Russia with 3 million German troops who poured in from the Arctic Circle to the Black Sea. The Russians had plenty of information about troop movements eastward by the Germans, and couldn't help but notice the increased number of aerial surveillance flights Hitler was sending over Russia. Besides, U.S. intelligence had already told Russian intelligence of Hitler's plans to invade Russia back in 1940. Russia was convinced that similar intelligence leaked to them by the British was really counterintelligence. Hitler played two deception schemes. He first explained the buildup of his troops on the Russian border as being there for training purposes, to prepare for the invasion of England (Operation Sea Lion). He then explained them as being contingency forces against possible hostile Soviet action. Stalin bought all this because his own intelligence led him to believe that Hitler would not dare try to fight a war on two fronts. This case is instructive because it details the problems associated with sharing intelligence and counterintelligence.

Another famous failure was PEARL HARBOR, again in 1941, when a task force of 33 Japanese ships stationed themselves 200 miles north of Oahu and launched two successive waves of air attack (350 planes). By the time the attack was over, the U.S. had lost 18 warships, 200 airplanes, and over 2,000 personnel. The case of Pearl Harbor is regarded as the worst case of intelligence failure in history. No intelligence agency had prepared a report for the possibility of an attack there, although everyone talked about it. Naval intelligence (ONI) did not even have a minimal amount of strategic or tactical intelligence. They thought Japan would attack Thailand about that time of year. The problem was that America lacked Human Intelligence (HUMINT) on Japan. The U.S. had a few geisha girls on the payroll, but no agents in the Japanese elite. The U.S. had broken the Japanese code, but what they were intercepting was just diplomatic and espionage information (movement of spies), nothing of the nature of military plans, and anyway, they changed their codes a day before the attack. Japanese radio transmissions deceived the Americans into thinking the task force was assembling for training maneuvers. This case stands as a testimony to the need for collecting human intelligence, and not relying upon technology so much.

FAMOUS INTELLIGENCE SUCCESSES

In 1962, photographs from U-2 overflights had been monitoring the military buildup in Cuba, and to the United States, the difference between defensive weapons and offensive ones was a dramatic one. Soviet ships had been arriving at night, unloading big cargo, and leaving behind troops. Specifically, the Cubans were assembling IRBMs (Intermediate Range Ballistic Missiles). The incident was known as the Cuban Missile Crisis (October 15-28, 1962), and it showcased the best of American technology: NSA intercept; photo reconnaissance; and intelligence analysis. The CIA produced several reports, all along the lines of titles like "The Military Buildup in Cuba". HUMINT was also coming in regarding Soviet ships headed for Cuba, and the size of the missiles being installed. The eighty-foot long missiles were identified as SS-5s by American intelligence, and from photo interpretation, it could be seen that two sites were already operational and could carry 5 megaton warheads (although no nuclear warheads were identified, nuclear storage bunkers were). The CIA started producing reports entitled "Possible Soviet Reactions to Certain U.S. Courses of Action in Cuba", and a blockade was recommended. The Soviets were confronted in the world press about their activities, and Khrushchev and Kennedy squared off against one another with threats. Eventually, the Russians backed off, and removed all the missiles from Cuba. They even packed up the launch pads. Naval intelligence monitored the removal process. This case shows the effectiveness of intelligence agencies in a time of crisis.

In 1967, Israel started the SIX-DAY WAR, a battle with Egypt, Jordan, and Syria. Israeli intelligence predicted an attack by Egypt on Israel the next day, so the Israelis timed their attack to take place right before the Egyptian troops woke up that morning. It was a devastating blow, wiping out almost all of the Egyptian air force. Israeli intelligence based their hunch on the fact that Nasser had ordered the return of Egyptian forces from Yemen and the entire mobilization of the Egyptian military. Israeli ground forces secured the Sinai peninsula, and its air force also struck Jordanian and Syrian planes while they were still on the ground. The chief Israeli spy was Ali al-Atfi, personal masseur to Nassar and his aide, Anwar Sadat. Because the Israelis had broken the Egyptian code, during the war they were able to issue false commands to Egyptian tanks, ordering them to circle around the desert harmlessly.

In 1973, an Egyptian attack triggered the YOM KIPPUR WAR, a battle between Israel, Egypt, and Syria. It was a war that made extensive use of intelligence operations, most importantly the first use of satellite hookups to guide fighters to their targets, and the use of deceptive SIGINT by the Israelis to deceive the Soviets that the U.S. was ready to step in if the Russians intervened.

Going back to 1968, one of the most famous cases of good intelligence analysis involved the Russian Invasion of Czechoslovakia. Russia typically installed so many bugging devices, wiretaps, and spies in their satellite countries that they could easily tell when it appeared likely that the communist leaders were about to lose faith. The Russians would then storm in with their tanks to reassure people that they were indeed a satellite nation. This pattern of control was used successfully by the Soviet Union for many years, keeping countries like Romania and Bulgaria in check. The only nation in which the CIA even thought about trying counterintelligence with this Russian pattern was in Albania.

TRAINING TO BECOME A SPY

Almost all nations operate schools, institutes, or academies to train their espionage agents. In the late 19th and early 20th century, the largest known spy school in the world was operated by the German Secret Service in Berlin, itself a city that had always been an espionage hub for different countries. Berlin's role as a spy center continues to this day, although Munich and Hamburg are close seconds.

Hitler's rise to power from 1920-1933 is associated with his consolidation of Germany's intelligence apparatus. He started out with a gang of street fighters and thugs (the SA – initials for Sturmbtielung – "storm detachment"), then an elite personal guard (the SS – initials for Schutzstaffel – "protection detachment"). An intelligence unit grew out of the SS (the SD – Sicherheitsdienst – "security service") with duties to discover the enemies of National Socialism. The SS was also a secret police and terror organization that ran concentration camps. Out of the SD grew an espionage unit (the RSHA – Reichssicherheitshauptant – Reich Security Organization) which infiltrated most of the world with a vast network of spies, agents, and informants. The RSHA worked closely with the Gestapo (acronym for Geheime Staatspolizei – secret state police), and was, in fact, organizationally under the RSHA, but since the RSHA was so involved overseas, the Gestapo acted with impunity at home. The RSHA operated two major spy schools, one in The Hague and one in Belgrade. The German military war machine also had intelligence units that worked with the SD, but these mostly involved expertise in cipher and coding. By contrast, RSHA agents were trained in topography, trigonometry, engineering, disguises, deception, and seduction.

Although Russia has a history of spying going back to 1565 with Ivan the Terrible, it was the first country to respond to Germany by creating its own spy schools. The Russian intelligence apparatus consisted mainly of the NKVD, MVD, and KGB, who each ran their own spy schools. The NKVD (Narodnyy Komisariat Vnutrennnikh Del – People's Commissariat for Internal Affairs) were Stalin's secret police, and in many ways, the world's most efficient internal security and repression agency. The NKVD was responsible for both domestic and foreign intelligence, and grew so large that it eventually took over the Gulag – a vast constellation of prison camps spread across the Soviet state. The MVD (Ministry of Internal Affairs) was the name given to the NKVD in 1946 after some of its foreign intelligence operations were spun off into Smersh (a "Death to Spies" agency), the MGB (Ministry of State Security – military counterespionage), and K1 (economic intelligence). The KGB (Committee for State Security) was established in 1954 to undertake any and all state security and foreign intelligence operations not assigned to another agency.

Russian spy schools include the main one at Pushkin, near Moscow (which also trained terrorists), and the Military-Diplomatic Academy in Moscow itself which poses as a research university but is a KGB training school. All in all, there are dozens of Russian spy schools throughout Russia and the world.

England has had deep roots in espionage, mostly in detection of treason, domestic surveillance, and cypher codes (in fact, the British Cypher School – GC&CS – Government Code & Cypher School – is well known as the birthplace of cryptography). Foreign espionage and British spying really had its start with the American Revolution (1775), and evolved rather haphazardly up to 1909 when two agencies were created in the Secret Service Bureau of the War Office. Those two agencies were the

Home Section (called "MI5" for the fifth branch of Military Intelligence) and the Foreign Section (designated "MI6"). The MI5 became famous for its counterespionage successes (catching German spies), and today operates as a counterterrorism agency. The MI6 operates today by sending agents into foreign lands on dangerous missions. It is not known exactly where British spy schools are located, presumably on military bases.

The United States operates several formal spy schools. The CIA trains its agents at Camp Peary, Virginia, and the FBI at its academy in Quantico, Virginia. Both agencies use a variety of military schools, including the Polygraph School at Fort McClellan, Alabama. The Army, Navy, and Air Force all offer intelligence curricula at their respective war colleges and postgraduate schools. All military and non-military intelligence services make use of private educational institutes, like the Defense Language School in Monterey, California, for foreign language training. Other agency training school locations, like those of the NSA, are classified.

CAREERS IN SPYING

Job titles come in many forms. At the top of the hierarchy are officers in the various intelligence agencies. An intelligence *officer* position is usually an executive position, which means they get to stay home at headquarters most of the time. Underneath this career level are junior officers who are known as *legals* or *illegals*. A legal junior officer is one sent overseas under cover as a diplomat or attache. Illegal junior officers have more deceptive covers, usually as a business or sales person. Among the junior officer ranks, there is usually one *spy master*, who acts as the head controller. Almost all junior officers stationed abroad serve as *case officers*, or controllers.

They are expected to recruit and run agents who come from the host country, setting up what is known as "assets", or a spy ring. The people who work in various supporting capacities at the home office are called *analysts*.

The persons recruited in the host country to work as assets, spies, or traitors are called agents. One of the defining characteristics of all agents is that they're expendable. There are different types of agents: penetration agents, or *moles*, who work under deep cover and are well-placed; *double agents*, who work for both sides; *cut-outs*, who act as intermediaries or mercenaries; *feedback agents*, who provide running commentary on political events, and may consist of *stay-behinds*, which are those left in place by retreating troops in wartime; and all-purpose *agents of influence*, who are provided with little direction and operate fairly independently.

INTERNATIONAL INTELLIGENCE AND SECURITY SERVICES (SELECTED)

ARGENTINA

Presidency of the Nation
Presidencia de la Nación
SIDE Secretariat of State Intelligence
CNI National Intelligence Center
ENI School of National Intelligence
Ministry of the Interior
Ministerio del Interior
Federal Police of Argentina
Policía Federal Argentina
Gendarmería Nacional Argentina

AUSTRALIA

Parliamentary Joint Committee on the
Australian Security Intelligence Organization
Parliamentary Joint Committee on the
National Crime Authority (NCA)

Office of National Assessments (ONA)
Department of Foreign Affairs and Trade
Australian Secret Intelligence Service (ASIS)
International Security Division
Strategic Policy and Intelligence Branch (SPI)
Intelligence and Counter-Terrorism Policy Section (ICT)
Department of Defence
Strategy and Intelligence (S&I) Program
Defense Intelligence Organisation (DIO)
Defence Security Branch (DSB)

BELGIUM

Ministry of Justice
Veiligheid van de Staat (SV) (Dutch) or
Surete de l'Etat (SE) (French)
(Federal intelligence and security agency)
Ministry of Defense
Algemene Dienst Inlichtingen en Veiligheid (ADIV) (Dutch) or
Service General de Renseignement (SGR) (French)
(Military intelligence and security agency)

CANADA

Privy Council Office (PCO)
Security Intelligence Review Committee (SIRC)
Department of National Defence and Canadian Forces
Intelligence Branch
Communications Security Establishment (CSE)
Solicitor General
Canadian Security Intelligence Service (CSIS)
Royal Canadian Mounted Police (RCMP)
Criminal Intelligence Service Canada (CSIC)

CHILE*

National Intelligence Directorate
(Dirección Nacional de Inteligencia—DINA)
National Information Center
(Centro Nacional de Información—CNI)
Ministry of Defense
Directorate of National Defense Intelligence
(Dirección de Inteligencia de la Defensa Nacional— DIDN) Army
Navy
Air Force Forces of Order and Public Security
Carabineros (Carabineros de Chile)
Investigations Police

Ministry of Interior
Directorate of Public Security and Information
(Dirección de Seguridad Pública e Informaciones)
* Some services now under review

CHINA

Communist Party Central Committee
Ministry of State Security [MSS]
Guojia Anquan Bu [Guoanbu]
Ministry of Public Security
People's Armed Police
People's Liberation Army
8341 Unit - Central Security Regiment
General Staff Department
1st Department [Intelligence]
3rd Department
4th Department
General Political Department
International Liaison Department
[China Association for International Friendly Contacts]

Military Intelligence
PLA Navy

Naval Intelligence
PLA Air Force

CUBA

Communist Party of Cuba
America Department (DA)
Ministry of the Interior
Directorate General of Intelligence (DGI)
Ministry of Revolutionary Armed Forces
Military Counterintelligence Department
Security Bureau
Ministry of Foreign Affairs [MOFA - Gaimusho]
Intelligence and Analysis Bureau
Ministry of Justice (Homusho)
Public Security Investigation Agency [Koancho]
Wasp Network/Red Ovispa - Cuba - Florida-eastern US seaboard-based Cuban spy network.

FRANCE

SGDN - National Defense General Secretariat
Secretariat General de la Defense Nationale
Strategic Affairs Delegation
DGSE - General Directorate for External Security
Direction Generale de la Securite Exterieure (previously SDECE)
SDECE - France - Service de Documentation Exterieure et de Contra-espionage 1945-1981.
DRM - Directorate of Military Intelligence
Direction du Renseignement Militaire

DPSD - Directorate for Defense Protection and Security
Direction de la Protection et de la Securite de la Defense
BRGE - Intelligence and Electronic Warfare Brigade
Brigade de Renseignement et de Guerre Electronique
SCSSI - Central Service for Information System Security
Service central de la sécurité des systèmes d'informations

DISSI - Interministerial Office for Information Systems Security Service
Delegation Interministerielle a la Securite des Systemes

HUNGARY

National Security Office
Nemzetbiztons·gi Hivatal
INDIA
Joint Intelligence Committee (JIC)
Research and Analysis Wing [RAW]
Intelligence Bureau (IB)
Ministry of External Affairs
Defense Ministry
Joint Cipher Bureau
Directorate of Military Intelligence
Directorate of Air Intelligence
Directorate of Naval Intelligence

IRAN

Ministry of Security [SAVAK]

Joint Committee for Special Operations
Ministry of Intelligence and Security [MOIS]
Vezarat-e Ettela'at va Amniat-e Keshvar VEVAK
Jerusalem Force, Guardians of the Islamic Revolution
Qods, Pasdaran-Enghelab-Islami, (Military Intelligence)

IRAQ

National Security Council/Bureau
[Maktab al-Amn al-Qawmi]

Special Security Committee
Special Security Service - SSS
[Jihaz al-Himaya al-Khas / Al Amn al-Khas

Iraqi Intelligence Service - IIS
General Intelligence Directorate/
Department - GID
[Jihaz al-Mukhabarat al-Amma]

Project 858
Al Hadi Project

Air Force
Military Intelligence
[Al-Istikhbarat al-Askariyya]

Military Security Service
[Al Amn al-Askariyya]

General Security Service
[Mudiriyat al-Amn al-Amma]

Special Republican Guard (SRG)
Republican Guard (RG)
Saddam's Martyrs ["Men of Sacrifice"]

Fedayeen Saddam

ISRAEL

Mossad - Institute for Intelligence and Special Tasks
ha-Mossad le-Modiin ule-Tafkidim Meyuhadim
Shin Bet - General Security Service
Sherut ha-Bitachon ha-Klali (Prime Minister control)
Aman - Military Intelligence
Agaf ha-Modi'in
Lekem -Bureau of Scientific Relations
Leshkat Kesher Madao
Center for Political Research
IDF - Israeli Defence Force - mainly military
but with threads to MOSSAD.

ITALY

SISDe Intelligence and Democratic Security Service

JAPAN

Security Council
Cabinet Research Office [Naicho]
Defense Agency / Japan Self-Defense Force (Bôeichô)
Defence Intelligence Office DIO [Jouhou Honbu]
Defense Intelligence Headquarters DIH Chobetsu
Ground Self-Defense Force [Nihon Rikujyo Jieitai]
Intelligence Office
Maritime Self-Defense Force [Nihon Kaijyo Jieitai]
Fleet Intelligence Command
Air Self-Defense Force [Nihon Koku Jieitai]
Intelligence Division
Tactical Reconnaissance Group
National Police Safety Commission (NPSC)
National Police Agency [NPA - Keisatsuchô]

JORDAN

General Intelligence Department

LITHUANIA

STT Special Investigations Service
Organizacija Kovai su Kurupcija

LUXEMBOURG

Ministry of State
Service de Renseignements de l'Etat (SRDE) (French)
(National intelligence agency)
Haute Commissariat de la Securite Exterieure (HCSE) (French)
(High commission for foreign security)
Ministry of Defense
2ieme Bureau de l'Armee (French)
(Military intelligence and security agency)

NETHERLANDS

Binnenlandse Veiligheidsdienst (BVD)
(National intelligence and security agency)
Ministry of Defense
Militaire Inlichtingendienst (MID)
(Military intelligence agency)
Koninklijke Marechaussee, Bijzondere Dienst en Veiligheid (Kmar/BD&V)
(Military police, Special section for intelligence and security) Veiligshield Dienst)

NORTH KOREA

Central Committee Korean Workers Party
Cabinet General Intelligence Bureau (Departments)
Liaison Department
Research Department for External Intelligence (RDEI)
General Association of Korean Residents in Japan (Chosen Soren)
General Staff Department
Reconnaissance Bureau
State Security Department
Ministry of Public Security

NEW ZEALAND

Parliament
Intelligence and Security Committee (I&SC)
Security Intelligence Service (SIS)
Government Communications Security Bureau [GCSB]S
New Zealand Police
Criminal Intelligence Bureau [CIB]
Financial Intelligence Unit [FIU]

NIGERIA

Provisional Ruling Council (PRC)
Nigerian Security Organisation (NSO)
National Intelligence Agency (NIA)
State Security Service (SSS)
National Guard
Special Bodyguard Unit
Defence Intelligence Agency (DIA)
Ministry of Internal Affairs
Nigeria Police Force (NPF)
Federal Investigation and Intelligence Bureau (FIIB)
National Drug Law Enforcement Agency

NORWAY

Control Committee for the Intelligence and Security Services
Kontrollutvalget for overvåkings- og sikkerhetstjenesten
Police Intelligence Service
Politiets overvåkingstjeneste
Joint Defense Security Service
Forsvarets sikkerhetstjeneste
Joint Defense Intelligence Service
Forsvarets etterretningstjeneste

PAKISTAN

Intelligence Bureau (IB)
Ehtesab [Accountability] Bureau
Ministry of Defense
Directorate of Inter-Services Intelligence (ISI)
Directorate of Inter-Services Public Relations
Army
Military Intelligence (MI)
Special Services Group (SSG)
Surveyor General of Pakistan [SGP]
Ministry of Interior
Federal Investigation Authority (FIA)

PERU

SIN* - The Security Service (*under review)

POLAND

Special Services (KSS) of the Sejm
Military Intelligence Organisation (WSI)
Office of State Protection (UOP)

ROMANIA

Ministry of Interior
Department of State Security
(Departamentul Securitatii Statului - Securitate)

Department of External Information (Departamentul de Informatii Extern . . DIE)
Directorate for Military Intelligence
(Directia de Informatii a Armatei—DIA)
Office of the President
Romanian Intelligence Service [SRI]
Guard and Protection Service (SPP)
Ministry of Foreign Aff airs
Foreign Intelligence Service (SIE)
Ministry of National Defence
Special Telecommunications Service
Counter-intelligence Directorate
Intelligence Directorate of the Army
Ministry of Internal Affairs
Intelligence Directorate - UM 0215
Ministry of Justice
General Police Inspectorate
Operative Surveillance and Intelligence Directorate
General Directorate of Penitentiaries (DGP)
Independent Operative Service (SIO)

SOUTH AFRICA

National Intelligence Co-ordinating Committee [NICOC]
South African Secret Service [SASS]
National Defence Force Intelligence Division
National Intelligence Agency [NIA]
South African Police Service [SAPS]

SOUTH KOREA

National Intelligence Service
Agency for National Security Planning (ANSP)
Korean Central Intelligence Agency (KCIA)
National Police Agency
Presidential Security Service (PSS)
National Security Council (NSC)
Ministry of National Defense
Defense Security Command

SPAIN

Ministry of Defense
Higher Defense Intelligence Center
(Centro Superior de Informacion de la Defensa—CESID)
General Headquarters of Information
Army
Staff Second Section
Air Force
Staff Second Section
Navy
Ministry of Interior
Ministerio del Interior
State Security Secretariat

Dirección General de Administración de la Seguridad
Civil Guard
Guardia Civil
Information Service
National Police Corps
Cuerpo Nacional de Policía
General Commissariat of Intelligence
Comisaría General de Información
Foreign Intelligence Brigade

SERBIA*

Council for Security
Federal Ministry for Foreign Affairs
Savezno Ministarstvo za Inostrane Poslove [SMIP]
Information and Documentation Service
Sluzba Informaitvna u Dokumenti [SID]
Ministry of Defense
Ground Forces
General Staff Security Directorate
Counterintelligence Service
Kontraobavesajna Sluzba [KOS]
Military Police
Special Forces Corps [Red Berets]
Navy
Air Force
Ministry of Interior
Ministarstvo Unutrasnjih Poslova [MUP]
State Security Service
Sluzba Drzavne Bezbednosti [SDB]
Public Security Service
Sluzba Javne Bezbednosti [SJB]
Special Force Police [Red Berets]
Specijalnih Jedinica Policije [SJP]
Special Anti-terrorist Force
Specijalna Antiteroristicka Jedinica [SAJ]
Special Police Unit (PJM)
* Some services reorganising

SWEDEN

SISD Swedish Intelligence and Security Directorate

TURKEY

MIT Secret Service of Turkey (Domestic)

UKRAINE

Intelligence Directorate
The Security Service of Ukraine (SSU)
(Sluzhba Bespeky Ukrayiny (SBU)

ZIMBABWE

CIO Central Intelligence Organisation

RUSSIA

Special Dedicated Section

Committee for State Security [KGB] (now defunct)
Komitet Gosudarstvennoi Bezopasnosti

Foreign Intelligence Service (SVR)
Sluzhba Vneshney Razvedki

Central Intelligence Service [CSR]
Centralnaya Sluzhbza Razvedky

Federal Security Service (FSB - replaces KGB)
Federal'naya Sluzhba Bezopasnosti

Federal Counterintelligence Service (FSK)
Federal'naya Sluzhba Kontr-razvedky

Federal Agency for Government Communications & Information (FAPSI) [surveillance]
Federal'naya Agenstvo Pravitel'stvennoy Svayazi i Informatsii

State Technical Commission [GosTekhKomissiya]
Gosudarstvennii Tekhnologiam Komissiya

Federal Protective Service (FSO)
Federal'naya Sluzhba Okhrani

Main Administration for the Protection of the Russian Federation (GUO)
Glavnoye Upravlenie Okhrani Rossiiskoy Federatsii

Presidential Security Service [PSB]
Prezidentskaya Sluzhba Bezopasnosti

Federal Border Service [FPS]
Federal'naya Pogranichnaya Sluzhba

Security Ministry of Russia (MBR)
Ministerstvo Bezopasnosti Ruskii

Ministry of Defence (MOD)

Main Intelligence Directorate (GRU)
Glavnoye Razvedyvatelnoye Upravlenie (GRU)

Ministry of Internal Affairs (MVD)
Ministerstvo Vnutrennikh Del

GERMANY

Special Dedicated Section

Federal Intelligence Service [BND]
Bundesnachrichtendienst

Defence Ministry

Office of Intelligence of the Federal Armed Forces [ANBw]
Amt für Nachrichtenwesen der Bundeswehr
Office for Radio Monitoring of the Federal Armed Forces [AFMBw] (Amt für Fernmeldwesen Bundeswehr)
Military Security Service [MAD]
Militaerischer Abschirmdienst

Interior MInistry

Federal Office for the Protection of the Constitution [BfV]
Bundesamt für Verfassungsschutz
State Office for the Protection of the Constitution [LfV]
Landesamt für Verfassungsschutz
Federal Office for Information Technology Security [BSI]
Bundesamt für Sicherheit in der Informationstechnik

UNITED KINGDOM

Special Dedicated Section

Joint Intelligence Committee (JIC)Joint Air Reconnaissance Intelligence Centre (JARIC)
Strike Command

Foreign and Commonwealth Office (FCO)
MI6 Secret Intelligence Service (SIS)

TOS/AC (MI6/SIS) - UK - Technical and Operations Support, Agent Comms
Government Communications Headquarters (GCHQ)

Home Secretary
MI5 Security Service
MI5 - t-branch UK -investigates terrorism in Britain
National Criminal Intelligence Service (NCIS)
Metropolitan Police [Scotland Yard]
UK Intelligence Messaging Network (UKIMN)Defence Intelligence Staff [DIS]
Royal Air Force
Ministry of Defence
Defence Advisory Committee (D-Notice)
JARIC Joint Air Reconnaisance Intelligence Centre

SAS Special Air Service
SBS Special Boat Service
CRWW - UK - Counter Revolutionary Warfare Wing - based in Hereford trains MI6 agents in various techniques
12th Military Intelligence Company - UK - unit formed with merger of several smaller intelligence organisations including the FRU

UNITED STATES OF AMERICA

Special Dedicated Section

Executive Office of the President
National Security Council
Senior Director for Intelligence Programs
National Coordinator for Security,
Infrastructure Protection and Counter-Terrorism
President's Foreign Intelligence Advisory Board
Office of National Drug Control Policy

Chemical and Biological Defense Information Analysis Center [CBIAC]
Critical Infrastructure Assurance Office [CIAO]
Interagency Operational Security Support Staff
National Infrastructure Protection Center [NIPC]
National Interagency Counterdrug Institute (NICI)
National Response Team
Security Policy Board
Technical Support Working Group

Director of Central Intelligence
National Intelligence Council [NIC]
Community Management Staff [CMS]
Arms Control Intelligence Staff (ACIS)
Counterintelligence Center [CIC]
DCI Center for Security Evaluation [CSE]
DCI Crime and Narcotics Center [CNC]
DCI Counterterrorist Center (CTC)
DCI Nonproliferation Center [NPC]
National Counterintelligence Center [NACIC]
Central Intelligence Agency (CIA)
National Security Agency (NSA)
National Reconnaissance Office (NRO)
National Imagery and Mapping Agency
The United States Defense Department
Assistant to the Secretary for Intelligence Oversight
Under Secretary of Defense for Policy
Office of Emergency Preparedness Policy
Assistant Secretary of Defense for C3I
Defense Dissemination Program Office (DDPO)
Defense Support Program Office
Defense Intelligence Agency
Central MASINT Office
Defense Information Systems Agency
National Communications System

Defense Advanced Research Projects Agency
Defense Protective Service
Defense Security Service
US Special Operations Command

Army

Army Deputy Chief of Staff for Intelligence

Intelligence and Security Command
US Army Intelligence Center
Office of the Surgeon General - NBC Defense
Chemical, Biological Defense Command
United States Army Medical Research Institute of Infectious Diseases (USAMRIID)
United States Army Medical Research Institute of Chemical Defense (USAMRICD)
Military Police Corps

Navy

Office of Naval Intelligence

Naval Security Group Command
Naval Criminal Investigative Service

Marine Corps

Marine Corps Intelligence Activity

Chemical, Biological Incident Response Force

Air Force

Air Force Technical Applications Center
Air Intelligence Agency
9th Reconnaissance Wing
55th Wing
93rd Air Control Wing
Air Force Office of Special Investigations
Air Force National Security Emergency Preparedness Agency
Air Force Security Forces [Security Police]

Various United States Federal Agencies

Commerce Department

CIAO - Critical Infrastructure Assurance Office
NIST - National Institute of Standards and Technology
NIST - Computer Security Division

Energy Department

Non-Proliferation and National Security
Nuclear Emergency Support Team

Health and Human Services Department

PHS - Public Health Service
PHS/OEP - Office of Emergency Preparedness
PHS/OEP - Metropolitan Medical Strike Teams

Justice Department

Office of the Inspector General
OSLDPS - Office for State and Local Domestic Preparedness Support
OIPR - Office of Intelligence Policy and Review
FBI - Federal Bureau of Investigation
NIPC - National Infrastructure Protection Center
NDPO - National Domestic Preparedness Office
DEST - Domestic Emergency Support Team
DEA - Drug Enforcement Administration
NDIC - National Drug Intelligence Center
USNCB - U.S. National Central Bureau

State Department

INR - Bureau of Intelligence & Research
INL - Bureau for International Narcotics and Law Enforcement Affairs
S/CT - Office of the Coordinator for Counterterrorism
FEST - Federal Emergency Support Team
DS - Bureau of Diplomatic Security

Transportation Department

USCG - US Coast Guard
USCG - National Response Center
USCG - Intelligence Coordination Center
FAA - Federal Aviation Administration
FAA/CAS - Civil Aviation Security

Treasury Department

Office of Intelligence Support
Office of the Under Secretary (Enforcement)
ATF - Bureau of Alcohol, Tobacco and Firearms
USCS - US Customs Service
USSS - US Secret Service
FINCEN - Financial Crimes Enforcement
OFAC - Office of Foreign Asset Control
FLETC - Federal Law Enforcement Training Center

General Services Administration

Federal Protective Service
(OIS) Office of Information Security

General Services Administration
Federal Protective Service
(OIS) Office of Information Security
National Archives and Records Administration
Information Security Oversight Office

WORLDWIDE ORGANISATIONS

INTERPOL

International Criminal Police Organization
OECD Financial Action Task Force
on Money Laundering (FATF)

USEFUL WEBSITE ADDRESSES

www.nato.int **- NATO** (numerous fields)

www.shape.nato.int - **SHAPE**

www.un.org - **UNITED NATIONS**

www.mod.uk - **Ministry of Defence**

www.dera.mod.uk - **Defence Evaluation & Research Agency**

www.gchq.gov.uk - **Government Communications HQ**

www.mi5.gov.uk - **MI5 The Security Service**

www.nsa.gov - **National Security Agency**

www.fbi.gov - **Federal Bureau of Investigation**

www.cia.gov - **Central Intelligence Agency**

www.odci.gov - **Director of Central Intelligence**

www.defencelink.mil/pubs/pentagon - **The Pentagon**

www.defencelink.mil - **US Department of Defence**

www.whitehouse.gov/nsc - **National Security Council**

www.nro.odci.gov - **National Reconnaisance Office**

www.dia/mil - **Defence Intelligence Agency**

www.nima.mil - **National Imagery & Mapping Agency**

www.odci.gov/ic/ni.html - **Office of Naval Intelligence**

www.af.mil - **United States Air Force**

PRIMARY IMAGING AND IMAGING ANALYSIS ORGANIZATIONS

AcronymService Name BranchCountry
AMAN Agaf Modiin (IntelligenceIntelligence Corps, Israel
Branch of Israeli DefenseLong-Distance
Forces) Observation Units,
and Air Force
Intelligence

CIA Central Intelligence AgencyIntelligenceUS
Directorate,
National Photo
Interpretation
Center, and Air
Force Intelligence

DMA Defense Mapping Agency Defense Intelligence US
Agency

ID Intelligence DivisionAir Self-Defense Japan
Forces

JARICJoint Air Reconnaissance - UK
Intelligence Centre

MID Military Intelligence- China
Department

Nibetsu Ground Self-Defense Forces Investigation Japan
Division,
Second Section, &
101st Survey
Battalion

NRO National Reconnaissance Under Secratary of US
Organization the Air Force, Air
Force Intelligence

PRIMARY COVERT ACTION SERVICES

Acronym Service NameBranchCountry
BND Bundesnacrichtendienst Division II West
(Federal Intelligence Clandestine Germany
Service) Technical
Operations

CIA Central Intelligence AgencyOperations USA

CSIS Canadian Security Counter- Canada
Intelligence Service Intelligence

DGSE Direction Generale deInformation France
la Securite Exterieure Directorate,
Action Service

HSR Hlavni Sprava Rozvedky Directorate B Czecho.
(Main Directorate of the Second Department
General Staff)

ILD International LiaisonReports to the China
DepartmentCCP Secratariat

MAD Militarischer ? West
Abschirmdienst Germany
(Military Screen Service)

Mossad Mossad Letafkidim Directorate forIsrael
Meouychadim (Central Political Action
Institute for Intelligence and Liaison (Special
and Special Duties)Operations Division)

SIS Secret Intelligence ServiceArea ControllerUK

SISDEServizio Informazioni? Italy
Generali e Sicurezza
(Service for Information and
Democratic Security)

SISMIServizio perle Informazioni? Italy
e la Sicurezza Militaire
(Service for Information and
Military Security)

UFWD United Front Work Department Reports to the China
CCP Secratariat

MILITARY INTELLIGENCE COLLECTION ORGANIZATIONS

Acronym Service NameBranchCountry
AMAN Agaf Modiin Under General Staff Israel
(Intelligence Branch)

ANFB Amt Fur Nachrictenwesen derUnder the Office West

Bundeswehr (Federal ArmedMinister of Defense Germany
Forces Intelligence Office) Intelligence Section

DIA Defense Intelligence AgencyOperations US
Directorate and
Directorate for
Foreign
Intelligence

HVA Hauptverwaltung Aufklerung MfS E. Germany

MND Militairsche Nachrictendienst Minister of Interior E. Germany
(Military Intelligence
Service)

Nibetsu Ground Self-Defense Forces Investigation Japan
Division,
Second Section

RUMNOIntelligence Division, - Bulgaria
Ministry of National Defense

VKF/II General Staff Directorate II - Hungary

WSW Wojska Sluzby Wewnetraznej Ministry of Defense Poland
Military Internal Service
tasked with Military
Counterintelligence

Z-II ZARZAD-II, Second General Staff Poland
Directorate of the General
Staff, tasked with Military
Intelligence Collection

ZSGS Zpravodajska Sprava General Staff Czecho.
Generalniko Stabu
(Intelligence Directorate
of the General Staff)

PRIMARY SECURITY SCREENING (BACKGROUND CHECKS) ORGANIZATIONS

Acronym Service NameBranchCountry
CSIS Canadian Security Security Screening Canada
Intelligence Service Branch

BfV Bundesamt fur Secrets Protection West
Verfassungsschutz Section Germany
(Federal Office for the
Protection of the
Constitution)

FBI Federal Bureau of ? US
Investigation

DGSE Direction Generale deSecurity France

la Securite Exterieure Branch

MAD Militarischer ? West
Abschirmdienst Germany
(Military Screen Service)

SISDEServizio Informazioni? Italy
Generali e Sicurezza
(Service for Information and
Democratic Security)

SS Security Service ? UK

PRINCIPLE COUNTER TERRORISM ORGANIZATIONS

Acronym Service NameBranchCountry
BfV Bundesamt fur Counterespionage West
Verfassungsschutz Section Germany
(Federal Office for the GSG-9
Protection of the
Constitution)

DELTASpecial Forces Detachment Army Special Forces US
Delta

CT CounterTerrorism Federal Bureau of US
CT Investigation

MAD Militarischer ? West
Abschirmdienst Germany

Mossad Mossad Letafkidim Directorate forIsrael
Meouychadim (Central Political Action
Institute for Intelligence and Liaison, and
and Special Duties)"The Unit"

SAS Special Air Service - UK

SISDEServizio Informazioni? Italy
Generali e Sicurezza
(Service for Information and
Democratic Security)

SISMIServizio perle InformazioniFirst Division Italy
E la Sicurezza Militaire
(Service for Information and
Military Security)

PRIMARY ECONOMIC INTELLIGENCE GATHERING AND ANALYSIS ORGANIZATIONS

Acronym Service NameBranchCountry
AMANAgaf Modiin Under General Staff Israel
(Intelligence Branch) Production Branch

BND BundesnacrichtendienstDivision I West Germany

(Federal Intelligence Service) Collection of Information

BNR Bureau of Intelligence and US Department of US
Research State

CIA Central Intelligence Agency Operations
Directorate, and the
Domestic Collection
Division (travelers)

DIA Defense Intelligence Agency Research Directorate US

DIS Defense Intelligence Staff Directorat of UK
Economic Intelligence

FIB Foreign Intelligence Bureau Economic IntelligenceCanada
Division

IARPB Information Analysis, Under Ministry of Japan
Research and Planning Bureau Foreign Affairs

MITIMinistry of International MITI itself, and Japan
Trade and Industry JETRO (Japanese
External Trade
Organization)

Mfs Ministerium fur Minister of Interior East
Staatssicherheit (Ministry Germany
for State Security)

Mossad Mossad LetafkidimDirectorate for Israel
Meouychadim (Central Collection
Institute for Intelligence
and Special Duties)

NSA National Security Agency US

OFS Office of Foreign Statistics Foreign Ministry Italy

RG Direction de Renseignement Under the Ministry France
(General Intelligence of the Interior
Directorate)

RI Research Institutes Party Research Off., China
various offices and
research institutes,
and colleges

RPPC Research and Political- Israel
Planning Center

FOREIGN ORGANIZATIONS RELATED TO STRATEGIC INTELLIGENCE

ADIO (Australian Defence Intelligence Organisation)
ADSD (Australian Defence Signals Directorate)
IGIS (Australian Inspector-General of Intelligence and Security)
ASIS (Australian Secret Intelligence Service)
ASIO (Australian Security Intelligence Organisation)
ONA (Australian Office of National Assessments)
PJCAAD (Parliamentary Joint Committee on the ASIO, ASIS, and DSD)
BFCO (British Foreign and Commonwealth Office)
MI-5 (British Security Service)
CCSE (Canadian Communications Security Establishment) [Commissioner's Site][Annual Reports]
CFIBA (Canadian Forces Intelligence Branch Association) [Intelligence Notebook]
The Canadian Intelligence Community: Control and Accountability
Canadian Intelligence Resource Centre (unofficial)
CSIC (Canadian Security and Intelligence Community) (or local pdf format)
CSIS (Canadian Security Intelligence Service)
CSIS Public Reports (several annual reports available)
SIRC (Canadian Security Intelligence Review Committee)
AIVD (Dutch General Intelligence and Security Service (Algemene Inlichtingen- en Veiligheidsdienst, formerly BVD) Annual Report, 1998 (BVD), 2001-(BVD), 2002 (AIVD) local pdf format)
IS (Intelligence Stratégique - unofficial site in French)
BfV (German Bundesamt fuer Verfassungsschutz / Counterintel)
BND (German Bundesnachrichtendienst)
MAD (German Militärischer Abschirmdienst)
NSO (Hungarian National Security Office)
SISDe (Italian Intelligence and Democratic Security Service)
GID (Jordanian General Intelligence Department)
GCSB (New Zealand Government Communications Security Bureau)
NZ-SONS (New Zealand: "Securing Our Nation's Safety" 2000)
AW (Polish Foreign Intelligence Agency) (also in English)
ABW (Polish Internal Security Agency)
SIS (Portuguese Security and Information Service)
AGENTURA (Russian Language Site on Intelligence; some pages in English)
FSB (Russian Intelligence)
SVR (Russian Foreign Intelligence)
ANSP (South Korean Intelligence -- unofficial)
CESID (Spanish Intelligence)
SISD (Swedish Intelligence and Security Directorate)
MIT (Turkish National Intelligence Organization)
NIM (United Kingdom National Intelligence Machinery)
GCHQ (United Kingdom Government Communications Headquarters)
CESG (United Kingdom Communications-Electronics Security Group)

ORGANIZATIONS RELATED TO STRATEGIC INTELLIGENCE

AAA (Air America Association)
AFCEA (The Armed Forces Communications-Electronics Association)
AFIO (Association of Former Intelligence Officers)
AI (Africa Intelligence)
AIPIO (Australian Institute of Professional Intelligence Officers)
BEAIF (Bulgarian Euro-Atlantic Intelligence Forum)
CASIS (Canadian Association for Security and Intelligence Studies)

CICENTRE (Center for Counterintelligence and Security Studies)
CIP (Center for International Policy: Intelligence Reform Program)
CONET (Numbers Stations Around the World) Also, the project booklet
CRYPTOME (On-line archival site, via JYA/Urban Deadline)
CSP (Center for Security Policy)
FASIRP (Federation of American Scientists Intelligence Resource Program)
IF (Intelligence Forum: Academic Discussion Group on Intelligence)
IIHA (International Intelligence History Association)
INT-ONLINE (Intelligence Online -- Newsletter Index)
IRSN (International Relations and Security Network)
ISS (Intelligence Studies Section of the International Studies Association)
IWP (Institute of World Politics, Graduate School of Statecraft and National Security)
Kim-Spy (Kim-Software Corporation Intelligence Page)
MASTA (Measurement and Signals Technology Association)
MCCIA (Marine Corps Counterintelligence Association)
NCMS (National Classification Management Society)
NSArchives (National Security Archives)
NCVA (U.S. Naval Cryptologic Veterans Association)
NSG (Naval Security Group Alumni)
NISA (Netherlands Intelligence Studies Association)
OLIN (Online Intelligence Project -- OSINT around the world)
OSS (Open Source Solutions)
PDA (Project on Defense Alternatives - Intelligence Issues page)
SECINT (UK Security and Intelligence Studies Group)
SPOOKS (The Spooks' Newsletter - Numbers Stations around the world)
USIC Guide (Document Service Center, Columbia University Library)
64 Baker Street (Women of the S.O.E.)

BASIC INTELLIGENCE TERMS

ACCESS AGENT	a talent spotter, performs reconnaissance for recruiters.
ACORN	slang for someone who is performing an intelligence function.
ACTION DIRECTE	an underground group in France.
AGENT	a person under the control of an intelligence agency or security service.
AGENT-OF-INFLUENCE	a deep-cover agent with influence among the members of a target group.
AGENT PROVOCATEUR	a deep-cover agent who feigns enthusiastic support while tempting the target to incriminate himself/herself through action or words .
AIS	Argentina's intelligence agency.
AL AMN AL-KHAS	Iraq's security service.
AMAN	one of Israel's intelligence agencies.
AMERIKA	underground metaphor for a fascist USA remeniscent of Nazi Germany.
ANALYSIS	drawing conclusions about raw information by assessing its significance and by collating it with other information.
ASALA	underground group in Armenia.
ASIO	Australian Security Intelligence Organization.
ASIS	Australian Secret Intelligence Service, a department of ASIO.
ASSAULTER	a member of a SWAT team responsible for making a forced entry.
ASSET	an agent.
AUM SHRINKYO	underground group in Japan with expertise in germ and chemical warfaire.
AVB	Hungary's security service, the Allami Vedelmi Batosag.

BACKSTOP	an arrangement between two persons for the express purpose of substantiating a cover story or alibi.
BAG JOB	surreptitious entry, break and enter.
BAKIN	Indonesia's security service.
BATF	a US security service, the Bureau of Alcohol, Tobacco, and Firearms.
BETTY BUREAU	FBI slang for a female support person who has worked for the FBI her entire career.
BfV	Germany's security service, the Bundesamt fir Verfassungsschutz.
BIOGRAPHICAL LEVERAGE	blackmail info.
BLACK-FLAGGED	an agent or intelligence officer who is to be interrogated and summarily shot if apprehended.
BLIND DATE	the first meeting with an unknown person.
BLACK PROPOGANDA	a smear campaign, usually consisting of character assassination.
BLOWBACK	unexpected negative consequences of spying activity.
BLOWFISH	a mathematical algorithm for computer encryption of text that purportedly can only be cracked by brute force if the passphrase is unknown.
BLOWN	detected.
BLUE-ON-BLUE	friendly fire, inadvertent hostile engagement between allies.
BND	Germany's intelligence agency, the Bundesnachrichtendienst. Literally translated as the Federal News Agency.
BOX	slang for Britain's security service, MI.5.
BREVITY CODES	a system of code-words used by members of a surveillance team.
BRICK AGENT	an FBI agent who works inside a field office. Also see STREET AGENT.
BRUSH CONTACT	a clandestine, momentary contact between two agents who are passing information, documents, or equipment.
BRUSH PASS	same as brush contact.
BSS	Belgium's security service
BUCAR	an FBI car.
BUG-ON-A-CHIP	slang for USA's Clipper chip.
BUPO	Switzerland's security service.
BURNT	burned, completed exposed. See BLOWN.
BVD	Netherlands' security service.
CALL-UP	a police term meaning a situation where a SWAT team has deployed.
CANNON	a thief who steals back the inducement offered by the spies to an informant, defector, etc.
CARIBINIERI	Italy's federal antiterrorist police.
CASE OFFICER	operations officer, controller.
CBI	India's security service.
CHASE CAR	a security detail or bodyguard vehicle that follows the subject.
CHEATING	command of the target from *in front of* the target during floating box surveillance. See also COMMAND OF THE TARGET.
CHENG PAO K'O	China's intelligence agency.
CHICKEN FEED	low grade information fed through a double agent to one's adversary with the intention of building the credibility of the double agent.
CHOBETSU	One of Japan's security services.
CIA	a US intelligence agency.
CNT	an acronym for crisis negotiation team. CNTs are used by police in situations involving hostage-takers or barricaded suspects. The name CNT is a misnomer
their true role is not to negotiate, but	

rather to obtain intelligence to facilitate an assault by the SWAT team, and to distract the suspect to divert his attention from the coming assault.	
COMINT	acronym for communications intelligence.
COMM	a small note or other written communication from an underground organization or one of its members. They are typically written on cigarette wrappers, chewing gum wrappers, etc.
COMMAND OF THE TARGET	active visual observation of the subject of the surveillance operation. Used during pedestrian and vehicle surveillance. See also CHEATING and FLOATING BOX.
COMMANDO	a civilian, military, or paramilitary combat group using irregular tactics. Commando can refer to an individual, a cell, a squad, or the organization as a whole.
COMMIT	a surveillance operative performing the commit function is watching a location to determine the direction that the target takes (or "commits" to).
COMPROMISED	breached security status.
CONG AN BO	Vietnam's security service.
CONSUMER	a person or an organization on an intelligence agency's distribution list. Also see PRODUCT.
COOKED	a mixture of genuine and fake material provided via a double agent to one's adversary.
COORDINATION DE LA SECURITE DU TERRITOIRE	Algeria's security service.
COUNTERESPIONAGE	activities designed to impede the efforts of hostile intelligence agencies engaged in espionage against one's own nation, allies, and citizens.
COUNTERINTELLIGENCE	activities designed to impede or thwart the efforts of hostile intelligence agencies attempting to penetrate or compromise one's own intelligence agency.
COUSINS	slang for CIA.
COVER	persona, profession, purpose, activity, fictitious image maintained by an undercover operative.
COVERT ACTION AGENT	a spy who works to reorient an entire nation's politics in favor of his country.
CS GAS	a form of tear gas, full name ortho-chlorobenzalmalanonitrile, used by cops, SWAT teams, and the military.
CSE	Canada's sigint intelligence agency, Communications Security Establishment. http://www.cse.dnd.ca/
CSIS	Canada's security service.
CUT-OUT	a go-between used to preserve the safety or anonymity of the principals. Same as LETTERBOX.
COURIER	delivers documents, money, etc.
DAM	France's military intelligence agency.
DANGLE	a spy who poses as a walk-in to penetrate the other side. Also see WALK-IN.
DARPA	Defense Advanced Research Projects Agency (USA).
DATA RECOVERY	bureaucrat-talk for the backdoor built into *all* US-exported crypto software since 1998.
DCSS	Denmark's security service.
DDIS	Denmark's intelligence agency.
DEAD DROP	a physical location where communications, documents, or equipment is covertly placed for another person to collect without direct contact between the parties.
DEAD-LETTER BOX	same as dead drop.
DEAD-LETTER DROP	same as dead drop.
DECOY	distracts adversary's attention.

DEEP-COVER AGENT	permanent cover.
DEFECTOR	a person who has renounced his/her country of citizenship.
DGI	Cuba's intelligence agency.
DGSE	France's intelligence agency.
DIA	a US intelligence agency, the Defense Intelligence Agency.
DIRTY TRICKS	covert sabotage carried out by a security service or intelligence agency, ranging from pranks to assassination.
DIVERSION	distracts adversary's attention.
DLB	acronym for dead-letter box. Also see DEAD DROP.
DOPE BOOK	a notebook kept with a sniper rifle for the purposes of recording the atmospheric conditions, range, lighting, and resulting hit or miss of every shot fired.
DOPPELGANGER	a lookalike. See also LOOKALIKE.
DOUBLE-AGENT	simultaneously serves two adversaries (often with their knowledge).
DRY CLEANING	active countersurveillance and antisurveillance against pavement artists and wheel artists.
DS	Bulgaria's security service, the Drzaven Sigurmost.
DSD	Australia's sigint agency, Defence Signals Directorate. http://www.dsd.gov.au/
DST	France's security service.
DUBOK	Russian term for a dead-letter box. Also see DEAD DROP.
E&E	escape and evasion.
ELEMENT	a five-man SWAT team. Consisting of a team leader, scout, rear guard, and two assaulters. The rear guard provides cover for the scout and is usually armed with a 12-guage shotgun. The assaulters usually carry Heckler & Koch 9mm MP-5 submachine guns. See also ASSAULTER.
ELLIPTICAL CONVERSATION	says one thing but means another.
EQUESTRIAN POSTURE	an effect produced by *rigor mortis* whereby the cadaver sits upright as if riding in a saddle, with arms outstretched.
ESPIONAGE	clandestine collection of intelligence by a non-domestic intelligence agency.
ESS	acronym for environmentally stable strategy, a concept used in strategic game-theory.
ETA	an underground group in Spain.
EVOC	an acronym for Emergency Vehicle Operation Course, taught at the FBI academy in Quantico.
FALN	an underground group in Puerto Rico.
FALSE FLAG RECRUITMENT	impersonation by a spy while recruiting an informant, defector, agent, etc.
FBI	a US security service.
FDS	One of Mexico's security services.
FIBONACCI SYSTEM	a system of non-carrying addition used for one-time pad codes. For example, (Fib) 999 + 222 = 111.
FILLING	the act of inserting material in a dead drop.
FLIP	a U Turn made by the target during a vehicle surveillance operation.
FLOATING BOX	a method of surveillance where a team of operators establishes a containment box around the target wherever he/she goes.
FMLN	Frente Farabundo Marti para Liberacion Nacional, an underground group in El Salvador.
FOLLOW	a surveillance team is executing a follow when they are shadowing a moving target. See also FLOATING BOX. A follow begins when the target exits the stakeout box and a surveillance operative attains command of the target. See also COMMAND OF THE TARGET.
FOOTFALL DETECTOR	vibration sensor designed to detect walking humans.
FOUR-BAGGER	disclipline of an agent by FBI headquarters, consisting of

	censure, transfer, suspension, and probation.
FRA	Sweden's military signals intelligence agency.
FREQUENCY FLOODING	a technique that allows an ordinary telephone to become a covert listening device.
FRIEND	slang for an agent, informant, or mole providing information to a handler.
FRIENDS	slang for Britain's secret intelligence service, MI.6.
FRONT	a legitimate-appearing business created by an intelligence agency or security service to provide cover for spies and their operations.
FSB	Russia's federal security service, responsible for counterespionage.
FUNKSPIEL	impersonation during electronic communications. Derived from the German phrase for "radio game".
FUNNY PAPER	slang for the counterfeiting and forged documents section of an intelligence agency or security service.
GCHQ	Britain's sigint agency, Government Communications Head Quarters. http://www.gchq.gov.uk
GIA	an underground group in Algeria.
GID	Iraq's main intelligence organization, Da' Irat al Mukhabarat al-Amah.
GRU	Russian military intelligence, the Glavnoye Razvedyvatelnoye Upravleniye.
GSS	Israel's security service (also called Shin Beth).
GUAN-XI	an access agent for China's intelligence agency
GUOANBU	one of China's security services.
GUSTAV WEBER	Hitler's double, used by the Fuhrer's bodyguards to stymie the Allies as to his whereabouts. Shot in the forehead immediately after Hitler's death.
HAMAS	an underground group in Palestine.
HARD MAN	an experienced operative who can survive in a hostile environment and who has killed.
HARD TARGET	a surveillance target who is actively maintaining secrecy and may not reveal that he/she has detected the surveillance team.
HEZBOLLAH	an underground group in Lebanon, alleged to have operating units in Latin America with links to major drug dealers.
HONEY POT	Mata Hari, Raven, lady, femme fatale; a female agent using romance to compromise a target.
HOOLIGAN TOOL	a specialized tool much like a crowbar, developed by fire departments for prying open doors and windows. Also used by SWAT teams.
HOSTILE RECRUITMENT	recruitment by threat or force of an uncooperative informant, mole, or agent-in-place.
HUMINT	intelligence activities involving people rather than electronic eavesdropping or communications interception.
HUNTING PACK	slang for surveillance team.
IAKHBAL	Israeli police unit that fights organized crime.
ICBM	an acronym for instant calm breath method, a way to overcome the flight-or-fight reflex (panic). Also reduces hyperventilation.
ILD	one of China's security services.
ILLEGAL	an intelligence officer operating in a foreign nation without the protection of diplomatic immunity.
IMINT	acronym for image intelligence.
INFORMANT	a legitimate member of a target group providing intelligence to the surveillance team.
INTELLIGENCE OFFICER	a trained member of an intelligence agency, an employee on salary.
INTERPOL	international police body that coordinates the intelligence gathering and investigative activities of member police forces.

INVESTIGATIVE SPECIALIST	the FBI's name for a surveillance operative (vehicle or foot). Pay grade GS-7 to GS-10. See also SSG.
IRA	an underground group in Northern Ireland.
ISTIKHBARAT AL ASKARIYA	Libyan military intelligence.
ITAC	an acronym for International Terrorist Assessment Center, located in Washington DC.
JARKING	bugging a weapons cache, often rendering weapons unusable.
JETRO -- one of Japan's intelligence agencies.	
JIHAZ AMN AL DAOULA	Egypt's security service.
JOE	a deep-cover agent.
JRA	Japanese Red Army, an underground group in Japan.
KEMPEI TAI	Japan's secret police.
KGB	Kometet Gosudarstvennoi Bezopasnosti.
K-LINE	SVR internal security and investigations section.
KOANCHO	Japan's counterintelligence and security service.
L5	4096 bit encryption algorithm
LADY	honey pot.
LAKAM	one of Israel's intelligence agencies (Ministry of Defense).
LEGEND	the faked biography of a deep-cover agent.
LETTERBOX	a person who is acting as a go-between. Also see CUT-OUT.
LINK DIAGRAM	connections being analyzed in a complex police investigation or counterespionage case. See problem-solving matrix.
LLB	an acronym for live-letter box, an address used to receive communication to be forwarded to an intelligence agency. See also DLB.
LOOKALIKES	decoys used to confuse hit squads and surveillance teams.
LSD	an acronym for d-lysergic acid diethylanide, a hallucinatory drug discovered in 1943 by Dr. Albert Hofmann, a researcher at Switzerland's Sandoz corporation, a pharmaceutical manufacturer. Subsequently monopolized by the CIA for its MKULTRA project that developed methods for secretly controlling people. Still used today by numerous intelligence agencies and security services for the following functions
1. disturbance of memory; 2. discrediting by aberrant behavior; 3. eliciting of information; 4. creation of dependence; 5. suggestibility. At the CIA's request, in 1954 Eli Lilly & Company developed a method for manufacturing LSD from publicly available chemicals. The CIA's bungling of MKULTRA allowed the drug to escape from the lab, where the CIA lost control of it. LSD subsequently ruined two generations of young Americans. No CIA officer or contractor was ever reprimanded or punished.	
M-19	underground group in Columbia.
MASKIROVDA	Russian name for deception techniques designed to fool US spy satellites. Recently used by India's counterintelligence agency to conceal nuclear testing from the CIA.
MATA HARI	honeypot, femme fatale,
MBRF	one of Russia's intelligence agencies.
MERCURY FULMINATE	an initiating agent for detonating PETN. See PETN.
MI.5	Britain's security service. K Branch is responsible for counterespionage, F Branch for countersubversion, C Branch for security of sensitive government installations.
MI.6	Britain's intelligence agency.
MICE	an acronym for money ideology compromise ego (methods

	used by intelligence agencies and security services to ruin a target).
MINI MANUAL OF THE URBAN GUERRILLA	an underground operations manual by Brazilian freedom-fighter Carlos Marighella. Contains 41 chapters. Banned in many countries.
MIN/MAX	a concept in strategic game-theory.
MITI -- one of Japan's intelligence agencies.	
MOLE	a penetration agent.
MONTENEROS	an underground group in Argentina.
MOSSAD	one of Israel's intelligence agencies, noted for its expertise in wet affairs. Literally translated as "institute". Never referred to as *the* MOSSAD, but rather simply called MOSSAD.
MST	Landless Rural Workers Movement, an underground group in Brazil.
MUKHABARAT	Libya's intelligence agency.
MUSLIM UIGHUR	an underground group in China.
NAICHO	one of Japan's intelligence agencies.
NARCOTHERAPY HYPNOSIS	CIA interrogators use hypnosis to force regression in the prisoner to make him believe he is talking to his spouse. The prisoner is first prepared by pharmaceuticals according to the following protocol. 1. An injection of 10 mg sodium pentothal to render unconscious. 2. Wait 20 minutes. 3. An injection of 10 mg benzodrine to revive the prisoner to a state partway between waking and sleep. 4. Repeat step 3 if required. At the end of the interrogation a hypnotically induced amnesia is invoked.
NEUROLINGUISTICS	a branch of psychology used by intelligence agencies and security services to covertly manipulate unsuspecting human targets.
NEUTRON BOMBARDMENT	used by security services like Britain's MI.5, America's FBI, Germany's BfV, and France's DST to detect microdots and invisible writing in postal mail. Originally developed by the Atomic Weapons Research Establishment in Britain for use by MI.5.
NIGHTCRAWLER	a talent spotter who prowls bars and nightclubs looking for government employees, military personnel, etc. who can be compromised using booze, drugs, or sex. Also see TALENT SPOTTER.
NINJAS	slang for members of a SWAT team.
NITROUS OXIDE	an anesthetic inhalant used to render sleeping targets unconscious during surreptitious entry by goon squads.
NMI	Norway's security service.
NPA	National Peoples' Army, an underground group in the Philippines.
NSA	US sigint intelligence agency and security service, the National Security Agency. http://www.nsa.gov:8080/
NSS	Bulgaria's security service.
NSTL	the FBI's national security threat list.
OBS	Croatia's intelligence agency, the Obavestajna Bezbednostna Sluzba.
OP	observation post.
OFFENSIVE PENETRATION OPERATION	infiltration of an agent into a target group or organization.
OFFSITE	a covert FBI site or facility situated away from a field office.
OG	an acronym for original gangmembers, now in their thirties and forties, who supply cocaine and heroin to street gangs.
ONE-TIME PAD	an unbreakable code system that works by adding the numeric value of the plaintext with a randomly-generated code string

	(the one-time pad). Also see FIBONACCI SYSTEM.
OSA	official secrets act, usually a law to enable governments to conceal their mistakes from their own population.
OUTRIDER	a wheel artist responsible for ensuring that the target does not get outside the floating box of surveillance vehicles. See also FLOATING BOX.
OVERT TARGET	deliberately attempts to draw attention and drain the resources of an intelligence agency or security service. Occasionally a decoy.
PARALLEL-LINE/INCIDENTAL-CAPACITANCE	a method of telephone, telex, and communications eavesdropping that is virtually undetectable.
PAVEMENT ARTIST	outdoor surveillance specialist operating on foot.
PEEP	photographer.
PERIMETER SURVEILLANCE	is used to alert the surveillance team when the target enters or leaves a specific area.
PETN	Pentaery-thritol tetranitrate, a plastic explosive favored by intelligence agencies and security services. See mercury fulminate.
PFLP	an underground group in Palestine.
PHOTINT	acronym for photo intelligence.
PICKET SURVEILLANCE	focuses on times and places when target is likely engaged in activities of interest to the surveillance team. Also called chokepoint surveillance. Named after the openings in a picket fence.
PICKUP	when the target of a surveillance operation is first spotted inside the stakeout box.
PINHOLE CAMERA	video camera with fiber-optic lens attachment.
POSSE COMITATAS	a Latin phrase that loosely means *power of the people*.
PROBLEM-SOLVING MATRIX	a grid-based notation system used by police investigators and counterespionage officers when dealing with complex cases.
PRODUCT	finished intelligence that has been evaluated by an intelligence agency and is ready for distribution to consumers. Also see CONSUMER.
PROFESSIONAL-NAME	nom de guerre of a spy.
PROFILE STOP	a random stop and search by police, based on a suspect's race, minority status, economic status, religion, physical appearance, travel status, location, etc. Previously inflicted on minorities and poor whites, but currently being expanded by bureaucrats to include all US citizens.
PSB	one of China's secret police agencies.
PSIA	one of Japan's security services.
PSYCHIC COMBAT	a condition of active psychological warfare operations between two covert adversaries.
PSYCHODYNAMICS	the CIA's psychological profiling system, used in combination with psychobiographic analysis.
QUANG BO	Vietnam's military intelligence agency.
QODS	One of Iran's security services.
QRF	quick reaction force.
RADINT	acronym for radar intelligence.
RAID	an acronym for Rapid Assessment and Initial Detection, consisting of teams of National Guardsmen who assist civilian authorities after a suspected biological/toxin/chemical attack on a population center.
RAVEN	a honey pot.
RCMP	police agency in Canada similar to the FBI in the USA. Acronym for Royal Canadian Mounted Police. Also known as RCM Police.
RCMP SECURITY SERVICE	counterespionage, counterintelligence, and counterterrorist branch of RCMP. Also known as RCMP SPECIAL SERVICES.

RED BRIGADE	an underground group in Italy.
RENT-A-GOONS	operatives proficient in hand-to-hand combat, used as muscle support when direct physical confrontation is likely.
RESISTANCE	a civilian underground organization, consisting of cells (1 to 10 persons), circles (a group of cells), and sections (a group of circles).
RG	France's police intelligence security service, Renseignements Generaux.
RING	a network of spies or agents.
ROSCOE	handgun.
RUSE DE GUERRE	subterfuge.
RZ	an underground group in Germany. Literally translated as revolutionary cells.
SA	FBI special agent.
SAFEHOUSE	a dwelling place or hideout unknown to the adversary.
SAPO	Sweden's security service.
SASHA KVAP	Russian mole inside Hitler's bunker during the final months of World War II. Subsequently poisoned by the KGB in 1955.
SAVAK	one of Iraq's security services.
SCIF	acronym for Secured Compartmentalized Information Facility (in Fort Gillem, GA, USA) where Clipper is housed (rumored to have already been penetrated by agents of China's intelligence agencies).
SEMTEX	a military explosive suitable for sabotage and terrorist operations.
SECRET CLASSIFICATIONS	Confidential, Secret, Top Secret, and (SCI) Special Compartmentalized Information.
SERE	an acronym for survival, evasion, resistance, and escape.
SERVICING	the act of removing material from a dead drop.
SET UP	to begin to conduct surveillance on a target.
SEVENTY-ONE YARDS	according to FBI statistics, this is the distance at which a typical police sniper will get you. Although the SR60 .308 sniper rifle used by most police departments is designed for distances up to 600 yards, most police snipers do not fire at suspects beyond 400 yards. (Of course, at any distance an *execution* is still an execution.)
SHIN BETH	Israel's security service (also called GSS).
SHINING PATH	an underground group in Peru.
SMERSH	KGB assassination group. Officially disbanded ;) The name derives from the Russian phrase "death to spies".
SIDE	Argentina's security service.
SIGINT	signals intelligence (interception of electronic communications)
SINN FEIN	the political arm (party) of the IRA.
SIS	one of Britain's intelligence agencies, the secret intelligence service.
SIT REP	situation report.
SIX	slang for a police officer, police cruiser, or a police patrol. Used as a warning in the criminal community.
SLEEPER AGENT	an inactive deep-cover agent.
SLUZBA BEZPIECZENSTWA	Poland's security service, also called the SB.
SOFT TARGET	an easy surveillance target, untrained and not looking for surveillance.
SOG	an acronym for Special Operations Group, FBI agents who conduct surveillance. In contrast, SSG is composed of non-agents. See also SSG.
SOS	dot dot dot dash dash dash dot dot dot.
SPECIAL BRANCH	the security branch of the British police.
SPLASHED	describes a bodyguard whose client has been assassinated. Also see WET AFFAIR.

SPOOK	a spy.
SPY	any member of an intelligence agency, security service, police agency, resistance movement, guerrilla group, or other organization engaged in covert intelligence-gathering activities.
SRI	Romania's security service (rumored to be made up of former members of Ceausescu's secret police).
SSG	an acronym for Surveillance Specialist Group, which is what the FBI calls a surveillance team. See also INVESTIGATIVE SPECIALIST. See also SOG.
SSS	Georgia's security service.
StB	Czechoslovakia's security service, the Statni Tajna Bezpecnost.
STINGBALL	a flashbang grenade used by SWAT teams to disperse crowds and disorient barricaded suspects. Throws off rubber fragments when detonated. It is standard police procedure to cover up the deaths of suspects inadvertently killed by stingballs.
STREET AGENT	an FBI agent whose work takes him to various locations. Also see BRICK AGENT.
SVR	one of Russia's intelligence agencies, the Slnzhba Vneshnei Razvedaki.
SWARMING	overfilling a location with surveillance operatives. Often used in psy ops as a means for controlling the target's environment.
SYNTHETIC HEMOGLOBIN	a component used in carbon monoxoide detector alarms. The radiation weapons recently developed and deployed by DARPA will set off these alarms.
TALEBAN	underground group in Afghanistan.
TALENT SPOTTER	same as ACCESS AGENT.
TARGET	the victim of surveillance, the subject.
THERMAL IMAGER	a heat-sensitive surveillance video camera and display.
THREE Bs	Booze, broads, and bucars. The three temptations of FBI agents. (If the choice of words offends our women readers, please remember that this is a phrase originated and used by FBI agents. We are merely reporting it.)
THROW PHONE	a cellular telephone thrown to a barricaded suspect by the SWAT team.
TRIADS	Asian organized crime gangs.
TRIGGER	a surveillance operative who is watching the target's vacant vehicle, home, garage, office, restaurant etc. and who alerts the rest of the surveillance team when the target is spotted.
TUPAMAROS	an underground group in Uruguay.
UACB	FBI acronym for Unless Advised to the Contrary by the Bureau.
UNITED RED ARMY	an underground group in Japan.
UNS	Croatia's security service, the Ured za Nacionalnu Sigurnost.
UNSUB	an unknown subject in a surveillance operation.
UOP	Poland's security service.
USSA	slang for a USA reminiscent of the oppressive totalitarianism of the former USSR.
VCP	vehicle control point.
VEVAK	Iran's intelligence agency.
VICKIE WEAVER	American citizen probably murdered by the FBI. A landmark case for many concerned Americans.
WAHABI	a Saudi Islamic underground group .
WALK-IN	an unsolicited volunteer.
WATCH-LIST	people targeted for routine surveillance.
WET AFFAIR	results in death of target. Also see SPLASHED.
WHEEL ARTIST	an outdoor surveillance specialist operating in a vehicle.
WILDERNESS OF MIRRORS	a spy operation so complicated that it is no longer possible to separate truth and untruth.
X RAYS	used by intelligence agencies and security services to pick key-

	locks and to deduce the settings for combination locks. Equipment fits in a standard briefcase.
ZAPATISTA NATIONAL LIBERATION ARMY	an underground group in Mexico.
ZERO-OUT	the range at which a weapon's sights will produce a bull's eye hit. Handgun fixed sights are usually zeroed-out at 25 yards. A sniper rifle scope is usually zeroed-out at 100 yards. The term *cold barrel zero* refers to the calibration of a SWAT sniper rifle so that the first (cold) shot will hit a target at 100 yards. Subsequent rounds will diverge due to barrel heating.
ZHONGYANG LIANLUOBU	one of China's intelligence agencies.
ZOU-HOU-MAN	back door access to a protected target (as used by China's intelligence agencies).

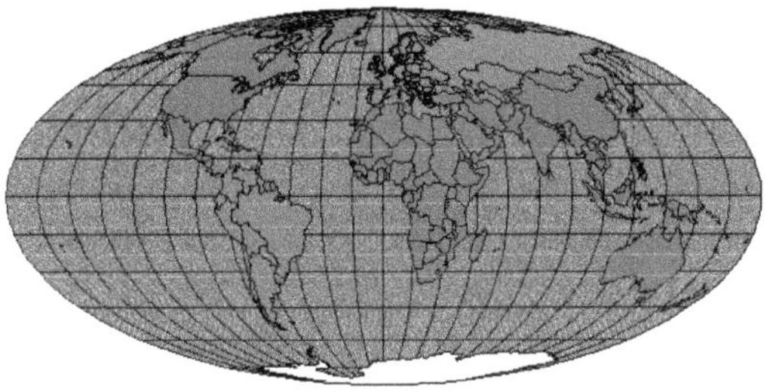

INTELLIGENCE, SECURITY ACTIVITIES & OPERATIONS HANDBOOK LIBRARY

Intelligence, counterintelligence, national security and related operation, conducted by specific countries. National security and intelligence agencies operations and structure

TITLE
1. Albania Intelligence, Security Activities & Operations Handbook
2. Argentina Intelligence, Security Activities & Operations Handbook
3. Australia Intelligence, Security Activities & Operations Handbook
4. Australia Intelligence, Security Activities & Operations Handbook
5. Bangladesh Intelligence, Security Activities & Operations Handbook
6. Canada Intelligence, Security Activities & Operations Handbook
7. Canadian Security Intelligence Service (CSIS) Handbook
8. China Intelligence, Security Activities & Operations Handbook
9. Cuba Intelligence, Security Activities & Operations Handbook
10. Czech Repuiblic Intelligence, Security Activities & Operations Handbook
11. Estonia Intelligence, Security Activities & Operations Handbook
12. Estonia Intelligence, Security Activities & Operations Handbook
13. EUROPOL – EUROPEAN POLICE OFFICE Handbook
14. Finland Intelligence, Security Activities & Operations Handbook
15. Finland Intelligence, Security Activities & Operations Handbook
16. France Intelligence, Security Activities & Operations Handbook
17. German Intelligence, Security Activities & Operations Handbook
18. Germany Intelligence, Security Activities & Operations Handbook
19. Global Counter-Terrorism Handbook
20. Global National Intelligence and Security Agencies Handbook
21. Global Terrorism Attacks Encyclopedic Handbook
22. Greece Intelligence, Security Activities & Operations Handbook
23. Hungary Intelligence, Security Activities & Operations Handbook
24. Hungary Intelligence, Security Activities & Operations Handbook
25. India Intelligence, Security Activities & Operations Handbook
26. India Intelligence, Security Activities & Operations Handbook
27. India Textime Industry Investment and Business Guide
28. Iraq Economic Sanctions, Customs, Trade Regulations and Procedures Handbook

TITLE
29. Ireland Intelligence, Security Activities & Operations Handbook
30. Ireland Intelligence, Security Activities & Operations Handbook
31. Israel Intelligence, Security Activities & Operations Handbook
32. Israel Intelligence, Security Activities & Operations Handbook
33. Italy Intelligence, Security Activities & Operations Handbook
34. Japan Intelligence, Security Activities & Operations Handbook
35. Japan Intelligence, Security Activities & Operations Handbook
36. Jordan Intelligence, Security Activities & Operations Handbook
37. Korea North Intelligence, Security Activities & Operations Handbook
38. Korea South Intelligence, Security Activities & Operations Handbook
39. Korea South Intelligence, Security Activities & Operations Handbook
40. Latvia Intelligence, Security Activities & Operations Handbook
41. Lebanon Intelligence, Security Activities & Operations Handbook
42. Lesotho Telecommunication Industry Investment Guide
43. Lithuania Intelligence, Security Activities & Operations Handbook
44. Macedonia National Security, Army and Defence Policy Handbook
45. Malaysia Intelligence, Security Activities & Operations Handbook
46. Myanmar Intelligence, Security Activities & Operations Handbook
47. New Zealand Intelligence, Security Activities & Operations Handbook
48. New Zealand Intelligence, Security Activities & Operations Handbook
49. Norway Intelligence, Security Activities & Operations Handbook
50. Pakistan Intelligence, Security Activities & Operations Handbook
51. Pakistan Intelligence, Security Activities & Operations Handbook
52. Philippines Intelligence, Security Activities & Operations Handbook
53. Poland Intelligence, Security Activities & Operations Handbook
54. Portugal Intelligence, Security Activities & Operations Handbook
55. Romania Intelligence, Security Activities & Operations Handbook
56. Romania Intelligence, Security Activities & Operations Handbook
57. Russia Intelligence, Security Activities & Operations Handbook
58. Russia Intelligence, Security Activities & Operations Handbook
59. Russian KGB Handbook: Past and Present
60. Russian Navy Handbook: History and Modern Situation
61. Russia-NATO Cooperatiion Handbook
62. Singapore Intelligence, Security Activities & Operations Handbook
63. Slovak Republic Intelligence, Security Activities & Operations Handbook
64. South Africa Intelligence, Security Activities & Operations Handbook
65. South Africa Intelligence, Security Activities & Operations Handbook
66. Sri Lanka Intelligence, Security Activities & Operations Handbook
67. Starting Business (Incorporating) in India Encyclopedic Guide
68. Sweden Intelligence, Security Activities & Operations Handbook

TITLE
69. Switzerland Intelligence, Security Activities & Operations Handbook
70. Switzerland Intelligence, Security Activities & Operations Handbook
71. Taiwan Intelligence, Security Activities & Operations Handbook
72. Taiwan Intelligence, Security Activities & Operations Handbook
73. Thailand Royal Intelligence, Security Activities & Operations Handbook
74. The French Foreign Legion Handbook
75. The INTERPOL Handbook
76. The United Stated Ambassadors Yearbook
77. Turkey Intelligence, Security Activities & Operations Handbook
78. Turkey Intelligence, Security Activities & Operations Handbook
79. UK Department of Trade and Industry (DTI) Handbook
80. UK Intelligence & Counterintelligence Handbook
81. UK Intelligence, Security Activities & Operations Handbook
82. UK Intelligence and Security Policy Handbook
83. UK MI5 Security Service Handbook
84. UK Military Intelligence Handbook
85. UK National Intelligence Service Handbook
86. UK National Police Handbook
87. UK Royal Airforce Handbook
88. UK Royal Army Handbook
89. UK Royal Navy Handbook
90. Ukraine Intelligence, Security Activities & Operations Handbook
91. Ukraine Intelligence, Security Activities & Operations Handbook
92. United Kingdom Intelligence, Security Activities & Operations Handbook
93. US Arms Sales to Foreign Countries Handbook
94. US Business Intelligence Handbook
95. US Counterintelligence Operations against Cuba Handbook
96. US Defense Policy Handbook
97. US Federal Grant Management Handbook
98. US Military Intelligence Handbook
99. US Ocean Transportation Companies Directory
100. US Political Intelligence Handbook
101. US War Against International Terrorism Handbook
102. US War Against Iraq Handbook: Political Strategy and Operations
103. US-Russia Cooperation Against Terrorism Handbook
104. US-Russia Economic & Financial Cooperation Handbook
105. US-Russia Military Cooperation Handbook
106. US-Russia Political Cooperation Handbook
107. US-Russia Scientific & Technological Cooperation Handbook
108. US-Russia Space Cooperation Handbook

INTERNET AND CYBER SECURITY HANDBOOKS LIBRARY

Price: $99.95 Each

World Business Information Catalog: http://www.ibpus.com

Please contact ibpus3@gmail.com to request the latest ISBN numbers for each publcation

TITLE
Albania Internet and Cyner Security Laws and Regulations Handbook - Strategic Information, Programs, Regulations
Algeria Internet and Cyner Security Laws and Regulations Handbook - Strategic Information, Programs, Regulations
Angola Internet and Cyner Security Laws and Regulations Handbook - Strategic Information, Programs, Regulations
Argentina Internet and Cyner Security Laws and Regulations Handbook - Strategic Information, Programs, Regulations
Armenia Internet and Cyner Security Laws and Regulations Handbook - Strategic Information, Programs, Regulations
Australia Internet and Cyner Security Laws and Regulations Handbook - Strategic Information, Programs, Regulations
Austria Internet and Cyner Security Laws and Regulations Handbook - Strategic Information, Programs, Regulations
Azerbaijan Internet and Cyner Security Laws and Regulations Handbook - Strategic Information, Programs, Regulations
Bangladesh Internet and Cyner Security Laws and Regulations Handbook - Strategic Information, Programs, Regulations
Belarus Internet and Cyner Security Laws and Regulations Handbook - Strategic Information, Programs, Regulations
Belgium Internet and Cyner Security Laws and Regulations Handbook - Strategic Information, Programs, Regulations
Bolivia Internet and Cyner Security Laws and Regulations Handbook - Strategic Information, Programs, Regulations
Bosnia and Herzegovina Internet and Cyner Security Laws and Regulations Handbook - Strategic Information, Programs, Regulations
Botswana Internet and Cyner Security Laws and Regulations Handbook - Strategic Information, Programs, Regulations
Brazil Internet and Cyner Security Laws and Regulations Handbook - Strategic Information, Programs, Regulations
Bulgaria Internet and Cyner Security Laws and Regulations Handbook - Strategic Information, Programs, Regulations
Cambodia Internet and Cyner Security Laws and Regulations Handbook - Strategic Information, Programs, Regulations
Cameroon Internet and Cyner Security Laws and Regulations Handbook - Strategic Information, Programs, Regulations
Canada Internet and Cyner Security Laws and Regulations Handbook - Strategic Information, Programs, Regulations
Chile Internet and Cyner Security Laws and Regulations Handbook - Strategic Information, Programs, Regulations
China Internet and Cyner Security Laws and Regulations Handbook - Strategic Information, Programs, Regulations

TITLE
Colombia Internet and Cyner Security Laws and Regulations Handbook - Strategic Information, Programs, Regulations
Croatia Internet and Cyner Security Laws and Regulations Handbook - Strategic Information, Programs, Regulations
Cuba Internet and Cyner Security Laws and Regulations Handbook - Strategic Information, Programs, Regulations
Czech Republic Internet and Cyner Security Laws and Regulations Handbook - Strategic Information, Programs, Regulations
Denmark Internet and Cyner Security Laws and Regulations Handbook - Strategic Information, Programs, Regulations
Dominican Republic Internet and Cyner Security Laws and Regulations Handbook - Strategic Information, Programs, Regulations
Ecuador Internet and Cyner Security Laws and Regulations Handbook - Strategic Information, Programs, Regulations
Egypt Internet and Cyner Security Laws and Regulations Handbook - Strategic Information, Programs, Regulations
El Salvador Internet and Cyner Security Laws and Regulations Handbook - Strategic Information, Programs, Regulations
Equatorial Guinea Internet and Cyner Security Laws and Regulations Handbook - Strategic Information, Programs, Regulations
Estonia Internet and Cyner Security Laws and Regulations Handbook - Strategic Information, Programs, Regulations
Fiji Internet and Cyner Security Laws and Regulations Handbook - Strategic Information, Programs, Regulations
Finland Internet and Cyner Security Laws and Regulations Handbook - Strategic Information, Programs, Regulations
France Internet and Cyner Security Laws and Regulations Handbook - Strategic Information, Programs, Regulations
Germany Internet and Cyner Security Laws and Regulations Handbook - Strategic Information, Programs, Regulations
Greece Internet and Cyner Security Laws and Regulations Handbook - Strategic Information, Programs, Regulations
Guatemala Internet and Cyner Security Laws and Regulations Handbook - Strategic Information, Programs, Regulations
Guernsey Internet and Cyner Security Laws and Regulations Handbook - Strategic Information, Programs, Regulations
Honduras Internet and Cyner Security Laws and Regulations Handbook - Strategic Information, Programs, Regulations
Hungary Internet and Cyner Security Laws and Regulations Handbook - Strategic Information, Programs, Regulations
Iceland Internet and Cyner Security Laws and Regulations Handbook - Strategic Information, Programs, Regulations
India Internet and Cyner Security Laws and Regulations Handbook - Strategic Information, Programs, Regulations
Indonesia Internet and Cyner Security Laws and Regulations Handbook - Strategic Information, Programs, Regulations
Iran Internet and Cyner Security Laws and Regulations Handbook - Strategic Information, Programs, Regulations
Iraq Internet and Cyner Security Laws and Regulations Handbook - Strategic Information, Programs, Regulations
Ireland Internet and Cyner Security Laws and Regulations Handbook - Strategic Information, Programs, Regulations
Israel Internet and Cyner Security Laws and Regulations Handbook - Strategic Information, Programs, Regulations
Italy Internet and Cyner Security Laws and Regulations Handbook - Strategic Information, Programs, Regulations
Japan Internet and Cyner Security Laws and Regulations Handbook - Strategic Information, Programs, Regulations
Jordan Internet and Cyner Security Laws and Regulations Handbook - Strategic Information, Programs, Regulations
Kazakhstan Internet and Cyner Security Laws and Regulations Handbook - Strategic Information, Programs, Regulations
Kenya Internet and Cyner Security Laws and Regulations Handbook - Strategic Information, Programs, Regulations
Korea, South Internet and Cyner Security Laws and Regulations Handbook - Strategic Information, Programs,

TITLE
Regulations
Kuwait Internet and Cyner Security Laws and Regulations Handbook - Strategic Information, Programs, Regulations
Kyrgyzstan Internet and Cyner Security Laws and Regulations Handbook - Strategic Information, Programs, Regulations
Laos Internet and Cyner Security Laws and Regulations Handbook - Strategic Information, Programs, Regulations
Latvia Internet and Cyner Security Laws and Regulations Handbook - Strategic Information, Programs, Regulations
Lebanon Internet and Cyner Security Laws and Regulations Handbook - Strategic Information, Programs, Regulations
Libya Internet and Cyner Security Laws and Regulations Handbook - Strategic Information, Programs, Regulations
Lithuania Internet and Cyner Security Laws and Regulations Handbook - Strategic Information, Programs, Regulations
Macao Internet and Cyner Security Laws and Regulations Handbook - Strategic Information, Programs, Regulations
Macedonia, Republic Internet and Cyner Security Laws and Regulations Handbook - Strategic Information, Programs, Regulations
Madagascar Internet and Cyner Security Laws and Regulations Handbook - Strategic Information, Programs, Regulations
Malaysia Internet and Cyner Security Laws and Regulations Handbook - Strategic Information, Programs, Regulations
Malta Internet and Cyner Security Laws and Regulations Handbook - Strategic Information, Programs, Regulations
Mauritius Internet and Cyner Security Laws and Regulations Handbook - Strategic Information, Programs, Regulations
Mexico Internet and Cyner Security Laws and Regulations Handbook - Strategic Information, Programs, Regulations
Moldova Internet and Cyner Security Laws and Regulations Handbook - Strategic Information, Programs, Regulations
Mongolia Internet and Cyner Security Laws and Regulations Handbook - Strategic Information, Programs, Regulations
Morocco Internet and Cyner Security Laws and Regulations Handbook - Strategic Information, Programs, Regulations
Namibia Internet and Cyner Security Laws and Regulations Handbook - Strategic Information, Programs, Regulations
Netherlands Internet and Cyner Security Laws and Regulations Handbook - Strategic Information, Programs, Regulations
New Zealand Internet and Cyner Security Laws and Regulations Handbook - Strategic Information, Programs, Regulations
Nicaragua Internet and Cyner Security Laws and Regulations Handbook - Strategic Information, Programs, Regulations
Nigeria Internet and Cyner Security Laws and Regulations Handbook - Strategic Information, Programs, Regulations
Norway Internet and Cyner Security Laws and Regulations Handbook - Strategic Information, Programs, Regulations
Opportunities
Pakistan Internet and Cyner Security Laws and Regulations Handbook - Strategic Information, Programs, Regulations
Panama Internet and Cyner Security Laws and Regulations Handbook - Strategic Information, Programs, Regulations
Peru Internet and Cyner Security Laws and Regulations Handbook - Strategic Information, Programs, Regulations
Philippines Internet and Cyner Security Laws and Regulations Handbook - Strategic Information, Programs, Regulations
Poland Internet and Cyner Security Laws and Regulations Handbook - Strategic Information, Programs, Regulations
Portugal Internet and Cyner Security Laws and Regulations Handbook - Strategic Information, Programs, Regulations
Romania Internet and Cyner Security Laws and Regulations Handbook - Strategic Information, Programs, Regulations

TITLE
Russia Internet and Cyner Security Laws and Regulations Handbook - Strategic Information, Programs, Regulations
Saudi Arabia Internet and Cyner Security Laws and Regulations Handbook - Strategic Information, Programs, Regulations
Serbia Internet and Cyner Security Laws and Regulations Handbook - Strategic Information, Programs, Regulations
Singapore Internet and Cyner Security Laws and Regulations Handbook - Strategic Information, Programs, Regulations
Slovakia Internet and Cyner Security Laws and Regulations Handbook - Strategic Information, Programs, Regulations
Slovenia Internet and Cyner Security Laws and Regulations Handbook - Strategic Information, Programs, Regulations
South Africa Internet and Cyner Security Laws and Regulations Handbook - Strategic Information, Programs, Regulations
Spain Internet and Cyner Security Laws and Regulations Handbook - Strategic Information, Programs, Regulations
Sri Lanka Internet and Cyner Security Laws and Regulations Handbook - Strategic Information, Programs, Regulations
Suriname Internet and Cyner Security Laws and Regulations Handbook - Strategic Information, Programs, Regulations
Sweden Internet and Cyner Security Laws and Regulations Handbook - Strategic Information, Programs, Regulations
Switzerland Internet and Cyner Security Laws and Regulations Handbook - Strategic Information, Programs, Regulations
Taiwan Internet and Cyner Security Laws and Regulations Handbook - Strategic Information, Programs, Regulations
Tajikistan Internet and Cyner Security Laws and Regulations Handbook - Strategic Information, Programs, Regulations
Thailand Internet and Cyner Security Laws and Regulations Handbook - Strategic Information, Programs, Regulations
Tunisia Internet and Cyner Security Laws and Regulations Handbook - Strategic Information, Programs, Regulations
Turkey Internet and Cyner Security Laws and Regulations Handbook - Strategic Information, Programs, Regulations
Turkmenistan Internet and Cyner Security Laws and Regulations Handbook - Strategic Information, Programs, Regulations
Uganda Internet and Cyner Security Laws and Regulations Handbook - Strategic Information, Programs, Regulations
Ukraine Internet and Cyner Security Laws and Regulations Handbook - Strategic Information, Programs, Regulations
United Arab Emirates Internet and Cyner Security Laws and Regulations Handbook - Strategic Information, Programs, Regulations
United Kingdom Internet and Cyner Security Laws and Regulations Handbook - Strategic Information, Programs, Regulations
United States Internet and Cyner Security Laws and Regulations Handbook - Strategic Information, Programs, Regulations
Uruguay Internet and Cyner Security Laws and Regulations Handbook - Strategic Information, Programs, Regulations
US Internet and Cyner Security Laws and Regulations Handbook - Strategic Information, Programs, Regulations
Uzbekistan Internet and Cyner Security Laws and Regulations Handbook - Strategic Information, Programs, Regulations
Venezuela Internet and Cyner Security Laws and Regulations Handbook - Strategic Information, Programs, Regulations
Vietnam Internet and Cyner Security Laws and Regulations Handbook - Strategic Information, Programs, Regulations

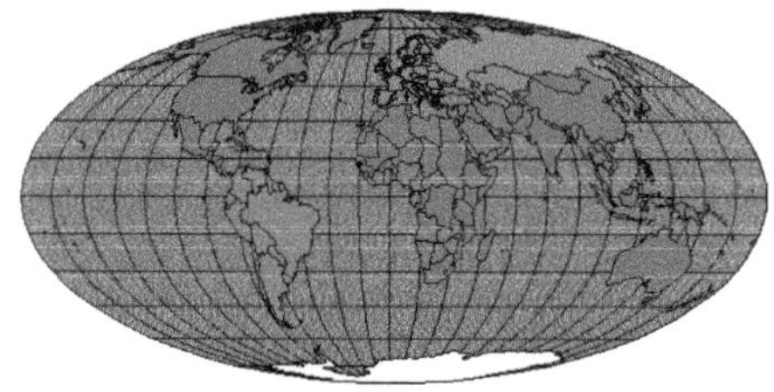

GLOBAL
NATIONAL SECURITY STRATEGY
LIBRARY

Price: $149.95 Each

1.	Albania National Security Strategy Handbook
2.	Algeria National Security Strategy Handbook
3.	Angola National Security Strategy Handbook
4.	Argentina National Security Strategy Handbook
5.	Armenia National Security Strategy Handbook
6.	Australia National Security Strategy Handbook
7.	Austria National Security Strategy Handbook
8.	Azerbaijan National Security Strategy Handbook
9.	Bangladesh National Security Strategy Handbook
10.	Belarus National Security Strategy Handbook
11.	Belgium National Security Strategy Handbook
12.	Bolivia National Security Strategy Handbook
13.	Bosnia and Herzegovina National Security Strategy Handbook
14.	Botswana National Security Strategy Handbook
15.	Brazil National Security Strategy Handbook
16.	Bulgaria National Security Strategy Handbook
17.	Cambodia National Security Strategy Handbook
18.	Cameroon National Security Strategy Handbook
19.	Canada National Security Strategy Handbook
20.	Chile National Security Strategy Handbook
21.	China National Security Strategy Handbook
22.	Colombia National Security Strategy Handbook
23.	Costa Rica National Security Strategy Handbook
24.	Croatia National Security Strategy Handbook
25.	Cuba National Security Strategy Handbook
26.	Czech Republic National Security Strategy Handbook
27.	Denmark National Security Strategy Handbook
28.	Ecuador National Security Strategy Handbook
29.	Egypt National Security Strategy Handbook
30.	El Salvador National Security Strategy Handbook
31.	Equatorial Guinea National Security Strategy Handbook
32.	Estonia National Security Strategy Handbook
33.	Finland National Security Strategy Handbook

34. France National Security Strategy Handbook
35. Georgia National Security Strategy Handbook
36. Germany National Security Strategy Handbook
37. Greece National Security Strategy Handbook
38. Guatemala National Security Strategy Handbook
39. Guernsey National Security Strategy Handbook
40. Hungary National Security Strategy Handbook
41. Iceland National Security Strategy Handbook
42. India National Security Strategy Handbook
43. Indonesia National Security Strategy Handbook
44. Iran National Security Strategy Handbook
45. Iraq National Security Strategy Handbook
46. Ireland National Security Strategy Handbook
47. Israel National Security Strategy Handbook
48. Italy National Security Strategy Handbook
49. Japan National Security Strategy Handbook
50. Jordan National Security Strategy Handbook
51. Kazakhstan National Security Strategy Handbook
52. Kenya National Security Strategy Handbook
53. Korea, North National Security Strategy Handbook
54. Korea, South National Security Strategy Handbook
55. Kuwait National Security Strategy Handbook
56. Kyrgyzstan National Security Strategy Handbook
57. Laos National Security Strategy Handbook
58. Latvia National Security Strategy Handbook
59. Lebanon National Security Strategy Handbook
60. Libya National Security Strategy Handbook
61. Liechtenstein National Security Strategy Handbook
62. Lithuania National Security Strategy Handbook
63. Luxemburg National Security Strategy Handbook
64. Macedonia, Republic National Security Strategy Handbook
65. Madagascar National Security Strategy Handbook
66. Malaysia National Security Strategy Handbook
67. Mauritius National Security Strategy Handbook
68. Mexico National Security Strategy Handbook
69. Moldova National Security Strategy Handbook
70. Mongolia National Security Strategy Handbook
71. Morocco National Security Strategy Handbook
72. Myanmar National Security Strategy Handbook
73. Namibia National Security Strategy Handbook
74. Netherlands National Security Strategy Handbook
75. New Zealand National Security Strategy Handbook
76. Nicaragua National Security Strategy Handbook

77. Nigeria National Security Strategy Handbook
78. Norway National Security Strategy Handbook
79. Pakistan National Security Strategy Handbook
80. Panama National Security Strategy Handbook
81. Peru National Security Strategy Handbook
82. Philippines National Security Strategy Handbook
83. Poland National Security Strategy Handbook
84. Portugal National Security Strategy Handbook
85. Romania National Security Strategy Handbook
86. Russia National Security Strategy Handbook
87. Saudi Arabia National Security Strategy Handbook
88. Serbia National Security Strategy Handbook
89. Singapore National Security Strategy Handbook
90. Slovakia National Security Strategy Handbook
91. Slovenia National Security Strategy Handbook
92. South Africa National Security Strategy Handbook
93. Spain National Security Strategy Handbook
94. Sri Lanka National Security Strategy Handbook
95. Sudan National Security Strategy Handbook
96. Suriname National Security Strategy Handbook
97. Sweden National Security Strategy Handbook
98. Switzerland National Security Strategy Handbook
99. Syria Export Import & Business Directory
100. Taiwan National Security Strategy Handbook
101. Tajikistan National Security Strategy Handbook
102. Thailand National Security Strategy Handbook
103. Tunisia National Security Strategy Handbook
104. Turkey National Security Strategy Handbook
105. Turkmenistan National Security Strategy Handbook
106. Uganda National Security Strategy Handbook
107. Ukraine National Security Strategy Handbook
108. United Arab Emirates National Security Strategy Handbook
109. United Kingdom National Security Strategy Handbook
110. United States National Security Strategy Handbook
111. Uruguay National Security Strategy Handbook
112. US National Security Strategy Handbook
113. Uzbekistan National Security Strategy Handbook
114. Venezuela National Security Strategy Handbook
115. Vietnam National Security Strategy Handbook

www.ingramcontent.com/pod-product-compliance
Ingram Content Group UK Ltd.
Pitfield, Milton Keynes, MK11 3LW, UK
UKHW051510290926
15471UKWH00008B/1534

9 780739 767078